The author's house and garden in the lovely bush setting of the Araluen Valley, New South Wales

The WILDERNESS GARDEN

Beyond Organic Gardening

COMPLETELY REVISED 2ND EDITION

JACKIE FRENCH

AIRD BOOKS

Cambridgeshire Libraries	
10010010275738	
Askews & Holts	25-Nov-2013
635.048	£20.99

This edition first published in 2007 by Aird Books,
an imprint of Manna Trading Pty Ltd
PO Box 122
Flemington, Vic. 3031

First published by Aird Books in 1992
Reprinted 1993, 1994

Copyright Jackie French 1992, 2007
National Library of Australia
Cataloguing-in-publication data

French, Jackie.
    The wilderness garden : beyond organic
    gardening.

    Completely rev. 2nd. ed.
    Includes index.
    ISBN 9780947214579 (pbk.).

    1. Gardening - Australia. 2. Organic gardening -
    Australia.
    I. Title.
635.04840994

All rights reserved. No part of this publication may be reproduced, stored in a retrieval system, or transmitted in any form or by any means, electronic, mechanical, photocopying, recording, or otherwise, without the written permission of the publishers.

Edited by Bet Moore

Design and layout by Pauline Deakin,
Captured Concepts

Illustrations by Greg Jorgenson and Dave Deakin

Printed by Everbest, China

CONTENTS

Introduction: the 'Not Quite a Miracle' garden 1
Questions and answers 4

1　The 'Magic Grove'　4
2　Different gardens for different places　17
3　Drought and bushfire　40
4　Gardens for kids　50
5　Feeding your garden　55
6　Easy garden beds　72
7　Dealing with pests and disease　82
8　Living with weeds　103
9　The vegetable garden　112
10　The fruit garden　148
11　The flower garden　184
12　Gardens by mail　197

Calendar　201
Index　222

I'd rather learn from one bird how to sing than
teach ten thousand stars how not to dance ...

                                      E E CUMMINGS

Introduction

THE 'NOT QUITE A MIRACLE' GARDEN, OR 'HOW NEVER TO WEED, FEED OR DIG YOUR GARDEN AGAIN, AND THROW AWAY YOUR LAWNMOWER.'

This is a book about ideas – about how to set up a garden that will look after itself – just as the bush doesn't need humans to look after it, but keeps fruiting, flowering and growing, endlessly prolific.

It's about how to grow avocados that will survive even as the snowflakes settle on their branches; about how to have a vegie garden that will still give you corn, tomatoes and parsley even if it hasn't been watered, either by you or the rain, for three months.

It's about how to have a garden that will delight you, the birds and the thousands of other species – mostly microscopic – that it's home to.

Above all, it's a book about how NOT to garden.

You don't have to dig your garden (I haven't for decades). You shouldn't have to feed it either, or weed it, or worry about those aphids on the roses (can't remember when I last did that, either). You don't have to mow your lawn. (Grass is there to be eaten. If you don't have 'roos or sheep, pave it or plant it!) You don't need to prune your trees or roses (as long as you grow the right ones), trim your paths, or spray for pests (let the birds and other beasties eat them instead).

Of course, if slipped discs and sweating legs mean ecstasy, go to it. But don't pretend you are doing it for your garden.

Most gardening is for masochists: digging, feeding, spraying, and the fanatical elimination of weeds are backbreaking, so they must be good for your garden. Righteousness means sweat. This is the Adam and Eve fallacy. Since Eden we've been supposed to tend our gardens instead of letting them take care of us.

So much of what we do to our gardens is bad for them; like medieval doctors prscribing powdered lead and leeches. Digging destroys soil structure and the bacterial associations that help create fertility. Weeding makes room for more weeds. Most pesticides just kill the natural predators that might have done the job for you. Herbicides are bandaids that simply cover up your problems. Most of the feeding you give your garden will probably end up in the air or the watertable, and won't do either any good.

A garden should take no more than ten minutes' work a week, not counting picking and lawn mowing. If your garden needs more than that, you're doing something wrong.

THE 'NOT QUITE A MIRACLE' WILDERNESS GARDEN

Our garden is about two hectares. We grow about 270 different sorts of fruit – I think it's Australia's largest fruit collection. There is never a time when there isn't fruit and vegies and flowers to pick. There are avocados, custard apples, cherries, macadamias, peaches, 125 varieties of apple, olives, pomegranates ... yet we live in a valley where the temperature regularly goes down to minus 7°C in winter, can climb to 52°C in summer. We've had at times three months of gale-force bushfire winds, an 11-month period with only 47 mm of rain ... and yet our garden had no watering. And it survived. (Well, most of it, anyhow. I'm not sure I did as well ...)

Our garden feeds us, the birds, three wombats, nine wallabies, two echidnas, a mob of visiting kangaroos, seven possums, and about 40 000 other species. (No, I haven't counted them all, I'm just estimating.) Weeks will go by without our doing any work in the garden at all, except to harvest. By most standards it is a mess; but it is a beautiful and productive mess.

So how do we do it?

By designing a gardening system that suits Australian conditions.

We have inherited our gardening designs from cooler, wetter and much cloudier places. In Europe you need to maximise sunlight with big gaps between trees and nice straight rows. If you do that here your garden dries out and/or fills with weeds.

So many of our ideas about growing fruit and veg come from farming, too. Farmers NEED nice big spaces to drive their tractors between the trees. And they want all their fruit to mature at once, too, to make picking and selling easier.

Backyard growers rarely have tractors and the last thing they want is six cases of apricots ripening on Tuesday. We need to change the way we think about our gardens – and throw out a heck of a lot of preconceptions.

I am an organic gardener: I don't use artificial fertilisers, herbicides or pesticides except to experiment. But I believe conventional organic ideas are not enough: they still allow backbreaking loads of mulch and harsh manures that may do as much damage as artificial fertilisers; rigorous digging and weeding; and organic pesticides that still kill the predators that might control the pests, or that eliminate the pest predators' food supply so their numbers never build up.

We need to develop new styles of growing things that suit our country. Australia has different soil structures and pest and predator relationships. Our plants respond to heat and light and pests and drought in ways that have scarcely been studied. Here, lack of water or harsh heat governs what we can grow; whereas in northern countries the limitations are set by the available sunlight.

We need to model our growing methods on the bush around us, not on outdated stereotypes from Europe and the United States of America. We need to move beyond such methods that originated when labour was cheap.

Nowadays, chemicals have replaced much of that labour, but the growing systems are still much the same. We need to look for radically different techniques.

This is what this book is about: new ways of growing things, based on the bush, on the way things grow naturally in Australia, instead of on imported stereotypes of neat orchards and flowerbeds with monocultures of ordered rows and rectangular regularity.

THE WOMBAT WAY OF GARDENING

I think it was a wombat that taught me how to garden. His name was Smudge. Many years ago he and I shared a shed and a clearing by the creek. I spent my days and most of my nights wandering around the bush, following him.

I think that sometimes when you spend long periods of time away from other humans and human structure you start to see things differently.

I watched how things really do grow here – away from all the myths perpetuated by most gardening books. I saw how fertility recycled, how nature balanced out the pest outbreaks, how the bush could stop a weed invading. I saw how plants survived in tiny microclimates where climatic lore said they should have died of heat or cold.

I watched broom and blackberry invade an orchard while one metre away the natural bush remained untouched. I watched an apple seedling in the bush outside my garden fence shoot and flourish and bear in almost half the time the pruned and fertilised and weeded ones did in my orchard.

I watched wild peaches bear year after year when conventional gardening practice said they need to be pruned or they won't fruit at all.

Why did I have to fertilise my apple trees to make up for the crop I took, when the wallabies and rosellas could feast on kurrajongs and not have to do a thing except wipe their beaks?

I learnt to watch, and to learn from what was around me. I learnt not to assume that what had been done for many years – especially in countries far away – was necessarily best for Australia. I learnt to be a wombat, taking what I needed, interfering as little as I could.

I learnt that the more work humans do in their gardens, the more they need to do. A wombat track through the bush doesn't need maintaining, a gravel road needs very little work at all. Make a super highway, and you have to employ machines and multitudes to keep it smooth.

It is the same with gardens. The more work you do in it, the more you have to keep on doing. Dig a bed, and next you'll have to weed it. Plant a lawn, and next you need to buy a mower. Prune your trees, and you have to keep on pruning (and feed the plant more to make up for what you've taken). Get rid of all your pests, and next thing you know there are more pest outbreaks than ever – you've probably killed the natural predators that might have controlled your pests for you.

We have all grown up with some idea of what a 'proper' garden or farm should look like. I shall always be grateful that a smudged, grey wombat showed me how things grow – away from human interference.

Forget about pesticides, organic or not, and learn instead to attract the predators that will clean up whatever's bugging you. Grow your own mulch and fertilisers where they are needed, instead of carting them for miles. Weeds? Most cultures don't even have a word for weeds. The Aboriginal languages certainly don't. Australians brought the concept of weeds with them – together with the seeds of Patterson's curse and milky thistle!

Instead of babying your garden for years, digging out the sorrel or the oxalis, like a parent wiping a grubby face, learn to develop systems that control their own weeds. And if you get the urge to dig and mow and re-create the world, just think of wombats dozing in the winter sun, and grazing through the night. Learn to plant your garden richly, and to love it, and to let it go.

QUESTIONS AND ANSWERS

These are the questions I am most frequently asked on air or in letters.

How can I stop my cat scratching up the seedlings?

Cats love fresh earth. Try a no-dig garden, or cover your seedlings with bird netting to catch their claws. (They won't try it again.)

Lion droppings also work. First find your lion.

How do I keep the dog out of the shrubbery?

Dogs use urine to mark their territory. You can mark it yourself instead, if your bladder is large enough or you use a chamber pot. Pretend you are a wolf: a bigger, fiercer carnivore than any dog around. Just don't tell the neighbours that I told you to do it.

What's killing my lemon tree?

Probably the cold; or lack of water; or it's starving to death. If it rocks it's root rot. Give the poor thing some companions to shelter it, and some mulch to cosset and feed it. Try a native lime instead.

How can I love a garden when it doesn't rain?

- Choose veg, fruit and flowers that will survive anything but a nuclear explosion.
- Mulch
- Design a garden that shelters itself from heat and wind and retains moisture.
- Mulch

How do I stop my mother weeding the garden? (She pulls out my favourite seedlings.)

Try the dog repellent above, and she'll probably decide not to. Ask her to sit down with a cup of tea under the roses, instead, and throw breadcrumbs for the birds.

How do I know if my garden's healthy?

- If there are at least six earthworms to every spadeful of soil. If there are lots of things flowering at any time during the year, and there are lots of small insects buzzing round the flowers.
- If your garden is host to lizards, birds, frogs and other species.
- If your soil always has organic matter decomposing on it.
- If there's no bare soil to be seen but just leaves and flowers and fruiting abundance.
- If it makes you, your visitors, passing kids, birds and animals feel like the world is full of joy.

Why is my garden boring?

Dunno. Maybe because you don't have the courage to be different from your neighbours and plant a glorious jungle of fruit and flowers.

How do I grow the biggest pumpkin at the show?

Why bother?

Why is my fruit falling?

Maybe it's too ripe. Maybe it's been infected by fruit fly or codling moth, or damaged by frost. (And damage to the core will cause fruit to drop.) Maybe it's too dry, too windy, or the birds have been partying up there with their boots on. Plant more trees to make up for fallen fruit, and introduce some chooks, geese or wombats to eat the fallen fruit to cure your pest problem.

How do I explain to the neighbours the mess my garden is?

Offer them a basket of fruit ... a bunch of flowers ... or a cup of tea while you watch the honeyeaters eat all your thrips (while their thrips are demolishing the blossom next door).

How do I afford all these plants?

Grow your own from seeds and cuttings. It's not hard! Gardens shouldn't cost the earth. See my book *New Plants from Old*.

Why doesn't my garden look like yours?

You just haven't planted enough. Add a few groves to your garden! Fill up every crevice ... and let time and your plants do the rest.

It all sounds very nice but it wouldn't work in my garden ...

Ha! Have you tried? And if these ideas don't work for you, use them as a basis to work out what will.

How do I kill ...

Don't. Spend your energy growing things, not killing things. That's the secret of wilderness gardening.

Doesn't your wombat eat the lettuces?

No, she prefers grass and weeds. But she devastates carnations.

Chapter 1
THE 'MAGIC GROVE'

WONDERFUL, GLORIOUS GROVES!

More than 200 years after white settlers first arrived here, we are still trying to grow gardens like European parks: lots of grass, straight garden beds of annuals, scattered shrubs and trees that fall down at the first big wind, because they've been grown in the lawn and their roots are poor shallow things.

The result? Gardens that must be pruned and tended, with pesticides to combat insect plagues, herbicides for the weeds, lawn-mowers, whipper snippers, leaf-blowers and other expensive paraphernalia ... plus large amounts of water or the gardens die in the first drought.

Australian gardens don't lack water. They just have too much evaporation. Cut down on the evaporation, and your garden can survive – and even flourish – with far less water than you ever thought possible.

Our garden survives the cold, heat and drought because it's planted in groves. And that is how we can grow such a lot without doing much – if any – work in our orchard, too. Groves look after themselves. And they give us – and the wombats, wallabies and so many other inhabitants of our garden – an extraordinary amount.

I believe that a garden – or a farm – should feed and shelter wildlife, too. We share the world, we don't own it. And the best way to do that is to grow LOTS – with, in my case, as little work as possible.

MORE 'GROVE MAGIC' – WHAT YOUR GROVES WILL GIVE YOU

Weather control

Groves cool the air when it's hot, and help keep it warm when it's cold. And they help keep it humid in dry times, too.

It's worth heading to Canberra just to go through the rainforest gully in the Botanic Gardens. There's a temperature and humidity measure just outside. It will tell you how hot/ cold/ dry it is outside the gully, and what it's like inside. And it is always amazing – even for someone who expects it – to see how the gully and the plants regulate their own temperature and humidity.

And that is what happens in a grove.

Without a grove there is no way we could grow avocados in the frost or snowflakes here, or custard apples, or even oranges in dry times. (Sometimes I think the neighbours assume there is something magic about this end of the valley. But there's not. It's just the groves.)

Drought protection

More shade means less evaporation. But it's more than that. In droughts often the only rain is 'mizzle', a cross between mist and drizzle. Not enough to wet the soil. But it WILL be enough to wet the leaves ... and groves have many levels of leaves. Each one gathers drips then drops them as they condense, and you'll find your groves have 'trapped' moisture from the air. Not a lot, but enough to keep your grove alive when the plants outside are dying.

Wind protection

The winds howl about. But in the grove the leaves hardly move. And even the outside trees are protected from gusty turmoil by their companions either side.

Pest control

Pests recognise their food by its shape (silhouette) or its smell. But trees in groves, with lots of vines growing up them, disguise both shape and scent. Result: very few pests.

Weed control

Weeds need space and light to get a toehold. And they won't find either in a grove.

Easy mulchability

Groves grow a lot in a small space, and a small space means less space needs to be mulched. Plus groves hide ugly mulch from view. We bung just about anything that has once lived under our trees. (We call it 'consigning it to the ecology'.) Dead foxes, old doormats, fallen trees, Aunties that have carked it ... only joking there, though honestly, if it were legally possible, that is how I'd like to be buried when I die. Under the corn stalks under the avocado trees, growing more fruit for my grandchildren.

Longer fruiting times

Most fruit trees fruit all at once – great for the orchardists who want to take their fruit to market, but the last thing a home grower wants is six cases of apricots all in one week.

Fruit in groves matures over a much longer time. Our 'groved' oranges fruit over three to four months, instead of two weeks. Our 'groved' peachcotts fruit over three weeks instead of one week. Groved apples can mature over six weeks instead of three weeks.

Possum control

Possums do NOT like climbing thickets with lots of vines.

Bird control

Well, not control ... sharing. It's a tithe system for wildlife. They get one tenth – the top fruit. I get the rest. Anyone can afford to give birds one tenth. And birds find it very difficult to find fruit deep in a grove.

Self-sufficiency

A grove means LOTS. Lots grown in a small space. Lots of varieties. Lots of fruit. Lots more for the wombats, wallabies, lyrebirds, and the birds who feast on the upper layers. Lots more in tough dry, hot or frosty times. And lots for you.

HOW TO START A GROVE

STEP 1

Start your grove with a single, very hardy tree that will survive severe frost, hellish winds, summers over 45°C and drought ... a bunya, loquat, macadamia, or plum, pears or apples NOT on dwarfing rootstock – you need the big vigorous ones for this. If the seasons are good you can get away with trees like lillypillies, calamondins or oranges, or any other trees that grow well for you.

Mulch your tree. Use Wettasoil. Cosset it all you can. If necessary, put it in a tree guard to keep it alive (see Chapter 10).

PS You can of course start several groves at once. In this case plant the trees about two or three metres apart.

STEP 2

Wait till it's established, at least three years old, more in tough climates. Plant another four hardy trees right at its drip line – where the drips fall off the outer leaves. (If you have lots of water, you can plant these at the same time as the first tree.)

Make it all a mix of deciduous and evergreen trees. This will mean that the evergreen trees will get more light when the deciduous ones lose their leaves in winter.

When they are established, continue, ad infinitum.

STEP 3

Now ... plant trees that aren't so hardy – citrus, which will die in dry times, or avocados that might die in frost – in between the other trees. Many, if not most, subtropical and tropical trees grow naturally under the skirts of their parents, that is, the young trees actually LIKE semi-shade. And yes, some of the trees in the middle will grow more slowly than trees planted outside the groves, as they get less light. But they WILL grow. And trees are very good at finding their own sunlight – they just keep growing up until they do.

Trees that actually prefer semi-shade include macadamias, tamarilloes, avocados, custard apples, lillypillies, ice-cream bean trees, sapotes, Davidson's plum, and quandongs.

STEP 4

Plant climbers, like passionfruit, hops, grapes, kiwi fruit (including wild kiwi fruit that don't need male and female) chilacayote, chokoes, rambling roses up the outer trees.

STEP 5

Plant shade-tolerating veg and other plants on the lowest level: native ginger, ginger lilies, ginseng, wild strawberries, Jerusalem artichokes on the outside where they get just a bit more light. But don't plant too much, as you need to leave a lot of space for mulch.

Groves are magic. Truly. You end up with a great glorious canopy of different fruits. You get the lower fruit. The birds get the top ones you can't get to. (They'll find it hard to reach the lower fruit in all that mass of branches.)

Groves are the best way I know to really intensify the productivity of your land, so there is enough for you, your friends, your chooks, and MORE wildlife than the place supported before.

Passionfruit vine

NINE GROVE HINTS

1. Avoid dwarf trees. An alternative phrase for 'dwarf varieties' is 'not very vigorous'. I've found that dwarf apple trees keel over in gales here whereas the full-sized ones are tougher than old boots. Trouble is, many trees you may buy as full-sized trees are really on semi-dwarfing root stock, as few gardeners or farmers want 20-metre-high lemons, limes, oranges, apples etc. The trees you grow from seed will be full-sized, and their roots will be too.

2. Don't plant in the lawn! Lawns get watered often … well, 'lawn' type lawns do (or did) and that means that the trees' root systems tend to be small and shallow, as they don't have to hunt down deep for moisture. Lawns are also often on shallow top soil, too, brought in and spread over the hard packed concrete stuff left after the house was built. Again, the result is trees that easily fall even in a stiff breeze.

3. Encourage roots to go deep down then spread. An old-fashioned way of doing this is to dig a deep hole, as deep as you can manage. Then plant your tree in a bucket or ten-gallon drum (excuse the lack of metric here) with the base cut out. The plant will need to grow DOWN before its roots can grow OUT … and the soft soil replaced in the hole will mean it's easy for the roots to penetrate. (IF you don't do this, your poor plant may sulk and stay root-bound.)

4. Water deeply. This means once a week or fortnight, a deep slow watering, so that in between the roots need to forage down deep for moisture. Or when you plant the tree, plant a two-metre piece of polypipe with it about one-and-a-half metres deep at the edge of the tree's hole.

   When you want to water the tree, pour water down the pipe … the moisture will head down deep to the root level. You'll waste less water (no run-off, no evaporation); the water will be going where it's needed, not wasted on the surface, and you'll also be encouraging the roots to forage downwards.

5. Don't stake trees. Instead take some old nylon stockings, or anything else with a bit of 'give' like polypipe or old hose, strips of T-shirts or other stretchy fabric, and tie four or five bits to the tree then stake them down about a metre out from the tree (the diagram in the magazine will be more helpful). This allows the tree to rock a bit, but still stops it being blown over till the root system has grown enough to anchor it well.

6. We prune the lower branches away from our trees: it keeps them out of wallaby reach and makes it easier to weed, mulch, plant or mow under them. But it makes them top heavy and liable to falling over in high winds. If you're in a windy area, don't.

7. Wet trees are heavy trees … if by any wonderful chance a windy wet season arrives, with lots of lush leaf and branch growth, it can be worth thinning trees out by pruning away thin or unwanted branches. This allows the wind to blow through them, rather than blow them over.

8. Trees protect each other. Winds may be blocked by stone or brick walls, but often 'dump' on the other side of them, causing turbulence and tree loss. But wind is slowed down as it blows through groves of trees and shrubs.

9. In very windy areas plant a line of tall, very deep-rooted trees like walnuts or pecans to help protect the others. (Assuming you have deep soil so they CAN be deep rooted.) But these are very large trees, and not suitable for a small garden except where you DON'T have wind and can prune off the lower branches to let in more light to other plantings.

GROWING IN THE SHADE

Hardy plants for shady gardens

Shady gardens can still be productive, colourful and capable of withstanding infinite neglect. Most gardens have large areas of shade: the compacted dull side of the house where no-one goes, areas under trees or next to high fences. As our garden grows I find that more and more of it is shaded – and more of it is planted out to shade-loving species, with vegies, flowers and herbs productive under the fruit trees.

Shade-tolerant fruit

Many plants will grow, or survive, in the shade, but not flower or fruit. Grow these on pergolas or trail them upward as much as possible, so that the tops reach the light. Tomatoes, for example, are unlikely to fruit in even semi-shade, but will grow with this treatment, at least in hot to temperate climates. They can be trained to grow on a trellis by continually pruning the lower branches and tying the top ones to the trellis.

NB: Generally, the hotter the climate the more shade many plants will tolerate. Conversely, in cold areas they will tolerate less shade.

Alpine strawberry – doesn't send out runners, grows from seed; look for good tasting varieties; some are bright red but taste like cardboard.

Apples – surprisingly shade tolerant, they fruit when they hit sunlight.

Apricot – shade tolerant in temperate to hot areas, but won't fruit without direct sunlight.

Bamboo – some species, but beware, they may become weed.

Avocado – will grow in semi-shade – in fact needs semi-shade to establish – but fruits best with at least some light.

Bilberry

Cape gooseberry – will fruit in quite deep shade in temperate areas or in cool areas next to a warm wall.

Chilean wineberry – like a raspberry with yellow berries, very hardy, fruits in temperate areas in medium shade.

Babaco – like a small not so sweet pawpaw. Will tolerate -6°C though it will lose its leaves and fruits in the semi-shade of deciduous trees.

Brambleberries – thornless blackberries, etc. Will grow in shade or semi-shade in warmer areas, but only fruit with at least two hours of daylight.

Blackcurrant

Chilacayote melon – will ramble up and down trees, grows in shade but needs sunlight to flower and fruit.

Elderberry

Feijoa – shade tolerant but won't fruit without some direct sunlight (and often a pollinator too).

Gooseberry – light shade only.

Hazelnut – light shade only.

Hops – will twine happily through trees.

Kiwi fruit – will twine through trees – and into your bedroom if you let it.

Loquat – will grow in semi-shade in warm areas, needs sunlight to fruit.

Monstera deliciosa – frost-free areas only.

Mulberry – in hot areas only, and needs sunlight to fruit.

Passionfruit – will ramble through trees.

Raspberries – light shade only in hot summers.

Strawberries – hot to temperate areas only and won't crop as well.

Tamarillo – will grow and fruit in semi-shade, but fruits best with some direct sunlight.

Quince – warm to hot areas only, fruits best with at least two hours of morning sunlight.

Walnut – shade tolerant when young, won't fruit without direct sunlight.

Herbs in the shade

If your herbs look dull rather than glossy, if their leaves are small and they seem to be literally 'shrinking', they need more sun. Transplant them or prune back foliage above them.

Alexanders (*Smyrnium olusatrum*) – See 'Salt-tolerant plants'.

Aloe vera – Needs semi-shade in tropical areas.

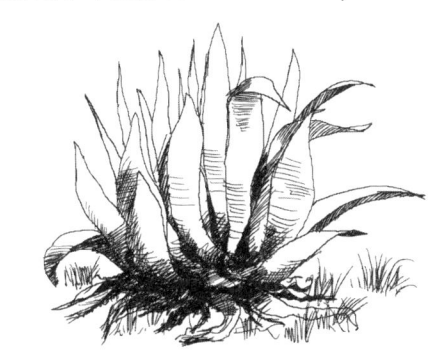

Aloe vera

Basil (*Ocimum* spp) – Most basils will grow in semi-shade in temperate to hot areas.

Bay (*Laurus nobilis*) – This slow-growing aromatic tree is often grown as a pot plant in semi-shaded spots in temperate to hot areas. It is best grown where it gets morning sun.

Bergamot (*Monarda* spp) – The perennial common bergamot (bee balm, Oswego tea – *Monarda didyma*) with its spectacular whorls of flowers – traditionally vivid red, though cultivars now range from white though all shades of pink and purple, will tolerate semi-shade to shade in temperate to hot areas.

Betony, woundwort (*Stachys officinalis*) – Betony needs moist, fertile soil and either full sun or partial shade. It won't tolerate dry exposed sites. Once established in the right spot betony is incredibly hardy. Betony often self-seeds. It is said to protect a house from evil and to provide sweet dreams if you sleep with it under your pillow.

Borage (*Borago officinalis*) – Borage grows anywhere except in a swamp, though it does best in deep soil; otherwise tall, well-grown plants have a tendency to fall over and may need staking. It tolerates semi-shade but does best in full sun.

Chamomile, dyers' (*Anthemis tinctoria*) – This bushy, dull green, incredibly vigorous mounding plant tolerates both heat and frosts, full sun or semi-shade and well-drained soil. Avoid over-watering.

Chamomile, perennial (*Anthemis nobilis*) – The perennial *Anthemis nobilis*, or Roman chamomile does best in moist fertile soils. It will tolerate semi-shade in cool to temperate area; in subtropical areas it MUST have semi-shade, preferably the broken light under trees. Annual chamomile needs full sun.

Chives (*Allium* spp) – The most common kitchen chives are *Allium schoenoprasum* – small tussocks that gradually thicken to large clumps with pretty purple flowers in summer. Garlic chives (*Allium tuberosum*) are flat-leafed, hardy plants, tolerating more frost before they die down in winter than most other chives. Chives will grow well in semi-shade in temperate to hot areas; it's the heat they need more than the light.

Coltsfoot (*Tussilago farfara*) – Tolerates almost any soil in sun or quite deep shade. Coltsfoot can become a weed and is best grown in a pot half buried in the soil if you don't want it to spread, especially in moist spots. Coltsfoot has been used for coughs, asthmatic and bronchial troubles but may cause liver damage. It is best to use alternatives.

Comfrey (*Symphytum officinale*), Russian comfrey (*S × uplandicum*) – Comfrey tolerates semi-shade in temperate climates. In subtropical and tropical areas it needs regular watering in the heat and does best with semi-shade.

Elder (*Sambucus nigra*) – These small trees or largish shrubs will grow in warm semi-shade.

Evening primrose (*Oenothera biennis*) – These plants prefer full sun and fertile soil (and can become immense under these conditions) but will also tolerate poor dry soil and semi-shade and grow quite well by the side of the road. Evening primrose sets hundreds of seeds and can easily self-sow and become a weed (I haven't bothered actually sowing any for years now).

Fennel (*Foeniculum vulgare*) – Tolerates semi-shade in temperate to hot areas, but if you want a tender sweet swollen base it is best grown in moist, slightly alkaline, fertile well-drained soil in full sun. If you just want the leaves, or are growing red (bronze?) fennel, stick it in the semi-shade under a tree and it will happily self-seed.

Feverfew (*Tanacetum parthenium*) – Tolerates semi-shade in temperate to hot areas.

Garlic (*Allium* spp) – Will grow in the semi-shade under trees in temperate to hot areas, but may not flower.

Ginseng, American (*Panax quinquefolius*) – This is one of the true shade lovers. Ginseng needs cold winters, warm to hot summers, semi- to dense shade (the harsher the light the more shade needed), masses of well-rotted organic matter in the soil and excellent drainage and moisture – in other words, ginseng is extremely temperamental and if not perfectly happy will die. Once you do manage to give it optimum conditions it will thrive, and in its native area is a hardy wild plant.

While ginseng can be grown from pieces of fresh root, I've never seen one for sale in Australia. Seeds should be sown in spring, after winter chilling. Fresh seed may not germinate for 18 months, and even when seed is stratified you may find that some germinates and starts growing while other seedlings appear from the same lot of seed next spring. Keep the seedlings in reliable shade (even half an hour of full sun can wither them) and, most important, KEEP THE SNAILS OFF. Snails appear to prefer ginseng to almost any other plant.

Ginseng seedlings grow very, very slowly and for the first year will remain as a single shoot with three small leaves with another two leaves appearing the following year.

Extremes of climate can cause ginseng to die back before winter. Don't throw it out. The hardiest thing about ginseng is its root and it may very well shoot again next spring. Ginseng may also shoot in early spring and be cut by late frosts. In this case the root often rots. Ginseng is perhaps the most celebrated of all 'tonic' herbs, hailed as an aphrodisiac, an aid to longevity and sporting prowess and many other attributes.

Goats' rue (*Galega officinalis*) – Sprawling, bright green perennial used in cheese making, has been used to promote milk flow and in conjunction with other treatments for diabetes. Needs moist fertile soil, tolerates sun or semi-shade and can become a weed.

Goldenseal (*Hydrastis canadensis*) – North American herbal remedy for a wide range of complaints. Needs moist, well-drained soil, preferably with broken light.

Gotu kola, Indian ginseng, wild pennywort, pennyweed (*Centella asiatica*) – Gotu kola needs moist soil and semi-shade though it will grow, but not thrive, in full sun. The better the soil the larger the leaves. It will grow in a sheltered spot in cold areas and vigorously in subtropical or tropical areas, where it an be an excellent ground cover for a damp place. Like ginseng, Gotu kola is valued as a tonic extraordinaire – as an aphrodisiac, an aid to longevity, to increase disease resistance, recovery from sores, wounds, illness and to help maintain mental and physical vigour in old age and under stress. The active ingredient, asiaticoside, is reputed to stimulate regeneration of damaged tissue. It may also be carcinogenic and large doses may lead to liver damage.

Herb Robert (*Geranium robertianum*) – Delicate looking, sprawling annual or biennial used as a weak sedative or for skin problems or as a gargle. Needs moist, fertile soil, tolerates semi-shade and full sun, a pretty ground cover but self-seeds enthusiastically and can become a weed.

Horseradish (*Armoracia rusticana*) – Tolerates semi-shade.

Kawa kawa (*Macropiper exelsum*) – Maori remedy for a wide range of complaints, used as a general tonic, for wounds, toothache and skin conditions. Needs deep, fertile, moist soil, plenty of well-rotted organic matter and broken light above.

Lemon balm (*Melissa officinalis*) – Lemon balm grows best in moist rich soil and partial light shade, especially in hot summers, but will tolerate drought, sun and exposure. It dies back after severe frost but recovers with warm weather and reseeds easily, so easily that lemon balm can become a weed.

Lemon grass (*Cymbopogon citratus*) – Lemon grass tolerates semi-shade in hot areas, or if grown in semi-shade in pots on a hot patio or warm windowsill.

Lungwort (*Pulmonaria officinalis*) – Leaves used for respiratory problems. Needs moist and semi-shaded soil, otherwise tolerant.

Marjoram and oregano (*Origanum* spp) – Both marjoram and oregano are vigorous, fragrant matting plants with tall flower stems. Both tolerating full sun or semi-shade; oregano can become a weed in moist areas or near wet forest. The golden-leafed form needs direct sunlight to maintain its bright colour.

Marsh or bog sage (*S. uliginosa*) – This has the brightest display possible of almost glowing blue flowers arranged in long spikes through most of summer in either full sun or semi-shade.

Marshmallow (*Althaea officinalis*) – Marshmallow will grow under trees.

Mints (*Menthus* spp) – Most mints tolerate semi-shade. We grow them as a carpet under trees. Vietnamese mint (*Polygonum mentha*) is not a true mint, but likes the same moist conditions. It tolerates light frost but heavy frost kills it. It will grow in light shade in warm areas to full sun in cooler districts. In humid areas choose a rust resistant culinary mint cultivar.

Mint bush (*Prostanthera* spp) – These bushy shrubs have dark green to grey-green very fragrant leaves and spike-like groups of purple, pink, mauve or white flowers at the end of branchlets. Mint bushes tolerate all but very heavy frosts and in hot areas they are best grown in semi-shade or with morning sun only. In temperate to cool climates they accept semi-shade happily. They prefer an acid, well-drained moist soil but will tolerate dryness.

Culinary mint

Parsley, curled parsley (*Petroselinum crispum*) – Though not as drought or cold hardy as flat-leafed parsleys, common parsley will accept semi-shade in temperate to hot areas. Japanese or perennial parsley (*Cryptoaenia japonica*) will also grow in semi-shade in temperate to hot areas or in a pot in cool areas on warm paving or patio.

Pleurisy root (*Asclepias tuberosa*) – Leaves and roots used for respiratory problems and needs dry, sandy soil in full sun or semi-shade.

Ramsons (*Allium ursinum*) – Perennial garlic-flavoured ground cover. Needs moist, fertile soil and semi-shade.

Salad burnet (*Poterium sanguisorba*) – Forms a small, ferny, fragrant clump with a strong cucumber scent. It will grow in dry sandy soil as well as more fertile loam in either full sun or semi-shade.

Soapwort, fullers wort, latherwort, tapestry plant, bouncing Bet (*Saponaria officinalis*) – Accepts semi-shade to quite deep shade in temperate to hot areas – see 'Hardy herbs'.

Sorrel (*Rumex* spp) – Both cultivated sorrels do best in semi-shade, with moist, fertile soil for the best tasting leaves

Sweet flag (*Acorus calamus*) – Root used in scent making, potpourris and has limited medicinal use. Needs rich, moist, fertile soil, only flowers when grown in or on the edge of water.

Vietnamese mint (*Polygonum odoratum*) – Vietnamese mint grows best in semi-shade, though it will tolerate full shade or full sun in cooler areas. It needs masses of water. Vietnamese mint will be knocked back by severe frost but usually recovers.

Watercress (*Nasturtium officinale*) – This grows well in semi-shade. See 'Wet gardens'.

Woodruff (*Asperula odorata*) – See 'Herbal carpets'.

Vegetables in the shade

The amount of shade your veg will tolerate depends on your weather and climate. In hot summers here our lettuce grow well in the dappled shade under the kiwi fruit pergola; in spring and winter they just seem to fade away.

The only way to know what will grow in your version of shade is to try it. The following are a starting point only.

Asparagus (semi-shade)

Celery (in temperate to hot areas; we grow celery under our kiwi fruit pergola in a tub by the kitchen door, very handy, with basil, garlic, chives and mizuma).

Dandelion

Garlic (hot areas only and filtered light in temperate areas)

Jerusalem artichokes (dappled light)

Lamb's lettuce

Leeks (hot summers only – good under deciduous trees)

Lettuce (hot summers only)

Mizuma (Japanese salad green or green veg)

Onions (filtered light in hot areas)

Parsley

Potato (hot summers in dappled light under trees or pergolas)

Silverbeet (dappled light in hot areas; ornamental chard and other chard varieties are more shade tolerant than the common 'Fordhook Giant')

Spinach – English (dappled light in hot areas)

Tomatoes (dappled light in hot areas)

Hardy colour in the shade

(*Note that the asterisked plants may become weeds in some areas, but not in others.*)

* Ajuga (plum-coloured leaves rather than flowers)
* Arum lily
  Autumn crocus (cool areas only)
  Begonia spp
  Bauera rubioides
  Calico bush (*Kalmia latifolia*)
  Coleus spp (variegated foliage rather than flowers)
  Columbine (*Aquilegia* spp)
  Clivea, Kaffir lily (*Clivea* spp)
  Daylily (*Hemerocallis* spp)
  English bluebell (*Scilla* spp)
* Erigeron, seaside daisy (*Erigeron karvinskianus*)
  False iris (*Dietes bicolor*)
  Fuchsia spp and a huge range of hybrids
  Hypericum calycinum (Rose of Sharon)
  Helleborus spp (winter rose)
  Hosta, plantain lily (*Hosta* spp)
  Hovea acutifolia
  Hydrangea spp
  Impatiens, busy Lizzie (perhaps the most floriferous of all shade lovers)
* Japanese anemone (*Anemone hupehensis*)
  Kopsia (*Kopsia fruticosa*)
  Lily of the valley (*Convallaria majalis* – cool areas only)
  Wood lily (*Trillium chloropetalum*)
  Shade-tolerant roses, e.g. 'Shady Lady', 'Madame Alfred Carriere'
* Solomon's seal (*Polygonatum multiflorum*)
* Violets (*Viola* spp)
* Vinca minor

Climbers for shady spots

Most of these will grow in the shade, but flower only when they reach some sunlight.

False sarsaparilla (*Hardenbergia violacea*) – Tolerates sun or shade and any climate.

Jasmine (*Jasminum officinalis*) – Take care it doesn't become a weed.

Ornamental grape (*Vitis coignetiae*) – Incredibly tolerant except of heat (no further north than Newcastle for a good autumn display) and humidity.

Red-flowered honeysuckle

Wisteria – Will grow, but not flower, in the shade. Plant in a shady spot and let it climb to the sunlight and then flower.

Hardy roses for dappled or semi-shade

'Blue Moon' (blue)

'Brandy' (apricot)

'Carla' (pink)

'Gay Princess' (Pink)

'Gold Medal' (Yellow)

'Iceberg' (white with pink edges in hot climates)

'Lili Marlene' (rich red)

'Maria Callas' (hot pink)

'Montezuma' (orange pink)

'Oklahoma' (rich red)

'Queen Elizabeth' (pink)

'Scarlet Gem'

Hardy miniature roses for shady areas

'Green Ice' (white, pink and green – exceptionally hardy)

'Ko's Yellow' (Gold)

'Lavender Lace' (pale mauve)

'Mary Marshall' (pink)

'White Simplicity' (white)

Climbing roses for shady areas

These will grow but not flower in the shade – but when the rose reaches the sunlight above house or tree level it will flower wonderfully.

'Albertine' (salmon pink)

'Altissimo' (red)

'Black Boy' (deep red)

'Cecile Brunner' (sweet pink)

Climbing 'Iceberg' (white)

'Madame Alfred Carrière' (soft creamy pink)

'Mermaid' (Creamy yellow)

'Paul's Scarlet Climber' (scarlet, naturally)

Yellow Banksia

Sweet scents in the shade

Daphne (*Daphne odora*)

Gardenia – Semi-shade in hot areas, full sun in cold climates.

Port wine magnolia

Mandevillea – Tolerates semi-shade in hot areas.

Wisteria – Won't flower in the shade but will clamber up to sunlight.

Flowering annuals for semi-shaded areas

(* will tolerate slightly deeper shade)
(# will naturalise in shady areas)

Ageratum (a weed in hot areas)

Aquilegia, columbine (avoid weed varieties)

Bedding begonia

Bellis perennis#

Coleus (probably won't flower but the foliage is usually attractive)#

Heartsease#

Impatiens* (perennial in frost-free areas)

Lobelia

Primrose

Primula*#

Snapdragon

Chapter 2

DIFFERENT GARDENS FOR DIFFERENT PLACES

THE IDEAL

Garden design should be as personal as underwear. (Who wants to wear white cotton knickers every day? Or have a garden like everyone else's in the street, or like those in garden magazines?) No-one can design a garden for someone else – a garden should be an intensely personal thing. Forget about the stereotyped gardens you see all around you, and just work out what you love and what you need.

What do you want to do in your garden? Sunbake or frolic with your lover? You need a sheltered courtyard and high shrubs around the border.

Do you have an urge to roller skate? Try paving inter-planted with hardy herbs like thyme and chamomile and rosemary. Or maybe play cricket? You need a long, tough smooth lawn – try the thyme lawn, which doesn't need mowing (see Chapter 11). Burglar proofing? Sun in winter and shade in summer?

Look at the designs that follow.

A BASIC GARDEN DESIGN

Three-tier planting

Most gardens are badly under-planted. We have inherited our garden spacing from Europe, where plants need space between them. Australia needs more leaves, not sunny patches. Our soil needs protection from sun and rain. (Our skins do too.)

Don't try to emulate an English park. Remember those fat drops of rain that wriggle down your neck if you stand under a tree? They help compact and erode Australian soil. Break up the raindrops, and the harshness of the sun, by planting trees, then shrubs, then small plants, with animals all around and birds all through the branches.

This 'three-tier' planting is the most important lesson in designing a garden.

Groves

A garden can have one grove, or several groves … or just become one great big grove! If I were to starting gardening in a conventional suburb now, I'd have a grove out the front, to shield us from the gaze of passers by, noise pollution and air pollution, plus a grove down the back. (See Chapter 1)

Fences

Plant tall trees around your fence, for privacy. Plant shade-tolerating shrubs under them to complete the courtyard effect: rhododendrons, mint bushes, blueberries, ginger lilies. Carpet the ground under them with strawberries or violets or mint or other ground covers.

Let banana passionfruit and other climbers ramble over your fences and up your trees (trees make wonderful 'living pergolas').

Don't bother with a fence at all: grow a living fence of prickly rugosa roses (intertwined with jasmine for winter greenery) or *Grevillea rosemarifolia*, or a thick, trimmed wormwood hedge to repel dogs and cats.

Place tall reinforcing mesh or other trellises against your fences and grow 20-metre high forests of passionfruit, kiwi fruit or climbing beans or chokoes.

Lawn

Don't bother with a lawn if you're not going to use one; pave the area, with shrubs and herbs in strategic places, or make a 'bush garden' instead. Try the 'no-mow' lawns in Chapter 11.

Don't have any more lawn than you need – fill the space with shrubs and minimum-effort beds.

Paths

Paths need to curve: they give more privacy, and make the space seem bigger, as straight lines attract the eye. Love chamomile paths, or yarrow paths (see Chapter 11). Or don't bother with paths – just have paving stones set into the garden. Plant herbs between your paving stones; line the paths with lavender bushes or a hedge of low-growing rugosa roses that don't need pruning.

Vegetables

Don't bother with a vegetable bed if you don't have time to plant and cosset veggies; instead put in asparagus and artichokes and the perennial and self-seeding vegetable beds in Chapter 9, so you have fresh luxuries to harvest whenever you want – without having to worry about who's going to pick the tomatoes.

Flowers

Plant flowering shrubs and perennials instead of lots of annual flowers. I only plant annuals next to the house – and even those are now self-seeding. I usually don't have separate flowerbeds; the flowers are planted with the vegetables, underneath the trees and shrubs.

Pergolas

Every house should have pergolas, supporting vines and climbers: tall stretches of green with paving underneath. Extend them as far as you can – even cover the driveway with them. They cool the house; then help warm it when the leaves fall in winter and the sun beats on the paving. Deciduous plants for pergolas include kiwi fruit (very fast and sprawling), grapes, hops, chokoes, perennial climbing beans or sweet peas, wisteria. Evergreens include pepper (in frost areas), clematis, wonga vine, passionfruit and banana passionfruit (for cool areas).

If you don't have room for a pergola, consider:
- a lattice archway over the front door or the front gate, covered again with roses, passionfruit, etc.
- an 'arbour' down the back – something vine- or rose-covered to sip iced tea under on hot days
- a lattice wall to cover up an ugly laundry or the neighbour's shed, and again, cover it with roses or clematis or jasmine.

Rules for pergolas and lattices:
- Use sturdy or treated timber ... or else when they rot everything will come crashing down.
- Make any arch or pergola at least two metres tall and also wide enough to pass through un-groped. Wet foliage is heavy and lattice droops, and in wet weather will drape damp fingers over your neck.
- Plant *two* roses, jasmine bushes, etc. – one on either side. No matter how vigorously they grow, most plants don't like to go DOWN a pergola ... only up.
- Prune the stuff on your pergola, lattice, etc. every year after it flowers. If you don't, you'll end up with mess and tangles, not beauty.

Useful tip: You can buy ready-made archways and arbours, but for about the same amount of money you can hire an expert to make one EXACTLY as you desire.

Waste areas

Most gardens have waste patches: the shady bit round the side of the house, the bare patch down the back, places that aren't planted and aren't used. Make every bit of your garden count:
- Grow a rosemary hedge around the Hills Hoist.
- Grow strawberries or asparagus down the driveway.
- Espalier fruit trees against your warm house-walls, or let grape vines clamber up them.
- Carpet the shady areas under your trees with strawberries.
- Plant out your footpath with loquats, lillypillies, quandongs, pistachio nuts, Himalayean pears, crab apples or kei apples – fruit trees that don't need much maintenance. Most passers-by won't recognise the fruit, so won't pinch it.
- Hang BIG hanging baskets of rhubarb, lettuce, parsley and other veg from the eaves, all at different heights. Even a small patio can have 20 baskets at different heights from its eaves.
- Avoid naked fences and tree trunks!

GARDEN LUXURIES

The writer Norman Douglas once said about food that 'nothing is too good for everyday'. The same goes double for gardens. Everyone deserves luxuries in their garden – for many of us it's the only place we can afford them.

Many years ago I decided I'd never feel poor if I had armloads of flowers to give away whenever I wanted to. It's hard to feel broke when you're eating your own asparagus or avocados; it's difficult to miss having a video as you watch blue wrens peck around your roses instead.

Try:
- A birdbath – endless entertainment.
- A romantic archway covered in roses, wisteria or pink flowered banana passionfruit.
- A thyme lawn to roll on.
- Climbing 'Papa Meilland', big fat perfumed dark red roses up any spare deciduous fruit tree.
- A grape- or kiwi fruit-covered arbour from which to contemplate the world.
- A greenhouse made from windows scavenged at the dump for raising winter cucumbers.
- A tree house (for you, not the kids – the world looks different up a tree).
- Four walls of Boston ivy so you need never paint the house again.
- A hot tub in a copse of shrubs, easier than a pool or a spa. Make your own of wood and plastic liner, fill it with a hose connected to the laundry tap, and empty it onto your fruit trees.
- A walled garden made of stone or brick, outside your kitchen, preferably so it catches the morning sun. This hot, sheltered area is

perfect for growing tomatoes through winter or quick crops of basil – or sitting in the winter sun.

- Window boxes filled with colour, or with climbing sweet peas trained up strings to the top of the window: a living curtain to keep out summer sun and fill the room with dappled light.
- Any luxurious vegetable: a packet of asparagus, frilled lettuce, artichoke or snow pea seeds costs less than a packet of frozen chips, but gives a lot more luxury for your money. You can buy the seed for a decade of flowers for the same price that you rent a video. Be extravagant and buy $50 worth of bulbs – then recoup your cost by selling half the flowers to the grocer, or pot up half and sell them when they flower.

Gardens are the best investment I know. Bank interest has recently varied between 10 and 15 per cent a year. Flowers and shrubs can more than double in a year – 100 per cent interest or more – and give seeds and cuttings for countless offspring too.

Never feel guilty about spending time or money on your garden. Humans once lived closely with the world around them. For most of us our gardens are the only contact we have with the natural world. Gardens give beauty and happiness and health – for you and the world around you.

Never stint on anything you want to do in your garden. Remember, too, plants needn't cost money: take cuttings of anything you fancy and stick them in the ground. Don't worry if it's the wrong time of year, they may grow anyway. Pluck seeds and stick them in your pocket. Plants have grown and fruited for millennia without humans helping. Even if you do everything wrong you'll be surprised how much grows and how luxuriantly. Most plants are very hard to kill.

There is only one rule for a good garden: just keep planting. It's easy to pull out unwanted growth; you've then got free material for mulch or compost. It takes much longer to grow something.

Start planting now. If you change your mind about the sort of garden you want – or the roses get crowded out – it doesn't matter: you've added greenery to the world, at least for a little while, given shelter to birds, and trapped a few pollutants from the air. Nothing that is grown is ever wasted.

SIMPLE SOLUTIONS FOR PROBLEM SPOTS

The shady side of the house: fill it with ferns. Or tree ferns. Or native ginger. (Make cordial from the roots or use them in cooking. Bake fish in the leaves. Eat the berries.) Or a hedge of tamarillos that love shade. Or ferns AND tamarillos AND native ginger. Or lillypillies.

A hot wall under the eaves: lavender or rosemary: they're one of the few plants that don't get mangled by mites if they don't get rained on. But do water them sometimes; even lavender and rosemary like to drink and to have dust washed off. Or hellebores. A lot of fruit salad sage, or pineapple sage or tequila sage, masses of flowers and scented leaves and birds after the nectar. Or dragon fruit, a climbing fruiting succulent that loves heat.

A steep slope: fill it with hardy trees like olives, ice cream bean tree, pears, plums, quinces, loquats; then plant fast-spreading hardy ground covers underneath prostrate grevilleas, rosemary or juniper, gazanias, a groundcover rose or six. Ask your local nursery for suggestions for your area. Or for a more labour- and cost-intensive solution, design and build some terraces.

We had a bank of blackberry. I planted fast-growing silver poplars, then as they shaded out the blackberry, planted ginger lilies under the trees; then planted avocados which are now crowding out the poplars.

An ugly laundry, shed, compost bin, etc.: put up some lattice and cover it with jasmine, clematis, wonga vine, kiwi fruit, passionfruit, choko ...

Hot paving: cover with a pergola planted with deciduous grapes, kiwi fruit, wisteria ...

A barren garden: find a nursery where it looks as if they love their plants. Smile sweetly and ask for two dozen low-maintenance shrubs, then spend the afternoon getting your hands dirty and having fun.

Nasty neighbours

Grow a hedge of stinging nettle trees ... only joking (sigh). But even very nasty neighbours don't deserve a giant leylandii hedge, blocking out all sunlight. Try fast growing passionfruit or Chinese star jasmine growing on a trellis – easily trimmed, still lets in a bit of light, and doesn't take up much space.

GARDENS FOR WET AREAS

(When I first wrote this book, it was wet! Actual, wet stuff falling from the sky!)

At the moment our roof's off (being replaced), black drips are oozing down the walls as the plastic leaks, and Lurk (the wombat from the artichoke bed) kept us awake last night rollerskating on the old tin on the ground. The raspberries have rust, the lavender downy mildew, the roses are nodding wet petals groundwards and if the grass gets any longer it'll sneak in one night and strangle us in our beds. (I hope it gets Lurk first.) But things are growing.

There are ways to cope with wet weather in the garden. The classic orchardist's trick is to add potash. Potash helps new growth 'harden off', so it's less disease prone and more frost resistant. You can buy this and apply it at about a tablespoon to the square

Plant trees 'above-ground' on a mound, and build 'above-ground' garden beds to keep roots away from waterlogged soil; dig ditches to drain away the water, and plant casuarinas and willows in low areas to soak up the moisture.

metre (or about a matchbox full for every good wide pace) or add a sprinkle of wood ash instead. Comfrey is also rich in potash: use it as mulch or add it to the compost. Also fertilise with mulch and compost, which will steadily decompose when and where the plants need it. Don't dig mulch or compost in when its wet though – digging wet ground destroys soil structure, and undecomposed organic matter encourages root rots. Leave it on top for the worms and bacteria to return to the soil.

Cut the grass, even if it's raining and you'll wrench half of it out by the roots. In weather like this it doesn't matter. It'll raise its head again soon enough. Long grass encourages mildews and fungi, increasing humidity where it's at its worst – down by the plants. You may think there's good air circulation in your garden, but stick your head down to plant level; its probably stiller and much more humid. Short grass means more breeze at ground level, less moisture and less disease.

Avoid transferring infections. Many disease spores are wind blown, but others are spread on skirts or trousers or hands. Don't brush past infected plants, then wander down to have a look at the next lot. Practise garden quarantine.

Don't apply nitrogenous fertiliser (you'll just get more soft wet growth); try spraying seaweed spray, green manure or casuarina spray. All of these will strengthen resistance to fungal infections, make plants more frost hardy and hopefully improve fruit set. (We've had a bad citrus set this year – it's been too wet for the bees to stick their noses out of doors.)

In very wet areas:
- Build drains above your gardens to channel off moisture; these may have to be a metre deep.
- Plant deep-rooted moisture draining trees above garden level, like casuarinas and willows (slash the branches for mulch).
- In very bad areas build your gardens up instead of down, so the plants' roots are out of water.
- Try planting trees above ground level; build up a small heap of soil and arrange the tree roots over it, then build up soil over the roots so there is a nice gradual slope on either side.

A GARDEN FOR POLLUTED AREAS

Gardens in polluted areas don't grow so well (humans don't either). They are also more vulnerable to pests: the plants are weaker, and fewer predators survive.
- Grow barriers of high trees, then shrubs to catch dust and other pollutants, as well as stopping noise.
- Hose down the shrubs every few days so that caught material falls to the ground.
- Keep up high levels of organic matter in the garden to 'fix' heavy metal pollutants and to break down others.
- And, of course … groves!

If you are in a heavily polluted area (either by a busy road, under an airport flight path, or have factory or mine dust blowing onto you) do not grow plants you are going to eat in the soil that has been there for years; it will have accumulated pollutants and these may be passed on to you. Make above-ground gardens instead by bringing in soil or organic matter for compost from elsewhere.

This is one case where it's not a good idea to recycle nutrients from your own garden; use garden refuse on ornamentals. Keep a separate compost bin of brought-in kitchen scraps and other scavenged material for your vegetables and fruit.

Wash vegetables well before you use them; add a little vinegar to the water.

In very bad areas you may need a glass-house or shadehouse to keep polluted dust such as lead-bearing dust from your garden.

A thick border of trees and some old mosquito netting reduce the amount of air-borne pllutants to reach your crop

An old mosquito net above your garden will catch most of the dust without excess shading; but wash it every few days (away from the garden) and take it down before it rains.

Use water filters if you're not sure of the purity of your water supply, or catch your own rainwater for your garden (though in city areas this is likely to be more polluted than the tap water as your roof collects pollution dusts).

Avoid herbicides and pesticides as your garden will be polluted enough without them. Little has been done on the cumulative effect of several different pollutants.

A GARDEN BY THE SEA

Seaside gardens suffer from wind and salt. Treat salt like the pollutant it is and follow the advice for a polluted garden. Use barriers of trees and shrubs, mosquito net or shadecloth, etc. As well:
- Choose plants with hairy leaves or thin leaves: they'll probably stand up to salt, winds and drying.
- Try and find out what grew naturally in your area before it was cleared and plant those species as windbreaks.
- Build stone, brick or sleeper walls wherever you can. Walled gardens are the traditional safeguard against wind. Make high walled courtyards for trees and shrubs, or just low walls above your vegetable areas.
- And, of course … groves!

GARDENS IN FROST ZONES

There are two things to remember about frost. Firstly, it isn't the freezing that kills, it's the thawing. Secondly, the main problem with cold stress is dehydration. If you can't avoid frost you can minimise its effects.

Avoiding frost

Look for frost-free sites. Learn to judge the frost potential of your garden. Even in a small area frost damage can vary enormously. Imagine frost as a body of cold air flowing like water. It will settle in hollows, flow down drains and air channels, be easily blocked by fences, hedges and other plants. If frost can drain away it may leave the higher spots in your garden clear – especially if they are north facing and thus warmer.

Frost also settles on mulch and bare soil. Mulch may stop plant roots from freezing – but it will increase the frost damage to leaves.

My garden is on a slight slope with a ridge behind it. There are enough differences in microclimate for me to grow raspberries and sugar maples in one part, where the sun is blocked till late morning and the frost stays till midday, yet have avocados ripening metres away where the frost drains down a sunnier slope.

Watch how the frost settles in your garden before you do major plantings. Work out if your intended garden design will change the frost pattern – a new fence, for example, might block the frost and burn off plants previously untouched, while clearing a hedge could let frost drain away, or the slow growth of a large tree may gradually protect the plants beneath it.

You can create your own frost-free sites by planting shelter trees. Go out in the garden on a frosty morning and peer under low, spreading trees. Unless the frost is extremely severe these areas will be frost-free. Use them for frost-sensitive plants like passionfruit (the leaves will twine up through the tree to find the light) or early strawberries – or as a place to keep your early seedlings safe.

Increase your frost-free area. Clear away any blockages if you can (weed piles, fences or at least long grass or bracken round the fences) so that frost can drain away. If you don't want to remove your hedge or other shrubbery, try cutting low drainage holes in it.

Predicting frost

Some gardeners swear they can smell a frost, a clear, sharp smell. It is the smell of cold, dry air. Frost is less likely when the sky is cloudy, when there is fog or other moisture around. Frosts can often be predicted by gazing at the sky at night. If the stars are particularly bright and twinkling there will probably be a frost.

Lighting fires around the garden is an old-fashioned way to keep off frost. The smoke from the fires is actually more useful than the heat from the flames. Orchardists once used specially designed braziers that burnt all night with a lot of smoke. Cover a good bed of coals with green wood for a smoky fire. (This is not a remedy in suburban areas.)

Keep frost records from year to year. The dates of the first and last frost each year should be fairly consistent. It's helpful to know, for example, that last year your first frost came in late April and your last at the end of September.

(Snow will act as an insulator, and do less harm than the frost. Don't clear it away from your garden – heap it up instead.)

A weekly spray of seaweed or nettle tea is said to increase plants' resistance to frost and to help fruit set in cold areas. Either can be easily made: just cover seaweed or nettles with water, leave for a few weeks and dilute to the colour of weak tea.

Overhead irrigation releases the latent heat of the water during spraying. For this to effectively help your crops you must start spraying when the temperature is still at least 2°C or more. You don't necessarily need large scale commercial equipment for this: a garden spray or even microjets can also work well.

Wind machines are used commercially to mix cold air with the warmer air above it. These are available commercially, or can be made at home. A 10 horsepower motor driving a propeller on a 10-metre tower is claimed to raise the temperature over a hectare by 2°C in a few minutes.

SOME FROST-PREVENTION GARDENS

A LOW mulch around your plants will INCREASE the frost damage, but if you mulch very deeply, so that most of the greenery is covered, you'll insulate the leaves from cold.

A highly mulched garden

Surround your garden with wire mesh or tomato stakes with string around them. Fill this circle with dry leaves or lightly packed hay so only the tops of the plants show through. The mesh should stop the leaves blowing away. Harvest crops through the mulch. Plants can dry out under this mulch, and can eventually rot.

Leave the garden covered only for the most dangerously frosty times, about six weeks in late autumn or in early spring for late harvesting or hardening off early plants.

Bodies of water

A pond in the middle of your garden will keep the area around it slightly warmer through the night. Keep your swimming pool full in winter and use it as heat storage for frost sensitive plants around it. Anyone who has watched steam rising from a lake or river in the early morning sees how a body of water can act as a heat sink.

The sheltered garden

Orange groves in England used to be planted in specially designed groves of other trees, tall and thick, which kept them sheltered. Use larger trees to protect smaller shrubs below.

Gardening out of frost's reach

Get some old tyres from the local garage, pile them high, as high as you need to get your plants out of the reach of the frost. If this means a pile of more than three tyres, stake down the middle so they don't fall over. Now fill them with earth, compost, or old hay or manure, still decomposing, if you have it: the decomposition will give a bit of added warmth. Plant your crops up top; even fruit trees work with this method, as long as they are well staked till the roots grow down below the level of the tyres. Water well though – drainage can be too good in tyre gardens.

You can of course build up your above-ground frost-free garden from materials other than old tyres, but these are easy to come by and, being thick and black, absorb and retain heat well.

The flooded garden

An emergency method of keeping frost from your crops is to flood them. This is easy in a garden with waterproof (i.e. concrete or mortared stone) permanent edges. Otherwise edge the garden with boards, making sure the ends abut firmly.

Now line the garden with newspaper, at least six pages thick, making sure that the pages overlap and rise up to the top of the boards. Just before you go to bed, on any clear starry night that seems to smell of frost, fill the bed with water, as deep as possible. Leave the hose just dripping into it. Take the boards away in the morning to drain away the water. As long as you drain the water off in the morning you can use this method even with plants that are susceptible to collar rot, especially if you give them their own collars of newspaper to stop soil-borne spores from infecting them.

The manure-heated pit garden

Dig a hole about 60 cm deep, pile in leaves or decomposing manure. Cover with sandy soil. Plant your vegetables. Now lay a few stakes over the pit and balance old windows or clear plastic on a few bricks so that they are orientated to the morning sun.

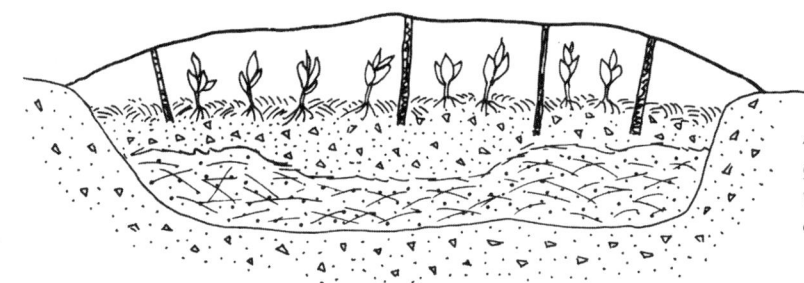

A manure-heated pit garden will give your plants extra warmth in winter, and get seedlings or cuttings off to a good start.

These beds can also be used to help strike cuttings needing bottom heat or to get early seedlings for spring planting. The heat generated by the decomposing material should mean that this pit cold frame is relatively frost-free.

Heated frost frame

Make a manure or compost pile about 60 cm high. Lightly cover it with soil. Carefully fit a cold frame over the top of it, so the top is level with the top of the pile and the main slope is orientated to the morning sun. A good mix for the compost pile is equal parts of coarse leaves (not gum leaves) and fresh cow or horse manure. This mixture produces a good, long-lasting heat, but do experiment with any suitable compostable material on hand.

Wait about a week before planting out, so the soil inside can warm up.

Repairing frost damage

The worst frost damage occurs when plants thaw rapidly. It isn't the freezing that injures the plants as much as the thawing, as the frozen cells expand and burst. If you are an early riser give your plants a thorough gentle watering before the sun hits them. This way the plant cells gradually relax instead of bursting. Even totally frozen plants can be restored.

Also try covering your plants, either the night before or race out and do it as soon as you see frost on the ground, to increase the thawing time. Use blankets, old newspaper; just get your plants covered. Often this may save them.

As a last resort rely on frost-hardy plants and ones that have been hardened to your area. Any plant you buy from an area hotter than yours, or from an indoor area in a nursery, may well tolerate less frost than a local plant. You can harden plants gradually by leaving them outside for longer and longer periods each day. Better still, raise your own from cuttings or seed you have saved yourself from plants growing happily in your area.

THE PRIVATE GARDEN

Homes should not just be secure, they should feel secure. If your house is buffeted by traffic noises, you'll soon get used to them – consciously – but your unconscious won't. People who live with constant noise are simply more stressed.

There's a corollary to this too. The more unpleasant the noise you live with, the more you block out sounds, not just brake grinds and accelerator roars, but the sounds of trees and the cracking as the roof expands on a hot day and rain on the roof or pavement ...

Plant tall trees around the front, back and sides – try melaleucas or fruit trees (preferably evergreen). Tall trees won't block out noise, but they'll create 'white noise', a pleasant murmuring of the branches and leaves, that will hide unpleasant sounds.

Don't worry about how you'll pick the fruit from these tall trees – you'll scramble through some way. Plant them closely. Fill in the space behind until they grow with trellises and climbers like passionfruit (banana passionfruit in cold areas), honeysuckle, jasmine or clematis. Don't leave a space for a path; you can cut some branches back as the trees grow, and the path can wind beneath the trees.

In front of the trees plant shrubs, such as small wattles, grevilleas and buddleia. Now plant smaller plants like ginger, canna lilies, blueberries, daisies, lavender or roses. This will leave you with irregular courtyards in the middle. Leave some as lawn, or try lawn alternatives. Otherwise pave the lot, leaving spaces in the paving for small plants and vegetables. Mark out the sunniest spots for sun-loving vegetables and flowers. In small gardens you may have to raise the beds so they get more sun.

Turn your fences into hedges, or even faster, fasten trellis to the fence and grow a passionfruit, banana passionfruit, jasmine, etc. for speedy protection. One of the best really thick evergreen low-maintenance hedges I know for frost-free – or light frost – areas is avocados.

Plant seedlings or grafted trees a metre apart and in five years you'll have dense cover that can be pruned to shape and a heck of a lot of fruit (see also 'Home-grown luxuries').

Photinia provides possibly the fastest hedge around (see 'Sound proofing'). Kumquats aren't bad either and camellias can be wonderful. Tea tree and callistemon, by themselves or together, make wonderful bird-attracting hedges if you want a more casual look.

Use lattice. If you're close to lattice you can see through it but passers-by at a distance can't. Lattice is wonderful to place in front of exposed rooms like laundries, or partially enclosed verandahs. It can be quite cheap but more expensive versions last longer. There's quite a range available, so shop around.

Plant shrubbery (I love that word) in front of your fence. Most passersby aren't Peeping Toms, just casual glancers, and if the space around your house is broken up by trees and shrubbery they won't crane to get a closer look. On the other hand, anyone sitting in your house (i.e., you) will get a good look at passersby because you're sitting still and can focus more easily through the greenery.

Curve all paths. People mostly look in straight lines and a curve will divert their glance from your front door or garage until they're well past.

Terrace your garden. Terraces look bigger than slopes and you feel you have more *Lebensraum*, even if you haven't. Install a few great boulders too, if it's possible and they don't look ridiculous. I don't want to go all *feng shui* on you, but boulders really do give a feeling of solidity. Solidity is contagious.

THE SELF-SUFFICIENT GARDEN

Turn your garden into groves – lovely productive thickets with vines growing up them and shade tolerant veg below. Even small gardens can have at least 50 fruit trees if you grow groves, and have a hedge of apples or other fruit out the front.

Hedge your garden boundaries with fruit trees. Plant them two metres apart – they'll grow tall to reach the sun and the branches will tangle, but this means birds won't find most of the fruit (though you will). Tall trees bear as much fruit as wide ones: you just have to climb the tree or use a fruit picker on a tall stick to get the crop. Plant dwarf fruit trees along paths as a hedge.

Hang BIG hanging baskets at uneven heights from your eaves. Even a small house can thus support about 200 big baskets of rhubarb, strawberries, silver beet, cos lettuce, herbs, spring onions, trailing climbing beans or peas, gooseberries, zucchini, mini pumpkin, cherry tomatoes, parsley.

Plant espaliered fruit trees – heat-loving varieties – next to the heat-absorbing wall of your house. Put frost tender plants like avocados and oranges so they face north. (This way even many Tasmanian gardens can grow subtropical fruit – walled gardens are good too.)

Make tiers for flowers, vegetables and small fruits like gooseberries and raspberries. Tiers give you much more planting space than flat ground. Build the tiers from old tyres or railway sleepers or bricks or rocks. Build them as high as you can be bothered – the more tiers, the more space.

Have as many climbers as you can. There should be no bare space on walls or fences; grow passionfruit and chokoes up the trees; grow climbing vegetables where you can.

Make your lawn productive, i.e., plant trees and shrubs instead, and mulch them.

Keep some animals, as animals mean fertility. They can help your weed problems (see Chapter 6) and your pest problems (see Chapter 7). Chooks and ducks mean eggs and meat.

Consider window boxes and hanging gardens (see Chapter 6). Stick poles in the middle of the garden for grapes to wander up (they don't have to be spread out). Try chokoes or passionfruit.

Rethink all your wasted space. Plant the drive with strawberries – you may squash a few berries sometimes, but that's better than no harvest at all. Plant out the nature strip, preferably with plants that passers-by won't recognise as edible. Use tea camellias, loquats, medlars, pomegranates, japonica (make jam or stew the fruit), Irish strawberries, guavas, hibiscus, kurrajong or elderberries. Grow oaks for acorns (for hen food), jojoba, white mulberries or bamboo (for shoots and building material). For more ideas, see the author's *Backyard Self-sufficiency*, published by Aird Books.

WHAT TO DO WITH A PATCH OF SHALE

Many gardens start without any soil at all – either because there wasn't any to start with, or because it was removed as the ground was cleared for building.

OPTION 1

Buy soil. This is the conventional solution. The soil probably won't be fertile, and you'll have to shovel it where you want it. It is also expensive, and for the same price or less you can try option 2. You'll also find your trees either blow over or die in the drought as their roots will be shallow, sticking to the thin layer of good soil.

OPTION 2

Make your own soil. Build up above-ground beds with hay if you can afford it – otherwise any organic material you can scavenge, from grocer's leftover cabbage leaves to old carpet. Put the most fertile on top: leaves, compost, other people's lawn clippings, manure, old sawdust, etc. Then plant in it. Water and feed with any of the 'extras' in the chapter on fertility till the mulch breaks down into the soil.

OPTION 3

This is a longer term, but cheaper, option. Soil will gradually build up on bare areas as natural vegetation breaks down. Speed this up – plant quick growers like wattle, and slash the young branches (most wattles 'fix' nitrogen and will help fertilise your area as well as add organic matter). Sow weeds like Patterson's curse, dock and anything else that grows rampantly in your area. (Weeds will grow where nothing else will – that's why they're weeds.) Slash them regularly. Water and feed with 'extras' – especially pelletised hen manure – as often as you can.

Terraces should not be like a staircase – they need a 'lip' to stop moisture run-off.

OPTION 4

Terrace your ground – by hand if it's small, with a bulldozer if it's large. The terraces should neither be flat nor level; they should gradually run around the slope, a bit like a round slippery dip gradually sloping to the bottom, and the terraces themselves should slope into the hill. This method catches any available water, and any soil that washes down will be caught on the inner terrace. Place small pockets of mulch on the inner terraces, and plant trees and shrubs with clover underneath, and herbs; plant native ground covers and hardy introduced ones like rosemary on the outer slopes; plant deep-rooting 'natural mulchers' like comfrey in between the two areas.

MAKING THE GARDEN PART OF YOUR HOUSE

When I was a child we played hide-and-seek in the garden and French cricket; now most kids seem to dash for the cartoons. Adults swapped gossip over the fence as they cut the evening cabbage; teenagers perfected their tans, toddlers romped with dogs. The garden was a source of evening vegetables, flowers for the table and friends (bought flowers were almost unthinkable except for a luxury corsage), and a large part of the family entertainment.

Now we have TV. We are focused inwards, not out. Most people no longer seem to regard their garden as part of the house – just as a frame, to look good to passers-by and to be enjoyed only as they trot up the path to an evening of Dynasty. Here we find our windows more engrossing than TV. This morning I started work late – the bower birds were cavorting in the kiwi fruit in the pergola and we stopped to watch them. Last night we observed an owl waiting for its prey on the tree by the gate.

Even if you spend most of your life indoors, your garden can still play an important role in your domestic comfort.

COOLING THE HOUSE

Natural air-conditioning

Somewhere beyond our garden it's 38°C in the shade, if there IS any shade that's not already full of hot kids and hotter dogs. But here, under the crabapple tree, as I write this (I LOVE laptop computers) it's ... well, I don't know how hot it is, as I'm not going to slog in and find the thermometer to find out. But it's a heck of a lot cooler than 38°C.

Our garden is cool partly because it's shaded by tall trees, carefully planted so they don't block the breeze (which smells of hot musk roses and curry bush at the moment).

The breeze is also flowing over a small fountain which is cooling the air too – literally.

Plants can lower air temperature by half. If it's a baking 40°C on the footpath, it can be a cool 20°C in your garden, as less sun radiates off the surfaces, and moisture evaporates and cools the air. In areas with hot summers and cool winters plant deciduous trees and vines around your house, angling them so they cut the summer sun but leave a path for winter sun. We have a pergola around our house – an excellent thing covered with kiwi fruit, wisteria, grapes and climbing roses. In summer they send a broken dappled green light into the kitchen and living room; in winter the leaves drop and strong sun pours in.

If you want an even greater cooling effect, string a drip irrigation line along your pergola – the breeze will evaporate the falling drips and cool the air around your house. A fine mist spray is even better – the more evaporating water, the cooler the air.

Cover the outside of your house with ivy or other creepers for added insulation; curtain your windows with window boxes of climbing plants like climbing geraniums, miniature climbing roses or sweet peas – train them up strings across your window. Consider a moist fernery or shade house next to your back door so cool air sweeps in when you open it.

Plants on the hot west side of your house will shade it; plants on the cool southerly side will mean cooler air – open the windows and let it in. Plants around your house will also catch dust, pollution, help shield you from noise and give you fruit, flowers and birds in season.

Houses in very hot areas are traditionally built around courtyards (these can be added to the side of your house): roofed with deciduous vines like grapes, with thick green shrubs around the walls – and a small pool and fountain for the breeze to flow across and cool the air.

Another traditional cooling method is to tunnel cool air from a shade house some distance away, under the earth to the house. These cool wind tunnels were reputed to become so cold that thin layers of ice could form at the other end of them. One of the coolest houses I know was in Brisbane, built on stilts with a fernery below, kept cool and moist by mini spray jets. The cool air seeped through the floorboards; vines drooped over the open verandah and the back door opened into a bougainvillea-covered shadehouse.

Deciduous climbers to cool your house

Roses, grapes, hops, kiwi fruit, chokoes (a falling choko can be a hazard, so keep them away from walkways), sweet peas (annual or perennial), climbing beans (annual or perennial), thornless blackberries, wisteria, and some clematis.

Evergreen climbers to cool your house

Passionfruit, banana passionfruit, jasmine, honeysuckle, bougainvillea, hardenbergia, wonga vine, and some clematis.

During hot days, the cool, moist air from a fernery around the perimeter of this house on stilts is drawn up through the floorboards as the warm air inside rises and escapes through high windows and vents in the pitch of the roof.

KEEPING LIFE BREEZY

Trees shade you, add a touch of moisture to dry air, and keep soil moister below them too. BUT … trees can also block breezes.

If you live in a humid area, i.e. near the coast, do have TALL trees – ones that are above your window height, not parallel to it. (Yes, I know trees take a while to grow but it is worth aiming for an ideal garden, even if takes a year or three.) Tall trees shade your house and garden, but unlike tall shrubs they allow breezes to cool the house too – or at least help some of the clammy moisture on your skin evaporate.

Look at the type of shade the tree gives too. Thick greenery above you can make a house dismal even in mid-summer, whereas more open canopies, the sort that a jacaranda gives you, for example, all green dapples (not to mention stunning flowers) will give you shade plus light. Look for umbrella-shaped trees as well, like palms, bauhinia, or Albizia (silk tree).

Just add water

If I could just remember my high school physics I'd be able to tell you why evaporating water really DOES cool the air down, which is why Coolgardie safes work. (Hands up those who remember what a Coolgardie safe is!)

But a breeze flowing over a fountain is also a delicious thing in its own right, softening the air with water smells and coolness. (Mostly, you only sense the smell of water on hot, still days.) In fact, even watering the paving around the house will cool things down! We have a polypipe and microjets watering system above our hanging baskets, and on hot afternoons these both water the plants and cool the air.

PS. Please, no-one write and tell me how a Coolgardie safe works! If I've forgotten for this long I don't need to know!

KEEPING THINGS GREEN

Okay, don't panic about that parched patch of grass. Grass recovers. Our grass turns brown here each summer (we just don't have enough water to keep it green), but even a few hours after the first rain green shoots appear.

Concentrate on watering the things that WON'T survive, like young shrubs and trees. But also consider planting a few 'stay green' climbers so you still have cool, green colours around you.

Our passionfruit and kiwi fruit and grape vines make the whole garden look green, and there's a comfortable feeling of abundance about it too (anyone like a passionfruit? a basket of grapes? twenty passionfruit and a box of peaches?).

Watch out for paving

Large areas of paving may be elegant, fashionable and low maintenance – but they do reflect a lot of light and heat onto the house. (Old-fashioned lawns were popular for a reason!)

If you do have large areas of paving, consider a pergola above them, with grapes or hops or kiwi fruit that will cover the area with greenery in summer and lose their leaves in winter. Of these, hops are the least messy, as the leaves wither up and mostly blow away, and kiwi fruit the most – their thick tough leaves drop through autumn and most of winter and the fruit can get a bit splodgy too.

Light up the darkness!

Install garden lighting! Why? Because the best way to enjoy your garden and stay cool is to do it at night. (A mozzie-proof 'cabana' in the garden, or mozzie-proof blinds on the verandah may also be a good idea!)

KEEP THINGS SMELLING GOOD

When the world smells of hot bitumen cool garden scents are immeasurably refreshing.

Hot days are also great for actually SMELL-ING your plants – perfume rises on hot days. One good fragrant plant can fill a garden with scent; half a dozen can turn your place into paradise. My midsummer scented favourites are hybrid musk roses like 'Prosperity', 'Penelope' or 'Buff Beauty', curry bush (our front steps smell like a good vindaloo at the moment), clary sage, mandevillea, boronia, lavender, rosemary plus thyme between the hot paving stones.

PLANT OUT YOUR SHADE

A shady garden doesn't have to be a dull one, especially if most of your trees are deciduous ones that lose their leaves in winter to let the sunlight in. As I look around our garden I can see deep purple impatiens flowers, purple pansies, blue and purple agapanthus, pink and purple fuchsias (well, I do like purple), blue and white hydrangeas, plus 'Green Goddess' lilies that keep blooming all year if they're kept cool and damp.

If you want a flash of orange, try clumps of bright clivias. Or the coloured foliage of cordylines in warmer areas or a carpet of hostas under fruit trees (watch for snails – install a blue-tongue lizard at the same time), or shade-loving natives like *Boronia heterophylla*, correa or native fuchsias, or the river dog rose (*Bauera rubioides*). I could go on for pages with colour in the shade. Seek and ye shall find!

HEATING THE HOUSE

Ivy and other clinging plants will help keep heat in your house as well as keeping it out. Paving around your house will reflect heat inside in summer. Consider a glasshouse at the north end of your house, or build a small glasshouse at the front or back door which you have to walk through to get inside. The heat from these glasshouses will spread through the house in winter. Replace the glass panels with shadecloth in summer, or make sure the windows open.

Trees can also be a sun trap and will block wind. Have a high belt of trees at the east and west, not so near the house they block sunlight, but near enough to make a sheltered glade around the house. Plant another lot of trees to block off the prevailing wind. In very cold areas walled gardens at the back or front provide extra reflected heat in winter (in summer they can be filled with annuals that shoot up in the added warmth) as well as protecting the house from wind.

BURGLAR PROOFING

Gardeners are often urged not to have thick gardens as burglars can hide in the shrubs. Plants can also give protection: thorny plants or hedges below windows, and thorny climbers like roses. Have movement-sensitive lights installed so that if intruders venture past your barrier of trees on the edge of the garden they'll be picked up in a sudden spotlight. Put pressure-sensitive alarms under bushes near windows where no-one (except an intruder) is likely to tread.

The prince may have chopped his way to Sleeping Beauty through a thorny hedge, but the casual burglar is unlikely to bother.

THE SECRETS OF GLORIOUS BALCONIES

(or how to turn those horrible stretches of concrete out the back or front of the house into flowers and greenery)

Balconies are probably the worst places on earth to grow things – deserts and Antarctica included. Balconies have no soil (and small pots of dirt soon turn into concrete unless lovingly tended). They're exposed to more glaring sunlight than the Sahara or, even worse, such depressing gloom that even an optimist would wither; and many get no rain either. They also receive an inordinate amount of wind.

If the plants on your balcony die it isn't your fault. No plant ever evolved on a balcony. How then can some people – glorious, green-thumbed people – manage to have balconies of such luxurious abundance? Read on ...

Six tricks to make your balcony flourish

1. Just add water ...
Do the plants on your balcony literally seem to shrink? You buy them all green and healthy and almost immediately it seems they start to dwindle and fade?

No, it's not your imagination, or your brown thumbs. It's simply that most balcony plants don't get rained on, and most gardeners virtuously water the base of their pot plants, not the new leaves.

After all, it's the roots that drink, isn't it? Well, not exactly. Most moisture is taken up by roots, and nutrients too, but leaves do 'drink' as well. Even more importantly, leaves get dusty. I dust my house (well, sometimes) and rain washes the dust off plants, except where they're sheltered by a balcony roof or eaves. Dusty leaves don't photosynthesise as well.

Leaves that aren't regularly 'washed' also get mite problems. Look more closely at the leaves on plants under eaves and on balconies. You'll probably see tiny 'tracks' or spots where mites have sucked the sap, and that is why your plants seem to shrink and fade. They literally are shrinking and fading – and the mites are to blame.

ALL plants need to have their leaves washed at least once a week. Water the whole plant, not just the base, and with a hose, not a jug, so you can spray UNDER the leaves too, where mites like to hide.

(Dedicated balcony growers can rig up a spray system. We have one on our pergola here – microjets attached to poly pipe and when they're turned on the whole area is watered with a lovely misty spray – wonderful on hot afternoons. You can make them up yourself or buy one prefabricated.)

Potted plants do dry out much faster than you'd ever expect. Even soil in most pots isn't wet much by rain; the leaves tend to direct the rainwater over the rim of the pot. A handful of water crystals added to each pot at planting time makes a huge difference to the pot's capacity to hold enough water to grow lush and beautiful plants.

2. Mulch!
Mulch in the garden breaks down into lovely rich soil. But your pots don't have room for more soil – so use a mulch that doesn't break down. Try coconut fibre. Tease out the fibre till it's loose and cushiony and tuck it round the plant. It won't absorb moisture, so it won't make the stems rot if you tuck it close in, but it will insulate the soil and stop it drying out and turning into concrete, which is too hard for moisture to penetrate when you do remember to water.

Many people prefer the neat look of small stones. You can buy lovely small white quartz rocks at many garden centres, or collect your own pebbles to use as heat retaining mulch. (They're not such a good idea where there are toddlers, either in permanent residence or visiting, as they are irresistible to small children, either for inserting in small orifices or, if the pebbles are too large for those fascinating games, for throwing over the edge of the balcony onto passing cars or pedestrians.)

3. Think BIG!!
Small pots dry out fast and get too hot or too cold (and ants and spiders love to crawl between them). Think big: one large pot or hanging basket instead of six small ones. Half-barrels or large concrete planters are good too.

When planting out a large pot remember that as well as the tall feature plant in the middle (be it bay tree, lemon or standard hibiscus) there is a host of small ground covers and low alpines that enjoy the free draining nature of a pot.

Small plants also help maintain soil texture and humidity around the feature plant. Try a variety of combinations. One of the best I can remember seeing was a beautiful round, full-bellied terracotta pot planted with a scarlet abutilon (Chinese lantern bush) and pale mauve brachycome daisies spilling over the edge. Erigeron daisies, violets, lobelias, alysum, parsley and violas are all worth trying as under-plantings.

If you can't bear to spend the large amount of money required for the purchase of the very beautiful terracotta, ceramic and concrete pots, group your pots. This way you can have the geraniums in the old pineapple juice tins and the lobelias in the anchovy tins lurking behind the more presentable containers. This also increases humidity and the plants give each other support and shelter.

4. *Feed your plants.*
Plants need to eat too. Slow release plant food is best – there's a wide range on the market. Just browse along the shelves. I like to give my pots a treat of seaweed-based fertiliser once they start leaping up in spring. Use according to directions.

5. *Be realistic.*
If you don't have time to tend your pots, or enough experience to really know what thrives where, stick to VERY hardy plants – pink, white or yellow daisies (the white ones are the hardiest), bamboo (ALMOST unkillable), poa tussock, geraniums/pelargoniums, weeping rosemary, oleander, weeping bottlebrush (*Callistemon viminalis*), heliotrope in frost-free areas, westringia, brachycome ... or even dull old ivy, which can look luxurious trailing from a hanging basket, and is almost maintenance free.

If the situation is really impossible (hot, dry, windy but you do get sun) stick with succulents and cacti, most of which have interesting leaf shapes in a good range of colours and some of which have spectacular flowers. (And not all are prickly horrors either.)

6. *Be extravagant (just a little).*
Yes, I know I just said to stick to hardy plants, but everyone should have just one extravagance to love and tend, one giant hanging basket for example, filled with a weeping miniature rose that'll weep bright petals all over the balcony. Or a standard bougainvillea – they adore heat, exposure, salt winds and they're terribly expensive, but gloriously vulgar purple most of the year (or even a discreet white if you prefer it).

Try tall liliums for a Christmas extravaganza tucked into a barrel, or a cascade of perennial petunias – they flower almost all year round at our place, with a little gentle pruning.

Have just one big tub for annuals or short-lived perennials like pansies; they'll bloom all winter and all through next spring and summer too. Tuck in a few bulbs for added spring beauty: tulips in cold areas or ranunculi or hardy dahlias in hotter areas. Most of Europe is made bright and cheery through summer and autumn by masses of potted geraniums flowering bravely and endlessly until cut by the return of cold weather. (And in most parts of Australia they'll bloom all year round, so you have no excuse whatsoever for a barren patio.)

Treat yourself to one wonderful urn, a strawberry planter or a giant barrel to fill with plants ...

Some (almost) indestructible plants for patio pots

Shade lovers: impatiens, pansies, ferns, many palms, fuchsias, polyanthus, Cape gooseberries, honeysuckle.

Hot and dry survivors: any cacti or succulents; geraniums/pelargoniums, erigeron, white or purple alyssum, daisies, rosemary, lavender, sage, calendula, petunia, gazania, tomatoes, wild, native or Warrigal spinach, marigolds, tiny golden nugget pumpkins.

Absolutely gorgeous: floribunda roses, especialy white Iceberg, clipped bay trees, cumquats or Tahitian limes, bright red pineapple or soft pink fruit salad sage (frost sensitive), standard bougainvillea, masses of nasturtiums, a froth of sambac jasmine, a miniature clipped box hedge, trailing strawberries.

Some luxuries for your patio

For a wandering vine, plant a grape or passionfruit or climbing rose in a very large pot, then train it along the railing, or fasten netting to the wall and let it clamber along that or even attach a false rail along the balcony ceiling and train wisteria or grapes along it. Both bunches of grapes and long tendrils of wisteria can look stunning.

A bowl of dwarf succulents (thick-fleshed plants – including cactus, but there are some other much prettier ones) can look spectacular on a patio table and no matter how much you neglect it, it will probably survive.

You need:
- a shallow earthenware or pottery bowl
- potting mix
- optional: white pebbles to mulch the surface
- a selection of pretty dwarf succulents from the garden centre.

Succulents are VERY tolerant of sun and glare and occasional drying out. They are also low growing, so you don't have to peer through the foliage at the person opposite you.

Standard weepers can be impressive – and are always expensive. Go and wander through the garden centre, and see what you fall in love with – a standard azalea, bougainvillea, weeping rose, weeping crab apple, weeping fig. Make sure they are suitable for your patio – need sun, shade, etc. When in doubt, ask.

Now start saving ... or ask Father Christmas VERY nicely ... or hint to your nearest and dearest from now till your birthday.

An orchard in a pot

Try tamarillos (stick a slice of fruit in a pot above the kitchen sink, water well and cover with Gladwrap till they sprout), Meyer lemons, pineapples, cumquats (the big juicy modern cultivars you can eat like a mandarin), dwarf 'Ballerina' apples or avocados (just dump a seed in a pot and wait ...).

Avocados can grow to be enormous, but if their roots are crammed into pots they won't, so don't worry about them lifting the ceiling off some night when you've left them unattended.

Give fruit trees the biggest pot you can and feed them very well and keep the soil moist but well drained – no saucers of stagnant water underneath. They may even fruit

A lemon tree in a pot

indoors – but you may have to pretend to be a bee with a paintbrush, transferring the pollen from the males to the females. If you're not feeling particularly bee-like, give your potted trees a holiday outdoors for a day or two, especially if they look a bit pale and need some sun.

GARDENS OF THE RIGHTEOUS

Beware of the gardens of the righteous! Trimmed edges mean a frightened soul. They're there to make a statement to the neighbours, not for the good of the garden. Neat lawns are mown for other people to look at. The lawn is not going to leap up and strangle you in your bed if you let it grow past carpet height. It might even seed and feed the birds, which will also eat the aphids on your roses.

How often haven't you seen a garden so neat it is depressing – how could you ever achieve the same? It's the sort of garden built to impress, the garden of someone who only imitates the joy of growing things. Gardens should not smell of sweat or be monuments to spadework.

Gardens are not to be admired – they're to be enjoyed! A garden should make you smile as soon as you walk into it. It should make you want to wriggle your toes in the grass, or sniff the roses, or sit beneath an apple tree to drink your tea and wonder what's around the corner. A garden should be as stable as the bush – as little work, and as prolific.

THE MESSY GARDEN

Four reasons to have a messy garden:

1. Fewer pests – spiders, tachinid flies, a whole range of different tiny wasps and many others all eat the pests in your garden, or their larvae do. Neat gardens don't have places for these beasties to live, or a few pests for them to munch. And you have to remember that one gardener's pest is another creature's lunch!

2. Birds – messy gardens have safe thickets where birds can nest, grass seeds for them to eat because the lawn isn't always kept carpet short, twigs, spiderwebs and dried grass for nesting material.

3. Relaxation – because the owners can sniff the daphne instead of worrying that the path edges need trimming, and guests don't have to feel that an alarm will ring if they leave a footprint in the perfection of the lawn.

4. Fun – because a messy garden ISN'T under your control and you never quite know what bird will next appear out the window, or what bulb will push its head up under the trees.

The wrong sort of mess

All right, there is good mess, and there is bad mess – a messy garden should still be a healthy, good-looking garden.

DO prune your garden. Most shrubs – including native shrubs – will be healthier and look better if they're regularly pruned. (Just don't go overboard and try to rework their entire shape.)

DO thin out your garden sometimes to let light in as trees and shrubs grow.

DO cut out dead wood SOME TIME – just don't go in for overkill and take each little bit!

DO feed your garden – if it doesn't get any tucker it won't grow much, or flower and fruit and feed its residents.

DO have stepping stones or wandering, informal paths that don't look messy if they're not trimmed.

Four ways to make your garden happy and messy:

1. Tolerate a bit of insect damage!
A garden isn't like your living room carpet

where every spot needs to be vacuumed up! A nibbled leaf here, a few brown splodges there mean your garden is healthy, with a good range of beasties living in it. Pesticides don't just kill the pests you spray – they kill others too, either by being sprayed directly or because there are no longer enough insects round for the birds, lizards, hoverfly larvae, etc. to feed on. Spray to save your plant if you must – but don't try to totally obliterate all insects from every cubic metre of garden.

2. Leave spiderwebs alone!
Every autumn and winter the webs build up on our windows – and every late winter and spring every single one is taken by the birds as 'gluing' and lining material for their nests. Okay, you don't have to be quite as fanatical about leaving the webs as we are, but do leave them alone for a few months in late winter and spring if you can. And NEVER worry about giant nests in the shrubbery – they're for catching tucker, not attacking humans.

3. Don't take trailer loads of rubbish to the dump!
Your poor garden has spent months creating that stuff! Compost it, or 'sheet mulch' it – which is a polite way of saying 'bung it sort of tidily under a large tree' so it can decompose into lovely tree tucker.

4. Don't over-prune.
Every tree and shrub has its own natural shape. Don't try to change it. Cut out dead wood and branches that tangle and rub against each other. Prune to encourage more flowers and fresh growth. But don't overdo it! (If you can see clear daylight through a leafy shrub, you've gone too far.)

Three stunning plants guaranteed to make a lovely mess:

1. Rambling roses have lots of thorns to protect birds' nests, lots of flowers to attract insects for birds to eat and wonderful thickets of branches – every rambling rose here has its own colony of small birds.

Plant roses up your walls, along pergolas. Any naked fence needs roses!

2. Chinese star jasmine and other scented thickets get wilder and more jungly every year, and birds adore them. Every garden needs at least one scented thicket.

3. Gums trees drop leaves and bark (and branches too – keep them down the back or front of the garden) and make an excellent clutter for lizards to rummage through and birds to find nesting material.

Many larger birds prefer perching on gum tree branches to anything else – and a nice mature gum tree will provide places for these excellent pest eaters to nest.

Look for smaller gums for your backyard! Your local nursery should stock several good backyard trees, including some of the new grafted improved selections that have reliable flowers and predictable growth types. You'll pay anything from $2.50 for tube stock to $30 or $40 for a grafted tree.

E. macrocarpa: 3–4 metres; bright red flowers; needs perfect drainage in full sunlight and a protected spot in cold areas.

E. leucoxylon ssp *megalocarpa*: 5–10 metres, pink, red or cream flowers; dislikes humidity.

Fuchsia gum (*E. forrestiana*): 3–5 metres, red flower buds and yellow flowers; protect from frost when young; best in low rainfall areas.

Rose mallee (*E. rhodantha*): 3–4 metres, red flowers and silver leaves; suits dry and warm climates; not frost hardy.

'Silver Princess' (*E. caesia*): 7–10 metres, weeping form, silver bark, red flowers, temperate climate, needs good drainage.

Snow gum (*E. pauciflora*): 3–20 metres, but in gardens is usually on the short rather than the tall side. Often multi-trunked with wonderful patchy coloured bark and dark red or bright yellow twigs; does well with pruning.

Great in cold gardens. Despite its name it flowers abundantly with large bunches of cream flowers.

THE HAPPINESS GARDEN

There are many reasons to have a garden: because every other house in the street has one, to increase the value of your home when you sell it, or even to grow your own veg. But the best reason of all is simply to make yourself – and others – happy.

Humans really are happiest with growing things around them. Even office pot plants reduce the number of 'sickies' taken each year, while greenery in shopping centres cuts down the rate of vandalism. But I reckon that the average backyard has the greatest potential of all to simply make you ... happy. So, what makes people happy?

Greenery – lots and lots of green leaves

Even though the modern trend is towards large areas of paving and succulents – nice, no-care plants – it can't compete with a sheer abundance of GROWING stuff.

The solution? Plant LOTS of shrubs, those that are suited to your area, so they don't need masses of water or attention. If you can see the fence, your garden is too bare. If you do have large areas of paving, consider a pergola above them, with grapes or hops or kiwi fruit that will cover the area with greenery in summer and lose their leaves in winter. Of these, hops are the least messy, and kiwi fruit the most.

Scent

Most flower scents raise your spirits, but so does the smell of newly mown grass, wet leaves and all the million subliminal odours from a garden. (There is a theory that it's the lack of these smells as much as the lack of sunlight that may trigger seasonal depression in winter.)

The solution? Plant shrubs to give you year-round flowers: a selection of roses, late and early camelias, and grevilleas will do it, but there are a thousand other choices. Plant pansies, primulas, Iceland poppies or calendulas for winter cheer, and any of the whole host of annuals you can choose in summer.

Colour

All of us have our favourite colours, the ones we like to wear and are happiest around, and those are the colours you need in your garden. You can find flowers and fruit in ANY colour if you look hard enough, even blue (blue roses, cornflowers, the blue flowers of garlic chives ...). I love purples, and deep, purple-red – which anyone would guess if they saw my collection of deep flushed roses and glorious purple bottlebrush in spring, not to mention the anise hyssop, the ... well, that's enough of that.

The solution? Work out what colours you love best, and plant them! I don't just mean flowers here. Fruit gives colour too. Remember though that you may prefer different colours in different seasons – even I adore bright daffodil yellows and cumquat and calendula orange hues in the miserable depths of winter and the cold winds of early spring.

Water

The sound of water is relaxing, the smell of water lifts your spirits, the look of water – trickling, splashing, or birds playing in it or just drinking – is one of the joys of a good garden.

The solution? Well, I refuse to live anywhere without a pond, with a tiny fountain when we're not in drought. But even a birdbath will do the trick – or in extreme cases a garbage bin lid hanging from a branch and regularly filled with water.

Rocks

There is something solid and comforting about rocks: giant rocks as features in themselves, rock pools, rock paths, rock walls.

The solution? Add rocks! You can buy excellent 'fake' rocks too, which normally I'd avoid like canned vegetable soup (the sludgy, salty kind), but modern fake rocks really look like rocks! Plus they are cheaper, lighter, and you're not destroying the homes of lizards and other beasties when they are removed from paddocks or creek beds.

Rock gardens are a great way to break up a boring, flat bit of ground. Another phrase for rock garden is 'big pile of dirt with rocks attractively arranged in and around it'. Try a mound at the front of your garden, to help keep out traffic noise, or a formal 'wedding cake' design in the middle of the lawn. In fact just buzz off to the library and get a book on rock gardens for masses of ideas to choose from.

Something to pick

You only have to watch a child's face as they pick their first piece of 'real' fruit to realise we humans are really still hunters and gatherers, even if the only gathering we can do is in the backyard.

The solution? Grow some tucker – the easy-care kind, like mulberry trees, passionfruit vines, kiwi fruit vines, lilypillies, or 'plant it and pick it' veg such as lovage (like a small, wild perennial celery) or watercress. (Keep this in a pot under your tap so it stays moist. Good in salads, sandwiches and soups, but a bit too peppery if you use too much.)

Garlic chives are TOUGH, and unlike common chives don't die down in winter or shrivel in heat and drought. They are flatter and coarser than common chives, but great in stir fries, sandwiches and salads where you want an onion/garlic flavour.

Plant some spring or bunching onions (*Allium fistulosum*) too. I rarely bother growing ordinary onions. If we want an onion flavour I pick a bunch of these and chop them fresh into salads or sauté till soft for other dishes. The clumps grow larger year by year, and tolerate sun or semi-shade.

Mitsuba, or Japanese parsley (*Cryptotaenia japonica*) is mostly grown as an annual, but it's really perennial, and will reseed itself happily too, coming up in bare spots all over the garden. It's like a very coarse parsley; chop the leaves and stems, and use in salads or stir fries or anywhere you would use chopped parsley. The more you pick the more tender new leaves you get.

Add to that some easy herbs like oregano, rosemary, peppermint, pineapple mint, winter savoury, marjoram and thyme and you've got scents as well as tucker, and green leaves.

This one is up to you.

What sort of garden do you dream about? A paradise of roses? Formal pools and topiary? A backyard cricket pitch? The garden that you dream about is the one that will make you happy. So get daydreaming ... and go to it.

An idea for a rock garden

Chapter 3
DROUGHT AND BUSHFIRE

Australian gardens do not suffer from lack of water. There are many (cooler) places in the world where our rainfall would be regarded as quite enough, thank you very much. Our problem is too much evaporation!

Our own garden survives with no extra watering. I wish it DID get more watering. But since our creek dried up – just too many local bores, which means the animals die of thirst too – there hasn't been any of that lovely wet stuff to use. Hand-watering once a week? Recycled water from the washing? I wish we could! It would be luxury ...

But our garden is still (mostly) alive. We still grow fruit, veg, flowers, and the grass comes back when it rains.

So how do we manage it?

SURVIVAL STRATEGIES

Groves

Plant groves, and use the other methods in Chapter 1 to stop moisture evaporating from your garden! This is the most important of all – and the way we have kept our garden alive.

I can't emphasise it enough: plant a garden that will protect itself!

Increase the area of shade, too. This will cool the garden generally (the more greenery, the less heat and light will be reflected) and in hot areas broken light will keep plants and soil below moist. Most flowers and vegetables tolerate broken light. Shade can be from a pergola above; a tall trellis facing the afternoon light (which is stronger than morning light); or from a tree above or tall plants like corn, Jerusalem artichokes or sunflowers liberally planted through your flower and vegetable beds.

Mulch

Mulch!!!!!!. Mulch can be a miracle. I wish every plant sold in a drought had to come with its own sack of mulch. No matter how often garden writers keep muttering 'mulch, mulch, mulch' – most Australian gardens are still baking hot and naked under cloudless skies!

Mulch is always my first line of defence in dry times – a good thick layer, at least 30 cm deep. My favourite mulch is lucerne hay –

things really seem to grow better with leafy lucerne. But pea straw, sugar cane slash, old horse or cow manure, compost, chopped up young wattle trees, etc. are also great. If possible mulch over DAMP soil, as mulch will also stop drizzle penetrating.

Our giant avocado trees are just mulched with mess – any old corn stalks, cabbage stems, prunings are all tossed under their wide skirts where no-one can see them. I toss in Dynamic Lifter or old chook poo once every year or two, and the mess breaks down into good rich soil.

Mulch stops the soil from drying out. It also helps stop soil turning into concrete, so any water just rolls off. Soil that has been mulched also retains moisture better, so even last year's mulch and the year's before is still helping to keep my trees alive.

I love using rocks as mulch. Sounds odd, but it works. The moisture condenses on them even from dry air at night and a little trickles down onto your plants – and the rocks stop it from evaporating next day.

There are a great range of pebbles and rocks available now. Arrange large rocks around your shrubs, so they look like they are growing out of a rock garden, or spread a layer of pebbles about two or three deep around shrubs or in flowerbeds or even vegetable gardens. If you want to plant new flowers or veg just scrape away the pebbles, plant and replace. You can even feed pebble-mulched plants with fertilisers like dynamic lifter – scatter and water well till the pebbles are clean again. And rock mulch doesn't burn in bushfires.

Be aware though that rocks and pebbles (particularly light-coloured ones) will reflect extra heat back onto plants (which in a hot, dry summer may already be stressed), so make sure that the plants in your pebble mulch are those that are tough enough to wilt and recover rather than those that are so tender that a real blast of heat will wither them irretrievably. Or use your rock mulch under established trees, where the rocks will be shaded.

You may find that except in very hot dry times you don't have to water mulched trees or shrubs at all, once they are well established and a year or two old.

Dense mulches like lawn clippings can stop moisture penetrating. Mix them with old branches, leaves or anything coarse.

Water efficiently

Work out what HAS to be watered. Like General Macarthur, grass WILL return! You can let it brown or even mostly vanish, then, a few days after it has rained, the ground will be green again. But give trees and shrubs you've cosseted for years a good soak every couple of weeks, or once a week if you haven't mulched them.

Water only to root depth when water is scarce – any more means you're watering the soil, not the plant! Seedlings may need only a gentle watering, but they'll need to be watered often. Big trees will need a longer soak.

When I put the sprinkler on, I leave an empty jar under the spray. When it's about one-eighth full I know I've watered the seedlings enough; a quarter full is about right for veg and grass, half full is a decent water for a small shrub, and totally full is a good soak for trees.

Get into dribbling. Let the hose drip on large trees, the smallest possible drip. The soil is probably too hard-baked for water to soak in ... but a drip ... three second pause ... drip ... will. Or install drip irrigation. Or buy two-inch polypipe, cut it about a metre long, dig it into the ground with the end poking up and pour water down that, to get to root level. Two or three will do a large tree.

Plant survivors!

The best way to see what survives in your area is to look at old neglected gardens. Or try a bushwalk, in autumn when you can see where an old garden was as the leaves turn yellow and red.

You'll find the great survivors aren't native shrubs. They're the ones with big roots, like rambling roses, apples, pears, persimmon, medlars, quinces, figs, bulbs like daffodils, japonica, camellias ...

It's a myth that natives survive drought best. They don't. Most native shrubs flower, seed, and die in a drought. Then, when it rains in five, or 10, or 50 years, the seeds germinate. (On the other hand, you'll get more flowers for a small amount of water from natives than from most exotics. If you have SOME water, natives may well be best. And young natives may survive when young introduced shrubs die, too. But old native shrubs don't survive as well without water as the big rooted plants.)

Many natives also come from rainfall areas originally and need just as much water as exotics, or may only grow deep drought-resistant roots in sandy or light soils, and need constant watering on clay or shallow soil.

How do you find large rooted plants?
- Avoid dwarf and semi-dwarf trees – and most fruit trees these days are grafted onto semi-dwarf stock. An alternative for 'dwarf' is 'doesn't grow very fast'.
- Grow your own fruit trees from seed, or have them grafted onto full-size stock.

Among the great survivors are the following.

Fruit: apples, pears, quinces, figs, mulberries, pistachios, almonds, bunya nuts, quandongs, native citrus, pomegranate, medlar, citronelles, olives, kei apple. Avocados are drought hardy once well established, i.e. about 10 years old. Avoid all the other citrus – very shallow rooted.

Vegetables: anything red ... red Freckles lettuce, red ribbed chocroy, turnip rooted parsley, most Asian leafed veg like mizuna and mitsuba, tomatoes, basil, chillies, capsicum, perennial beans, choko. Plant corn under 30 cm of sand and mulch to its leaves. Mulch beans, tomatoes and capsicum to their leaves too. Avoid lettuce, apart from Freckles, and celery (will survive but goes stringy).

Flowers: I find most of the salvia family wonderful survivors – amaranth, agapanthus (avoid the old, tall varieties that become weeds), dahlias. Avoid all annuals except for salvia bonfire and, at a pinch, petunias.

You can be reasonably sure your plant will be drought tolerant if it has a deep, fleshy root system; has tough, thick leaves to reduce evaporation, or a waxy or hairy coating; has small leaves that point up and down to reduce the surface area exposed to sunlight; sheds leaves during water stress and regrows them after; or opens its stomata (pores in the leaves through which water can pass) only at night, like cactus and pineapple. Grey- and red-leafed plants are also mostly drought tolerant.

Feeding

Feed, and otherwise cosset your plants, when you DO have water.

The bigger the plants' roots are, the better they'll survive droughts – and cold, heat and wind. Only plant when the weather bureau predicts rain, or you have enough stored water to trickle moisture onto plants for at least three months. Feed them, water them, mulch them ... and when the time comes, they'll be tough survivors.

Have less lawn!

Lawns use about 95 per cent of garden water. A hundred years ago only a few rare great houses had big lawns – other mansions had gravel, which was raked every day, and smaller gardens were filled with gravel and garden beds too.

Replace most of your lawn with paving, leaving small circles of grass for greenery, or plant massed mulched shrubs and trees instead.

Treat the small amount of grass you DO keep carefully. Remember that well-tended plants survive better! Make sure your lawn is very well fed – good grass roots help grass stay green longer. It's also a good idea to set your lawnmower at a higher level in summer, as short grass dries out sooner.

Hard-packed soil dries out faster, so keep cars off the grass, put down paths or stepping stones where grass gets lots of wear and tear, and use a product like Wettasoil so that water penetrates and doesn't just run off into the gutter.

Irrigation

Use drip irrigation, instead of overhead sprinklers. In hot areas more water evaporates from sprinklers than gets to the soil, and the water that does will be high in dissolved salts. Use drippers instead and you'll use perhaps a tenth of the water with better results.

Drippers and black polypipe are actually less expensive than garden hose and much more flexible. You can move them around the garden or leave them in place so you only need to turn on the tap to water your garden.

Tanks

Put in a tank! There are tank designs now for just about every area: under the steps, slimline ones next to walls, flexible plastic 'bladders' that can take on just about any shape that's needed. Seek and ye shall find!

Three years ago we had no rain for eleven and a half months – and at the end of it two and a half of our three tanks were still full. (Now, if I'd known WHEN the drought would break I'd have been able to use the lot!)

Many country gardeners find they can keep a good-size garden alive just on tank water, even in a drought. (As long as they also mulch, etc., of course.)

Grey water

Use only treated grey water! Grey water is waste water from the house, excluding that used to flush the toilet. Its major advantage is that it's wet, and will keep plants alive (mostly). But grey water can also be a real health hazard. Even without water from the toilet, small amounts of faecal matter can be flushed down showers, laundry tubs etc., and bacteria breed in the rich soapy water. Grey water is probably safe if used only on trees and ornamentals – never on grass where kids might play.

Grey water also contains fatty soap, grease from the kitchen, and salts from soaps and detergents. These can clog up the soil and if too much builds up, can kill plants.

If you plan to use grey water:
- Avoid detergents, highly perfumed soap and water softeners.
- Collect grey water discriminately – say from the rinse cycle of your washing machine, or your own shower when you don't wash your hair and can be fairly sure you've used the toilet paper efficiently.
- Install at least one filter, preferably two or three, and regularly clean out soap sludge.

- Avoid products containing boron or chlorine.
- Always share out the grey and the clean water – make sure the whole garden gets some of each rather than concentrating the grey water on a small part of the garden.

The easiest and safest way to collect some grey water is to stand a bucket next to you in the shower – just kick it away till you've washed off most of the soap. Fill buckets with rinse water from washing too.

Grey water systems cost about $4000–$5000, are trouble free (usually with a 'hot line' in case of break-down), and regularly inspected (this is a legal requirement). Some systems also recycle sewer waste. These systems are highly recommended for dry areas.

Efficient water use

- Water in spring! Plants do about 75 per cent of their growing in spring – and most of the rest in autumn. Don't bother doing more than just keeping your garden alive in summer. But try to keep a nice tank of water to get plants really growing in spring.
- Water when it's cool.
- Water AFTER rain – especially small amounts of drizzle. Water will penetrate best then.
- Try products like Wettasoil that help water to penetrate and stay in dry soil.
- Other products like Yates Stressguard will help stop plants losing so much moisture from their leaves.

Some useful products

Tree sleeves: these are plastic sleeves you put round your trees, shrubs or even tomatoes. They're mostly used to establish trees in paddocks or along roads, but even though they're pretty ugly in the garden they can really keep your young plants alive in bad times.

Water tubes: these are fat bulging tree sleeves filled with 20 litres of water that seeps around the roots of your plant over about 16 days. Like tree sleeves, you need three stakes to keep them upright. You get the advantages of a tree sleeve, plus the water.

Aqua spikes: you screw old soft drink bottles into the spikes, poke a few next to your shrub or one by your capsicum plant, then fill them up with the hose. The water drains out at about one litre per hour.

Home-made polypipe waterers: take about 1.5 metre lengths of black 50 mm polypipe, and bury one end of it about 30 cm deep near the plant you want to water. The rest of the pipe sticks up in the air. Once a week or once a fortnight, fill the pipe with water.

Upside-down old pots: these are great to keep seedlings alive in the heat. Cut the bottoms out of old pots, and wriggle them down to make 'collars' around each seedling. They'll keep plants cooler, moister – and keep off snails too.

Trench gardens: an ancient method of growing vegetables in areas where there is not much moisture is trench gardening. Dig a trench, as long as you like but no more than a metre wide or you won't be able to reach across it. Angle it east–west, so it catches the sunlight. Let it slope slightly, so moisture runs down it and doesn't just sit there.

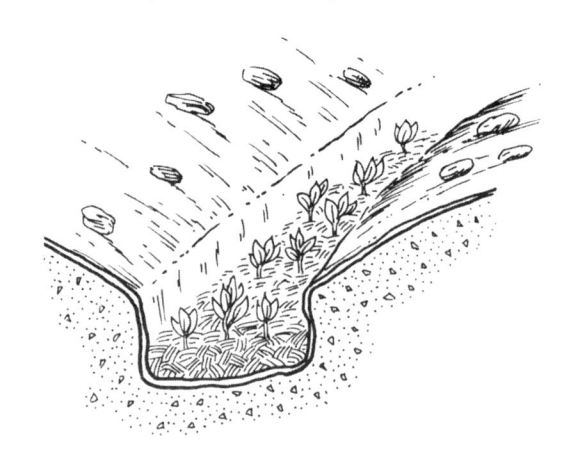

Slope the sides to catch any moisture. You can either leave these bare or, better still, line them with plastic; weigh the plastic down with rocks; cover with more plastic and secure with more rocks at the edges. At night the moisture in the air between the layers will condense and seep down into the garden.

Now either line it with a couple of centimetres of compost, or slightly disturb the surface. Plant your vegetables and mulch well.

Don't bother with the sprinkler – up to 90 per cent of the water will be lost to evaporation on a hot day. Just stick the end of the hose under the mulch at the uphill end of the trench, or at several points along it if it's very long. If you think your trench doesn't slope, trickle water down it and see – nearly all ground slopes somewhat, it may just be too slight a gradient to be easily visible.

PS One dripping tap loses 100 litres a day! Enough to water several gardens ...

And if your garden is thirsty, the birds will be too. Hang a birdbath from a tree, where cats can't reach it, and in the shade, where the water will stay cool. Refresh it often.

WHY DROUGHTS ARE GREAT FOR PESTS

Drought means pests – one of nature's little bad jokes, there to make things just a bit worse than they were before. Why? Well, it's partly due to dust. A light cover of dust on leaves will stop many predators from hatching and controlling the beasties for you.

Also it's hot: heat- and moisture-stressed fruit falls prematurely and rots faster and hot soil sends the lovely smell of rotting fruit higher and higher and further to attract pests to its lovely scent. Winds are stronger and pests like fruit fly can be blown 20 kilometres or more.

The answer? Again, grow your fruit trees in groves, and your veg between shelters of tall growing plants like perennial beans on a trellis. This will keep the dust from the leaves, and let the predators get on with their job of breeding more predators to control pests.

PS Sometimes mild water stress can be good for your garden. Plants are encouraged to send down deeper roots, and so are more drought tolerant; soft disease-prone growth is reduced; and plants can be gradually hardened off to the lack of water.

Mild water stress, for example, when flower buds are forming on many fruit trees, will increase the number of buds, though water stress shouldn't continue once the buds start to develop. Less water while fruit is growing usually means smaller fruit – but the fruit may also have a better flavour, improved keeping qualities and excellent texture. Too much water when fruit is ripening can cause it to split.

PPS Mulch!

PPPS In very bad seasons prune trees and bushes right back to reduce moisture loss, so they can grow again when it rains.

SURVIVING BUSHFIRE

Plants to slow down bushfires

The good news: a good garden or shelter belt CAN slow down a fire; a house in a good garden may be more fire resistant than one with bare earth around it. BUT – the plants chosen need to be the correct ones, grown in the correct way.

Why this works: the intensity of the fire around your home depends on two main things: the amount of fuel, and the intensity of the wind.

If you can grow an effective fire break – one that will cut down wind speed, not just around the lower part of the house but also at roof level, and also one that will catch burning embers before they reach your house – you will have a far greater chance of saving your house.

You also need to cut down fuel around the house – avoid ANY plant that burns well within 10 metres of your house; avoid flammable trees within 10–30 metres of your house, depending on slope. (The steeper the slope, the bigger a gap you need.)

Remember, as a rule of thumb, that flames reach twice as high and wide as the plant they are burning. A two-metre high and wide shrub will burn four metres high and four wide.

Plants to avoid: plants that go 'whoosh!' or 'bang!'

- Any plant with scented leaves – eucalypts are the classic scented leafed plant, but there are many others including most pines (a very few are far less flammable, like *P. Ponderosa*) and cypresses, casuarinas, citrus, lavender, etc. Scented leaves indicate a high oil content – and oil goes whoosh.
- Any plant with rough, thick or flaking bark that will burn even on the living tree.
- Any plant – like wattles – where the sap oozes out and dries in thick globules. Dry saps burns beautifully and can explode; trees with sap like this will also explode in a hot fire (wattles – acacias – are probably the best example of this).
- Any plant with lots of dead or dry material: jasmine, potato vines, Chinese jasmine, kiwi fruit, persimmon, giant rambling roses and many, many others accumulate dead wood as they grow larger, and even though the live plant may not be particularly flammable, the dead wood, especially by the house, can add enormously to the intensity of the fire.

    These plants CAN be grown (and most provide great spots for small birds to nest), but they DO need to be pruned and thinned each year, and dead wood removed. (This also makes the plant healthier and gets rid of black rat nesting sites!)
- Any plant climbing on the wall of the house where embers can lodge, i.e. ivy and ornamental grapes.

Warning: do not rely on any published list – including this one! I have tested most of the plants in this list (see notes against each species) but in many cases my testing has been incomplete – I haven't tested how they burn in situ, or if the leaves have been parched, for example, by weeks of gale-force hot winds. The flammability of some plants can really vary in different sites and conditions.

I have yet to see ANY list of 'fire-resistant' plants that agrees with the tests I've done here. Too often – as in other areas – a published list is repeated from publication to publication, and the contents simply aren't checked again.

Before you do large scale plantings, do check that:
1. The freshly picked leaves don't burn easily when one bowl full is mixed with one tablespoon of compressed kero – i.e., a commercial firestarter found at any supermarket.
2. The wilted leaves don't burn under the same conditions.
3. The dried leaves don't flare up and burn fast and hot (they will burn, just watch for flaring – a ZOOM effect – rather than smouldering).
4. When you burn a log of the dry wood the dried sap doesn't explode, and you don't get small flares of 'blue' flame.
5. The fresh bark from a living tree won't burn.

How to have a good windbreak or firebreak

I'm afraid I can't explain this properly without diagrams. But basically you need a belt of plants that the wind can still penetrate, but will be slowed down. A totally wind resistant firebreak dumps the wind on the other side. You want one that will slow down and deflect the wind and burning debris higher than your roof, and one that will also catch some of the debris before it reaches your house, and 'cool' the fire at least slightly.

How high should the trees be?

This depends how far away they are from your house, and how steep the slope is. The steeper the slope and the further away, the higher they need to be. It's probably safest to say the higher the better, preferably three to five times the height of the buildings they are supposed to protect.

As a very, very rough guide a windbreak will help protect your house for a distance of up to 25 times the height of the trees. The best windbreak design has a row of very high trees at the back, then a row of lower trees, then another of even lower trees.

POSSIBLE PLANTS FOR WIND BREAK/ FIRE BREAKS

Note: these plants will probably die in a major fire – sadly trees that survive fires are usually ones that add to the fuel load.

- Apples – again, make sure they aren't grown on semi-dwarfing stock. Apples like the old colonial 'twenty ounce' will grow to 10 metres.
- Boobialla or myoporum species? Haven't tested these. Native.
- Brachychiton (native – does this grow well in Canberra? Does for us.) Tall, lovely tree, but slow growing in cold areas.
- Bunya pine? Have only tested green leaves, not wood or bark or dry leaves. Native; nut producer; grand specimen in Goulburn's park. This definitely needs more testing before planting but is a possible.
- Hazelnuts, as long as dead wood is cut out. Sucker well and are very drought resistant.
- Honey locust? Need more testing. Choose thornless varieties. Very drought resistant.
- Lillypillies – we grow seven different lillypillies so far, all of which have proved drought resistant once established and tolerate seven degrees of frost. They are fire resistant when growing well. I haven't tested the dead or wilted leaves for flammability. They're native, and bird attracting.
- Linden trees (have only tested leaves here, not the wood).
- *Melia adzerach* (white cedar) – not fantastic, but better than many if you have to go native – one of the few deciduous natives. The moister the soil the less flammable it appears to be, but I'm still not sure about this.
- Mulberries – only if watered sometimes and dead wood pruned each year.
- Norfolk Island hibiscus? Haven't tested them.
- Oaks? Only leaf tests on green leaves so far.
- Pear – but not the ones you buy in the nursery, grafted onto quince rootstock to make nice, smallish backyard trees. Go for ones on *Pyrus calleryamna* stock – or just grow *Pyrus calleryamna*, which happily grows to 10 metres or taller (have seen them up to 20 metres in good soil), survives hideous drought, horrid frost, and is a bit less attractive to pear and cherry slug than many other pears. Seedling pears also usually grow large and hardy, up to 15 metres. Also try *Pyrus pryrifolia*, up to 15 metres (Japanese pear – selected varieties are 'nashi' pears), *Pyrus kawakammi*, and the Manchurian pear, *P. ussuriensisthe*, the largest commonly grown pear that grows up to 22 metres high.
- Pecan. Must be watered to establish in dry areas.
- *Photinia robusta* (haven't tested them – I hate the stuff).
- Pittosporums – native, *P. undulatum* is surprisingly drought resistant; can become a major weed in many areas.
- Plane trees
- Pomegranate – very drought resistant; haven't tested dry leaves. Don't plant the dwarf or semi-dwarf varieties by mistake. Dry, split fruit will burn.

- Poplars? Have only done leaf tests, not wood tests, and only on silver and lombardy poplars. Drought resistant.
- Port Jackson fig (Don't know though how flammable this is in very dry conditions – it's a native.).
- Rhododendrons (need shelter from other trees and water – a garden rather than a windbreak plant).
- Tamarilloes (but no chance whatsoever in frosty climates, except in a warm, moist courtyard!)
- Tree lucerne – smallish trees; haven't tested dry or wilted leaves or wood yet; their great advantage though is that they can be used for stock food if the stock get used to the green branches when young.
- Various rainforest trees – sadly, most, though not all of these, also need a rainforest. We have been trying some here in open ground with some success, and they are worth trialling. Some, like the fruit-producing Davison's plum, have even proved drought resistant.
- Walnuts
- Willows – but only the non-invasive dry land ones, whose name I can't recall at the moment!

Low firebreaks

Many fleshy plants will stop grass fires. These may only have to be half a metre wide – it depends on the height and density of the grass behind. The higher the grass, and the more dead grass, the wider the firebreak needs to be.

Wider low firebreaks (10–30 metres) help protect against bush fire. The most common firebreak is bare or ploughed earth, or gravel, rock, concrete, paving. (Paving is excellent around the house – you can see sleeping snakes, watch basking lizards and roller blade on it – though not at the same time.)

However, when fires are intense and winds high, houses can catch fire from burning embers hundreds of metres or even kilometres away. But at the very least a low firebreak will cut down on the amount of nearby flammable material.

These 'green firebreaks' need to be combined with making sure that any flammable material is at least 20 metres from your house on flat land, and 40 metres away on steep slopes and towards prevailing bushfire winds.

POSSIBLE PLANTS FOR WIDE, LOW FIREBREAKS:

- agapanthus (drought resistant), but avoid the seeding varieties that become weeds
- comfrey
- dahlias (only in summer, but then so are most bushfires – dahlias are also extraordinarily drought tolerant)
- chokoes or pumpkins as a ground cover
- dichondra (native)
- grapes in rows on metal frames with paving or gravel between them, not grass
- a green lawn (except, when your lawn is green, the danger of drought and fire is probably not high!)
- melons – the Siberian melon will grow and fruit even in frosty areas in summer, and grows in soil that literally appears to be dust; or in a sand hill – watermelons originated in South African desert country

- passionfruit grown as a ground cover – also banana passionfruit, ditto
- rhubarb (drought resistant – use large-stemmed, green varieties)
- well-watered veg gardens – but not dried corn stalks, etc.
- West Australian Jacksonia – haven't tested or grown this one

PS Lucerne is possibly the most fire-retardant of available pasture species.

Mulch

Avoid woodchips or bark – anything that might burn. Many mulches, though, stay damp and semi-rotten even in dry weather, and can actually slow down a fire. Use common sense – if it looks like it will burn, don't let it.

Remember too that rocks are also great weed suppressing, heat storing and moisture retaining mulch – and things have to be very hot indeed for rock to burn.

Summary

1. Avoid plants that go 'whoosh!' around your house.
2. Have a high 'green' windbreak/firebreak.
3. If possible, have a low 'green' firebreak to help protect from grassfires.

Postscripts

- There are many garden features that can help radiate heat, like white-painted garden walls, or slow fires, or water gardens and bog gardens – these are another subject! There are some, however, that are both drought- and fire-resistant.
- Most native shrubs are NOT drought resistant, and will die – or at least have lots of dry wood – in dry conditions. Some however, are both drought- and fire resistant, but I've done too little work to really expand on this yet.
- No, our garden isn't fireproof. Though I've tried to surround our place with fire retardant plants I never expected to have to plan for current conditions!
- Beware of wooden pergolas next to the house – they may catch alight and their heat set your house burning. Beware of vines against walls – they can harbour burning debris. Keep an eye on downpipes against your walls – they can hold debris too
- In fact ANY bush or wooden object (or gas bottles) near your house can either catch burning embers or burn in the heat. **Keep your house – and gutters – clean.**

And yes, it IS possible to build a bushfire-safe house. (Although now we don't have one, if there is ever a next time, we will.) Underground houses, houses made from fireproof materials – they ARE possible and good to live in! And anyone who says that there is nothing we can do to protect ourselves from fire except burn the bush each year is talking through their hat. (Very hot fires can actually INCREASE the likelihood of the bush burning again, as it dries out the soil and leaf litter, and encourages the germination of fire-loving – and very flammable – shrubs.)

In the last big fires here I saw bushfire pass over ground that had been burnt four times. The last time it was almost as though the ground itself was burning. 'Burn-offs' won't necessarily protect you. But, rethinking what a house in the bush should look like, will. And if one day our house or garden burn, our next one will be that supposedly impossible dream – a fireproof house.

Chapter 4

GARDENS FOR KIDS

When I was a kid, dragons lurked at the bottom of our garden, somewhere behind the mulberry tree, and if I dug deep enough in my sandpit I might just make a tunnel down to China ... or at least find a fossilised dinosaur.

Nowadays, gardens are smaller, and more carefully designed too. The grass we played cricket on has become a courtyard and paving, and there's more likely to be a flower-bed along the front than a tree to climb to spy on the teenager next door when she meets her boyfriend at the gate.

But kids need gardens! A place in which to play, to imagine, to be active, instead of sitting in front of a TV or computer. And even a small garden can have places to tempt kids outdoors.

Kids don't destroy gardens (it's important to remember this). They just wound them a bit. Gardens are living places, and damage repairs itself.

Yes, kids do leave great gashes on the lawn with their bicycles, trip over pots with roller blades, balance on garden edges so they crumble, or pluck great handfuls of flowers and rip some up by the roots.

But before you weep for your dahlias decide whether it's more important to teach them about other people's flowers, or let them enjoy the garden without guilt.

LET KIDS OWN THE GARDEN TOO!

Let kids share some of the garden. Let them choose the colors for the garden furniture, and do the painting! Okay, you may have to live with bright pink chairs or a purple and silver striped table for a year – but another coat of paint will cover it!

Next time you go to the nursery let them choose a shrub of their own ... even if it's yellow and yours is an all-white garden.

Teach kids how to prune, weed and pick flowers ... and don't stress if they make a mess of it! Gardens heal ... but sharp words when kids pick your prize roses may turn them off gardening for years.

Let kids use the garden, even if they damage it a bit. Branches torn from shrubs can be horses to ride, or lions' tails. A few pansies ripped from the soil are a small price for a bunch of flowers in your child's fist, given to you with love and pride.

Plants for kids to nibble

Kids love picking and eating veg straight from the garden, with a quick wash under the tap. Ask kids to pick the peas for dinner – even kids who hate peas on their plate will eat most of the crop, then hand you a measly three or four pods for the saucepan.

Kids love to pick and eat:
- Peas and snow peas
- Tiny carrots (try the small round ones) and beetroot
- Parsley
- Tiny fresh beans
- Tiny chokoes no bigger than their finger nail, all crunch and sweetness
- Tiny cucumbers or zucchini, no bigger than their little finger
- Passionfruit, hot from the sun
- Fresh strawberries and raspberries
- Any apple or orange they pick themselves!

Pots for kids

Kids love a row of pots, like insect-eating Venus fly traps or Pitcher plants, or a row of really spiky cacti, especially those multi-coloured ones with red and yellow grafts like beanies on their heads.

Some kids like pots of bulbs. A pot of bulbs is a 'secret pot' because no-one else knows what is going to come up and flower.

HOW TO TEMPT KIDS INTO THE GARDEN

A sandpit

Small 'shell' sandpits are great for very little kids, but bigger kids need good, deep sandpits so they can build a giant castle or a fort.

A simple sandpit is easily made by digging out as big a space as you have room and muscle for, but should be at least 30 cm deep and 2 metres square; line it with weed-mat, so that water can drain out. Fill with clean sand; keep a roll of bird netting to spread over the pit when it's not being used, to stop cats from using it. This type of sandpit has no hard or rough edges, and can be filled with soil to make a veggie garden once the kids have outgrown it.

A clothes line cubby

Props needed: lots of sheets or blankets. Lower the clothes line; drape over spare blankets, sheets or whatever else is handy. Hills Hoist clothes lines can amaze with a dragon at their centre, if you hang blankets from every line – and peg them tight to stop them blowing off.

A styrofoam palace

Props needed: masking tape, lots of empty styrofoam or even cardboard boxes – ask for them at the supermarket. This is a bit like playing Lego, but bigger. Tape the boxes together. Pile them up to make walls, then tape the corners of the walls to make a house. Add a roof, and don't forget a space for the doors!

A garden table zoo

Props needed: a table, blankets, chairs. This is where the wild creatures dwell, so be careful passing in case they bite your ankle. Drape blankets over the table – use a few books so they don't slide off. Line up chairs, too, and drape blankets over them as well, to make caves deep into the heart of the jungle.

A bicycle track

Even a small garden can have a long track that winds around the outside of the garden, in and out of shrubs. It need only be wide enough for two feet or a bicycle.

Step 1. Mark out the path with string.

Step 2. Dig down to about 100 mm, then use 120 x 7 mm boards along the edges to make formwork for the concrete. Make sure each side is level with the other.

Step 3. Insert strips of plywood every 2 metres to make an expansion joint.

Step 4. Place 20 cm of sand on the base, level.

Step 5. Pour the concrete – this doesn't have to be done in one day! Add ochre so it isn't all grey and boring.

Step 6. Level it with a float, then rough over the surface with a broom or brush so it's not too slippery. Pull out the expansion joints.

Step 7. When the concrete is set, pull out the formwork.

Swings, seesaw, slippery dip or trampoline

These are all great fun, and safe ones are available ready made or in kit form. Make sure there is soft tanbark, sand or at least grass below … and no hard or protruding objects that kids might fall onto! Trampolines can be sunk flush with the level of the garden, too, so there isn't as far to fall

A climbing frame

These can be bought, but they can also be made far more cheaply by anyone who can lift a pile and drill a hole. There are some great 'how to' books at the local library.

Sports' spots

- A prefab basketball hoop with backboard from a sport's store.
- A shed wall that they can bounce a ball against with concrete or paving underneath.
- A net to hit balls into so they don't fly over the fence.
- Concrete or paving marked out for hop-scotch … or long, painted snake with the letters of the alphabet so they can hop and learn at the same time.

Trees for kids

Give kids a fruit tree each birthday. Kids love picking fruit – and this tree is THEIRS and no-one can pick its fruit without permission. As they grow, so does their tree! Good trees include lemon trees, oranges, cumquats, mandarins, dwarf apples, dwarf peaches, a passionfruit vine … anything that will give at least one fruit in the next year!

Kids love carrots (sometimes)

Somewhere in Australia, right this minute, there's a desperate parent telling their kid, 'Of COURSE you like carrots, Jason. Open up now …' Except Jason just KNOWS he'll be sick if he eats that carrot. Carrots are soft and squishy. How can any parent expect him to eat squish?

What kids need

- Shade, hats, and suncream. Either put shade sails over sandpits and play areas, or have lots of trees!
- Flexibility. Kids get bored with the 'same old … '! A tent that can be put up and down is better than a fixed cubby; big packing boxes or old sheets are even more fun, as kids can turn them into rocket ships, boats or submarines!
- Mess. Yes, boxes all over the lawn are messy, but they are also the basis for lots of creativity and fun!

Most parents forget how deeply kids feel about food. When you're a kid a chocolate biscuit is the most important thing in the universe – or you really will throw up if you have to eat that carrot. So how do you get kids to eat their veg? Easy. Grow special, kid-friendly veg, just for them. This method is infallible. Food that kids will reject on a plate becomes irresistible if they've helped grow it – or even if grandpa tells them he's grown it just for them and lets them pick it. (Eating it freshly washed and outdoors can be important sometimes, too, not all squishy on a plate.)

I can't count the number of kids who've wandered around our garden, eating every type of veg in sight, while their parents look on amazed. THIS WORKS!

Great 'pick your own' veg for kids

Tiny tomatoes: look for red, cherry-sized fruit, like Cherry Cocktail, Sweet 100 Hybrid, Tumbler which has cute little red peach-shaped fruit (each with a little pointy bit on their ends), or Tiny Tim or baby Red Pear or tiny yellow egg-shaped tomatoes like Yellow Baby. One gulp and they're gone.

Round carrots, like Mini Round, Thumbelina or French Round: these are small, round and crunchy. Kids are entranced by their weird shape. But mostly a small carrot isn't intimidating – two crunches and it's gone.

Mini capsicums: red, yellow, green or chocolate coloured – one bite and they're gone too.

Round zucchini, like Rondo de Nice: pick them tiny, no bigger than a thumbnail. Zucchini are best eaten outdoors, straight from the bush, or very lightly stir-fried so they don't go squishy.

Vegetable spaghetti: this marrow has interesting wriggly innards. Call it 'worms' and serve with tomato sauce.

Baby corn: OK, this one doesn't always work. But most kids love freshly picked, stir-fried

Things kids learn from gardening

- Hard work achieves things.
- Patience ... those strawberries WILL get ripe.
- Fresh food tastes better (but remove the slugs first).
- Yes, you can grow your own.
- Real life is more satisfying than TV (except for 'The Simpsons').
- It's possible to have a two-hour conversation with your relatives.
- Things GROW – without the aid of computers or microchips.

baby sweet corn with a bit of piquant sauce. Nor have I ever met a kid who doesn't love freshly picked, big sweet corn, especially one like Honey and Cream with yellow and white kernels, dashed from garden to pot then smothered in butter and salt. Just like corn chips but sweeter and messier.

Snake beans: these metre-long beans may not attract kids on a plate. But freshly steamed, stir-fried or boiled snake beans can be sucked down like spaghetti. They just become fun. Especially if you say 'no hands'.

Magic beans: these are purple beans, like Purple King or Queen, that turn green when they're cooked. Magic ...

Snow peas: somehow, when there are kids in our garden there are never any snow peas on the vines. Maybe the wallabies get them ...

KID'S FOOD GAMES

Forget about the saying, 'Don't play with your food.' Food games get kids eating!

The 'How far can I spit' game

Make it a rule that kids have to taste every food on the table. But if they hate it they can spit it out the window. (Make sure the cat and Aunt Ethel aren't in spitting range.)

Most kids (and adults) need to try a new food several times before the taste becomes familiar enough to like it. And spitting means they don't have to worry about swallowing yuck stuff.

Lucky dip fruit and veg

Take kids around the markets every week or fortnight, and let them choose one new fruit or veg to try. Their choice, no prompting, and you agree to try it too. (That makes it fair – and allows kids to have some real sense of power over their choices – especially when they manage to choose something that is new for all of you!)

Pick and choose

Get a couple of seed catalogues and a good book on cooking veg – one with lots of pictures. Let kids choose what THEY want to eat. You may be surprised what they choose.

Keeping kids safe!

You need to be able to see small kids at all times from the kitchen or living room window, but older kids need a bit of privacy with shrubs and hedges. Other garden dangers include:

- Trees. Kids love to climb ... make sure any tempting trees have soft landing places below.
- Steep retaining walls and steps – toddlers may fall down them.
- Loose rocks around gardens or on banks that might come loose if kids jump on them.
- Ponds. Either keep water fenced off from kids, or have a solid reinforcing mesh cage just under the water – or both. (This also discourages Golden Labradors from leaping in there.)
- Dirt. Let kids get dirty, but also teach them that dirt too can harbour dangers. Make sure they wash (and dry) hands before eating; make sure all dogs who visit your garden are wormed; keep kids' tetanus shots up to date (and yours too).
- Pesticides, fungicides, herbicides, snail pellets and potting mix – keep them out of reach of kids and pets.
- Poisonous plants – see the web pages for more on poisonous plants.
- Make sure that kids can't run onto the road. Even older kids may impulsively run after a ball. A gate they have to open at least gives them time to think!

Six Games for Bored Kids

- Make a cubby with blankets on the clothesline.
- Paint all the garden furniture different colours. (Who cares if it's tacky? It can be repainted again next year). PS Use a waterproof paint.
- Paint each step a different colour.
- Paint a big mural on the shed wall.
- Mark out a cubby shape, then plant it with giant sunflowers.
- Make a teepee of poles and grow climbing beans up them.

Chapter 5
FEEDING YOUR GARDEN

THE IDEAL

The ideal garden relies on bush-style fertility: leaves and bark and debris return to the soil and grow more plants, with animals an integral part.

In our garden the birds leave white, phosphorous splotches; geese recycle greenery; wombats leave their droppings; clover and lucerne fix nitrogen under the trees; wattles drop fertile leaves; dark-green comfrey leaves decay in winter, while in summer their roots draw up from deep down nutrients that would otherwise be lost. Sometimes I think 'fertility' is the most beautiful process there is.

- Instead of artificial fertilisers ... use homemade liquid manure, pelletised hen manure or blood and bone. Buy hay or other mulch. It's cheaper and gives you better results than fertilisers, controls weeds, and regulates moisture, among other things.
- Instead of buying manure ... let small animals manure your garden.
- Instead of buying organic fertilisers ... recycle kitchen and garden waste. Plant green manures, add free nitrogen from the nitrogen-fixing bacteria associated with plant roots and other free-living bacteria, and use deep-rooted perennials to bring up leached nutrients.
- Instead of compost and mulch ... grow your own 'living mulches', which can be slashed down to decay back into the soil where they grow.

Fertilisers are a racket – most gardens don't need fertilisers. You only need to add fertiliser if you crop your garden, taking out flowers or vegetables. Otherwise, once your soil is fertile, it will stay that way – as long as you let leaves and lawn clippings decay back into the soil.

Even if you do take flowers or vegetables out of the garden and into the house you probably needn't buy fertiliser unless you are entirely self-sufficient. If you buy groceries you are also buying nutrients – scraps to turn into compost or liquid manure. Even your own urine, used fresh and thrown out in the morning before the neighbours are up – or tactfully tipped into the compost – will give your garden the fertility it needs.

It may take time before a garden can accumulate its own fertility, but there are many ways in which to help that process along.

HOW TO FEED YOUR GARDEN

Artificial fertilisers produce soft, sappy pest- and disease-prone growth – and may destroy both soil structure and useful soil organisms. Try this for yourself: grow two plots side by side, one fertilised with mulch, one with artificial fertiliser – and count the pests. Measure too, how much water each needs before plants wilt! Organic fertility relies on the steady release of nutrients from decaying organic matter: mulch, green manure and compost.

Yet, conventional organic fertilising can be a lot of work. There's an enormous amount of energy involved in transporting lucerne hay, seaweed or manures – both your energy and fuel. It's also a form of mining the soil: too often your organic fertility is robbing some other area of its organic matter.

The alternative is to grow your own: to provide your own organic matter from the plants you grow, your own nitrogen 'fixed' from the air. Phosphorous, potash and trace elements, recycled or made available as your soil becomes more 'active', or brought in as extra food for the animals in your garden – whether they be native birds attracted to your jungle, or chooks in a mobile yard down the back.

Nothing feeds the native figs, the kurrajongs and gum trees in the bush above our house – or rather, everything feeds them. Leaves and other plant material decay and recycle, wombats leave their droppings, nitrogen-fixers like indigophera and casuarina flourish all around.

FIVE WAYS TO FERTILISE YOUR GARDEN

- Buy fertiliser – either artificial fertilisers, 'organic' fertilisers like manures, blood and bone, or mulching materials.
- Recycle garden and kitchen wastes, urine, animal waste, paper – anything that will decompose except human, dog and pig faeces and any other waste that may be infected.
- Grow your own fertilisers: algae or deep-rooted perennials, green manure and 'nitrogen-fixing' plants, for example, rhizobium bacteria fix nitrogen in association with legumes and other roots, while other free-living bacteria like azobacter and *Clostridium pasteurianum* fix nitrogen from the air.
- Keep small animals, whether sheep, chooks or earthworms. Keep them for their dung and the increased nitrogen-fixing soil microflora associated with it.
- Make nutrients that are already in your soil more available to the plants.

OUR GARDEN REGIME

Our fertility system is simple: mulch once a year (or every two or three years for some trees). Plus the occasional scatter of hen manure or other fertiliser.

Everything that can be is recycled. Weeds get thrown under trees or are used as mulch, scraps go into the compost. Urine is used in liquid manure or as a herbicide. Nitrogen-

Buy animal feed instead of fertiliser, and let the animals' manure fertilise your garden.

fixers like wattles (which we slash for mulch), bracken, indigophera, sweet peas, lupins, broom and many others add fertility. Animals like wombats, birds and bees add their dung.

Most of our 'bought' fertiliser comes from the manure from our chooks. We feed the chooks; they feed our trees and garden. (I think I'd have chooks just for their droppings even if they never gave us eggs.) And every few years I bring in some hay and commercial pelletised hen manure or similar to replace the nutrients we've given away as gifts of flowers or vegetables, or that have escaped in our faeces through the septic tank.

HOW MUCH FEEDING?

Once your soil is fertile you only need to replace the nutrients you take out, as flowers, vegetables or lawn clippings. Otherwise your garden will recycle itself: fallen leaves fertilise the trees and shrubs, flowers that die down become mulch for the next lot.

Many gardens suffer from being over-fertilised: too much nitrogen that causes soft, sappy, pest- and disease-attracting green growth, and well-fed shrubs and flowers which produce more leaves than blooms.

The best fertility is natural fertility. Mimic the way soil is naturally created from organic matter (mulch), the breakdown of rocks, and accumulated nitrogen in the soil by nitrogen-fixing bacteria – often associated with so-called 'nitrogen-fixing' legumes.

ADDING FERTILITY: QUICK FIXES

Quick fixes are sometimes needed: maybe when your garden is just beginning, and you need to get a crop in while your natural fertility accumulates; or perhaps as 'extra' feeding for a hungry crop like celery that turns stringy if you don't force-feed it.

Forget about artificial fertilisers, or you'll eliminate many small organisms in the soil, and end up with 'nitrogen-flushed' plants, pest and disease prone. If your plants need feeding fast – they are small, stunted, yellowing with narrow leaves – or you know your soil is lousy but have planted anyway; or if you want extra feeding for a hungry crop like lettuce or celery, try:

- Running chooks through your orchard – and feed the chooks.
- Running chooks through the vegie garden after a crop is harvested (i.e., divide your garden into four or more parts, so chooks can be kept out of areas that are still producing).
- A thick mulch of lucerne – green as possible with lots of leaves, or pea straw – any high-nitrogen mulch.
- A thick mulch of home-made compost.
- Blood and bone – scatter it on the garden like icing sugar on a cake, once a fortnight.
- Pelleted hen manure – scattered once a month should be enough.

Home-made liquid manure

This is the best of the quick-fix options. Fill a bucket with any of the following: weeds, lawn clippings, green leaves (strip them from a tree if you must), green vegetable scraps (lettuce or cabbage leaves, carrot tops, etc), or garden scraps. Get hold of comfrey leaves, seaweed or nettles if you can – they seem to help make plants healthier too. You can also add manures if you have them – any manure, fresh or stale – or a spadeful of compost. Fill the bucket with water; wait a week or two till it starts to turn brown; and pour it onto your plants once a week. Add more water to the bucket and let it brew again. After a month or two you can use the gunk at the bottom of the bucket as mulch – it'll be decomposed and even weeds will then be safe.

Urine

If you really want to put backbone in your liquid manure add a little urine – your own, and must be fresh. Fresh urine doesn't smell – as long as it's your own. You can also add the urine just before you pour the liquid manure onto your garden. If you do add urine make sure it is diluted – no more than one part urine to 10 parts water – and you only apply it once a fortnight, and not onto bare ground – it is better to pour it onto mulch. Urine is reasonably safe as long as the donor doesn't have a urinary tract or other major general infection and hasn't recently returned from the tropics. But it ISN'T sterile, so treat it cautiously. And it CAN be high in salt if you have a high salt diet – not good for you or your soil. Too much urine can also make your ground sour and useless – and it can pong!
If it pongs, you've added way too much.

Human, dog, cat and pig faeces can be used only by composting at a high temperature (20 years in a septic tank doesn't make them safe), then dug in well, to fertilise a deep-rooted non-edible crop, like comfrey, lucerne or trees. Use the residues of this crop to fertilise other areas: recycled fertility without danger. Never graze this area or walk on it in bare feet, and make sure it will not pollute the water table.

Manure

Hen manure is richest – don't use it fresh or it may burn plants. Try soaking manure in water for liquid manure and using the sludge remaining a few weeks later. This method also kills weeds – and many manures are weedy.

Comfrey leaves

These are 17 per cent nitrogen and break down quickly – though of course they are not as 'fast' as the products above. Let comfrey leaves wilt in the sun so they don't blow away, then use as a thick mulch.

Rich sources of nitrogen for 'quick fixes'

- Hen and other bird manure.
- Urine, hair, and blood and bone.
- Seaweed and algae.
- Lucerne hay (green, not stalky), fresh grass clippings, and comfrey.
- Fresh bean, broad bean or pea plants.
- Leaves from 'nitrogen-fixers' like tree lucerne, casuarina (very acid), robinia, etc.

MULCH

This is the best way to feed the garden, especially if it's home grown. It not only adds nutrients, it helps soil structure, both retaining more moisture or draining waterlogged soil. It tones down extremes of heat and cold for plant roots underneath, prevents erosion of bare ground, keeps down weeds, and encourages earthworms which make phosphorous more available to plants. It also increases disease resistance and provides a good environment for mycorrhizas (associations between plant roots and fungi which can help roots take up more nutrients, especially phosphorous).

What to use for mulch

Even stones are better than nothing – and in many cases can be excellent (see 'Drought gardens'). Anything that has once lived – leaves, sawdust, old doormats, old gardeners – will eventually break down and their nutrients can be used by the plants. But if the mulch is low in nitrogen to begin with, it may take nitrogen from the soil while it is breaking down. If you are using a low-fertility mulch, use the 'quick-fix additives' outlined before for a year or so, until at least the first lot of mulch has gone back to the soil.

High-fertility mulches

The following mulches can be used without any additives – they will fertilise your garden by themselves AS LONG AS THE SOIL IS FERTILE TO BEGIN WITH. Try to avoid using just one mulch though, in case you get trace element deficiencies over the years – use as many sorts as you can get hold of.

- Seaweed. Wash seaweed that has been above the high-tide line, as the sea wind will have impregnated it with salt. It is weed-free! (But it can also be illegal to gather it – check. And if too many people gather too much it can affect the area's ecology.)
- Gunge from ponds and creeks (be careful that it's not blue-green algae – toxic to humans, it can cause illness and skin problems).
- Lucerne hay. The more green leaf matter in the hay, the better it is – avoid bales that are all stalk. Watch out for weed seeds in poor hay: give it to the chooks for a week first if you can.
- Comfrey leaves.
- Lawn clippings. These are good, as long as the lawn is short and green.
- Small, soft, green weeds. These are good too, as long as they don't have roots or seeds.

Poorer mulches

- Stones (i.e., not much use as fertiliser, but great for keeping in warmth and moisture).
- Sawdust
- Garden debris. Debris like corn stalks and old radish tops, prunings and autumn leaves can also be quite good, as they break down quickly.

Add liquid manure, urine, or blood and bone to all of these. They break down faster with added nitrogen.

NEVER USE PAPER!!!!!!!!

And never be tempted to use paper under your no-dig garden, either. It prevents rain from penetrating the soil. It stops the soil micro-organisms spreading up into the mulch to help it break down too, and soil can become sour with paper on top. I have lost count of the gardens and plants I've seen die where someone has mulched with paper. Avoid carpet, cardboard and all other water repelling mulches too!

Homegrown mulches

The best mulches are homegrown – they save time and energy, and you're not robbing some other system of its nutrients and organic matter.

Green manure

Plant a crop of peas, beans, broad beans, sweet peas, lupins, peanuts or any other 'nitrogen-fixer'. (It is actually the bacteria associated with the roots that fix the nitrogen from the air.) Slash the plants as they start flowering and use them as mulch.

DON'T DIG MULCH OR GREEN MANURE INTO THE SOIL. Digging is hard work, bad for the soil structure, and may cause root rots. Leave the plants on top to return to the soil naturally.

Other plants, like sunflowers (plant cocky seed), radish, buckwheat and oats can be grown as mulch. They won't add nitrogen, but they'll be good for your soil and plants.

Deep-rooted plants

Deep-rooted plants, like comfrey, and trees, bring nutrients up from deep down where shallow roots can't reach. As their roots and leaves decay, the nutrients go back into the soil. Other deep-rooted plants – like chicory, parsnips, and even dock – can also be used to bring fertility back to the surface.

Comfrey

Comfrey is a high-fertility mulch: a thick comfrey mulch should provide enough nutrients for a garden.

We grow comfrey in a border round our gardens. I slash the dark green leaves three or four times a year, leaving the leaves where they fall for instant mulch. In winter the leaves die back and fertilise the garden again with the nutrients brought up by the thick deep roots.

Our main asparagus bed is grown with comfrey. Every year the asparagus spears come up before the comfrey shoots. When the comfrey is in full leaf I stop picking – then in winter the comfrey dies down and mulches the asparagus. This association has been working for 12 years – with no other fertiliser. Some year soon, though, I'm going to have to add some nutrients to make up for the asparagus harvest we remove ... maybe next year. A comfrey border will also stop grass invading your garden.

Comfrey will keep rooting deeper the longer it is left. Our early plants wilted in dry weather, now they soar through it. Comfrey can be used as a complete fertiliser, either by using the roots as mulch or letting them soak in water until it turns deep tea-coloured, and using that as a liquid tonic for plants.

Comfrey is about 17 per cent nitrogen. This compares with horse manure at about 14 per cent. Comfrey has about the same phosphorus as horse manure and twice the potash.

Comfrey grows from root divisions. Buy a plant in the nursery, wait for it to multiply, or take a bit of root from someone else's garden. Never rotary hoe comfrey – it keeps spreading as the roots divide and is impossible to get rid of. Comfrey has tall blue flower spikes and is quite pretty around the garden. It stops growing in winter, and dies back in frost.

It is now illegal to advise eating comfrey – although the evidence this is based on is controversial. But a lotion from the leaves or roots, or just the juice, is excellent for wounds, bruises and sprains.

Lemon grass

This is a quick-growing, low-fertility mulch for warm areas. Grow the lemon grass in rows between your crops – it will also act as a windbreak and a sunscreen and stop grass invading the garden. Slash as often as you need to. It also has some pest repelling qualities.

Wattles and other 'nitrogen-fixing' trees

Wattles grow naturally around our garden. The bacteria associated with their roots fix nitrogen from the air; the small branches can be used as high nitrogen mulch. Slash your wattles when they are no thicker than your wrist – they'll sprout again. Don't let them get too big, or they may damage the garden when you cut them down, and root rotting fungi can spread from their decaying roots to the rest of your garden.

Lawn clippings

Sprinkle these thinly – they can compact and either burn or stop moisture penetrating. Flies like them too. But if you have clover in your lawn mix, lawn clippings can be rich source of fertility.

Perennial sweet peas

We let these ramble up trellises in the garden and through trees. They are nitrogen-fixers – and the debris returns excellent fertiliser to the soil to feed the nearby plants. They are also beautiful.

Clover

Strongly growing plants like corn, potatoes, beans and cauliflowers can be planted directly into clover, as long as it is regularly mown. (I use a whipper snipper.) You can also cover clover with weed-mat and plant more vulnerable seedlings like lettuce and celery onto it. Or try a winter-growing clover that will die down in hot weather, leaving a ready mulched and fertilised garden bed.

Lucerne

Lucerne makes a good lawn, if you mow it often. Good lucerne hay has more than enough nitrogen to decompose without robbing the soil of nutrients. It is the basis for the classic 'no-dig' garden.

Lucerne can be brought in. It should be as green as possible and not smell musty. If it does, don't inhale the dust. Have as much leafy material as stalks. Don't buy 'first cut' lucerne if possible as it probably contains more weed seeds than later cuts. Large weed seeds can be shaken out over a few sheets of newspaper; or give the bales to the chooks for a few days to fluff out the hay, eat the seeds and deposit a bit more nitrogen for your garden.

Lucerne seed is small and rarely reseeds from hay, though we do sometimes get a little in the garden. It isn't any trouble. Lucerne seed can be bought at any stock and station agents, along with its 'inoculator', the bacteria needed to associate with the lucerne to fix nitrogen. 'Alfalfa' seed, bought at health food stores, is really lucerne seed. You can plant alfalfa seed for sprouting, but without an inoculant it will probably be less use for nitrogen fixing.

Lucerne roots will continue to grow downwards. I have heard of them reaching 22 metres. Lucerne can be cut from a lucerne lawn and sprinkled thinly (fresh) on the garden or around trees.

GATHERING QUICK FIXES

If you are beginning your garden you may want to increase your fertility quickly. As well as the 'quick fixes' listed above, forage for:
- Seaweed. See above for cautions. Don't spread it too thickly or it may suffocate your plants.
- Algae from dams. This is high fertility, is weed-free, and fish will bless you for getting rid of it. Again, see above for cautions.
- 'Garbage'. Taken from greengrocers and restaurants, this should be composted first, either conventionally, with chooks, or with any of the 'compost alternatives' (see below).
- Fish waste. This stinks, but is very high in nutrients. It must be composted.
- Wool tailings
- Lawn clippings or old leaves. Beg them from a neighbour or get them from a park.
- Waste from food-processing plants
- Hair. This is rich in nitrogen. Beg it from the local hairdresser.

And remember that any mulch is better than no mulch. Anything that has once lived will add fertility to your garden – though it may take some time to break down and become available to your plants. Even newspaper will eventually add its nutrients to the fertility of your garden (see above for cautions).

NITROGEN-FIXERS

The best way to add fertility is with nitrogen from the air recycled back into the garden when the nitrogen-fixing plants die and decompose.

Nitrogen-fixing plants

It is the bacteria associated with nitrogen-fixers' plant roots that actually do the 'fixing'. To maximise this you will need to apply an inoculant to your nitrogen-fixing crops. Ask for the correct inoculant wherever it is sold.

Legumes are nitrogen-fixing plants:
- A soybean crop will fix about 60 to 90 kilograms of nitrogen per hectare per year.
- Cowpeas will fix 80 to 90 kg.
- Clover will fix 100 to 160 kg.
- Lucerne will fix 120 to 600 kg.
- Lupins will fix 150 to 170 kg.

Other nitrogen-fixers include honey locust, judas tree, woad, broom, black locust, mesquite, casuarinas, peanuts, robinia, sweet peas, bracken, wattles, indigophera, and tree lucerne.

Clover garden

Grow your garden on a clover-rich lawn as clover is nitrogen-fixing. Put weed-mat strips down the lawn leaving clover in strips in between. Every year in autumn or early winter move the weed-mat to the clover strips. The clover will break down and feed that year's vegetables.

If you don't have a convenient clover patch, weeds will do almost as well – but you will have to add some nitrogen in the form of liquid manure, blood and bone.

GROWING ALGAE

Algae are nitrogen-fixers, as are various plant algae associations, including azolla, which produces most of the nitrogen in various rice-producing areas in Asia.

Most algae produce at least 25 kg of nitrogen per year per hectare. This compares with azolla, which can produce up to 300 kg, and lupins which 'fix' (or their associated bacteria do) about 160 kg of nitrogen a year.

Even though algae is low on the nitrogen-fixing ladder it has several advantages. It can be grown where other crops can't: on roofs for example, or concrete or any waste ground at all. It will grow all year round – and it is a weed-free, instantly usable mulch or fertiliser, breaking down quickly.

One small algae-harvesting pond in the backyard can be quite an addition to the vegetable garden, and may even supply all the extra nitrogen you need if scraps and garden waste are also recycled.

BEWARE OF BLUE-GREEN ALGAE – it's toxic and can also give you dangerous skin problems. Most of the algae in garden ponds isn't blue-green algae – but do be careful! And NEVER harvest algae from a creek or dam unless you are sure it isn't blue-green algae.

Equipment

You will need a shallow pond, either bought from a place that sells small ornamental ponds, or made yourself. This can be made in a sand 'mould', then moved wherever you need it.

Dig a shallow depression in the ground, as wide as you want your pond to be, and no more than 30 cm deep. Line it with a couple of centimetres of clean sand, or a few sheets of overlapping newspapers. Mix a strong mortar of cement and sand. Check the cement packet for quantities. Smooth it over the sand or newspapers, about 5 cm thick. It doesn't have to be even.

While still wet, press some chicken mesh into it. This makes it less liable to crack. Keep it covered with wet sacking while it dries.

After a week or so lift it out. It should come quite easily, covered with sand or scraps of newspaper – either leave them or wash them off with a scrubbing brush.

Method

Site your pond somewhere out of the way. Shed roofs are excellent if the hose will reach up there, and you can reach it with a ladder. Simply make sure it has full sun and can easily be refilled.

Algae need light, nutrients and water. Once your pond is full and exposed to sunlight, add some food, rich in nitrogen and phosphorous. Hen manure is ideal. Garden soil and urine, or blood and bone will get the process going.

Mix the food into the water. Quantities will vary according to the strength of the food. As a rule of thumb mix in as much as you can without the mixture turning darker than fresh straw. Remember that algae need light, and they won't get that in dark water.

If there are mosquitoes in the area, cover the water with mosquito netting stretched on a wire or wood frame for easy removal.

Starter

You can either wait, and trust in the impurity of your water system to add algae for a starter, or go off to a polluted creek or dam and take home a bucket full of green stuff. CHECK WITH YOUR LOCAL DEPARTMENT OF AGRICULTURE OR COUNCIL HEALTH OFFICER THAT IT ISN'T BLUE-GREEN ALGAE. Use most of it on the garden. Pour a little into the pond, and wait.

Stir once a week, top up with water as necessary. If it dries out completely it will probably still be all right when you fill it up again, as long as conditions haven't been too hot. A drip irrigation system over the pond is fail-safe. It also helps add oxygen.

To harvest the nutrients just bucket out the slimy water and use it straight on the garden. Like seaweed, there will be no weed seeds and it will decompose very quickly. The amount of nutrients you harvest in your pond will depend entirely on what species you are growing there – experts on algae are hard to come by outside academe and government laboratories.

COMPOST

Compost is wonderful. It is also a lot of work. But sometimes it is a great help: in recycling material like kitchen scraps; in killing weed seeds; in destroying pollutants like herbicides; and in breaking down large stalks or branches.

What is compost?

A compost heap is a pile of rotting layers of various organic materials: garden or kitchen waste, manure, soil, paper or next-door's dead cat. A good compost heap is a dynamic living body, a mass of bacteria, actinomycetes and fungi breaking down plant fibre.

Why make compost?

Because it makes your plants grow better. Compost gives a better result than a mulch of the same materials would give. Compost is cheap. It recycles nutrients that might otherwise have been lost. It adds more nitrogen from nitrogen-fixing bacteria. It encourages earthworms and can neutralise excess acidity or alkalinity. It may provide spores, living bacteria and fungi that suppress pathogens like phytophthora root rots, eelworm and potato scurf, or supply fungal spores for mycorrhizal associations that help plants grow better with more resistance to disease.

Inorganic forms of plant nutrients like phosphorous and potassium are released by the organic acids produced by the micro-organisms in compost. A good, hot compost heap will also help control disease in garden wastes and kill off weed seeds.

What not to add to compost

- Pig, dog, cat, rat and human manure. These can spread disease, unless they get to very high temperatures. Human urine is fine as long as the donor is healthy.
- Too much newspaper – it clags together and won't rot. Try shredding it and mixing with something high in nutrients like hen manure with leaves to stop it sticking together.
- Plastic, including disposable nappies and plastic bags.
- Big bones – unless you don't mind bones in your garden, because bones will compost but take longer than most other stuff. Try keeping the bones in the oven for a week or two. After a few roastings they go brittle and decompose much more quickly. They are an excellent source of phosphorous.
- Fat, oil, salt, borax, disinfectant, antibiotics, herbicides and pesticides – they'll kill the organisms that make the compost.
- Weed seeds, unless you're confident the compost will warm up and kill them. The same goes for diseased leaves and material that might be infected with herbicides or

pesticides. A good compost heap will break down most herbicide and pesticide residues – but be safe.
- Meat – unless the container is fly- and rat-proof, or you tuck it in the centre where the beasts won't smell it. Meat is the basis of blood and bone. If you have a carcass don't waste it. If it's not safe to compost it, bury it near a tree.
- Thick layers of leaves, grass clippings, old oranges or apples – anything which will stick together. Mix them up with other stuff and they'll be fine.

What you do add to compost

Anything else that has once lived. In the last year our bin has been fed with a dead fox, an old hat, scraps, weeds, a no longer functional doormat, newspapers, jeans that even the rag bin didn't want, many bones, some rotten hessian that the rats got into before I could make tree guards, and a handful of Lego. The Lego survived. The rest is soil.

Should I add anything special to my compost?

You can add wood ash or eggshells if you want to, or rock phosphate for phosphorous deficient soil. But unless the plants you put in your heap are very phosphorous deficient this may not be necessary.

Compost tends to be slightly acidic. But remember that the problem with acid soil is not the acidity itself, but the fact that in acid or alkaline soil some nutrients are not available to meet the plants' needs. You may well find that this doesn't matter in compost-enriched soil. Don't add lime or dolomite. This speeds up nitrogen loss. If lime is really necessary add it after the compost is finished, not while it's decomposing.

Why has my compost failed?

It might be too wet. It might be too dry. It mightn't have enough air. But probably it didn't have enough nitrogen. Most compost material is scraps – which are low in nitrogen – or weeds or woody residues. If your compost fails to heat up add nitrogen – like urine, diluted hen manure, blood and bone, or green leafy lucerne. Wait a few days. If it fails to heat up, add more. A bit of phosphorous helps compost speed up too – try a sprinkle of ground rock phosphate.

How do I know if my compost is working?

Compost should start to heat up after three days. If it doesn't, check that it isn't too wet, or too clagged together with old porridge or rotten oranges; that it isn't too dry, or needs air or nitrogen. Compost should stay warm, not hot, until it is a solid mass. If it smokes or turns grey inside it's too hot – toss it around a bit to cool it down.

When is my compost ready?

When you can no longer tell what went in it – except for a few oddments like Lego, teaspoons and extra large bones.

Won't it breed flies and cockroaches?

If it does, it isn't working. Compost should start to heat up in three days – at most a week in cold weather. It should be too hot for flies and cockroaches. Add more nitrogenous matter.

HOW TO MAKE COMPOST

Basically, compost making falls into two methods – aerobic, that is, with air; and anaerobic, without air. The airless method includes the commercial Gedye bin, as well as compost made in trenches and plastic bags. The main advantage of the airless method is that it doesn't smell (which badly made aerobic compost does) and there is minimal loss of nitrogen to the air. Airless methods, however, are much slower than the others – unless heat is generated from outside. That's why Gedye bin compost is faster in summer. Always put your Gedye bin in full sunlight.

Plastic bag compost

This is the easiest compost of all. Buy heavy-duty garbage bags. Fill them a third full with a mixture of kitchen and garden waste (this is a good way of getting rid of fruit that may be infected with fruit fly or codling moth), and seal it. Now put it out into the sun. It may be ready in a fortnight or six weeks – it will depend on the amount of nitrogen in your waste, the moisture level, the weather and a few other things. Open it every week or so. If it stinks (and it should as it processes) it isn't ready yet. When there is no odour you have compost.

Trench compost

The advantage of a trench compost heap is that it's unobtrusive, though you have the work of digging the pit, and nutrients can leach and be lost.

Dig your pit about a metre square – any wider and deeper is too hard to reach into. Drive a stake into the middle of the plot. Place a layer of old branches, corn stalks or anything coarse on the bottom, then a hand-span of green matter like garden waste, a few centimetres of manure or a sprinkle of blood and bone, then alternating layers of kitchen scraps and garden waste until the pit is full.

Cover with garden waste or a thin layer of soil. After three weeks, take out the stake to help ventilation. The pit should have subsided a good deal by then – add more material if necessary.

Pit composting can be either airless or aerobic. If you seal it off with dirt so that the neighbours' dog can't dig it up, you'll have anaerobic compost – if you let it breathe you'll have aerobic compost.

Aerobic compost

Aerobic methods include the classic Indore compost developed by Sir Albert Howard at Indore in India – and most aerobic composts are variations on his methods.

When making aerobic compost remember it has four basic needs – moisture, heat, nitrogen and air. Make sure your compost heap is kept moist – but not wet. Don't put it in the coldest spot in the garden. Under the broken shade of a tree is best. Keep up the nitrogen level. To every layer of compost add something like blood and bone, hen manure, urine or fresh grass clippings.

The more the material in your compost heap is shredded the faster it will work. Attack it with garden shears, or run the lawn-mower over it a few times. Give your compost air by turning it, or make 'chimneys' by building the pile round stakes and pulling them out later.

If you follow these rules you should get good fast compost.

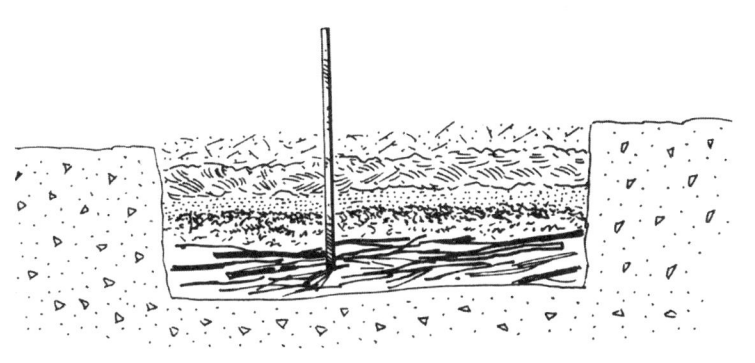

Trench compost: keep filling the trench with additional layers as the organic matter decomposes and settles. When it is full, plant your garden on top.

Classic compost heap

Drive a stake into the ground. Remove some of the grass around it or sprinkle some old compost around the stake – this is to facilitate the entry of natural 'starters' present in soil or compost.

Pile on the coarsest material you have, like branches or corn stalks. Add a handspan of garden wastes, old hay or other green matter. Add some nitrogenous material like blood and bone or hen manure or a wider band of cow or horse manure. Now add more green matter, a layer of kitchen scraps, a thin layer of soil, and repeat. Make the pile all in one go if you can. Now water till it's moist, turn every three or four days, watering if it's dry and adding more nitrogenous material if it fails to heat up after a week.

The compost should be ready in six weeks.

Two-week compost

Shred together vegetable matter and garden waste with a shredder, mower or garden shears. Pile it about a metre high and wide. Moisten the pile with liquid manure. This is made by suspending green garden waste, seaweed or manure in a bucket and leaving it for a few weeks. Dilute to the colour of weak tea and take out the liquid as needed.

Turn the compost every two days, adding more liquid manure if it needs moistening. If it isn't heating after two days add more nitrogen – use a stronger liquid manure solution. The secret of this method is the frequent turning, the finely chopped ingredients and the high nitrogen level.

Kitchen compost

Take a large bucket with a lid: nappy buckets are excellent. Every day toss your kitchen scraps into the bucket. Every evening add a layer of sawdust. Press down after every addition. The sawdust should soak up the excess fluid, but keep the scraps as dry as you can.

When the bucket is full – and you'll be surprised how much fits in as the stuff compacts – top it with a layer of sawdust or soil, up-end it in an out-of-the-way spot in the garden, and leave it for six weeks to three months, depending on the weather. (Summer compost is quicker.)

ALTERNATIVES TO COMPOST

Sheet mulch

This is when you just lay down the materials where they are to be used.

Mulch is not compost, and the results aren't as spectacular – but they are still good. Mulching is less work: you only have to move your recycled nutrients once, not twice, and while the mulch is breaking down it is also keeping moisture and heat in and weeds down.

Weeds in a basket

This is when you just toss your weeds into a basket and wait till they decompose. Then you plant. You now have a simple above-ground garden. Weeds in a basket may sprout. But without watering and contact with the soil all you have to do is turn them over once or twice to kill the regrowth.

Weeds under plastic

This needn't be plastic – old carpet, waterbeds, sodden newspapers – anything that won't blow away will do. Pile up your weeds or scraps or whatever, cover and weigh the cover down, close to the ground. Leave for anywhere between one and 12 months, depending on the weather and the amount of moisture and nitrogen in your pile. Weeds under plastic don't decompose as quickly as compost, but at least the plastic helps keep most of the nutrients in.

Don't just leave the weeds in a pile uncovered – you may lose a lot of your nitrogen to the air, more weeds may sprout on top and you'll just end up with a great weedy heap in the garden.

Chook pen 'compost'

Take your weeds and scraps, and feed them to the chooks. Use the old manure in the garden – or use it fresh, diluted one part manure to 50 parts water and never more than once a month. When the hens die recycle them too – in the compost bin, or bury them under the fruit trees.

FERTILITY – THE 'BUDGY METHOD'

Backyard stock-keeping

There used to be an old farmer's saying, 'Keep ten sheep an acre till you can keep ten sheep an acre.' In other words, don't buy fertilisers – buy food for your stock instead. Their end products – manure and urine – will return to the soil and build up its fertility, and you'll still make a profit from the stock.

The same process works in the backyard. Keep hens, geese, and ducks. Buy food for them – and use the manure. Don't think of hen food as an expense to be weighed against the cost of eggs – remember that you are buying fertility with every bag of wheat.

A little gentle grazing in your growing area is the best way I know to get active microflora in your soil. Crop yields from areas that have had animals grazing on them are always higher than the nutrient input would suggest, partly because of the bacterial and other activity created.

SMALL ANIMALS FOR SMALL GARDENS

Bees

Like birds, bees bring nutrients from elsewhere to your place. Don't underestimate the droppings of a million bees – or their honey or pollen. Bee pollen can also be rubbed on pest-prone plants to attract lacewings and hoverflies. However, to raise bees needs care and knowledge; and some people are allergic to them.

Birds

Even a pair of budgies produce enough fertiliser for half a dozen pots of silver beet and strawberries. Better still – attract wild birds to your garden. Imagine the manure given by six hens: it's enough for a good-sized vegetable garden. You can easily attract 20 or 30 wild birds to your garden and get the same amount of added fertility. This may not be in the exact place you want, but if you use the recycling methods described before – using tree leaves, etc for mulch – you'll be able to make use of the added fertility.

Attract wild birds with birdbaths (out of the reach of cats); with thick bushes for them to nest in; with year-round flowers for nectar and insects; and with a bird table with old bits of bread, stale muesli, dripping or cheese on it.

Don't underestimate the manure a flock of wild birds will give you. Anyone who has kookaburras perching on the clothesline can tell you: wild birds are good dung-producers. You'll also have year-round help with your pest control – and the joy of the birds as well.

Ducks

Ducks provide meat and eggs. They are also good snail hunters if trained and given other green stuff to free-range on before being let into the garden. Try letting them into your garden for only an hour before sundown. Don't give them any concentrates until after they have hunted for snails through your vegies – but give them as much greenery as they want all day. That way they will ignore the vegetables and guzzle the snails.

Ducks are very decorative. But they will

Worms turn garbage into fertiliser: breed them in layers of scraps and soil arranged in an old bathtub or in a bucket with drainage holes in it.

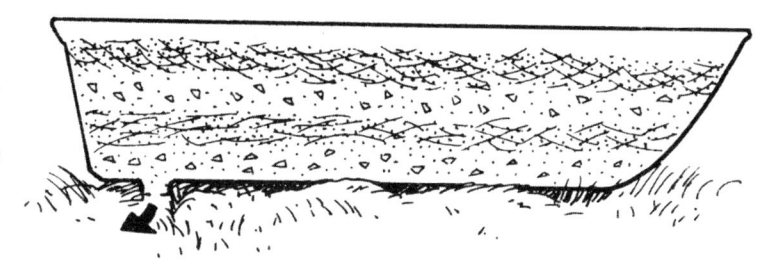

pollute any swimmable water nearby, must be protected from dogs, cats and foxes, and their droppings can be messy and attract flies.

Earthworms

(See also under 'Making phosphorous available' later in this chapter.)

Earthworms help organic matter decompose. They increase the availability of nutrients, and improve the texture of the soil. They will turn garbage into nutrients (and can be eaten). But many bought varieties don't survive in the wild; they will need regular feeding and tending. It is best to catch them wild or answer an advertisement in any gardening magazine.

Fish

Goldfish and other fish are wonderful concentrators of fertility – just scoop out the dirty water and use it on the garden. They need less care than many other livestock, and can be eaten. But to thrive they need a clean water source – most city water isn't. Aquariums range from small bowls to complex infrastructures.

Geese

You don't need a lawnmower if you have geese. They provide meat and eggs, are excellent watch dogs, and can be hilarious to watch. They are wonderful in orchards. They are also noisy and messy. Their droppings are runny and attract flies. The males may attack your pets and your best friends.

Geese love company – especially if that company feeds them – fence them away from the house or be prepared for messy verandahs. Never get geese unless your neighbours can stand being woken at 4 a.m. by a horny gander yodelling in triumph.

Geese need swimmable water, or at the very least water they can puddle in and duck their heads under. Give them a handful of wheat every night to keep them tame.

Goats and sheep

These provide hair, meat, milk and concentrated fertility, and can be tethered for short periods. They should be trained to this when young, and given plenty of free-ranging as well. A whole life spent on a chain is cruel.

Goats and sheep need care and are vulnerable to dogs. Both will eat gardens, fruit trees and anything else – given a chance.

Guinea pigs

These are small, make good pets, and can be eaten. But they are vulnerable to dogs and cats, heat and cold. Like hens, they can be moved in mobile pens around the garden.

Hens

They provide eggs, meat, and a friendly presence. Hens in the orchard eat fallen fruit, spread nutrients, catch grasshoppers and act as general pest controllers. Organic wheat and other grains to feed them are relatively easily obtained. But they must be protected from dogs and foxes, whilst neighbours dislike roosters (though roosters need not be kept). Hens will scratch up vegetables unless you only let them into the garden after a day's free-ranging on other green stuff, so they simply go for slugs and snails. See *Jackie French's Chook Book* for more on keeping chooks (Aird Books). A backyard can probably support about six free-range chooks with kitchen and garden scraps, more if food is imported. Hens can be housed in mobile pens and moved round the garden to control weeds and spread fertility. They can also be used as ploughs: make bottomless mobile pens and let them thoroughly scratch any area that needs to be dug. This can also be done on a wider scale: I have used chooks to scratch and weed a potato field.

Peacocks, guinea fowl, pheasants

These provide concentrate fertility and can be status symbols or pets. But they are noisy, garden scratchers, and provide few eggs. You need to be enthusiastic to raise these.

Rabbits

Rabbits are small and can be fed on kitchen and garden scraps. They breed quickly and are easily tamed. They are also vulnerable to dogs, cats and too much food from kids. Their rapid breeding is a problem unless you want to eat them or keep them celibate.

Like chooks, rabbits can be housed in small pens but let them out often) and moved around the garden for weed control and mobile fertilising.

Rats and mice

These are small, breed quickly and will eat almost anything – but they can escape. Both the dung and corpses of rats and mice are good fertiliser. Whilst not advocating that you keep them for either product, they are worth considering if you happen to be looking for a pet.

Turkeys

Again, these provide meat and eggs. They are great fertiliser spreaders and provide a good moral lesson on the disadvantages of too much dignity. But turkeys are more temperamental and disease prone than other poultry. You do need to know what you are doing – so subscribe to *Australasian Poultry Magazine* (Grass Roots Publishing) for advice.

Wombats

Wombats bring fertility into your garden by excreting round your trees what they've eaten outside. They eat weeds in succulent mulched patches under your fruit trees and like grass, young oats and other garden weeds. They will eat your fallen and wasted fruit – but they will also eat lettuce, peas and other garden produce you would rather they didn't; and rabbits may come through the holes they make in your fences.

Some wombats eat anything, some are selective. The first garden wombat we had was a pest; the present one ignores all our valued crops except carnation buds and the odd lettuce heart – but only when there is a glut of them. You could try making a wombat gate out of a netted car tyre which rabbits can't push open.

ACIDITY AND PHOSPHOROUS DEFICIENCY IN SOILS

Australian soils are said to be mostly acid and deficient in phosphorous. Well, they're not necessarily – ask any gum tree – it's just that most of our imported plants can't make use of the phosphorous that is there, or gather the nutrients they need from an acid soil.

If you use compost and mulch regularly in your garden, you should find you have no problems with acid, alkali or phosphorous-deficient soil. There are many ways this can happen. You may have healthy mycorrhizae (fungal root sheaths that help take up nutrients); and you may have more earthworms (their droppings make nutrients more available). There are many other factors, all leading to healthy plants.

If you are starting your garden, though, you may find that compost and mulch don't break down well if the soil is very acid or low in phosphorous. So, for the first year only, to add phosphorous, use some of the plants listed below round the garden. And sprinkle some dolomite or wood ash to make the soil less acid.

Phosphorous sources

All plant waste contains phosphorous:
- Use bones and eggshells. Crush eggshells and add them directly to the garden or compost heap; dry bones in the oven, then pound them with a hammer. If your family are egg- and meat-eaters this should provide enough phosphorous for a home garden.
- Ground phosphate rock will release phosphorous slowly over a five-year period; unlike superphosphate, it is not readily washed out of the soil and won't greatly affect the bacterial population of the soil.
- Blood and bone contains about 8 per cent phosphorous (superphosphate has about 10 per cent).
- Other sources of phosphate include lobster shells, fish waste and sewage sludge.
- Run ducks or hens around the orchard for self-spreading phosphorous applications.

Making phosphorous available

1. Make your soil less acidic. Phosphate can be locked up as insoluble iron or aluminium phosphate in very acid soils. Add lime, dolomite or wood ash.
2. Make your soil less alkaline. A very alkaline soil will also bind up phosphorous. A fairly neutral soil, between a pH of 6 and a pH of 7.5, is best for the release of phosphorous.
3. Make your soil more active. The acids produced by certain micro-organisms (usually found in compost or decomposing mulch) will also release phosphorous fixed in the soil. Add compost, mulch and organic material liberally. Superphosphate and other artificial fertilisers will kill many of these micro-organisms, and tend to inhibit any that remain.
4. Use deep-rooting plants and green manures. Various deep-rooting plants and green manures also make phosphorous more available to plants.
5. Earthworms. Earthworms are killed by the application of superphosphate. Worm casts contain seven times more available phosphate and five times more nitrogen, more potash and 40 per cent more humus than is available in the soil around them. Worm casts can make a considerable difference to soil fertility.

HOW TO GROW EARTHWORMS

Worms convert organic matter – mulch and scraps – into soil. Worm casts are more fertile than surrounding soil, and they also make the soil looser and easier for roots to penetrate.

Any container with good drainage and a lid to keep off rain can be used to breed worms. (Worms can drown too.)

Place about 10 cm of soil at the bottom of the container, then 5 cm of scraps – old bread, cabbage leaves, weeds, manure, prunings. Then add another 5 cm of soil, 5 cm of scraps. Repeat till the container is full. Keep the container moist (not wet) and dark. Add more soil and scraps as the level gets lower as the worms eat the scraps, and as you remove the worms.

You can 'seed' your worm farm with a few worms from your garden – or buy them from a number of suppliers in any state.

Check your phone book under 'worms' or 'vermiculture'.

NB Most 'commercial' earthworms may not survive in your garden – they need protected worm farms to survive.

MYCORRHIZAE

Plants with mycorrhizal infection round the roots are less prone to stress and seem more resistant to pests and diseases. This is partly because they are healthier, but also because mycorrhiza can inhibit pathogens like *Phytophthora cinnamomi*. The phosphorous uptake of plants with mycorrhizal infection will also be enhanced. To encourage this:
- Dig as little as possible.
- Use mulch and compost.
- Avoid harsh artificial fertilisers and soil sterilants.

FEEDING NATIVE PLANTS

Most native plants like acid soil, and are adapted to soils low in phosphorous. Many respond well to high phosphorous/nitrogen fertilisers in the short term, but become more susceptible to pests and disease. If you are growing natives like grevilleas, banksia and many of the protea family near plants that need richer feeding, try giving them a low-nutrient mulch like sawdust or bark or casuarina needles. Otherwise, feed your natives with compost (without rock phosphate in it), rotted manure (avoid hen manure if possible, though a little does no harm), and blood and bone in spring. Don't give a lot of blood and bone to any of the protea family – a yearly mulch is all they should need.

Generally, try to limit the amount of nitrogen that native plants get – too much makes them pest- and disease-prone and will shorten their life.

An Easy Feeding Regime

1. Mulch everything in late spring.
2. Feed young or plants which give lots of fruit or veg with 'quick fixes'.
3. Add rock phosphate every 10 years.
4. Add trace elements every 20 years.
5. Use everything that will decompose (except maybe Grandma and the dog) as mulch or compost – weeds, logs of wood from fallen trees, prunings, hair ... whatever you can grow or scavenge.
6. And just keep mulching!

PS A seaweed or fish-based foliar spray is a great comforter for hungry or stressed plants.

Chapter 6
EASY GARDEN BEDS

THE IDEAL

These are beds that take only a few minutes to prepare and plant, and minimum work thereafter. Most no-dig gardens are quick to assemble, but it takes time and money to buy and haul in their ingredients. The ideal garden beds make use of the material everyone has plenty of: lawn clippings, weeds and garden rubbish.

- *Instead of digging your garden beds* ... make no-dig beds from hay or lawn clippings or weeds.
- *Instead of neatly dug garden beds, which must be mulched and weeded* ... create weed-mat gardens on the lawn, or terraces.
- *Instead of gardens that are planted out in spring and whenever the last crop is finished* ... plant a mixture of perennials and flowers and vegetables left to reseed and sow themselves.
- *Instead of spending your time sweating in the garden* ... sit back and watch the carrots swell.

DO NOT USE NEWSPAPER! (See Chapter 5, 'Poorer mulches'.) You'll end up with shallow-rooted plants that die in droughts.

Our garden beds haven't been dug for ten years (except for the wombat hole in the artichokes and a few lyrebird scratchings). Digging breaks your back, breaks up the soil structure, kills earthworms, destroys nitrogen-fixing bacteria and mycorrhizal associations, while the dust kills natural predators, and weeds start filling up the bare patches as soon as your back is turned.

We use a range of garden beds – weed-mat gardens in one spot, frost-resistant terraces of car tyres in another, potatoes growing in rubbish piles under the apple trees, pumpkins in the lawn down one end, and a self-seeded jungle that grows itself year after year down the other ... and many more.

None of these gardens is much work, much less than conventional dug or no-dig gardens. None of them requires much weeding, and very little – if any – mulching and fertilising. These are garden beds for anyone who's rich in weeds and grassy spots, but short of time ... or who'd rather use their time in watching the tomatoes swell, instead of digging and throwing mulch around.

WEED-MAT GARDENS

This is the easiest garden of all: no digging, no weeding and no carting mulch. It is an instant garden – ready in no time at all. In spite of the fact that it relies on bought material (weed-mat) it still mimics a natural system. There are no bare spaces for weeds and erosion, no digging to break down the soil structure, plenty of leaf cover, and it relies on decaying organic matter for most of its fertility.

Weed-mat is a woven fibre mat, not black plastic, though it is also black. Water can't get through black plastic and plant roots sweat underneath. Weed-mat is reasonably cheap and lasts for years.

If you are worried about the temporary stretches of black mesh you can sprinkle on lawn clippings, hay, old leaves, or bark. They are not necessary but will look better, and they'll help mulch the seedlings.

It's often hard to get people to try the weed-mat garden: it looks too easy. We're too used to having to sweat on our gardens. Weed-mat gardens need no sweat at all – neither to make nor to maintain. And they work.

STEP 1

Buy some weed-mat.

STEP 2

Spread the weed-mat on the grass or patch of weeds – wherever you want your garden.

STEP 3

Weigh it down with a few rocks, bits of wood or garden chairs – anything to stop it blowing away. (Once the plants grow you can take these weights away.)

STEP 4

Make cuts in the mat for planting your seedlings. (Later you can make them larger if needed.)

STEP 5

Dig small holes in the ground under the cuts with a sturdy tablespoon.

STEP 6

Plant your seedlings.

STEP 7

Water the seedlings and – you now have a garden.

Alternative materials

Any woven fibre material can be used instead of weed-mat, though weed-mat is the cheapest if you have to buy it. You can make a garden from old wool sacks, or from woven fibre bags that have held dog food, wheat or laying pellets. Old carpet can be used instead of weed-mat. But make sure first that water will soak through it: I have seen plants die of water stress in beds of old carpet. Old sea-grass matting makes an excellent garden, as do coiled raffia or rope mats.

A weed-mat garden needs almost no maintenance or preparation.

Disadvantages of weed-mat

The main disadvantage of the weed-mat garden is that a stretch of black over the grass looks ugly, but I actually find a stretch of dug or ploughed ground ugly too. I think of the soil eroding and blowing away, the germinating weeds, the death of earthworms and soil bacteria. However, most people are so used to dug ground they no longer find it unnatural.

The soil can also compact under them – move the weed mat every two or three years.

Plant close together

Weed-mat gardens are quickly covered with greenery. Weed-mat gardens can be planted two or three times closer than normal gardens. Seedlings won't have to compete with weeds and will have plenty of moisture under the mat – and plenty of food if you keep up their feeding.

Caring for the weed-mat garden

Weed-mat gardens don't need weeding. They also need less watering than other gardens: the mat helps to keep in moisture. The black mat also absorbs heat, so you'll find your plants are growing faster. They will, however, need feeding.

The soil under our weed-mat beds is rich in earthworms – they curl away whenever you lift up the mat – and it turns a dark, rich brown as the organic matter decays back into it. Both soil and plants are far healthier than in conventionally dug beds.

Don't buy artificial fertilisers. As well as being expensive they are bad for your soil and your health. Instead, water your seedlings once a week with home-made liquid manure (see Chapter 5), or scatter blood and bone or old hen manure on the mat: the nutrients will seep through to the soil. Gradually, the grass and weeds under the mat will break down and their nutrients will be available for your plants – but this takes a few months and meanwhile your seedlings need to be fed. You can also mulch on top of the weed-mat: many of the nutrients will gradually travel down.

After the first year you can take up the weed-mat and move it somewhere else, to a new crop of grass and weeds. This will leave you a bare, friable garden that can just be raked and planted with carrot seed or beetroot – the only two vegetables that are hard to grow in weed-mat.

Otherwise you can just leave the weed-mat where it is and stuff some compost or weeds or old leaves underneath it, to break down and add nutrients and organic matter to the soil.

WEED GARDENS

STEP 1

Throw on any old weeds, leaves, lawn clippings or other green scraps you have around. Lucerne hay is even better, but it is expensive and bulky to handle. The weeds will also help mulch the seedlings and decompose gradually into plant food and humus.

STEP 2

Leave for two months to kill the grass or other weeds below.

STEP 3

Push the weeds or mulch away so there are bare handspans of soil.

STEP 4

Plant your seedlings in the holes.

STEP 5

Water.

Maintenance

Feed your weed like a weed-mat garden. Add more mulch as the first lot breaks down. Water it often until the weeds break down.

Be wary of slugs and snails – they may hide in the mulch. Use a snail fence or one of the traps described in Chapter 7.

'Pile of weeds' garden

Suitable crops

Almost anything except carrots, beetroot and radishes grows well in the weed garden. Potatoes are excellent: just take one small potato or part of a potato with an eye and bury it in a hole. Keep piling on mulch as it grows. Garlic grows large and fast in a weed and paper garden; so do nasturtiums, sweet potatoes, pumpkins – and nearly everything else.

Planting directly into grass

Many vigorous plants will outgrow grass if they have a chance to get going before the grass chokes them. Any plant with a large bulbous root will outgrow grass if the grass is kept cut for a few months. I have planted Jerusalem artichokes straight into the lawn, and dahlias, rhubarb (mulch it well as it comes up and the large leaves will gradually shade the grass around), comfrey, gladioli, and most other large bulbs.

Our major flower garden – a bank outside the kitchen – was directly planted into grass. The secret here is to plant very thickly, and to keep the garden well fed and watered, so the small seedlings grow fast and out-compete the grass. A little grass still comes up each year – some we pull out if we get round to it – but mostly the thickly planted flowers themselves control the weeds.

Pumpkins in grass

Place a large spadeful of compost on the grass, at least 30 cm high and wide. Plant a pumpkin seedling in the compost. Water well and keep the grass mown until it gets big. The vine will gradually sprawl all over the place. As long as the soil is moist and fertile it will grow strongly enough not to be intimidated by the grass. I find that grass-grown pumpkins mature a week or two earlier than similar vines in a nearby garden bed.

THE 'PILE OF WEEDS' GARDEN

Most gardens have piles of weeds, euphemistically called compost heaps. They aren't, but they can be useful gardens. Place a few pockets of soil or compost on the weeds. Plant seedlings, or a potato or a piece of sweet potato in them. Let them grow. The heat from the decomposing weeds will help them flourish – as will the nutrients in the pile. Ramblers like cucumbers, beans and chokoes do wonderfully with this method, but so do other crops like silver beet. Note that weed piles need to be partially decomposed for this to work. Don't try to grow lettuce in a pile of old corn stalks, or beans in a pile of grass clippings – the grass clippings may heat up and kill the lot.

CLOVER AND/OR LUCERNE BED

This is perhaps the most sustainable method of all. You are growing your own mulch, and 'fixing' most of your nitrogen right where your plants are growing. It works excellently with long-maturing vegetables like corn and cauliflowers. Short-term vegetables like lettuce can be grown with this method, but need extra feeding – see Chapter 5.

Establish either a cover crop of clover, or a combination of clover and lucerne. This can be done in spring or autumn. Now plant your seedlings.

It is essential to keep the clover or lucerne cut short. This can be done with a mower between the rows, with a whipper snipper or, even better, with animals like hens, geese or sheep, or even wombats. Unfortunately the animal method only works with certain vegetables that the animals won't eat. I have grown pumpkins and melons successfully with all the animals mentioned above. Corn can be grown with geese or wombats grazing in between, but only when the corn is knee-high before they are let in.

The mown clover/lucerne becomes the mulch for the vegetables – and the clover flowers also attract predators and bees to help your crop.

I have used this method for about ten years, both in the garden and for a hectare of commercial crop. It has recently been refined by researchers at CSIRO, but I think the principles are much the same. In the CSIRO method only clover is used, sown in autumn. It is then left to grow during winter, and dies down naturally in summer when you sow your crops directly into the rich clover debris.

HANGING GARDENS

These are for anyone who can't bend, for anyone with arthritis or high blood pressure, for anyone who's confined to a wheelchair or just wary of slipped discs. And hanging gardens are for people who do not have a garden, but who do have nice, sunny walls on their patio, balcony, or paved terrace.

The hanging garden is also good for frost-tender plants in cold areas. Hanging gardens can be hung in the warmest place you have: the wall will absorb and hold the heat. The higher up a plant is, the less liable it is to be affected by frost.

Starting small

Hanging gardens can be enormous but it is best to start small until you get used to them. Hang a little garden on the windowsill or door jamb: one metre wide by one metre long.

STEP 1

Buy some weed-mat (see above).

STEP 2

Cut it into metre wide strips. The length depends on the height of your wall and how high you can lift the garden.

STEP 3

Sew the edges together – bottom and sides, but not the top. If you're lazy or can't use a needle, staple them instead. Use lots of staples. (The staples may rust in time but then you can staple up the holes.)

STEP 4

Hang up the mat. You can:
- nail it to the top of the wall; use several nails, as it gets very heavy;
- fasten ropes to the top and fasten the ropes to the other side of the wall; this is good for brick walls where you can't hammer in nails;
- hook it on to the top of the wall with several pieces of bent wire (again, use a lot as it'll get heavy);
- nail it to a post; or

Less glamorous but more productive than the hanging gardens of Babylon: pierce holes in old cans and nail them to fence posts or walls; fill them with soil and plant them with strawberries, cucumbers, or anything else that likes to trail. Paint the cans if you don't like the shiny metal.

- hang it to a frame (see diagram – this is a good way to have several hanging gardens at once).

STEP 5
Stuff the garden with potting mixture, or silt or compost if you have some. Don't stuff in too much or it'll spill out later.

STEP 6
Cut small horizontal slits on the weed-mat. Holes should be about a hand length apart.

STEP 7
Plant one seedling in each hole.

STEP 8
Water. This is easy. Just stand back – or sit back – and spray the whole thing with the hose.

What to plant in a hanging garden

Almost anything can be planted in a hanging garden, though I'd avoid things like carrots that take up a lot of room without much crop. Strawberries, raspberries and loganberries are excellent. So is silver beet: just keep pulling off the leaves. Try any of the lettuce varieties that you can harvest one leaf at a time. Broccoli is good; as long as you keep picking it, it will crop for years.

Grow nasturtiums, convolvulus and other trailers. Plant a miniature rose at the top, climbing beans in the middle and a pumpkin or cucumber vine on the bottom. (Always plant heavy yielders like vines on the bottom so the watermelons or rockmelons, etc. can rest on the floor and not weigh down the garden.)

Slip in dahlia bulbs, geraniums, passionfruit vines, mint and basil. Try a potato at the bottom: when the plant dies down, feel round inside with your fingers for the potatoes.

Feeding the hanging garden

Feed your hanging garden with a watering can, or with a pump-action sprayer – you can buy these at most hardware stores. Just pump it a few times and it'll reach about six metres up. Use any of the liquid manures described in Chapter 5, and there are also some proprietary organic liquid fertilisers on the market. Feed your garden at least twice a week: the plants will grow quickly and need regular food.

EASY GARDEN BEDS

Watering

Make sure your garden is near a hose. Hanging gardens dry out quickly and most have to be watered every day in summer. If you need to go away for a while, get a friend to help unhook the garden and take it home to babysit.

Styrofoam hanging gardens

Collect styrofoam boxes and wire them on top of each other in steps and stairs so that the ones below support the ones above but are not quite overshadowed. Angle the boxes to get the sun – you may have to move them a couple of times a day. This is a lot of work, but the styrofoam garden is a space-saver and plants can grow very quickly if it is set up properly. It can also be taken with you when you move house. Fill the boxes with soil and compost and plant them with your favourite plants.

Hanging gardens from the supermarket

Collect tin cans or plastic ice-cream containers. Wire or staple them together and punch a few holes in the bottom. Lean them against a bank or stake them upright. Fill each with a little compost and plant herbs or strawberries. These are for cool areas only, as they can overheat; or just use them to get a strawberry crop through winter.

I have used these heat-collecting gardens to grow lettuce through winter on the shed roof. Watering was easy – I just sprayed the roof – but picking wasn't. Make sure all the cans have a hole in them or the water will collect and the plants rot.

BOX GARDENS

These are neat and productive. They don't need weeding and can be taken with you when you move. Even if you have only concrete and gravel you can have a box garden.

STEP 1

Fill an old box with compost or potting mix. Any box will do as long as water can drain from it. Punch some holes in the base if needed.

STEP 2

Plant 'thickly', as these beds will be well fed and watered. One styrofoam box could contain a cucumber plant, three lettuces, two silver beet plants and a few radishes.

STEP 3

Water and feed well. Any liquid manure can be used in a box garden, or try mulching with lawn clippings, lucerne hay or cow manure.

TYRE GARDENS

Tyre gardens are a form of simple terracing, using recycled materials. The black tyre absorbs heat, and the height of the beds makes them frost resistant. (We grow potatoes all through winter with temperatures down to minus 5°C in our tyre beds.) Tyre gardens are also a way of getting more to grow in a small space – plant climbers like beans or peas or cucumbers or melons in the tyre bed, and let them ramble down the sides. (This is also a good way to get early melons – you can plant them earlier.)

STEP 1

Scavenge old tyres from the local garage; they'll be glad to get rid of them.

STEP 2

Pile the tyres on top of each other. The height depends on you – higher gardens need more filling, but they are also out of reach of light frosts, animals and rising watertables. I usually have beds two tyres high, but you can use only one or even twenty. After two, though, it's a good idea to place a stake in the middle so they don't fall down.

STEP 3

Half-fill the tyres with weeds, grass clippings or anything else that will rot, even screwed-up newspaper.

STEP 4

Place a thick layer of soil or compost on top.

STEP 5

Plant seeds or seedlings.

STEP 6

Water well.

Tyre gardens can be fed with any liquid manure, or can just be well mulched. For a simple garden, make it only one tyre high:

- Dig a small hole in the middle of the tyre and plant your seedling.
- Mulch around the seedling with newspaper, then clippings – hay, grass clippings, etc.
- As the seedling grows add more tyres to protect it from wind, frost, etc.

This method is excellent for potatoes. I have covered a potato plant with mulch as it grows, making it up to three tyres high, until only a little green was showing. The plant continued to grow and produce potatoes, and the eventual crop was massive.

Warning: some heavy metals may leach out of tyres, at least in the first two years.

Never grow more than 5 per cent of your food in them – best kept for a treat like out of season basil or tomatoes. And tyres can be VERY dangerous in bushfires – they burn with a thick, toxic and choking smoke, and may keep burning for a long time.

MODIFIED JUNGLES

This garden grows and mostly seeds itself. It is the most productive part of our garden – even easier than the weed-mat garden, though it takes a few years to establish.

YEAR ONE

1. Dig your garden or use the clear ground under last year's weed-mat garden.
2. Plant radishes, turnips and parsnips thickly.
3. Let them go to seed.

YEAR TWO

1. Pull out most of the plants now gone to seed. The ground beneath should be reasonably weed free and well dug. (The bed will get more and more friable and weed free as the years go by.) Leave a few plants to set seed.
2. Plant crops that will reseed themselves, such as tomatoes, potatoes, sweet peas, turnips, radishes (try daikons), foliage turnips (eat the sweet, mild tips), mignonette lettuces, all-season carrots (don't plant varieties that may germinate mid-winter and go to seed in spring), silver beet, dandelions, leeks, perennial beans, kumaras, sunflowers and calendulas.
3. Mulch well.
4. Let the plants spread their seed over the bare places in the garden. They'll fill up the spaces, so the weeds won't get a toehold, and keep germinating as you use the vegetables.
5. Always leave some plants to go to seed to produce next year's crop.

In a 'modified jungle' plants do the weeding, the digging and planting, and the pest control: flowering tops attract pest-eating predators, seed falls for next season's vegies, and deep roots do the digging, leaving a weed-free space after harvesting for later plantings.

Maintenance

This garden will grow itself. Harvest what you need. When you need more space pull out some radishes, turnips, etc. Don't have bare ground unless you are going to plant in it. Don't dig; let the radishes do the digging. Don't weed; let the radishes crowd them out, or just cut them for mulch.

Feed your modified jungle with mulch. Once it gets established it will need very little feeding if you return all the scraps as compost or mulch. Our modified jungle garden gets the scraps from the rest of the garden thrown into its compost piles – and needs no other fertiliser.

VERTICAL GARDENS

Vertical gardens save space – instead of growing out you grow up. Two metres of vertical space should give you the same crop as two metres of garden – but as the plant roots take up only a small line there's less watering and weeding.

Vertical gardens also get more sun and mature faster; they need less mulch; and are slightly more frost resistant (cold air sinks, warm air rises).

If you search you will find many climbing varieties – not just beans and peas, passionfruit, chokoes and berries, but climbing tomatoes (one plant feeds a family). Train broccoli, eggplant, capsicum or ordinary tomatoes up a trellis; cut off the lower shoots to encourage more top ones. They'll fruit faster and take up less room. Let cucumbers, melons and small pumpkins grow up a trellis instead of sprawl over the ground: you'll get more fruit and the plants will be more mildew resistant.

Trellises

You can buy wooden trellises – expensive but neat. We mostly use steel reinforcing, held up with steel star pickets. You can also use:
- an old bicycle wheel on a stake;
- wire or string strung between posts;
- wire netting;
- old mosquito net tacked onto posts (this lasts only a year);
- an old wire bedstead on its side; or
- anything your imagination can put to use.

Plants for fences

A bare fence is a waste. Try:
- perennial climbing beans;
- chokoes;
- hops – hops die down in winter and ramble all over the place in summer: eat the young shoots, make beer from the flowers, or use them to stuff hop pillows;
- passionfruit in frost-free places and banana passionfruit in cold areas;
- loganberries, marionberries, boysenberries and other climbing berries;
- perennial sweet peas, pink or white – they come up every year;
- grapes – there are hundreds of grape varieties in Australia, suitable for any area from snowy winters to tropical summers;
- flowering climbers like clematis, wonga vine, bougainvillea, jasmine, rambling roses,

to attract birds, predaceous insects, and for pleasure;
- edible Chinese convolvulus;
- sweet potatoes (temperate areas only);
- use your fence to stake up tomatoes, peas, or broad beans.

CONVENTIONAL GARDEN BEDS

Double-dug organic garden bed

I don't advocate this. But if you really want an old-fashioned organic garden, and you're into digging, sweating and getting dusty, and you don't care how many earthworms you slaughter, here it is.

Dig your bed deeply: at least 30 cm down. Pull out all weeds and sift the soil through the tynes of your garden fork to make sure there are no bits of root left. Leave the bed alone for two weeks, watering occasionally to germinate any weed seeds. Dig again. Plant your seedlings, water well, and apply mulch as soon as the seedlings 'harden' – that is, as soon as the stems can be snapped instead of bent. If you apply mulch too early, the seedlings may 'dampen off' – that is, rot at the stem.

An alternative 'dug' bed

If you must have bare soil – and it is good for carrots, onions and other root vegetables unless you have a 'self-seeding' garden – try this instead.

Cover your lawn, or weeds, with clear plastic. Leave for at least a month. Don't worry when you see the plants underneath grow like mad: they'll grow so fast in the heat and moisture that they'll start to rot, and the roots will rot too.

When this happens pull up your plastic, leave for two days in the sun, then scratch gently and scatter your seed – or, even better, scatter your seed thickly and cover the seed with a light sprinkle of sand, compost or old sawdust. I like to mix my seed with the sand first, and scatter sand and seed together. This spreads the seed more evenly, and stops it clumping together.

Conventional above-ground bed

This is very effective, though it does involve buying hay – which can be both expensive and hard to transport – and is mining after all, as it involves depriving another area of its organic matter.
- Do not use newspaper. You may end up with an impermeable layer between mulch and soil. I've seen hundreds of plants die in drought because of this silly idea that you need to lay newspaper below mulch. Avoid it!.
- Lay a sandwich of lucerne hay on top. (Hay naturally breaks into 'sandwiches' – you'll see what I mean when you try it.) The greener it is, the better the hay.
- Top with compost, or even with a thin layer of potting mix or soil.
- Plant your seedlings.

This method needs more watering to begin with, but grows superb vegetables and flowers. Even carrots grow well in this system, though they might have a bend or two.

Chapter 7
DEALING WITH PESTS AND DISEASE

THE IDEAL

This would be a garden where diverse predators keep pests under control without resorting to any pesticide, organic or not, a garden where rich, undisturbed soil and compatible planting means pests rarely build up to problem levels, and where the gardener understands that pest plagues are usually the fault of humans – and works to correct the cause, not to exterminate the result.

- *Instead of spraying when pests appear ...* wait as long as possible for predators to build up to control the pests.
- *Instead of worrying whenever you see a pest ...* accept that a few pests all year round mean that the predators are around too – because they have a reliable food supply.
- *Instead of using 'organic' pesticides ...* rely on healthy garden design and healthy soil – and sprays like glue to slow pests down so predators can find them.
- *Instead of having nice straight rows and rectangular garden beds ...* grow groves of tangling shrubbery, climbers up trees, a medley of herbs, flowers and veg to disguise your crops from pests.
- *Instead of using bird nets or loud noises ...* use groves to keep birds from most of your fruit, and use decoy fruits that birds adore to keep them from your crops.

PEST AND DISEASE CONTROL

Most garden pest control is unnecessary. Some causes more problems than it solves. We are taught to hate insects: to scream at spiders, to shiver at centipedes and, at the sight of a cluster of aphids, to race to the garden centre shelves for a can of expensive, polluting, and usually unnecessary pesticide.

Pesticides and fungicides don't only pollute your garden: some harm your health. Many harm the health of people who make them or live near their factories. (Pesticide tankers overturn, and fires, leaks, or explosions in manufacturing plants can lead to even greater disasters – like that in Bhopal, India, for example.)

Pesticides can increase your pest problem by killing useful insect predators like spiders, hoverflies and ladybird larvae, which can keep control of the pests for you. By denying such predators a year-round supply of pests (at a non-problem density) you may not have year-round predators either. Instead of trying to wipe out those pests completely, the natural grower does the opposite by trying to have a small, year-round supply of pests, preferably on plants where a small amount of damage won't matter.

I'd rather grow things than kill things. A lot of effort is wasted in killing pests when the same effort could have been put into better feeding and watering with better results. Most pests don't need to be controlled: control will happen naturally, due to predators and the weather, and through disease.

You can also make your plants more pest and disease resistant:

- Avoid high-nitrogen fertilisers, whether artificial or in the form of too much hen manure or urine. They all create soft, green, sappy growth which attracts pests.
- Use compost and mulch. Through various interactions, both increase plant resistance to pests and disease.
- Plant year-round flowering shrubs and flowers to attract birds and other insect predators.
- Grow plants suited to your area.
- Don't panic. Most pests will worry you more than the plant. Pests usually disappear in a couple of weeks. If they don't, try some of the controls given in this chapter.

TWO GARDEN STORIES

The tale of a healthy garden

This is the story of Harry and Charlotte who moved onto their two hectares three years ago. They wanted to be self-sufficient, and they'd had plenty of gardening experience in the city. They knew the soil in their new garden had been abused with artificial fertilisers, digging and all weeds removed. They were looking forward to cosseting it back to health.

The first year was a disaster. There were bugs in the citrus and caterpillars ate the cabbages and bean fly killed the beans and there were aphids on everything. Harry and Charlotte bought their carrots from the supermarket and resorted to frozen peas. They kept on mulching.

Things were better the second year. Harry and Charlotte threw out the last of the frozen peas when the broad beans started producing. There were still pests galore – but at least the garden produced enough for Charlotte and Harry to eat too.

This is the third year. The soil has turned from anaemic grey to a rich black. There are at least half a dozen worms to every spade of soil. There are still pests – enough to keep the pest-eating predators fed and happy through the year, but not enough to badly damage the crops. When I last saw Charlotte she was trying to give away lettuces. Harry was buying a pig to eat the last of the pumpkins.

Healthy soil means healthy plants. If you doubt it, try it yourself. Grow two patches: one with artificial fertiliser, the other with compost or mulch. Count the bugs; measure the produce. Then throw away your bag of Multigrow.

The tale of the plant pathologist

He's the brother of a friend and he loves tomatoes. He grows them every year. They get bugs every year, too, and spots and diseases. Every year he has to haul them out. His sister also grows tomatoes. She reckons hers get as many pests and diseases as her brother's. But she doesn't worry about them. She knows that the tomatoes will fruit anyway – and if the crop is reduced, she'll just plant some more.

The moral of this story is: concentrate on growing things, not killing things. Healthy crops survive pests – and pests prefer weak plants. Put your energy into feeding your plants, and watering them – and planting more. Gardens should be places of fecundity, not destruction.

OUR PEST CONTROL REGIME

I don't bother about pests unless they are killing a plant, or we will lose most of our crop. Then I use glue spray. Just dilute 'Clag' glue or mix one cup of flour with one cup of boiling water and dilute with cold water until it is sprayable (see below). Glued-up pests aren't going anywhere. Birds love aphids or scale in batter. Actually, I haven't had to worry about pests here for years.

There is no need to identify most of the pests in your garden. All you need is a basic knowledge of the damage they do – specifically their eating habits.

Leaf eaters

Earwigs, grasshoppers, caterpillars, leaf-eating ladybirds: look for holes in leaves, ragged leaves, and large green droppings.

Control: Encourage birds. Use glue spray – the birds will find that battered caterpillars are delicious and very slow moving. Pick them off by hand or hose them off. Spray Dipel (a bacterium that kills only caterpillars) against caterpillars.

Sap suckers

Aphids, bugs, cicadas, scale, thrips, mites, leaf-hoppers: look for skeletonised foliage; foliage browned or curled at the edges; or leaves that appear mottled or pitted. Sap suckers may also damage new shoots: they wilt and die off suddenly. Sap suckers excrete a lot of sugary wastes, which can promote sooty mould and attract ants.

Control: Encourage birds and other predators. Clean up sheltering weeds below trees, and get rid of overripe fruit and vegetables as these can attract pests. The best spray for sap suckers is glue spray, as it suffocates pests. Use oil sprays in cool weather. Only glue, oil spray or a spray of mustard and water will kill scale.

Borers

(See also below.)
Look for shoots and even branches that die back, and look for holes and sawdust deposits.

Control: Poke out the borer with wire. Plug up holes or inject them with eucalyptus oil mixed with soft soap. Encourage large predator birds like magpies. Bordeaux will repel the borer's moth parents. So will a paint of wood ash and eucalyptus oil. But mostly just accept that borers infect trees and shrubs that are past their prime.

Root rots

(See also below.)
Look for plants that are yellow or die back suddenly, usually from the top; plants will rock unsteadily when you shake them.

Control: Cut back the tree as a temporary measure and feed it with foliar spray while you mulch with compost and correct the drainage. Compost inhibits many root rots, and compost made with wattle bark is even more effective. Use a mulch of 2 parts lucerne hay to 1 part wattle bark, with a light scatter of rock phosphate. You may prefer to dig out the tree to stop the rot spreading to other plants.

Fungal and bacterial problems

Look for leaf spots or blemishes, and fruit rots.

Control: Spray Bordeaux on old, tough foliage (not blossom or new shoots) or dormant trees. (Don't use Bordeaux too often as it also kills predators.) Spray chamomile tea on infected leaves and fruit once a week, or more frequently in wet weather when the disease may become rampant. Pick off all old dried 'mummies' at the end of the season, and thin out fruit if fruit rots are a problem. Use the milk spray below.

PEST-LIKE SYMPTOMS

Some pest-like symptoms are not caused by pests at all.

Leaf fall

Before you bother about root rots, check that the plant isn't waterlogged or starved of water, has been adequately fed, and isn't being overshadowed by a taller tree or bush. One of the most common questions I get from Canberra people is, 'Why has my lemon tree lost its leaves?' The answer is usually, 'Because of the cold.' Cold-stressed plants don't always look black and frost bitten. Cold-injured citrus may simply turn listless, yellow and finally defoliate.

No fruit

Young trees may not set fruit, or the fruit may fall off before it is ripe. Frost can destroy blossom so it falls before fruit sets, or young fruit can be damaged by frost, hail or birds. Try to remember if there was frost, strong wind or hail at blossoming time. Brown rot can also damage blossom so it fails to set.

Many fruit trees need a pollinator to set fruit. Even if your apple tree has fruited by itself for years, the neighbouring pollinator – perhaps several houses away – may have been recently cut down. The result is no fruit on your tree. Poor pollination may result in no fruit setting or premature fruit drop. Cut open a fallen fruit – if it has fewer or no seeds, or misshapen seeds, there is probably a pollination problem. Plant flowers and flowering shrubs to attract bees to your garden at the same time as your trees flower.

Codling moth and fruit fly larvae both head to the centre of fruit and damage the seeds. The fruit then falls prematurely.

Dieback

This can be caused by insect attack: see if the leaf edges are ragged or the stems chewed. It can also be caused by root rots: see if you can rock the tree. It may be caused by borers: look for holes and sawdust deposits. It may also be caused by sap suckers: see if the young shoots are dying back first. Sometimes dieback from sap suckers on new shoots will spread as a pathogen enters the injury.

Yellow leaves

If the oldest leaves are yellowing but not the young ones, you have a nitrogen deficiency. If the young leaves are yellow you may have a phosphorous or iron deficiency. Yellow young leaves with dark-green veins indicate an iron deficiency. In all cases feed with good mulch or compost and give a liquid manure spray to the leaves once a week in the evening until they turn green again. If all leaves seem to be yellowing evenly check that the plant isn't waterlogged or starved of water: plants need water to transfer their nutrients. Rock the plant to see if it seems loose – this would mean root rot. Cold weather will cause leaves to turn yellow; so will herbicide drift. Check the base of the plant for collar rot or injury from a motor mower.

Failure to grow

Even with the best treatment, plants that have been badly treated in the past may take several years to start to grow again. We had several apparently dormant trees in the orchard. They had been badly eaten by sheep for several years. It took three years for them to start to grow again – then they thrived. Warning: if a new tree isn't growing, always check for root rot. You may have imported it with the tree. Root rots are best dug out before they spread.

Otherwise, check that plants are well fed. If they are kept well mulched and watered, and are not suffering from competition with grass or larger plants, there isn't much doubt of it.

Old gardens and orchards may suffer from 'replant disease': new plants, grown where old ones have been, often don't thrive, possibly due to a gradual build-up of soil pathogens and soil deficiencies to which the old plants had gradually become tolerant. But again, a gradual build-up in soil condition from mulch and compost will, eventually, solve this.

Plants grown in areas that are too cold or too hot won't thrive either. Shading pergolas, an ice mulch on the roots, or hessian shelters may partially solve the problem, but in most cases the extra effort won't be worth the trouble. There are now so many species available in Australia for cold to tropical climates, that it is more sensible to keep to your climatic limitations.

Plants may also be stunted by leaking gas mains: check by sniffing in still weather.

SOME BASIC SPRAYS

Use sprays only if you have to. Any spray, organic or otherwise, will destroy the balance between pest and predator. Predators build up 'in response' to pest build-ups. Learn to wait. Every time you consider spraying, remember: 'When in doubt, do without.'

Make sure you spray under leaves too, in case pests are hiding there. Wash the sprayer out well when you've finished.

Preventive spray

This spray helps both pest and disease resistance, and helps plants recover from frost. Take as many of the following as possible: nettles, comfrey, chamomile, seaweed, waterweed, lucerne, yarrow, casuarina, horsetail and horseradish leaves. Cover them with water. Add water up to a weak-tea colour and spray onto the foliage. Add more water to the plants and use again when the solution is strong enough. The remnants can be used for mulch.

The best pesticide

The best pesticide of all is glue: ordinary billstickers' paste. Spray glue on your bugs and they stop eating your plants. They stop breeding too. In fact, they stop doing everything. The birds can see them easily and learn that your garden is a good place to get some easy tucker. The glue washes off in the first rain or watering.

Mix:
1 cup flour
1 cup boiling water
Add as much cold water as you need to make the mixture sprayable. Strain out lumps! Spray at once.
WASH OUT YOUR SPRAYER WELL AFTER USING IT, OR IT MAY BE GLUED UP FOREVER!

Glue spray may be sprayed with a small handheld mister. Large trees will need a pump action sprayer. If you spray often it's worth buying these, as they make spraying faster and much more thorough.

Pesticides you can eat for dinner

Pest killers don't have to be poisonous. Try the following:
- a mixture of skim milk and flour sprayed on sap suckers like aphids, bean fly and red spider mites;
- flour dabbed on cabbage leaves against caterpillars;
- a mustard-and-water spray on bean fly and red spider mites;
- chamomile tea against fruit rots, damping off and mildews. This tea is also a mild sedative. If the problem is really bugging you, drink it yourself.

A tasty fungicide

(Well, actually, it isn't. It tastes bloody horrible, but at least it won't kill you!)

9 cups water
1 cup full cream milk (goat, sheep, yak or camel milk will do – in fact, camel milk is even better as it greasier)
1 tsp bicarbonate of soda
Mix well, spray at once, under and over the leaves, every three days for 21 days, then every two weeks.

This is great for downy mildew, okay for black spot, even works for powdery mildew, but in all cases it's best at the start of the problem. Once the leaves are wilting or shoots are dying back it's hard to regain control. So spray as a preventative when you suspect the problem is lurking.

Black spot spray

The Rose Society of the USA recommends the following organic spray:

Mix 3 teaspoons bicarb with 2.5 tbs PestOil (a commercial oil-based spray), then mix into 4.5 L of water. Spray every four days for two weeks, then once a week.

Well-fed roses will outgrow black spot – at least most of them will (if you have a black-spot-prone Bourbon rose like 'La Reine Victoria', for example, you'll need to stick it in a raincoat to entirely stop it getting black spot). Take a look at your spotty rose bushes. The old leaves will look awful – but the newest leaves will be unblemished. Remember too that in most varieties, the more new growth, the more roses.

Bordeaux mixture

This is the standard organic fungicide. It is very effective against a wide range of parasitic fungi and bacteria. Unlike many modern fungicides, pathogens do not seem to develop resistance against Bordeaux. It sticks very strongly to trees once sprayed and if it has been made properly and used fresh even rain shouldn't affect it.

Always make Bordeaux mixture yourself. It doesn't keep, and commercial mixtures aren't traditional Bordeaux. Always use Bordeaux within an hour of making it, or before it starts to separate. If it has been allowed to stand for more than two or three hours it won't stick to the plants and may injure them.

Try not to use Bordeaux too often – try the other, 'softer' fungicides first. Too much copper can affect soil fungi (though high humus levels can mitigate this), and may also kill predators. If you have trouble with scale in spring, and you have been spraying with Bordeaux, that may be the reason. Try spraying every second bush, then spraying the rest ten days later so you still have a nucleus of predators for when pests start to build up. A good commercial Bordeaux alternative is Kocide.

To make your own Bordeaux, follow the directions below.

Bordeaux is made from copper sulphate (bluestone) and calcium hydroxide ('brickies lime'). Both can be bought quite easily from hardware stores. But note that calcium carbonate, or agricultural lime, doesn't work at all.

Try to get fine crystals of copper sulphate: they dissolve more easily than the coarse ones, which need a lot of stirring.

Make sure the lime is from an unopened bag. Once the calcium hydroxide has been exposed to the air it becomes calcium carbonate and won't neutralise the copper sulphate. The resulting spray may severely damage your trees.

Mix 90 g of blue copper sulphate with 6.5 L of cold water in a non-metallic container – plastic, glass, wood, or earthenware. NEVER use iron or galvanised iron for Bordeaux. In a second, non-metallic container, mix 125 g of slaked lime (not agricultural or garden lime) in another 2.5 L of cold water. If either is lumpy at all put each through a strainer. Lime may also come mixed with bits of sand and, unless it's strained, this may block the spray nozzle. The copper sulphate must be thoroughly dissolved in sufficient water or it may form a suspended precipitate that will sink to the bottom and not stick so well to the plants. Mix the two together, stirring well.

Test with an old nail. Dip it in the mixture for 30 seconds. If it comes out blue you need more lime – or more mixing to dissolve the lime. Don't use the spray until you have corrected the problem, or you may burn your plants.

Use within an hour, stirring occasionally. Use it with any spraying equipment, but have some water around to wash out the nozzles and stop them from clogging.

Bordeaux is used mostly at bud swell for deciduous plants, after blossoming for evergreens, and against downy mildew at half strength on grapes and vegetables through the season.

When spraying trees make sure you spray ALL the bark, including the crutch of the tree. If your trees are prone to canker or branch dieback, it is a good idea to spray them just before pruning – this will make all the remaining leaves drop off – and then again after pruning, so that infection doesn't enter where the leaves once were.

Bordeaux paste

This is useful for collar rot and tree wounds.

Dissolve 60 g copper sulphate in 2 L of water, then add 120 g of brickies lime also mixed in 2 L of water.

A tablespoon of powdered skim milk can also be added to this mixture to increase its effectiveness.

Clay spray

For this spray, don't use just any soil: it must be made with clay. Just squish up clay in water until you can spray it. It will suffocate aphids, scale and mites.

Compost spray

This will fight a wide range of diseases. It is even more effective if the compost has been made with at least 20 per cent black wattle bark, or 40 per cent comfrey, or 10 per cent chamomile or chives; or with all of them in the one brew. Cover the compost with water, drain it off and dilute it to a pale golden colour. Spray weekly.

Garlic spray

Garlic spray too, is for leaf eaters and sap suckers, and can be used as a general insecticide in a wide range of situations. But its effect is variable, from very effective sometimes to not effective at all. It is possible that harsh arid conditions make it less so. Remember that it's not a contact poison, and must be consumed to be effective.

Chop 85 g garlic (don't bother to peel it) and soak it in two tablespoons of mineral oil for 24 hours. Add 600 mL water in which 7 g soap has been dissolved (or as soapy a solution as you can make). Strain and store in glass, not metal, away from light. Dilute with ten times the amount of water to begin with – then make it stronger if it isn't effective. The smell isn't as bad as you would expect and doesn't linger when sprayed.

Oil spray

Commercial oil sprays like Pestguard are better than home-made sprays – they are lighter and can be sprayed when it's hotter. Oil sprays work by covering insects or their eggs with a light film of suffocating oil, especially in winter when their outer surfaces are more porous.

For this recipe you can use any oil in your cupboard – I use old oil I've previously used for frying. (The spray will burn young leaves and flowers when the temperature is likely to reach 24°C or above in the following 48 hours.)

Take 1 kg of soap for every 2 L of oil. Boil and stir vigorously until the soap has dissolved. Dilute with 20 times the volume of water. This spray separates quickly and doesn't store once it has been mixed with water.

Pyrethrum spray

This is a broad spectrum spray, worth trying on most pests. It will kill some predators but has a low toxicity for humans. Spray it at night to avoid bees and other beneficial insects. It breaks down in sunlight in two hours to two days.

You can use any one of several commercial pyrethrum sprays or make your own. The easiest method is to pick the pyrethrum flowers before they are fully open, dry them, then use the resulting 'insecticidal dust'.

The active ingredients in pyrethrum are not water soluble, though a pyrethrum 'tea', made with boiling water, will have some insecticidal effect. For the best result, though, cover the flowers with brandy or other alcohol, mineral oil or eucalyptus oil, or a combination of these. Shake well, then add three times the quantity of hot water. Put the lid on at once. Leave until cool. Strain only when needed, and spray. Store in a cool dark place. I have also made pyrethrum spray by covering the flowers with hot vinegar.

Feverfew flowers can also be used instead of pyrethrum flowers, but you will need to use two or three times the amount of flowers to get the same strength spray, and even then the effect will be variable as active ingredients will vary.

Warning: some people may be allergic to both sprays, resulting in either rashes, asthma or even more severe reactions.

Repellent spray

This may or may not work – I include it here only because many people claim a good effect. Place handfuls of wormwood, chilli and other strongly scented plants (like peppermint-scented or ivy-leafed geranium) in a container. Cover with boiling water. Cool, strain, and spray. You can also cover them with cold water and wait until it turns pale brown, then spray. If the spray is dark brown, it may burn the plant: dilute it until it is just a pale golden colour.

Seaweed or 'green' spray

This can be made of seaweed or from a mixture of comfrey, seaweed, casuarina leaves, horsetail, chamomile, garlic tops, yarrow or nettles. If you don't have all these ingredients, use what you do have. There is no need to wash the salt from seaweed, unless it has been above the high-tide mark and collected salt from days of spray. Cover the ingredients with cold water and wait three weeks. Dilute the liquid to a pale golden colour and spray every week. Warning: collecting seaweed may be illegal.

SOME COMMON DISEASE PROBLEMS

Black spot

For black spot and other leaf blotches, spray roses, when dormant, with Bordeaux, Kocide or other copper spray. Use black spot spray in summer.

Brown rot of fruit

Spray Bordeaux or a copper-based spray like Kocide in winter, when the tree is dormant or, in bad cases, at leaf fall and just before bud burst. Make sure all dried fruit 'mummies' are picked off the tree. They probably didn't fall off because they were infected the previous year. Seaweed or green spray or compost water applied every fortnight in summer will increase resistance. In bad (damp) seasons, thin fruit and spray weekly with chamomile tea. Dip picked fruit in hot chamomile tea, and dry them thoroughly before storing. Or dip them in boiling water for a few seconds: this requires good timing or the skin will shrivel. Then dry and store.

Collar rot

Trees die back; bark is lifted at the base. Don't mulch to the very base of the tree – leave a breathing space. Avoid injury from mowers or when weeding. Cut back affected bark to healthy wood, and paint with Bordeaux paste (a less dilute Bordeaux 'spray') or some other copper spray. Spray seaweed or 'green' spray on the leaves of the tree every ten days until the wound begins to close over and new growth and green leaves appear.

Curly leaf

This causes pink, blistered leaves. New shoots may die back. Brown rot control will also control curly leaf. LOTS of garlic planted around the tree for at least a metre will help control curly leaf, but will take up to five years to be effective.

Damping off

This causes seedlings to suddenly die, with a dark rim around the stem at soil level. Dip seedlings in chamomile tea before you plant them, soil and all, or drizzle strong chamomile tea around the base. Make sure all organic matter in the soil is decomposed. Use solarisation before planting (see Chapter 8). Try a green manure crop of broad beans in winter, but do make sure it's all decomposed before planting again.

Downy and powdery mildew

Downy mildew makes plants shrivel, with white clumps of fungus underneath. Powdery mildew leaves a grey film over the leaves. Mulch, to keep spores from splashing up from the soil onto the leaves. To increase resistance, spray every ten days with seaweed, 'green' spray or compost water. Spray every three days with equal parts of milk and water, or use black spot spray.

Root rots

(See also above.)
Improve drainage and mulch well. A compost made of 30 to 40 per cent wattle bark and 50 per cent lucerne hay inhibits many root rots. So do most composts, though to a lesser degree. In bad cases, prune the tree back and feed it with a spray while the compost keeps the pathogens in check and the roots re-establish themselves so they can feed the tree.

THE MOST COMMON PESTS

Aphids

These small insects have a wide colour range. Leaves wilt or are malformed as their sap is sucked. Aphids also secrete honeydew, which stimulates sooty mould and can transfer virus diseases.

Use grease bands as an ant barrier at the base of shrubs. Encourage ladybirds and their larvae, lacewings, hoverflies and birds: all consume aphids. If this isn't enough, try spraying strong jets of water on top and under leaves, or glue spray. In bad cases, use an aluminium-foil mulch under the plant to scare them off.

The same treatment can be given to thrips and to woolly aphids, or these can be squeezed by hand or dabbed with metho. A soapy water spray will often control both thrips and aphids, but be careful not to burn foliage when it's over 200°C.

As with any organic control, always wait to see if predators will do the job for you before you start control measures. And with native plants you at least can be sure that just as the pests have evolved with the plants they are munching in your garden, so have the predators evolved to prey on the pests.

Borers

(See also above.)

Borers are beetle or moth larvae which tunnel into stems or roots and often cause a great deal of damage. You may not notice them until the damage is done and you have a dying tree or branch. Small piles of sawdust are an early indication.

Sickly and old trees are more prone to borer attack. (Borers may be an indication that your short-lived tree is nearing the end of its life.) A good repellent, if you know your trees are susceptible, is to paint trunks and branches in spring with Bordeaux paste diluted with four parts water. This deters the females from laying eggs. Lavender bushes grown around your plants may act as a moth repellent.

If you are desperate, you could also try the following borer repellent, which is not really organic but should save your tree without harming any other species around: a slurry of wood ash and eucalyptus oil.

Christmas beetles

These summer visitors munch through an enormous amount of eucalypt leaves, eating the young ones first and then the older ones. Young trees with young foliage, especially bright-blue young leaves, seem particularly susceptible, and can be defoliated or even killed. Strongly scented species like lemon-scented gums seem less prone to attack. In beetle-prone areas avoid blue gums or any tree with bright-blue young leaves.

Immature Christmas beetles are large white grubs with reddish heads. They eat plant roots.

The best prevention is growing understorey plants. Here we have a tree by the road that is eaten every year. A few metres away trees are untouched, but they have smaller trees and bushes around them. Disguise your tree with a bush-like understorey – and encourage the birds that eat the beetles and their grubs.

As a last-ditch control, try shaking the tree, and stamping on the results. Use glue spray and a pump action sprayer.

Codling moth

Plant parsnips or fennel round the garden. Let them flower to attract predators that will help control the codling moth. Look for the moths – small, browny-grey ones – and spray with derris spray once a week, under the leaves as well. Check the fruit every two weeks: look for small holes in the top or bottom. Pick off affected fruit. Stew it or seal it in a plastic bag, but don't compost it. Most

• •

Recycled pests

European forests lose their leaves every winter – and their nutrients are recycled back into the soil. This doesn't happen in eucalypt forest – the nutrients are recycled partially by burning (in some areas), but even more by pests.

Pests eat the leaves or suck the sap, die, fall back to the soil and decay. Don't shudder when you see a partially defoliated gum tree – it's part of the natural cycle of 'what's up there needs to come back down here so Junior can grow'. (This isn't to say that devastating Christmas beetle plagues are natural – they're not – they're a result of our bad land management, but that's another story.)

Don't worry about some pest infestation in your garden. As long as it isn't killing or stunting the plants – or depriving you of a needed crop – it is helping to recycle nutrients. (The sappy sweet secretions of many sap suckers like aphids will also stimulate nitrogen-fixing bacteria in the soil, but that's another story too.)

• •

codling moths breed in fallen fruit, and codling moth-infected fruit falls early. Pick up fruit at once and get rid of it. Check ladders, boxes and wooden fences for cocoons in winter. Run chooks or geese under trees.

Earwigs

Catch these in balls of damp newspaper. Make a collar from an old tin-can lid or use a grease band on the trunks of shrubs like roses, to stop them climbing and chewing the buds.

Fruit fly

(See also under 'Baits and traps' below.)
Any fruit or soft vegetable can be attacked by fruit fly. Look for small 'maggots' and brown rotting patches. Most fruit fly breed in fallen fruit, so pick it up and dispose of it. Make sure every bit, every squashy, overripe tomato, is picked up within a day. Either feed them to the animals, or place them in an airtight, sealed garbage bag in the sun, or cover them with water until the fruit decomposes.

Avoid early ripening crops like loquats in bad fruit-fly areas. These may attract the fly to your later crops. Avoid late maturing varieties that fruit when large numbers of fruit fly are likely to be around. Be careful too of late summer fruits like quinces, figs and medlars: they can host fruit fly and provide a 'bridge' for them to breed in, ready to infect winter crops like citrus. A 'fruit-fly free gap' of a couple of months may be enough to save later crops from infection.

Repellent: I have been experimenting with a repellent of 1 part sour milk to 1 part wormwood tea, sprayed on apples once a week. It seems successful, but it is too early to be sure.

Grasshoppers

(See also under 'Baits and traps' below.)

Plant in groves. Grasshoppers are just that – GRASS hoppers. They don't like groves.

The more thick greenery round your garden (especially lavender, grevilleas and other tough plants), the more it will be protected. In bad cases use a barrier of microjets or sprayer hose: grasshoppers dislike crossing water. Rows of tall perennial pineapple marigolds may deter grasshoppers in good seasons. But in a plague, the grasshoppers will eat these too. You can also try turkeys or some athletic free-range chooks.

Pear and cherry slug

If yours is an adult tree, try to forget about it: even a bad plague probably won't kill the tree, which will fruit as well next year. Use glue spray and a pump action sprayer. It's probably better to plant pear and cherry trees where you won't be bothered by the pests.

Red spider and other mites

Water frequently. This will probably be all that is needed. As a last resort, spray on top and below the leaves with a mixture of half a cup of flour to half a cup of buttermilk and five cups of water. Use oil spray in cool weather, or a clay or pyrethrum spray. Feed with compost. For long-term control improve your feeding regime, or don't grow plants where the rain can't reach them.

Sawflies or spitfires

These resemble black, white-haired caterpillars. They hang in clusters during the day and eat the leaves at night. The adult is a steel-blue wasp with yellow markings on the head.

They are relished by cuckoo shrikes and other birds. Use glue spray and a pump action sprayer.

Scale

Scale inject a toxin that may cause trees to die. Use oil spray in cool weather (below 24°C), or try glue spray at any time of the year. Many small birds will clean up your scale for you. Grow grevilleas or sages like pineapple sage near susceptible trees.

Stink and other bugs

These are attracted by the smell of ripe fruit. Pick the fruit when it's semi-ripe. Pick up all that's fallen. Ivy-leafed scented geraniums wandering up the trees will repel bugs. So will a ground cover of reflective foil. Shake them out of the tree with a long rake, and rake them up (taking care to use gloves). Use glue spray and a pump action sprayer.

Slugs and snails

(See also under 'Baits and traps' below.) Look for seedlings that disappear or lose their tops, for holes in leaves, and for shiny tracks. Snails are only a nuisance inside the garden; outside, they are good bird and lizard food.

Birds and lizards will keep down slugs and snails for most of the year: snails are worse in spring before lizards become active. Gardens with resident cats that keep the lizards at bay will probably have more snail damage.

A snail-proof fence: take a piece of metal, bend it over into a V-shape at the top, and push the bottom into the ground; the slugs and snails won't get over.

Snails on shrubs and trees: keep them off the trunks with a thick band of grease, or a barrier of wool or material soaked in old sump oil.

The English method: put on your wellies (joggers will do). Go out with a torch on a wet night and stamp on them.

The easiest method of all: last spring I offered two small boys one cent for every snail they found. They brought me 260 snails in two days. That was $2.60 – much cheaper than snail bait, and the end of the snail problem for the year.

Eating snails

Snails are best eaten in autumn, when they are fattest, or in spring, when they are slow and heading towards the seedlings. Place your snails in a box of lettuce or vine leaves for three weeks; then in a box lined with bran or flour for three days. Change the bran or flour every day. On the fourth day, leave the box empty and let the snails starve for 24 hours.

Wash them well. Put them in a pan of cold water and leave them for an hour. Now slowly bring the water to the boil. Boil for an hour, then simmer gently for another half an hour. They should now slip out of their shells.

Dip your cooked snails in garlic butter, cover them with home-made tomato sauce, or toss them in spaghetti and call them meatballs. If your family is squeamish, mince them, bind the mince with a beaten egg, and make them into rissoles. Just don't mention what's in them.

NEVER EAT SNAILS FRESH FROM THE GARDEN – they may have been eating a plant that will poison you.

NEVER pick snails from any plant that may be toxic, especially oleander, hellebores, daffodils, tulips and other bulbs.

Staghorn frond beetle

These are small round beetles, with orange larvae about a fingertip in size, that tunnel into staghorn fronds. Simply cut off the infected fronds, or squash the larvae inside, and you'll very effectively break the breeding cycle.

Thrips

Thrips start at ground level and work up to the higher blossom. Grow lots of spring-flowering ground covers under your trees to stop thrips migrating from dying weeds to fruit tree blossom. As a last resort hose them.

Woolly aphids

These usually result from injury or too much pruning. Squash them with your fingers, paint them with methylated spirits or use glue spray.

BAITS AND TRAPS

Fruit fly

Baits and traps are very effective, and provide the continuous control needed. Their main disadvantage is that they may attract fruit fly into your area before they would have come normally.

Fruit fly are airborne for about a week before they mate and lay eggs: if you can kill them during this time you'll break the breeding cycle.

Fruit fly netting: use this on trees and veg crops.

Fruit fly bags: tie these on quinces and other late maturing but precious fruit.

Dak pots: these are a commercially available trap. Forget about them, though, as they only indicate whether you have fruit fly or not, and are of no use at all as a control. Also, Dak pots attract only male Queensland fruit fly. The Mediterranean fruit fly is the only one active in Western Australia and, anyway, it's the female that lays the eggs – one lone surviving male can cover an awful lot of territory.

Home-made ginger beer: boil 2 L of water, 2 sliced lemons, a pinch of fresh or dried ginger and 2 cups of raw sugar. Add a pinch of yeast when only lukewarm. Bottle. Drink half in two days and use the rest as fruit-fly bait.

Soft-drink bottle trap: take an empty plastic soft-drink bottle. Cut off the top at the shoulders, turn it round so that the spout is sticking into the bottle, and tape the edges firmly. Fill the bottle one-third full of bait, cover the hole with mosquito netting, and suspend it from trees or stakes in the garden. Alternatively, just half-fill a plastic bottle with bait, hang it spout downwards, and punch a few very small holes in the (now) top end.

Baits: these include bran, sugar and hot water; a banana peel in water; orange rind; human urine or a pinch of yeast and water. But I find home-made ginger beer is the best lure of all. It's sweet, wet and yeasty.

Splash-on baits: these are commercially available and, while not 'organic', at least do not affect the fruit; they are splashed onto the bark. Use them as a last resort.

Yellow traps: hang yellow fly-papers near the fruit. Paint yellow boards with commercial sticky glues, like Temobi.

Cutworm bait

Cutworms can be trapped with a sugar or molasses solution. Take some hardwood sawdust and soak it either in a strong solution of sugar and water or molasses. Leave it on the soil near seedlings. The cutworms will be trapped and dehydrate come daylight.

Grasshoppers

Trap them with dishes of molasses and water, or with yellow plastic floating in a dish of water, in a dam or in the swimming pool: they'll try to land on it and drown.

Slugs and snails

Snail bait: use commercial snail pellets in a margarine container with the lid on (so the rain can't touch it), and cut a few holes in the sides for the snails: they won't poison earthworms or pets as long as they are inside the margarine containers.

Traps: trap snails in hollowed raw potatoes or oranges, and squash them every morning.

THE BIGGER BRIGADE

Birds

Encourage birds; don't treat them as pests. They clean up from 40 to 90 per cent of pests. Also, they are beautiful, and the most obvious wildlife most suburbs have. Who wants to live in a human-only desert? But if birds eat your fruit:

- Grow fruit in groves (see Chapter 1).
- Grow decoy crops; birds PREFER sour fruit, which is why they eat your fruit ten days before you pick it; and birds are conservative – they'll keep eating one fruit rather than start on a new tree.

We have large mobs of rosellas, parrots and bowerbirds here, and lots of citrus in winter. But the birds ignore our oranges; they're eating the tiny, sour calamondins. Calamondins are VERY prolific, and small enough to be carried away or held in a claw.

Try:

Winter: calamondins, 'wild' kiwi fruit (the small, round ones that don't need male and female vines)

Spring: calamondins, lillypillies

Summer: lillypillies, native figs, mulberries, loquats

Autumn: wild kiwi fruit.

There are many other crops to tempt birds, of course: look at whatever native (sour) fruits grow well in your area, then use them to tempt the birds away from the nasty sweet stuff that we humans like.

- Provide fresh water every day – 50 per cent of fruit eating is a search for water.
- Provide other food – I put out last year's apples, kiwi fruit or stale bread to keep the birds away from other crops.
- Let your fruit tree branches tangle; mix up your vegetable garden so peas are overshadowed by corn, cabbages shield the beans, and fruit tree branches overhang the lot.
- Encourage resident birds – they'll help keep away seasonal invaders like white cockatoos.

Dogs and cats

Use a motion sensing water-spraying scarecrow to scare them off. Place bird netting over sandpits to deter cats.

Possums

Try feeding them old bits of bread and apple. They'll be too stuffed to eat your rose shoots. (Spray new shoots with wasabi mixed with water – the possums will learn quickly that the bits of bread are tastier.) Net them out of roofs. As a last resort, tune a radio to a sport's station and put it in your roof to evict them, or hire a disco service (noise and flashing lights) for stubborn ones. Possums are territorial: if you trap them and let them loose elsewhere, they may die trying to get back, or others may kill them. You either learn to live with them, or accept the guilt for their death.

Flying foxes or fruit bats

You can try grasshopper repellent, or try deterring them with paper bags or old nylon stockings filled with mothballs and impregnated with urine, wintergreen oil or tiger balm. Leave a radio on loud, or produce a high-frequency noise near the trees – though they will get used to this. You can also buy specially designed flying fox netting.

WHAT PREDATORS EAT WHAT IN THE GARDEN

Aphids

Wrens, silvereyes, firetails, Willie wagtails, grey shrike-thrush, some sparrows, eastern spinebills (sometimes), some finches (during nesting), yellow and other robins, honeyeaters, thornbills, kingfishers (sometimes), treecreepers, cuckoo-shrikes, wrens, pardalotes, whistlers, ladybird larvae, lacewings (especially the green lacewing), hoverflies, damsel bugs, stilt flies, paper wasps.

Beanfly
Damsel bugs, hoverflies, lacewings, ladybirds and their larvae, mantids, stilt flies, ants, various wasps, tachinid flies, assassin bugs.

Caterpillars
Cuckoos (eat hairy caterpillars too), rosellas, noisy miners, Richard's pipit, tillers, rufous whistlers, shrike-thrush, flycatchers, monarchs, cicada birds, pardalotes, magpies, choughs, magpie larks, currawongs, grey shrike-thrush, starlings (sometimes), yellow robins, scorpion flies, spiders, tachinid flies, chalcid, flower, paper and other wasps, ichneumons, centipedes, ants, assassin bugs, dragonflies (eat butterflies and moths).

Codling moth
Many caterpillar eaters eat the larvae stage of codling moth. The moths are eaten by owls, nightjars, swifts, lacewings and their larvae, spiders, tachinid flies, chalcid wasps (eat codling moth eggs), flower, paper and other wasps, at least one species of earwig (eat the larvae), tiger and other beetles, ants, ichneumons.

Cutworms
Calosoma beetles and tiger beetles, ants, spiders, various soil dwelling larvae, magpies, kookaburras, currawongs.

Fruit flies
Ants. Predatory flies may catch them on the wing. Predators probably play a very small role in controlling introduced fruit fly.

Grasshoppers
Bustards, strawnecked ibis, fantails, Willie wagtails, cuckoos, owls, kingfishers, noisy friar birds, Richard's pipit, scarlet and yellow robins, chooks (must be free-range chooks, used to hunting their food vigorously), honeyeaters, soldier beetles, assassin bugs, sphecid wasps.

Heliothis caterpillars
Assassin bugs, mantids, centipedes, dragonflies, hoverflies (eat small caterpillars), ichneumons, lacewings (eat the eggs), scorpion flies, spiders, various wasps.

Lerps
Honeyeaters, cuckoo-shrikes, firetails, blue wrens, some finches (during nesting), predator ants, various wasps, possibly lacewing larvae.

Lerp psyllids
Ants (*Myrmecea vurians*)

Pear and cherry slug
Cuckoo-shrikes, scarlet and yellow robins, silvereyes, currawongs, thornbills (sometimes), firetails, lacewings, ichneumons, paper wasps, probably various other wasps.

Sawflies
Hoverflies, ichneumons, pollistes and other wasps, spiders, lacewings (eat the eggs). See also pear and cherry slug predators.

Scale
Treecreepers, cuckoo-shrikes, pardalotes, silvereyes, firetails, honeyeaters, blue wrens, some finches (during nesting), ladybird larvae, lacewings, hoverflies, chalcid wasps, damsel bugs.

Snails
Kookaburras, currawongs, magpies (sometimes), owls (sometimes), pittas, trillers (sometimes), mynahs (sometimes), nightjars, butcher birds, glossy ibis, chooks, ducks, lizards (blue-tongue lizards love them), centipedes, various beetles (especially snail eggs), frogs, toads.

Thrips

Treecreepers, Richard's pipits, cuckoo-shrikes, pardalotes, firetails, honeyeaters, blue wrens, thornbills, whistlers, shrike-thrush, wood swallows (sometimes, as they dip for nectar), ladybird larvae, lacewings and their larvae, damsel bugs, spiders.

HOW TO ATTRACT PREDATORS

Have year-round flowers, and let some vegies flower too: the adult form of many predators like nectar, and their young eat the pests.

Remember that cats kill frogs, toads, birds, lizards, dragonflies, and other pest-eaters, and that bees will scare away hoverflies.

Tolerate a little sooty mould: many adult predators are attracted by it. Don't dig. You'll destroy many predator eggs and nymphae, and the dust too will kill predator eggs.

HOW TO ATTRACT BIRDS

Birds can clean up most of the pests in your garden. Once they have finished with one pest, they'll move on to another. Even nectar eaters will eat insects while nesting. As I write, I can see blue wrens eating the spiders above the door, yellow robins eating aphids on the roses, a kookaburra crunching snails, and a small brown bird (I can't see what it is) pecking the mites off the kiwi fruit under the eaves.

Give birds fresh, clean water out of cats' reach (and, if possible, freedom from cats), lots of thick bushes and high perches for safe nesting, masses of blossom year-round. Grevilleas and pineapple and other sages are especially good: they'll feed the nectar eaters and attract insects for the insect eaters.

For more information on pest and disease control, look for the author's *Natural Control of Garden Pests* (Aird Books).

COMPANION PLANTING

Most companion planting doesn't work. This is generally because we expect too much of it. Companion planting is a bit like romance – it's not enough to introduce basil to tomatoes to expect them to live happily ever after.

It is also because a lot of our companion planting lore comes from Europe or the USA – and what works there doesn't necessarily work here. Some companion planting works because one plant attracts a predator which then eats the pests on its companion. But if we don't have that pest or that predator in Australia – or they both happen to eat something else – there's not much point in planting the two together and expecting miracles. Forget about growing marigolds to control nematodes, for example: the main problem nematode in Australia isn't bothered by it. (They do like mustard though.)

Most companion planting advice is also imprecise. It doesn't tell you why an association works, or how.

To give just one example: it's common companion planting folklore that carrots planted with onions do well. This is probably because onions help repel carrot fly. So, if your carrots aren't affected by carrot fly there won't be any marked improvement resulting from planting onions with them.

Yet the matter isn't as simple as this. Onions may reduce carrot fly by up to 70 per cent, but only if the onions are actively growing – as soon as they stop growing tops and start to bulb, the protective effect is reduced to 30 per cent. As there are two or more carrot fly flights a season you will need more than one onion crop. In addition, there need to be twice as many onions as carrots if they are in alternate rows; though if the carrots are grown in a block surrounded by several rows of onions, fewer onions are needed.

A lot of companion planting lore is simply repeated from book to book without testing, such as having companion planted beds and non-companion planted beds growing in the same conditions. I've tried garlic under trees for curly leaf, chives for black spot, basil with and without my tomatoes, and many other associations: a lot of advice simply didn't work. If it doesn't work in my garden, it probably won't work in yours. (This is not to say it didn't work somewhere, once, nor that it will not work again – but unless you work out why and when it works, it is unlikely to be of much use to most gardeners.)

Some companion planting is incredibly effective, but there is no mystique about it. Follow the principles set out in this chapter, and you'll be able to work out your own companion planting strategies.

USING COMPANION PLANTING INSTEAD OF PESTICIDES

Grow year-round flowering plants

It's no coincidence that most of the recommended companion plants are long-flowering ones, like borage and nasturtiums. Flowers attract predators – either by producing nectar or by attracting other insects for them to feed on. Make sure you have flowers throughout the garden all year round. A variety of grevilleas is excellent for this, as are daisies, buddleia and elderflowers – or just let vegetables go to seed. Flowering umbelliferae like parsnip and fennel are particularly good at attracting predators that eat your pests.

Inter-plant

Arranging plants in big clumps or neat rows is like designing a smorgasbord for pests. They're easy to find and the pests can move along the rows. Pests either recognise their food by shape or by smell. Disguise the shape and they won't be able to find their target. It doesn't particularly matter what you inter-plant with – the more you mix your species the less of a pest problem you'll have.

Aphids, for example, recognise brassicas (cabbage, cauliflowers, etc.) by their silhouette. If other plants are grown among them the aphids fly on without landing. The companion crop, however, must cover at least 50 per cent of the soil area or it won't be effective. Almost any companion crop will do as long as the outlines are blurred – but beans or other legumes are best as they won't reduce the yield and grow quickly, so slower brassicas can get established before bean competition.

Plant 'trap crops'

Some plants may lure pests away from others. Chinese cabbage gone to seed, for example, may 'trap' aphids. Brassica weeds will trap cabbage white butterfly and cabbage moth caterpillars. Hollyhocks will lure harlequin beetles from other plants. Hawthorns, on the other hand, will lure pear and cherry slug, which will breed and spill over onto your pear and cherry trees: trap crops should be used with care.

Grow strongly scented flowers

These are mostly herbs like lavender, wormwood, pyrethrum, rue, lad's love, feverfew, lemon balm and nasturtiums. Some also contain pesticide substances, though these only kill the pests if extracted and sprayed onto the plants.

Strongly scented plants will help repel any pest that follows scents. Be wary though: many strongly scented plants may also inhibit plant growth as their oils are washed from the leaves. Don't put them near the roots of your plants – put them in hedges outside the garden bed, or move them around in pots.

Pest repellents

These include:
- bergamot
- catnip
- cedronella

- coreopsis (sap suckers especially)
- coriander (aphids and other sap suckers)
- clove pinks (while the flowers are blooming)
- daisy cress (also insecticidal)
- scented leafed geraniums or pelargoniums
- feverfew (also insecticidal)
- fleabane
- garlic (borers, mites and sap suckers, but must be regularly trimmed to be effective)
- horehound
- hyssop
- Indian beech (seeds are insecticidal, flowers repel insects)
- larkspur (aphids, thrips, sometimes grasshoppers and locusts unless in plague numbers)
- lavender
- marigolds (the root secretions also inhibit some nematode species. They do NOT repel sap suckers! Beware, they may also attract sap suckers to your plants)
- mustard (the root secretions also repel common problem nematodes)
- native and introduced pennyroyal
- nasturtiums (the leaves are a mild repellent for sap suckers like mites; the flowers deter aphids above them)
- southernwood
- rosemary
- rue (rue sometimes also deters dogs, cats, wallabies and rabbits)
- rhubarb
- sacred basil (also insecticidal)
- stinking roger
- sneezeweed (especially ants)
- tansy
- tea tree
- thistle (several varieties)
- tobacco (insecticidal and poisonous – treat with care)
- woodruff, and
- wormwood.

The flowers of many of these also attract pests like aphids. The effects only last while the flowers are blooming.

Always remember that these plants are deterrents, not cures. They will simply make other plants less pleasant to pests, but won't stop them attacking. If I see a shop that advertises 'hamburgers' I'll be deterred from going in – but it won't stop me if I'm hungry enough. Repellents are just one aspect of pest control.

PS Never believe any book that says marigolds will help keep sap suckers away. Marigolds ATTRACT sap suckers!!!

USING COMPANION PLANTING INSTEAD OF HERBICIDES

Beware of plants that inhibit growth. These include daffodils, jonquils, mugwort, sunflowers and ranunculi (these suppress nitrogen-fixing bacteria), most pines, most eucalypts, most cypresses, oak trees, walnuts, pittosporums, lad's love, couch, and bracken. They may suppress growth in plants around their drip line.

On the other hand, these plants can also be used to help control weeds: try a thick patch of sunflowers, dahlias, oats or gladioli to clear a weedy area. A mulch of bracken or gum leaves will help stop weeds germinating, but it may also stunt your plants. I use alyssum or strawberries between my plants to keep down weeds. Let brassicas like cabbage, radish or cauliflowers go to seed: they'll inhibit all other plants around them, and by early summer you'll have a weed-free bed which can be planted with seedlings.

USING COMPANION PLANTING INSTEAD OF FERTILISER

Some plants help the growth of other plants, either by substances washed down from their leaves, or because they are nitrogen-fixing or bring up leached nutrients. Nettles, for example, 'fix' nitrogen (or their associated bacteria do). Their leaves break down quickly and add humus to the soil; they are reputed to encourage earthworms and also to transmit some 'tonic' properties to plants (not yet specified but which seem to work). Plants grown with nettles really do seem less prone to pests and diseases and to grow better.

HOW TO USE COMPANION PLANTS

Grow them in hedges around your garden. Inter-plant them in garden beds: flowers, chamomile and borage. Move them round in pots wherever they are needed, especially fragrant herbs.

Most companion plants need to be planted at least 10 to 20 days before the pest-prone species is planted. Companion planting books are sometimes like introduction agencies – they assume that once carrot meets tomato they'll live happily ever after. Companion planting is a help to good gardening, not a cure for all garden problems. In my garden, for example, are two young orange trees, one planted around with nettles, the other without. The one with nettles is growing slightly faster and healthier than the other one – but the nettles neither save it from aphids in the spring, nor from stink bugs in the summer.

Don't expect too much of companion planting. It can be effective, sometimes startlingly effective – but not always. And if you follow the most important rules – plenty of year-round flowers and inter-planting – you will probably get as good or better a result than any close following of companion planting manuals might give you.

SOME GOOD COMPANIONS

Vegetable companions

Remember that any inter-planting will change the silhouette of your vegetables. Think like a pest. If you want to stump a cabbage white butterfly, for instance, change the shape and the smell of your cabbages with tall celery or tomato bushes. Just consider the shape and scent of the plant you want to protect, and how best to disguise it.

Grow flowers with your vegetables. They are usually of a different family from that of the vegetables, and have quite a different shape. If you grow flowers like marigolds, borage and nasturtiums, which have a pest-repelling foliage scent and predator attracting flowers, you're ahead already.

Vegetables gone to seed, especially parsnip, brassicas and radishes, are the best predator attractors I know, and underneath trees can also clear the ground of weeds.

Grow comfrey near whitefly-prone plants: the comfrey will help use excess nitrogen, and the leaves can be used as a potash rich mulch. Whitefly are more prevalent in potash-deficient soil.

If you have a nematode problem, try growing mustard around each plant you want to save. In other words, plant your seedling in a carpet of mustard. Plant the mustard thickly, 10 days before you plant the seeds or seedlings. Mustard germinates and grows very quickly, and can be planted at any time of the year. Trample it down every couple of weeks, or snip it, so it doesn't compete too much with the other plants.

Spent Chinese cabbage can be used as a trap crop for aphids. Try growing them around early broad beans.

Cabbage grown with red or white clover will have fewer aphids and fewer cabbage white butterfly caterpillars, due to interference in colonisation and more predators, especially ground beetles. Try growing a patch of red clover in spring, mowing it short, and planting your brassica seedlings in a narrow, deeply dug trench. Keep the clover short while the brassicas grow. Then, when they are a finger high, let the clover flower. If it has been regularly cut, it will flower while it is quite short, and not compete with the brassicas. But it will repel the cabbage white butterflies.

The scents of tomatoes and cabbages grown together appear to mask each other and will help reduce the number of aphids.

To cut down on leaf spot, try growing garlic among the celery, basil or silver beet: at least twice the area of garlic as celery. Plant out the celery seedlings and garlic cloves at the same time. Keep the garlic tops snipped. Either eat them, or use them as mulch around the celery. A ring of chives around each plant, again continually snipped, may also help. If you have the time, grow your celery in the middle of a carpet of chamomile. Nettles are an excellent leaf spot preventive and, if you don't mind working with gloves on, can be used as a mulch for celery.

Peanuts grown with corn tend to increase the number of spiders, leading to fewer corn borers as well as fewer other pests. Plant the peanuts at the same time as the corn, in early spring, and use the corn slashings as mulch for the ripening peanuts.

The shapes of pumpkins and corn grown together seem to confuse pests and interfere with the budworm moth's flight paths.

Try a broad bean crop before a potato crop. The bacteria associated with the broad bean roots will add nitrogen to the soil, and their residue will be an excellent mulch. It is possible that broad beans may reduce a number of fungal diseases that potatoes are susceptible to. An old remedy for fungal problems is to grow horseradish plants in between the potatoes, one horseradish tuber for every potato plant. Horseradish is a perennial; an alternative may be to push potato seed tubers into the horseradish bed.

An old reference book suggests Indian hemp as a companion crop to reduce potato blight. I haven't tried it. But if you can get hold of legal hemp seed – the sort used for cloth, not drugs – it's worth a go.

Inter-plant comfrey, beans, peas or broad beans for mulch to cover tubers and stems to keep out potato moth, and to disguise the shape of potatoes. Try a crotalaria hedge around the potato patch: crotalaria repels eelworm. Beware though: like any repellent, crotalaria may send the eelworm into the potato crop in greater numbers. Several species of fungi, encouraged by high levels of decomposing organic matter, trap eelworm in mycelium webs. Grow comfrey or other mulch plants between the rows.

Grow a crop of thickly planted broad beans to help control fusarium wilt in tomatoes: their root secretions will inhibit the fungus. The potash in a comfrey or lucerne mulch may help; so may a companion crop of garlic. Use the garlic tops as mulch.

Fruit companions

Let grapes, hops, perennial sweet peas, chilecayote melons, chokoes, etc. wander through your fruit trees to help repel pests (including birds), and to provide living mulch which gives insulation against frost and heat.

Grow nitrogen-fixing lucerne or clover underneath your trees. Legumes like clover are said to be stimulated by a small proportion (up to 10 per cent) of mustard in the mix. We mix mint, marjoram, thyme, nasturtiums, prostrate grevilleas, prostrate rosemary, and other pest repellents with the grass and clover under the trees.

Fruit trees grown with nettles seem to do better here, giving faster growth, fewer pests, and more frost resistance. Nettles increase nitrogen-fixing bacteria and improve the quality of the soil, though fruit picking with bare legs can be a problem.

Grow deep-rooted comfrey, chicory and dandelions. They will bring up nutrients leached deep down into the soil, returning them to the soil as their leaves decompose. Dandelions are also reputed to encourage earthworms and improve soil condition generally.

Plant hedges of tree lucerne or wattle. They can be regularly trimmed for nitrogen-rich mulch. But don't let the wattles get too tall, or you'll have problems with pests and sooty mould, as well as possibly armillaria root rot, and they'll compete for nutrients and water.

Grow parsnips, Queen Anne's lace, phacelia and dill, and let them flower under trees. Hoverflies and small wasps love them, and they help control codling moth and other pests.

If you are plagued by thrips, have plenty of low-growing spring flowers around the base of your fruit trees (bulbs, thyme, primulas), so the thrips stay down below instead of migrating upwards. Thrips are lazy: they'll stay on low-growing plants if possible, and usually only move onto fruit trees when winter-flowering weeds die off in spring.

Rose companions

The best plants to grow under your roses are small, flowering plants with strongly scented foliage. Tall plants may block air drainage and make your roses more susceptible to disease. Highly scented plants are often pest deterrents.

Flowering companions will attract predators which eat pests like aphids and caterpillars. Carpeting plants will keep out the grass which may stunt your roses or increase black spot.

My favourite rose companions are various scented-leafed salvias (to attract birds and repel sap suckers), parsley, strawberries, chamomile, dwarf lavender, prostrate rosemary or grevilleas under old-fashioned ramblers; alyssum for flowers and soil conditioning; carpets of thyme, catnip or catmint, and woodruff; and disease-inhibiting carpets like garlic and chamomile and mint (pennyroyal, ginger mint and apple mint are my favourites).

A thick bed of marjoram will keep out grass. Oregano is stronger, both in taste and as an insect repellent. Both are reputed to boost the growth and perfume of your roses ... dunno if they do.

Chives are a traditional rose companion and, like all the alliums (garlic, leeks, onions and shallots), are reputed to repel insects and help prevent disease, especially black spot and mildews, particularly if regularly cut. I have never found them successful.

Roses under elderberry bushes seem less prone to pests and black spot.

Our pest regime

Step 1. Do nothing.

Step 2. Wait a year and see.

Step 3. Plant lots more salvias and big grevilleas and winter-blooming red hot pokers to attract birds and pest-eating insects and spiders.

Step 4. And if birds eat your crops: grow decoy fruits, like small 'wild' kiwi fruit, lots of calamondins (harder, more prolific and longer fruiting than cumquats), six sorts of lillypillies, crab apples and clumps of sour cherries.

For more on companion planting, see *Jackie French's Guide to Companion Planting* (Aird Books).

Chapter 8
LIVING WITH WEEDS

THE IDEAL

A garden where weeds are valued as part of the natural system of regeneration of disturbed soil, but where the soil is rarely disturbed by harsh digging. A garden where plants grow in such close associations that weeds have only a very small role to play.

- *Instead of laboriously sifting out your weeds before you plant* … use no-dig gardens so weeds don't get a foothold, kill them with clear plastic, or use your weeds to make your garden beds.
- *Instead of weeding your garden* … mulch over your weeds (preferably with 'living mulch'); whippersnip them; use 'natural herbicides', or just encourage your crops to outgrow them.
- *Instead of throwing weeds away* … use them as plant tonics or fertiliser – or even eat them.
- *Instead of hating weeds* … see them as healers that protect our damaged soil.

WELL-PLANTED GARDENS DON'T GET WEEDS

Weeds are a problem because we don't know what to do with them. Think of your weeds as a crop, not a problem. They can give you free fertiliser and free mulch, bring up leached nutrients, and shelter tender plants. The flowering ones attract predators to clean up your pests. You can eat weeds, or use them as the basis for your medicine chest. Think of weeds as a bandaid, correcting some of the damage that people have done to the soil.

Our attitude to weeds is a hangover from 19th century Europe, when labour was cheap and the thirteenth gardener at the manor house could weed the flowerbed. There was no TV and sex was only for under the covers with the lights out, so what else would you do on Sunday afternoons but weed the cabbages?

After World War II labour became scarcer and chemicals (often war research by-products) became the answer to our prayers: 'dig them out' turned into 'poison them'. Until recently very little work had been done on evolving strategies to cope with weeds instead of wiping them out.

I love weeds. I wouldn't be without them. This is a good thing, as there's not much chance for a gardener to avoid weeds entirely. Weeds have an essential role, both in natural and in gardening systems. Weeds stabilise the soil. If it's dug by a spade or left bare when a tree's blown down by the wind, the weeds move in. They stop the soil eroding; they stop its structure breaking down. Their deep roots bring up nutrients and when their leaves decay the nutrients are there near the surface, ready to feed the young tree seedlings that will colonise in their turn. Weeds are the first stage in returning the forest to stability.

Gardeners have a habit of messing up the soil: digging it so that it forms a hard pan or horrible clumps; leaving it bare so it blows away or washes in the rain and bakes in the sun. Thank heavens for weeds. At least they correct some of the problems that too-avid gardeners create.

USING WEEDS

To make a garden out of weeds, see the 'pile of weeds' garden in Chapter 6.

Weeds as ground cover

If weeds are covering a bit of ground that you don't plan to use – leave it alone. We have hectares of blackberries here, glades of bracken, clumps of briars. We're gradually getting rid of them, but only as fast as we need the ground. If you clear a patch of ground you have to establish either grass or garden, and fast, or weeds will move back in. Weeds look after the soil. So leave them where they are until you need the soil.

Weeds as fertiliser

Harvest the weeds and cover them with water and use the liquid after a week as liquid manure. Slash the weeds and use their leaves as mulch – even dock is fine as long as there are no seed heads, and so are thistles as long as their prickles are covered by something else.

Weeds with seeds or roots should be added to the compost so they won't grow again – or stick them in water for liquid manure. The residue can be used as mulch after a month, when the seeds and roots have turned to mush.

Eating weeds

If you let carrots go to seed they'll start springing up everywhere. But carrots aren't a problem – because we know what to do with them. When potatoes were first introduced to Queen Elizabeth I she tried to eat them raw. That was the end of potato cuisine for a few years. Don't assume weeds taste revolting just because you haven't learnt how to use them.

There are too many edible weeds to list here. Try any or all of the following.

- Add chopped purslane leaves to your tomato salad instead of basil. Like all raw green veg (weeds or not) it's high in oxalic acid – don't eat more than a small amount.
- Sautée fat hen leaves gently in butter; scatter the seeds like poppy seeds or caraway.
- Sheep's sorrel, stuffed in fish – grill or bake the fish – is lovely; or add a very little, finely chopped, to buttery creamed potatoes; add a few chopped leaves to spinach soup for piquancy; heat in natural yoghurt as a sauce for fish, or serve cold with curry. Like all green veg it's high in oxalic acid, so don't eat more than a small amount.
- Scrub and bake dandelion roots like parsnips; the leaves can be eaten fresh in salads in early spring or steamed like silver beet in summer (you can get rid of most of the bitterness by covering the plant with a box or flower pot for a week before you pick it).

- Make nettle soup (very good!) – sautée an onion in butter, add three cups of nettles, cover with water and simmer until tender; add a little tomato purée, strain, and throw away the nettles; add milk or cream to taste, and serve warm;
- Boil oxalis 'nuts' for 20 minutes, throw out the water, boil again and use them like water chestnuts. Don't eat more than one serving a week.
- Cover dock leaves with a flower pot for a week, blanch in boiling water for 30 seconds, then simmer them in milk. Like all green veg it's high in oxalic acid. Don't eat more than a small amount.
- Cook burdock or bracken roots in butter and cider.

WEED CONTROL

None of the gardens in Chapter 2 should have much of a weed problem. The few weeds that appear can either be left or pulled out as you wander through the garden, but if you have traditional garden beds – lots of bare, dug ground waiting to be colonised by weeds – you will need to learn how to control them.

In conventional practice there are two things you can do with weeds:
- dig them out, which breaks your back; or
- use herbicides, which may not be healthy either, and is only a short-term solution.

The best weed control is knowledge: knowing your weeds and knowing your garden, and keeping it growing strongly. Learn to co-exist with weeds – if they become a problem, find out the reason so you can correct it. Unless you understand your weed problems they'll keep on coming back.

Keeping weeds out

Bare ground invites weeds. If you eliminate bare ground you'll eliminate weeds. By bare ground I also mean patchy bits of lawn under trees or where the mower has cut too short. Deep-dug neat garden beds with everything planted in rows are paradise for weeds.

Fill bare spaces

Plant creeping shrubs like prostrate grevilleas or rosemary under trees – weeds like oxalis love lawn that's been impoverished by roots underneath. Don't bother to dig out the oxalis – plant a daisy bush over it. In two or three years' time you can dig up the daisy bush and plant woodruff, pennyroyal or lawn chamomile instead: something that likes shade more than grass.

I plant alyssum or radishes in between flower or vegie seedlings. As they grow, the new plants overpower the alyssum, and we pull out the young radishes and eat them. Other flowers can be used too, but make sure they are shallow rooted and good survivors. (I once tried marigolds to fill up the bare spots between my onions – marigolds are great growth inhibitors and I thought they'd keep the weeds down. They did – but they kept the onions down too. We didn't get an onion crop that year.)

Mulch between flowers and vegetables

Plant them closer together. Fill up spaces in your garden with undemanding plants like white alyssum or strawberries – we let strawberries ramble through our vegie beds.

Keeping grass out

Keep grass out of your garden with deep-rooted plants like comfrey (will spread) or lemon grass. Chop the leaves for a free mulch. These days I use a thick row of garlic chives to keep out grass and weeds. Looks great. Also tastes good.

Try a 'grass barrier': a strip of metal bent over at the edges and pushed into the soil round your garden. This will also keep out snails.

Try a 'moving rubbish heap'

Start weeding at one end of the garden. Toss the weeds on top of other weeds further down. They'll kill them, gradually breaking down and adding to the garden's fertility. (Weeds that have gone to seed need to be composted or made into green manure. Weeds that may re-root should be placed on paper.)

Plant thickly

Plant much thicker than the rates recommended on seed packets. Thicker planting means no bare ground for weeds to colonise. Excess seedlings can be pulled out. Tiny carrots are sweeter than big ones, young beetroot leaves can be cooked like spinach, tiny lettuce leaves can be tossed in salads. Many plants will be stunted by their more vigorous neighbours, then start to grow when the neighbours have cropped. I find, with cauliflowers, red mignonette lettuce, carrots, beetroot, leeks and many other vegetables, that the smaller plants will stay dormant until I harvest the more vigorous. Then they start growing and cropping in their turn – an easy way to stagger your cropping.

Prevent weeds from spreading

Make sure you control undesirable weeds as soon as they appear. Weeds like couch, kikuyu, etc. won't co-exist with vegies. Pull out perennials before they seed. Slash annuals; cover them with mulch or use any of the weed control measures described before. Try not to introduce new weeds, whether in mulch or on your clothes. Grass seeds, bindii eyes, cobblers pegs, etc. stick to your clothes – that is their way of expanding their territory.

HOW TO GET RID OF WEEDS

Choke them out

I cleared a garden bed last year by planting gladioli bulbs thickly in the lawn. (I used a spoon to scoop them into the soil, not a spade.) The stored nutrients in the bulbs let the flowers compete against the grass. The bulbs won. This year I pulled out the bulbs and had a ready-dug, weed-free bed to plant in. Plants that grow from roots or bulbs are excellent weed clearers – try dahlias or rhubarb.

Choke weeds out with banana passionfruit. This grows well even in frost, and the fruit are

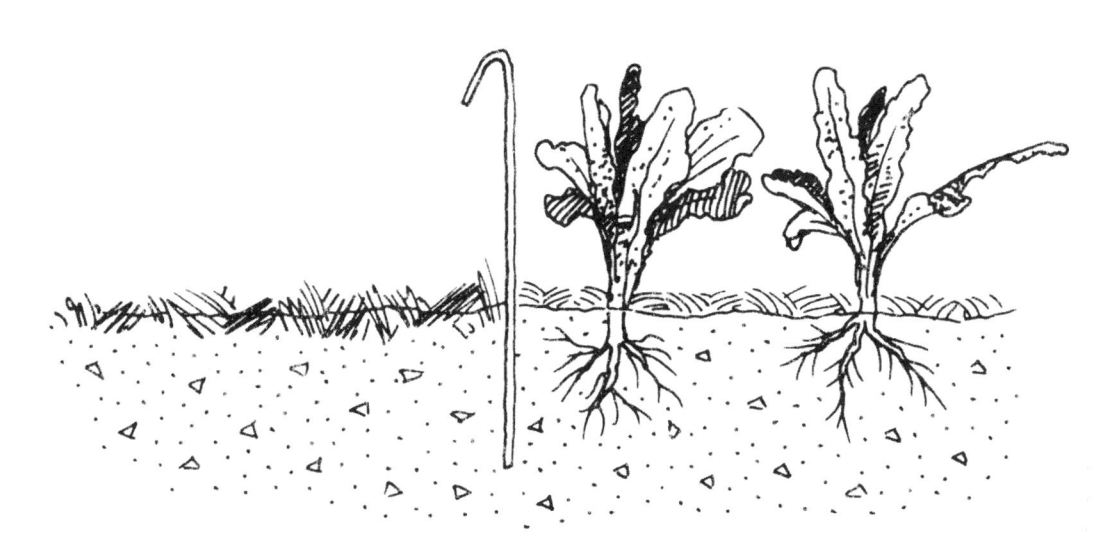

Keep grass out with comfrey or a strip of metal.

good too. Plant a hop vine and let it sprawl over convolvulus or wandering Jew or oxalis; even pumpkins can be trained over a weedy patch. I grow pumpkins round our corn and other tall growers to keep down weeds.

Weeding with radishes

Many plants suppress the growth or germination of other plants when they go to seed, especially cabbages, caulies and radishes. I plant radish and parsnip in autumn, and let them go to seed in spring. Then I water them well and pull them out. The ground below is almost weed-free and deeply dug by the radish roots: perfect for planting carrots or spring seedlings.

Weeding with chooks

Make a temporary pen with bales of hay around the weeds. Add chooks. Throw in laying pellets. Let them scratch (and go back to their roosts at night). After a week, you should have nicely dug up, weed-free and fertilised soil. Move chooks to a new patch of weeds. Plant.

Weeding with pigs

Substitute pigs for chooks, and electric fence for the bales of hay. A neighbour used to get rid of high blackberry bushes this way: surround the bushes with an electric fence, throw in pigs and pig nuts and add a water trough ... and a week later he had no blackberries and a lot of manure-rich mud.

Weeding with guinea pigs

Our guinea pigs are excellent ground clearers. We move their cage over a weedy patch and half a day later it's bare. All you need to do to get your guinea pigs to eat your weeds is to place the guinea pig cage over the weeds – with guinea pigs inside – and wait. The weeds will be nibbled to death. (I class couch and kikuyu grass as weeds when they're in my vegie garden.)

Grow pumpkins around corn to keep down weeds.

Nowadays I use the guinea pig method to clear small patches of ground for planting: a weekend of shifting the guinea pigs through the vegies means I've got enough cleared (and manured) ground to plant next season's peas or lettuces. I also place the cage over dandelions and other nuisance weeds in the lawn.

NB Don't expect your guinea pigs to eat tall, tough or poisonous weeds like bracken – they're good weed exterminators but they can't work miracles. Make sure they also get enough good food.

Hens in mobile cages, rabbits, and tethered sheep or goats can also be used to clear weeds in small areas.

Use green manures

Green manures are plants grown especially as fertiliser. Plant peas or broad beans or lupins thickly, then slash them just before they flower. They'll add nitrogen and organic matter to the soil. Don't dig them in – just part the debris and plant your crops. Some green manures like oats produce root secretions that suppress weed growth and germination. Sunflowers are a cheap, fast-growing green manure that suppresses weed growth. Sow cockie seed thickly.

Outgrow weeds

Use drip irrigation. This waters only the valuable plants, not the weeds. Once your crops have a well-watered head start, they should be able to out-grow the weeds.

Then keep your plants growing strongly. This is the most important strategy of all. Once a plant is about a third grown it can out-compete a weed. Feed and water your plants and they'll be the best weed protection you can have.

KILLING WEEDS

If weeds need to be killed try the following remedies.

Solarisation

Cover weeds with clear plastic. Don't use black plastic: vigorous weeds just grow out from the edges. The ground under clear plastic will be warm and moist, and the weeds grow soft and sappy, and die of rots and mould. This can take three to eight weeks, depending on the temperature. Solarisation also kills weed seeds and pathogens like fusarium wilt.

Urine

Don't shudder, it works on grass and reasonably soft-leafed, spreading weeds. Great on bindii eyes. Pour stale urine (store it in a covered bucket for two days) over weeds like bindii eyes and couch on a dry, hot day. Leave for 48 hours before watering.

Mulch

Cover your weeds with more weeds, old newspaper and hay – as thickly as you can. Even if they poke through the mulch they'll be weakened and easy to pull out.

I have tried nut tree leaf, oak leaf, cypress leaf, pumpkin leaf, mugwort and bracken mulches. They do inhibit the weeds – but may not be worth the work. A lawn clipping mulch is easier, though any mulch will help keep down weeds, if not as well as the weed-suppressing ones. You also have to be careful with weed-suppressing mulches not to suppress the growth of useful plants. Most weeds can be killed by covering them with newspaper for a few weeks.

USE NATURAL HERBICIDES

Some plants produce phytotoxic substances, either from their roots or washed down from their leaves, which inhibit plant growth. Use thickly grown poppies, oats, cabbages or mugwort to clean a weedy area.

Try a barley, oat or other grain 'green manure' to clear a patch of weeds. Slash it and let it decompose on top of the soil. All grains suppress weed germination. Oats works particularly well, but wheat, buckwheat and rye will also help 'clean' an extremely weedy paddock or garden bed.

Potatoes suppress the germination of many weeds around them. Many of the 'stately home' lawns were first planted with potatoes by gardeners who knew their value in 'cleaning' weedy ground.

Weeding with brassicas gone to seed

This is the most effective natural herbicide I know. Let brassicas go to seed – cabbage, caulies, though I prefer broccoli. As it goes to seed it will suppress the germination of all

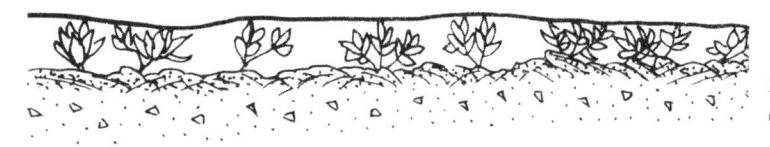

Solarisation with sheets of clear plastic kills weeds

other plants around it, and the growth of those already growing. When you need the space, pull them out. The roots will 'dig' the soil for you, and you will have a relatively weed-free spot to plant carrots, onions, etc.

I let most of my winter broccoli go to seed, then, as I need the space for spring planting, I haul it out and bung it on the compost. A couple of weeks later I plant, or staightaway if the seedlings are ready. But be warned, after a crop of gone-to-seed brassicas, seedling growth can be slow until the residues in the soil break down.

Gladioli as herbicide

I use gladioli to clean up grass- and weed-infested areas before I plant them out. I dig roughly, lay gladdie corms on top THICKLY, then rake. Most of the gladdies grow, though a good few die; but I buy them by the thousand as small bulbs so they are VERY cheap. The gladdies multiply over the next two or three years – and at the end of that time I have a bed of gladdies that can be easily pulled out after they flower and turn brown, leaving bare soil behind. Or I can leave the gladdies in place, thinning slightly so I have new gladdies to clean up other spots, until I need the land.

Dahlias as herbicide

Dahlias are thick- and tough-growing – and not really that ugly if they are growing in masses of other plants. I grow them at the edge of the garden to keep out weeds, or plant thickly, as above, to clear up grassy or weedy patches. Like gladdies, they multiply FAST, and sprawl so well that there is a good bare patch around each clump in winter.

Kiwi fruit as killers

If you have problems with briars or other woody weeds, and a lot of time, try poking two kiwi fruit cuttings in at either side. Let them grow – and sprawl – and eventually cover the weed and kill it. You then have to get rid of the kiwi fruit ...

Silver poplars

We once had a bank of blackberry and thorn bush. I planted very large silver poplar trees – their heads just topped the blackberry. We now have a bank of silver poplars, though there is still some blackberry at the edges (one day we'll get round to mowing it).

Hydrangeas, hibiscus, wormwood, ginger lilies

Take a steep, grassy, weedy slope. Stick in LOTS of hydrangea cuttings or hibiscus (depending on your climate), or wormwood or ginger lilies, depending on which will grow best in that spot. Then wait two or three years.

Climbing perennial seven-year or runner beans

These climb – but they also sprawl. Plant them around weedy areas, in small patches of compost. As they grow they'll suffocate the weeds. I'm sure you get my drift – select the plants that are ultra vigorous in your situation (but controllable by you), with a growth habit that will lend itself to suffocating, strangling or out-shading the target weed – and let them do your dirty work for you.

THE VAMPIRE METHOD

The Vampire Method involves pouring water that has just boiled onto weeds – they shrivel up and die at once. If they have deep roots, like dandelions, thrust a wooden stake into their hearts, just like killing a vampire, and then pour the boiling water down the hole. (I use a tomato stake – for the weeds, that is, not vampires. I suspect I'd have to sharpen the stake more to kill a vampire.)

The Vampire Method is a wonderfully therapeutic activity: just picture your favourite hate object instead of the weed, and cry 'Die vermin, die!' as you pour on the water. Then explain nicely to the neighbours that you were just killing the weeds (you don't have to mention my name) and show them how to do it.

MOW YOUR WEEDS

One mow will not kill weeds. Regular mowing will. Why? Weeds are weeds because animals don't eat them. (If they did, they wouldn't be weeds.) Grass evolved to be eaten. Weeds don't like having their heads cut off regularly.

We have got rid of about 20 hectares of blackberry by mowing it every month or so – just as you might a lawn – for two years. (We knocked the bushes flat first by slashing out the central stem).

A FEW STUBBORN WEEDS

Bamboo

Dig in a metal 'fence' about half a metre deep around the bamboo to stop it from spreading. Pick the bamboo shoots. Sell them, or boil them for 20 minutes, and eat them.

Bindii eyes

Pour on undiluted urine in winter when they stand out bright green against the grass. Don't water for a day.

Blackberry

Burn or hack back the clumps. Then scatter grass seed (this is essential), then either keep mowing or run goats or other stock to eat the soft regrowth. Cover small mounds with choko or banana passionfruit. Build a no-dig garden on top using the blackberry slash as mulch. Circle the affected area with an electric fence and throw in three pigs and a bag of pig nuts.

Bracken

Offer kids a cent a bracken fiddle in spring: a cheaper solution than herbicide. Just keep mowing small areas. In large areas pull an old wire mattress base across the bracken in spring, mid-summer and autumn to break the fronds. Repeat every three weeks for two years.

Briars

Graft on another rose, using stock like hybrid teas. Cattle, sheep, horses, goats or wallabies will eat them and kill the bush. Cut down, then mow.

Broom

Plough: broom doesn't like disturbed roots. Even incomplete digging is often successful. Then re-sow with a good mixed pasture selection. Don't burn it: you'll make the problem worse. A good grass or tree cover will keep an area clear of broom. Poor pasture or overworked land is vulnerable.

Couch grass

Keep it out with a grass barrier, either metal or comfrey. Kill it with clear plastic or undiluted urine. Scatter thickly with sulphate of ammonia, then cover with clear plastic. Leave a week.

Convolvulus, wandering Jew, and other spreaders

Cover with weed-mat, cut tiny holes for seedlings and plant a garden on top. Scatter thickly with sulphate of ammonia, then cover with clear plastic. Leave for a week.

Dock

Use the leaves as mulch until it starts to go to seed. Water very well, then pull it out just before the seed sets – it's easier to pull out then. If dock is slashed for mulch every week it'll die. Pretend it is a vampire: hammer a stake into its heart, then pour down boiling water.

Kikuyu

Fence it out with a metal or comfrey barrier. Ploughing or digging must be repeated at weekly intervals, as kikuyu grows fast. A heavy, temporary stocking of chooks or pigs is the best control.

Lantana

Slash it, or cover it with weed-mat and plant after a few months. Try the pig method (see under 'Blackberry'), then plant sweet potatoes. Grow banana passionfruit over it. Slash it and keep mowing it. There are dozens of ways to get rid of it. But don't even try to get rid of it unless you are going to use the area straight away: the bare patch will just fill up with weeds again.

Lawn daisy

I love lawn daisies. They are one of the earliest spring flowers, and mowing keeps them in check. If you hate them, dig out under the leaves and compost them, but be prepared for a few years of seedlings. Scatter thickly with sulphate of ammonia, then cover with clear plastic. Leave a week. Don't plough with your lawnmower or they will spread.

Nutgrass

Dig it out in late winter/early spring when the roots and tiny tubers are nearly exhausted. Take as much soil as you can and keep it under water for three weeks to kill the bulblets. Mulch must be at least 20 cm deep and maintained for a year to be effective, as the bulblets provide a good food supply for the plant. Repeated cultivation will get rid of nutgrass, but the best solution is to plant lots of thick shrubs like French lavender over it!

Oxalis

Cover with a daisy bush, grevillea, etc. Oxalis grows where grass growth is poor, like under trees. Either resow your lawn or grow something that does better there. If you must dig them out, do it in late winter when food reserves are low.

Paspalum

Cut it with a sharp knife just below the surface. The leftover roots won't regrow. One blow with a mattock should do this.

Sorrel

Good gardening will gradually get rid of sorrel. Mulch it deeply, then pull out the loose rooted regrowth. Run chooks for a few days over the garden bed: chooks love sorrel and will peck at it in preference to most other things. Add dolomite and improve the aeration of the soil with more organic matter. Or just ignore it, and wait until your good garden care eliminates it naturally.

Most important

Water your garden!

ANY plant can become a weed. A plant that is safe in one area may go feral in another. And even so-called 'sterile' varieties may set seed after a couple of decades. So, if a plant starts spreading, get rid of it – fast!

More details on weed management techniques can be found in the author's *Organic Control of Common Weeds* (Aird Books).

Chapter 9

THE VEGETABLE GARDEN

THE IDEAL

A generous producer demanding almost no work (ours gets about three two-hour periods a year). A perennial skeleton of spring onions, perennial beans, berry bushes, chokoes, perennial leeks, surrounded by other crops like parsley, misuba, mizuma, Freckles lettuce, and other veg that reseed themselves, using nitrogen-fixers for nutrition and a little mulch brought in around seedlings for other elements. Surplus plants are pulled out to make room for the few vegetables that need to be planted every year and to provide mulch around the other crops. The soil is so rich in organic matter that simply by pulling out old vegetables the ground is left prepared for the next crop – no digging, weeding, and very little extra fertilising is required.

- *Instead of watering every day or two* … increase the amount of shade in summer with climbing beans or choko on trellises. These will die down to let in winter sun.
- *Instead of neat rows* … grow a ramble of closely planted veg to disguise them from pests, protect from frost and heat, choke out weeds, and stop too much moisture evaporating.
- *Instead of dug beds or no-dig beds with bought hay* … plant seedlings directly into living mulch, or use the easy-care beds described in Chapter 6.
- *Instead of sowing your vegie garden every year* … try a 'self-seeding' or a perennial vegetable garden.
- *Instead of stale packets in the cupboard* … have a bed of fresh herbs by your back door, or a 'wall of herbs' on your patio.
- *Instead of conventional plant-weed-and-pick* … use growing methods like deep planted corn or climbing cucumbers that suit your garden's needs and the weather.
- *Instead of conventional European-based styles of growing vegies* … enjoy a ramble of self-sown vegetables and flowers, tyre terraces, pumpkins in the lawn and melons in the rubbish heap.
- *Instead of tender lettuce and celery* … grow hardy Italian chicory, Chinese celery or lovage, unkillable amaranth, burdock or warrigal spinach.

I can see our main vegetable garden as I write. The top half hasn't been dug for 11 years: the radish, borage, tomatoes, carrots, sweet william, leeks, turnips, sunflowers, spring onions, calendulas, parsley, kumaras, dandelions and perennial beans keep coming up year after year. Every spring I just pull up the surplus to let the seedlings through.

It's fertilised with nitrogen-fixers and last year's weeds as mulch, and the compost from the kitchen scraps is ladled over it in spring. Geese and wombats help manure it. It's dug as surplus radishes are pulled up.

It looks a mess (one visitor this year asked how long I thought it would take to get it 'back into order'), but it produces masses of vegetables – with almost no work.

TEN RULES FOR A HEALTHY VEGIE GARDEN

These rules apply to flower gardens too.

1. Don't plant straight neat rows. Pests can start at one end and march down the row munching, like guests at a smorgasbord. Break up plantings so there are no large groups of one plant; plant small plants near tall ones, shallow rooters like lettuce near deep rooters like carrots, climbers next to long-stemmed corn or sunflowers.
2. Grow flowers and vegetables together. Flowers attract predators to eat the pests, attract bees to pollinate, help break up groups of vegetables so that pests, which track their food either by shape or smell, will find it harder to attack your crops. Vegetables can be beautiful too: just look at ferny fennel (try the bronze variety) or bright yellow zucchini flowers for example. Potatoes were grown as ornamentals for their sweet blue flowers long before chips were even thought of. Try Swiss chard with multi-coloured stems; admire the bright-red flowers of climbing beans, more vivid than sweet peas.
3. Don't plant too early. Spring growth is soft and sappy – just what pests like – and is disease prone. Predators start to breed up some weeks after pests. Wait until the ground warms up, until you can sit on the ground for an afternoon in comfort. Vegetables and flowers planted later will mature at the same time anyway: a cold, slow start stunts them. Start seedlings in pots if you want big seedlings early.
4. Let the best vegetables go to seed. This will give you fresh, free seed next year, adapted to your garden, and the flowers will attract the adult form of many predators.
5. Don't worry about pests and disease. Worry only if they are killing the plant. Put your effort into growing things instead: plant more, mulch more and pick regularly, instead of worrying about killing things.
6. Pick often. Frequent picking stimulates more flowers, more leaves on the silver beet or lettuce, more flowerettes on the broccoli – and it takes you into the garden, to enjoy it.
7. Don't just plant annuals in your flower and vegie garden. Perennials send down deep roots and bring up leached nutrients. They are more drought resistant and their leaves will shade annuals in the heat. With a backbone of perennials your garden will be sure to have flowers or material for mulch – and a year-round food supply for a small number of pests and the predators that eat them: a background security system.
8. Plant nitrogen fixers like beans, peas, sweet peas and broad beans. Peanuts fix nitrogen from the air and add fertility to your garden as their residues break down. Most importantly:
    - Don't dig.
    - Rarely weed.
    - Concentrate on healthy plants, not killing pests.
    - Don't exhaust yourself in spring creating an enormous garden that you can't keep

up with. Unless you like weeding, mulching and thinning every week, use a minimum-work garden.

9. ADD MORE SHADE! In summer our veg are shaded by tall trellises of perennial beans and chokoes and kiwi fruit. The trellises stop the soil from drying out so fast, hide the garden from flying pests, and provide a heck of a lot of food in a small space.
10. Mulch thickly in dry times, right up to the leaves of beans, tomatoes, corn.

WATERING

Plants need water to carry their nutrients and to soften the soil. Water when the soil just below the surface or under the mulch is dry. Mulched plants need less water; deep-rooted perennials also need less water and their leaves will shade the annuals.

If water is scarce, mulch, even with rocks, to cool the soil and keep in moisture; install a drip irrigation system if you have the time and money (a drip system can actually be cheaper than the equivalent hose if you install it yourself).

In hot weather, if you are going to be away for a few days, try upending a bottle of water, with a small hole pierced in the lid, next to fragile plants or seedlings. Moisture will slowly trickle out of the hole. You can do the same with a bucket of water, preferably with a lid and, again, with a small hole in the bottom.

You can still have a vegetable garden, using almost no water at all!

FERTILISING

Feed your flowers and vegies with mulch, even in a weed-mat garden: dry lawn clippings, old leaves, straw, hay, or dry manure. Use 'additives' like blood and bone, liquid manure or hen manure only in an emergency, or if the mulch hasn't many nutrients. Mulches like comfrey, lucerne hay, seaweed, old lawn clippings and compost won't need much else. Try and vary your plants' diet with mulches of more than one ingredient if you can – and do try to give some compost at least every two years. It is almost impossible to give vegies and flowers too much mulch – just make sure the leaves are showing.

If your soil is poor, remember that your mulch may actually remove nutrients from the soil as it breaks down. Use a nitrogen-rich starter – a scatter of hen manure or urine – on top of the mulch until it begins to break down and feed your plants.

WEEDING

Weed-mat and other above-ground gardens will rarely get weeds. The few that appear are easily pulled up.

Annual weeds can just be cut or the tops pulled off. Perennial weeds can be dug out (often difficult), mulched over (try a thick paper mulch with a rock on top), covered with clear plastic (see Chapter 8), or just accepted as a source of fertiliser and mulch.

There is no place for grass in a flower or vegetable garden. Grass slows the growth of other plants, not just by competing for nutrients and water, but by releasing growth inhibitors. Keep grass out with a metal 'grass barrier' (this also keeps out snails, see Chapter 7) or with a thick line of plants like lemon grass (which can harbour snails) or garlic chives).

SPEEDING UP CROPS

- Keep them well fed and watered.
- Use a plant tonic made by soaking nettles, seaweed and chamomile in water for a week then spraying the strained liquid over the plants. This should give them an added fertiliser boost and increase their resistance to heat stress.
- A heat-absorbing dark mulch around plants will speed up their growth. Con-

versely, so will a white or reflective aluminium mulch. A mulch of small rocks will help retain heat, reflect heat, keep the soil moist and keep weeds down. You may also find that a VERY small amount of moisture condenses at night on the warm rocks and trickles down to your veg.
- Dandelions release ethylene, a natural ripener. Couch grass is said to do the same, but the root exudations of couch grass also inhibit the growth of other plants, so what you gain on the one hand with couch grass you'll more than lose on the other. Try to grow dandelions among any marginal crop like okra or eggplant or early tomatoes which you want to mature a little faster
- Weeding isn't a high priority. Contrary to common belief, by the time your plants are a third grown, 'new' weeds won't decrease their growth much; they should be easily able to out-compete them. In addition, the added leaf cover of weeds with their insulating warmth may actually speed other plants' maturing. Crops under apple trees are also reputed to come to maturity faster, though competition for moisture and light may inhibit this.

SEEDLING PROBLEMS

Seedlings disappear. This may be from snails or cutworms. See Chapter 7 or protect seedlings with cut-off bottle tops or cans.

Seedlings wilt. Water them and mulch them. Look for the brown rings at the base indicating 'damping off'. Water with chamomile tea if you find the rings.

Seedlings are yellow. Feed them with the 'additives' given in Chapter 5, until the mulch starts to break down.

Seedlings die. You have probably used too strong a fertiliser (or the neighbour's cat has chosen your garden as a toilet).

Damping off. If the seedlings have a brown ring around the base they are suffering from damping off. Water with chamomile tea, and make sure the mulch isn't too close to them.

Cats or birds scratch up the garden bed. Cover freshly dug soil with bird netting. Use a motion sensing scarecrow.

VEGETABLES

Amaranth

Possibly the most drought-, cold- and heat-hardy veg ever. Grow some varieties for their leaves, others for their seeds (amaranth grain). All grow tall and have gorgeous red flowers, which the birds adore in winter. Plant seed in spring, but once you have let one plant go to seed, seedlings will pop up unbidden. Just thin them out – ruthlessly. Use the leaves like spinach or young leaves in a salad, or a few flowers in a salad too (though they can be tough). The grain can be ground for flour, or boiled like rice, or a little added to rice for extra crunch and texture. Grow climbing beans or peas up the stems.

Arrowroot

The source of arrowroot flour, the fat roots can also be eaten like potato, or grated and added to stews, stir-fries or soups as a thickening agent. Full sun or dappled shade on the edge of groves. Grows the best and fattest roots in moist soil, but survives drought. Grows both in the tropics and temperate climates. Survives frost in groves.

Asparagus

Asparagus used to be grown in a deep trench filled with sifted manure and compost. It was mulched three times a year and weeded constantly. That's why asparagus is a luxury vegetable.

Our asparagus was planted in an old blackberry bed: I laid down mulch and planted in that, on top of the blackberries. The blackberries have grown through a bit, and the whole bed is filled with weeds. This is all to the good: I slash the weeds in late winter and they break down and mulch and fertilise the asparagus. I haven't fed, watered or weeded the bed in 12 years. I might feed it a bit this year if I get round to it, though I've said this for the last four years.

It produces enormous crops of asparagus. We gorge ourselves from September to November, then happily face life without it until next year.

SIMPLE ASPARAGUS

Asparagus is best grown from one- or two-year-old plants: the new seedlings are tiny and can get swamped by weeds. Sow asparagus seed in spring and set out the crowns in winter. Mary Washington asparagus can be harvested two or three years after planting. New varieties will crop after one or two years. The less you pick your asparagus in the first years after planting, the bigger the root system will grow, and the more asparagus you'll get later.

1. Buy some bags of potting mix and hay when you buy the asparagus crowns (or use your own compost).
2. Dig holes in the grass or weeds. Lay down the asparagus crowns, with the roots well spread out.
3. Cover with potting mix, compost, etc.
4. Cover grass or weeds between the plants with hay, old wilted weeds, grass clippings or old leaves.
5. Keep mulching! If there are weeds, there isn't enough mulch.

Don't pick any the first year, or the next year if the spears are spindly. Wait until the spears are as fat as your index finger as they poke through the soil in spring. When they get skinny, stop picking. Let the rest of the spears turn into ferns and wait until next year.

FEEDING

Feed your asparagus for the first two years, either by mulching, or by mulching and sprinkling with blood and bone, hen manure or any of the 'additives' described in Chapter 5. After two years of mulch the soil should be fertile and you need only mulch once a year.

Asparagus dies down in winter. Cover the whole bed THICKLY with mulch, at least ankle height. Use any mulch, as it'll have time to break down over winter. Though, if the mulch is very low in nutrients, scatter on some blood and bone, diluted urine, etc. as well.

Don't worry about weeds: asparagus has large roots and should survive the competition after three or four years, as long as it's fed and mulched in winter.

ASPARAGUS AND COMFREY

First year: plant a row of comfrey.

Second year: when the comfrey dies down in winter plant asparagus in the bare ground next to it. There's always a bare spot next to the comfrey because the leaves are so large they shade out grass and weeds. You can either dig in the asparagus or lay it flat on the ground and cover it with compost and mulch.

In summer: slash the comfrey often and use the leaves to mulch the asparagus. Comfrey and asparagus grow well together: comfrey is deep-rooted and brings up nutrients, and asparagus is shallow-rooted and tall enough to grow above the comfrey.

BEANS AND LENTILS

Try perennial beans. They die down in winter and grow each spring. Mulch them well, or after a few years the big roots will poke out of the soil and rot.

There are at least six perennial varieties of beans available, but you may need to hunt them out. Eat them young and tiny – no bigger than your little finger – or they'll be tough and coarse. Or wait and just eat the seeds of the big ones; they are quite delicious as 'fresh dried' beans. I also leave a lot to hang on the trellis over winter. They dry themselves, and we can cook them as we want them. I always leave just a few as extra seed for next year.

I prefer climbing beans as you get more crop in a small area, with no weeding. The plants grow above the weeds and you have only a small area to mulch and water. You also don't have to bend down to find the beans for dinner.

Plant beans in spring, then a new crop whenever the last lot is flowering: this'll keep you in beans all summer.

Dwarf beans grow well through weed-mat: use one seed per hole. Climbing beans can be sown at the bottom of a tyre garden – they'll trail all over the tyres and won't need staking. Tyre-planted beans grow quickly because of the warmth and moisture and to get to the light.

FEEDING

Don't fertilise beans or you'll get a lot of leaves and no crop. Mulch them instead, either on top of the weed-mat, against the trellis, or wherever you plant them. The higher you mulch the beans the more roots

The higher you mulch a bean plant, the more roots will grow from the stem, giving you more beans and increasing the plant's resistance to pests and disease

If your area is prone to bean fly, snails, or if frost could snap your early beans, try 'beans in a bottle'.

will form on the stem. Mulch up to the bottom leaves if you can, and they'll crop wonderfully. This is also a good remedy for bean fly: the beans outgrow the damage.

BEANS IN BOTTLES

Cut off the top of a plastic bottle. Thrust the top into the soil – water the soil first if it's hard. Throw in some mulch, then a bean seed, and cover with a bit of compost or potting mix.

The bean will germinate quickly in its own hothouse. As it grows, keep mulching – up to the top of the bottle first, then around the bottle.

The advantage of this method is that you don't have to prepare a bean bed at all, just plant them in the lawn. All you need are enough bottles and mulch. The beans grow fast and should be healthy.

INDOOR BEANS

Beans are an attractive indoor plant, especially in winter. Twine climbing beans up a pole, and keep them near a window – purple kings can look lovely.

BEAN SEED

You can grow dried beans and lentils from the supermarket or health food store. Choose fresh looking lentils or dried beans, ones with no dust at the bottom of the packet. Soak them overnight, and plant. I have done this with soybeans, chick peas, lima beans, red kidney beans, green and brown lentils. It doesn't work with dried peas though. They may have been partly cooked before they were dried.

PROBLEMS

Beans get bean fly. Try planting your beans later. Try growing purple king climbing beans and, most of all, add potash to your soil: sprinkle it with wood ash. If pests are bad try growing beans in pure compost and make sure you mulch them up to the bottom leaves. Beans put out new roots along the mulched stem. More roots mean more nutrients, and more pest resistance. As a last resort try glue spray.

Beetroot

Beetroot can't be grown in a weed-mat garden: it just isn't worth it, one plant per hole. Grow beetroot in the bare soil under last year's weed-mat garden. An alternative is to mow some lawn or weeds very close in autumn; rake it deeply and scatter radish seeds thickly. By spring the radish will have taken over the garden. Pull them out and your soil will be dug, ready for carrots or beetroot. Cover with clear plastic for three weeks if you want to be sure the bed is weed-free: weed seeds will germinate, then die under the plastic.

Don't feed beetroot unless the soil is very poor: nitrogen-rich soil means large leaves and no beets. Mulch, as beetroot plants are slow growers and can't stand weed competition when they are small.

BEETROOT IN BOXES

Take an old styrofoam box, fill it with compost or potting mix, and scatter on the seed – it needn't be buried. Water often and well.

This is a foolproof method: no weeds, no competition. All you need to do is water.

PROBLEMS

Don't give beetroot too much fertiliser – you'll get leaves, not root. Keep them weed-free with mulch (newspaper will do) until the roots start to swell: beetroot grows slowly and can be taken over by weeds.

Beetroot is not for the beginner, or for poor soil – no slow-growing plant is. If you haven't grown it before, try the box method. It's safer.

Broad beans

Plant these in autumn and winter. They are nice, big seeds which grow quickly in spring and will overtake any weeds around as long as your soil is good.

Broad beans do well with a deep mulch. They also do well planted against a fence or trellis: broad beans aren't climbers but do grow tall. Otherwise, plant them as close together as you can, they'll support each other. Plant a series of small clumps, not one big one, or else you won't be able to see the beans to pick them.

BROAD BEANS IN A TYRE

Throw down some mulch into two tyres placed on grassy ground. Throw in the seed, then more mulch. As the beans grow, add more mulch. The tyres help support the beans.

BROAD BEANS IN A WIRE GUARD

Make a wire netting tube. Stake it firmly. Throw in some mulch. Throw down the seeds

Broad beans fall over easily: plant them inside a circle of wire mesh, mulch well, and pick the beans through the wire.

in the middle – thickly, there should be almost no mulch showing – then add more mulch. Pick the beans through the wire. This method gives the beans support while maximising the amount of light they get. You will need six to 12 tubes of broad beans for a family of eager broad-bean eaters.

PROBLEMS

Aphids: broad beans may be attacked by aphids in spring. This may mean you've planted them too early. Pick off the tops, wash off the aphids and steam the tops like silver beet. This solves the aphid problems and gives you an extra feed.

Black spot: sprinkle broad bean beds with wood ash or use a comfrey mulch if you have black spot problems. Otherwise use any of the fungicides given in Chapter 7.

Broccoli

Sow this at Christmas for autumn, winter and spring eating. The more you pick your broccoli, the smaller the heads become – but there'll be more and more of them.

Broccoli can be grown in any type of garden. It is excellent in a weed-mat garden. You can even grow three or four broccoli plants in a corner of the lawn, by themselves in their own weed-mat square: just lay down the mat, cut four holes, and plant the seedlings.

Feed broccoli well: the more you pick it the more food it needs. Either keep it well mulched, or feed it every week with one of the liquid fertilisers listed in Chapter 5. For problems, see cauliflower.

Brussels sprouts

See under 'Cauliflower' for cultivation and problems. If your brussels sprouts aren't firm it's either too hot or you've used too much nitrogen to feed them. Mulch instead, for both problems.

Burdock

This is an improved form of the weed – a nutty, giant-rooted veg that tolerates drought, heat, and frost and is quite unstoppable. Play tag with the seed heads – they cling without prickling. I have only planted them once: since then the seedling plants give us all we need, and much more! Don't try digging up the whole root; they can be massive. Great baked with olive oil, or made into soup.

Cabbage

Cabbage can be sown at any warm time of the year, though the firmest heads come from cabbage planted at Christmas for autumn, winter and spring picking. Cabbage can go to seed quickly in hot weather. Pick them as soon as the head seems to elongate – that means it's getting ready to burst to seed.

Grow cabbage in any of the beds described in Chapter 6. See under 'Cauliflower' for problems.

If you pick the main cabbage head and leave the stem, you may get a crop of tiny cabbages growing later.

Capsicum and chilli

Try perennial chilli and bell peppers. They may lose their leaves in cold areas in winter, but will often grow again. Otherwise, grow in the warmest spot you can, by a stone or brick wall in plenty of sunlight, or protect in a plastic, water-filled tree guard.

Some bell peppers are hot as dragon's breath. Others are quite mild. It's worth hunting out both.

Sow capsicum in spring. In mild areas you can mulch them in autumn and they'll shoot again when it warms up. Keep capsicum well mulched, with a little urine or blood and bone added every month. The more you mulch the more roots will form, and the faster the plant will grow.

GETTING SEED

The seeds of dark red capsicum, so ripe it seems thin-skinned, can be dried and sown. Most capsicums in the shops, however, are still green. They can be left until they turn red. Then the seed can be dried in the sun and stored in a dry envelope.

PROBLEMS

Capsicum are frost tender: protect them with cut-off bottle 'greenhouses'. Dig up capsicum bushes in autumn and pot them so that you can ripen the fruit into winter inside the house.

Capsicum may be stung by fruit fly: the insides rot and the outside blisters and goes rotten. See Chapter 7 for fruit-fly control.

Carrots

Try white, red-skinned and yellow carrots. They are MUCH more drought, heat and cold hardy. Save seed from the best each year. You may find that yellow or white carrots seed themselves – ours come up each year.

See 'Beetroot' for carrot cultivation. Carrots also grow well in a box garden. It is a myth that carrots need deeply dug soil: carrots will do their own digging, though they may bend a bit in the process. Above-ground garden beds are excellent for carrots.

ABOVE-GROUND CARROTS

Spread a thick layer of compost (at least 30 cm). Sprinkle on the carrot seed. Scatter a thin layer of straw or dried lawn clippings over the seed. Water every day until the seedlings appear, as the soil or compost will dry out.

Don't thin carrots. Just pull them up when they are finger-sized and eat them: small carrots are very sweet. Then the rest will have more room to grow.

Carrots are best sown in spring for all-year eating, though they taste best after a frost. Red Changenay seem to resist going to seed longest in spring.

PROBLEMS

Don't dig in undecomposed organic matter or the carrots may rot. Leave it on top for mulch.

Carrot fly: See sap suckers. Grow nasturtiums or flowering clover around the carrot bed. Hose strongly every day and add compost, wood ash or a comfrey mulch to the soil. Use the repellent or pyrethrum sprays in Chapter 7.

CARROT SEED

This is a children's game. Choose a dark orange, thickish carrot. Cut off the top – it should be about as long as your thumb. Place it on wet cottonwool. It should start to sprout. Now plant it out in the garden so the top is just showing. By the end of the season it should have gone to seed. Keep it staked so it doesn't fall over.

Alternatively, plant the whole carrot back in the garden and wait for it to shoot again. This will give you a better base for the seed head.

Cauliflower

These can be planted through the year, but Christmas is best for planting cauliflowers to

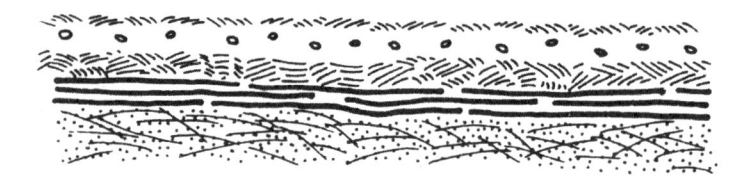

There's no need to dig at all to get a crop of carrots: just scatter the seed over some compost spread out on a layer of newspaper.

mature in autumn to spring. Summer cauliflowers turn purple and become tough.

Cauliflowers are excellent grown in any of the gardens described in Chapter 2.

Try cutting the head off the cauliflower instead of pulling it up. Small heads should form around the stalk, and these can be eaten too. Once the stalk starts to rot, though, remove it or it will inhibit other plants.

PROBLEMS

Caterpillars: use glue spray or Dipel. Grow lots of other plants in between the cauliflowers to disguise their shape: the butterflies that lay the eggs that turn into the caterpillars recognise plants by their shape. Grow nasturtiums or clover in between the plants, or pots of herbs like lavender.

Aphids: plant the cauliflowers later; you have probably planted them too early. Add potash to the soil with wood ash, comfrey or compost. Hose them strongly, or make a spray of glue and water to suffocate the aphids.

Molybdenum deficiency: many Australian soils are molybdenum deficient. If the leaves are tall and narrow, you may need to add this trace element to your soil.

Chokoes

We grow our chokoes up the trees. They take up no extra room in the garden, bear masses of fruit, and don't get watered, weeded, fed or tended. Just picked. Or fed to the chooks. Or ignored.

If you hate chokoes, try eating them when they are no bigger than your little finger nail and can be eaten peel and all, whole. They are delicious – far nicer than zucchini. A real luxury veg, and only available home-grown.

And with a choko ... well, civilisation may fall, but you'll still have chokoes to eat. Choose the largest choko you can, preferably with the seed or shoot just starting to poke out the top. Leave it in a dry, dark place, well ventilated, until it starts to shoot. Plant it in spring with the shoot upwards. If it is shooting strongly in mid-winter, plant it in a pot indoors in a well-lit spot. Shooting can be slowed down by putting it in the refrigerator. The shoot can also be trimmed if it gets too long.

Chokoes die down after frost and re-sprout only in warm soil. They will climb as high as the tallest pine tree. Chokoes can be grown as far south as Melbourne as long as they are grown near a warm wall and are heavily mulched in autumn so they don't freeze in winter. Even if the crop doesn't mature, the immature chokoes can still be eaten.

In very cold areas grow them as an annual and start the young plants indoors in a pot in late winter.

PROBLEMS

Chokoes are usually too abundant. Feed them to the chooks, compost them, or give them away. Don't feel you have to eat the lot.

Celery

Try Chinese celery – smaller, more drought hardy and very fast growing; or 'wild' celery, a small perennial; or celeriac, a big rooted, and quite delicious celery, again cold and drought hardy. Try a combined potato and celeriac mash. Or red stemmed celery – stunning.

Celery needs a lot of feeding or it becomes thin and stringy. Plant it in spring and eat it until next summer. Mulch it heavily in spring to stop it from going to seed too soon, and pick out the seed-head stalks.

Feed celery every week with liquid manure, urine or a little hen manure if you want tender fat celery. Celery and lettuce are the only two vegetables that really do need 'additives' for feeding. But if you end up with stringy celery, use it for soup or stock. It'll taste excellent – just throw the stringy stuff to the chooks.

Don't waste celery leaves either. Chop for salads. Bung in stews. Makes great soup.

PS Remember, don't pick the whole plant, like the bunches bought in shops. Just pick the stems you want and leave the rest to grow. Celery is great value in the garden; plant six or 12 plants and you can eat them until they go to seed next spring ... and even then you can eat the leaves and scatter the seeds on bread rolls before cooking.

CELERY IN A BOTTLE

As for 'Beans in a bottle'. Grows faster and is more tender.

BLANCHED CELERY

Wrap stems, not leaves, in newspaper for two weeks to make them softer and more tender before you pick them. Great when it's hot and dry.

PROBLEMS

Small hard celery: not enough food.

Spots and blotches: spray celery spot with Bordeaux. If you have problems with blotchy celery, grow it in a weed-mat garden or use a mulch between the plants to stop spores splashing up, and to lower humidity as moisture evaporates from the soil or mulch. You can also just pick off the affected bits and hope the new shoots are disease free. A weekly seaweed spray will help keep celery healthy.

Celeriac (turnip-rooted celery)

Grow this like celery, though celeriac is hardier. It likes frequent watering when young. Boil the roots and have them as a cooked vegetable (beautiful cold with mayonnaise), in soups, or you can grate them raw for salads. Sow seeds in spring.

PROBLEMS

See 'Celery'; but celeriac is even hardier and more problem-free.

Chrysanthemum, edible

Annual, very hardy. Eat the leaves in salads or cooked. Lovely flowers. Survives anything except wombats and wallabies. Sow any warm time of year.

Chicory

I grow masses of Italian red-ribbed chicory; looks lovely either growing or in salads, great steamed or stir fried, and much hardier than lettuce in cold, heat, and drought. See lettuce for cultivation. Sow any warm time of year.

Collards

Non-hearting cabbage type veg. Cold and drought hardy. Plant in summer, harvest leaf by leaf in winter when the leaves are sweetest. Can be a bit sulphurous in hot weather.

Corn

Think of corn as a grass. It needs plenty of feeding and watering to bear well. I try to mulch corn as high as I can, and I give it a little liquid manure every week for the first four weeks. Then I ignore it until it crops. Sow seed in spring and then every week until autumn.

High mulching will protect it from early frosts as well as help it through droughts. In very dry times cover seed with 30 cm of sand. The plant will find its way upwards, and the deep roots will help protect it.

CORN IN WEED-MAT

Plant one seed or seedling per hole. Feed with liquid manure every week, unless the soil is very fertile.

CORN IN TYRES

Place one tyre on top of another. Place spoonfuls of compost or potting mix inside, all around the edge and in the middle: a bit like the spokes on a bike. Plant the seed or seedlings. Keep moist. You'll get a clump of fast, tall-growing corn. Mulch it regularly, as it keeps growing until the tyres are full of mulch.

WINTER CORN

Corn is frost sensitive but can be kept ripening through winter. It won't be sweet but will be better than no corn at all. Simply mulch it right up to the top leaves with a loose mulch like hay or bracken.

CORN SEED

Don't bother keeping corn seed; most sold today is hybridised and won't come true-to-type – unless you have bought open-pollinated seed from a seed merchant who specialises in old varieties.

PROBLEMS

Caterpillars: Paint the tassels with mineral oil to repel caterpillars. Squeeze the tops of the cobs every day to kill caterpillars inside. Spray with Dipel, a commercialised caterpillar-killing bacterium.

CORN SALAD

This is a spicy salad plant. Sow seed in late summer to autumn. Pick the leaves as you want them. Corn salad is incredibly hardy.

Cucumbers

I grow cucumbers up a trellis. This gives them better air circulation so they are less prone to mildew. You also get more cucumbers and the plant takes up less space. Gherkins, Lebanese cucumbers, telephone cucumbers, apple cucumbers, Dutch yellow cucumbers: the cultivation is the same for all. Try Giant Russian cucumbers – very vigorous – or apple cucumbers in cooler areas. Sow seed after the frosts have finished and the soil is warm. Mulch. Give liquid manure for the first three weeks, then forget about them.

CUCUMBERS ON A PILE OF WEEDS

Place spadefuls of soil, compost or potting mix on the sides of a pile of weeds. Plant your cucumbers. The heat from the decomposing weeds will speed them along and they'll trail down the heap.

CUCUMBERS IN A HANGING BASKET

These are great in hot humid conditions, especially grown over paving. Also good in cold climates and of course on patios.

CUCUMBERS IN TIN CANS

Pierce a few holes in the bottom of a can. Fill it with potting mix or compost, or even soil. Nail it onto a post, wall or door jamb. Plant out the cucumber and let it trail down.

Water often and feed with liquid fertiliser every week. Cucumbers grown this way usually aren't affected by powdery mildew, and they bear earlier. They can even be grown through winter on a sunny window sill.

Cucumbers like to trail: grow them in cans nailed to a board which can be hooked over the window sill.

PROBLEMS

Powdery mildew: spray with milk spray. Cucumbers planted on weed-mat and then trained up a trellis are less likely to be affected, as are cucumbers grown to trail out of hanging baskets over paving. New plants are also less prone to mildew: so, plant a succession of cucumbers rather than trying to keep the old ones going. Compost-fed cucmbers are healthier. Test it and see! Cucmbers are also more mildew prone if they are alternately too wet and too dry – if it's a wet season, keep the soil moist in between deluges.

Snails: they love cucumber seedlings. See Chapter 7 for snail control.

Misshapen cucumbers: these haven't been pollinated properly; plant flowers to attract bees, and avoid using pesticides. Threaten to build a 6-metre brick dividing wall or plant a *leylandii* cypress hedge if your neighbours use pesticides.

Bitter cucumbers: these have been left to grow too big in hot weather – pick them small.

SEED

Take seed from a cucumber that is yellowing, and not dark green. Cucumber seeds can be washed from the plant, then dried in the sun. Germinate on blotting paper or cottonwool first, to test the seed and not waste potting space.

Dandelion

A perennial, grown for its leaves or roots. Use the large-leafed, improved varieties, which give a far better crop. Leaves are sweetest in winter or early spring; or cover with mulch (or an old box) for two weeks to remove their bitterness and make them more tender. (Heat and dry increase the bitterness.) Just pick the leaves as you want them and each plant will crop for years. Digging up the root kills the plant, and though they can be baked in cider or apple juice, or baked until crisp and ground for coffee, I find them too bitter. But others like them.

Eggplant

These grow like tomatoes but need more time to mature. Sow seed in spring. Pick fruit often, so more form. Mulch right up to the leaves, especially in dry weather. Grow well in pots and hanging baskets, especially the ones with small egg shaped fruit – as attractive as any ornamental.

PROBLEMS

Fruit fly: see Chapter 7 for fruit fly control. Fruit fly blotches are usually small in eggplant and can be cut out before you use the fruit.

No fruit: this is probably because of poor pollination. Grow eggplant in a sunny spot with a few flowers around: eggplant flowers seem less attractive to bees than many other vegetable flowers. Bees may need to be lured to the eggplant patch.

SEED

Choose an eggplant that is very dark and ripe, with dark seeds in it. Eggplant fruit can also be left in the cupboard until they start to wrinkle – the seed may ripen inside. Leave the seedy flesh in a jar of water until it starts to ferment, then wash out the seeds and dry them.

Globe artichokes

Hardy, love sun, survive drought. Plant seeds in spring and you may get an autumn crop; otherwise divide plants each winter. Perennial. Pick the chokes before they open into flowers – older big ones are tougher, tiny ones so tender you can eat the whole thing, baked with olive oil and potatoes, steamed or boiled or deep fried. A wonder survivor. Also stunning if you don't pick the chokes and they open into purple blue blooms.

Jerusalem artichokes

Plant these once and you'll always have them – they'll just pop up each year. DON'T grow them where you may need to get rid of them. Choose the fattest tubers you can. Keep them in a dark, dry place (not the refrigerator) and plant them in spring, or in a temporary pot on the window sill if they start to shrivel during winter.

Jerusalem artichokes can be sown in the lawn or in a bed of weeds. They may be small the first year if they have a lot of competition, but will gradually get bigger. They are attractive plants, like giant daisies or small sunflowers. We grow them for their appearance as well as for their tubers – and for the knowledge that once you have a bed of Jerusalem artichokes, you'll never starve. You will, however, 'break wind'. Eat Jerusalem artichokes only with close friends, or alone.

They also survive a surprising amount of shade. We grow ours at the edges of the groves. The yield is reduced – but they are so prolific this can be a relief.

Try them in the flowerbeds, too. If you didn't know they were edible you'd grow them just for the flowers – masses of tall bright yellow blooms. If planted in a thick row they also make good wind breaks for young trees or veg that need protection.

Kale

An ultra-hardy cabbage type veg. Pick leaf by leaf. Sow any warm time of year, cold to temperate climates only. Sweetest in cold weather. Best chopped fine and stir fried with onion, garlic and a touch of soy.

Kumaras

These are New Zealand sweet potatoes – not real sweet potatoes, but more a cold-tolerant cultivated form of oxalis. Choose fat tubers – from the supermarket if you can't get them from a seed supplier. Plant them after frosts are over and keep them weed free. They need six frost-free months for large tubers. Kumaras need a high-phosphorous/low-nitrogen diet. Harvest in autumn or after the tops die down. Kumaras must be exposed to light for at least two weeks after harvest or they will taste revolting. They are good baked or in soup.

KUMARAS IN THE LAWN

Dig a small hole with a tablespoon, just big enough for the kumara. Cover with soil. Surround the hole with mulch: hay or wilted weeds, or dry grass clippings. Water often, and keep the young plants mulched. Add more newspaper if the weeds threaten to take over.

KUMARAS IN A TYRE

Throw some hay or, better still, wilted comfrey into a tyre. Toss in a few kumaras. Throw on more hay. Harvest in autumn.

KUMARAS IN A BUCKET

See under 'Potatoes'.

Leeks

We mostly eat perennial leeks now. They are tiny if you let them grow into clumps, but large as normal leeks if transplanted every year. Very, very, very hardy and prolific. And the tiny ones make a great leek and potato soup.

Sow seed in spring to late summer. I let some leeks go to seed every year. They raise a large clump of small leeks around them. We use these little leeks instead of the fat whoppers – they are thin, but tender and sweet. This is much easier than planting out leek seedlings. Leeks grow slowly and are often lost under weeds or encroaching tomato bushes.

Our leeks simply absorb their nutrients from the mulch around them. The more you mulch, the better your leeks will be. In dry times, mulch almost up to the top of the leaves. In cold climates you can speed up a crop of autumn leeks with a rock mulch.

PROBLEMS

Tough leeks: these are going to seed. Let them – and let the seed sow itself, and harvest next year's crop instead.

Thin leeks: not enough food – according to the lore of the supermarket, that is, which says that leeks must be fat and soggy. Eat the thin ones anyway. The taste will probably be excellent.

Lettuce

Lettuce can be grown all year round – just choose your lettuce variety. I grow mostly Freckles lettuce as it is drought resistant and doesn't go bitter if it wilts. It will even come back from its roots if the tops die off in the dry. Also try mignonettes and cos and perennial lettuce. (You just pull off a leaf as you want it.) These grow at any time of the year, and I can let them go to seed themselves and harvest the self-sown ones.
Lettuce is tenderest if fed with liquid manure once a week and watered daily in hot times – after all, it's mostly water. Mulch lettuce thickly in dry times; speed up lettuce in autumn or winter with a rock mulch, or in spring with a miniature 'glasshouse' made from the top of a clear plastic orange juice bottle. These will also keep snails from eating the seedlings.

Miniature lettuce: plant lettuce thickly (seed germinates easily and one lettuce will give you thousands of seeds) and pick it finger high.

PROBLEMS

Bitter lettuce: these have been stunted at some time by too much heat, not enough water, or too little food. Slow lettuce is bitter lettuce. Grow mignonettes instead, or use 'liquid manure' weekly, and water daily.

Slimy lettuce: these have been watered too much in hot weather and have cooked. On the other hand, without the watering they would have turned bitter. Choose another variety with thicker leaves – it's usually the iceberg lettuces that go slimy.

Snails and slugs: these love lettuce. See Chapter 7 for snail and slug control.

Maize

A hard kernel corn, producing much more abundant crops than sweet corn. Great chook food, and a hardy drought survivor. Immature cobs can be eaten like sweet corn, or grind the dried corn into cornmeal. See under 'Corn'.

Marrows

See 'Zucchini'.

Melons and pumpkins

We grow lots of chilacayote melons these days. They are perennial melons that fruit in autumn and early winter, then die back and grow again in spring. They are VERY prolific, and will grow 20 metres up a tree; or they're great as ground covers. Drought hardy, pest free. Eat the tiny ones as zucchini, or the big ones chopped into fruit salad or stir-fried. They don't have any flavour, so are versatile, but have an excellent texture. Also make a great melon and ginger jam. And once you have them, you'll have lots! Great value in any garden, especially as they can take up very little room if you grow them up trees. Vigorous pumpkin varieties like Queensland blue and ironbark can also be trained up trees.

Sow melons and pumpkins in spring. Don't plant them in the garden bed: they'll spread and take up all the bed. Train them up a trellis instead, or plant them at the edge of the garden and train them outwards. In cold areas look for mini melons – they mature in about 10 weeks.

Just grow pumpkins on the lawn in a spadeful of compost; the sprawling vine will outgrow the grass.

Hang the vines up in the shed at the end of autumn: the pumpkins or melons will continue to ripen. Eat small pumpkins like zucchini – either immature ones or ones you don't need as whoppers. Pumpkin flowers can also be eaten. Stuff them or fry them. Nip off the ends of pumpkin vines in late summer to speed up the maturing pumpkins.

Pick melons and pumpkins when the stalks wither. If you want a giant pumpkin for the show, insert a little strand of cottonwool in the base of the stalk, and leave one end in a saucer of 9 parts water and 1 part urine.

Pumpkins should be matured for keeping by baking them in a hot, sunny place, such as a shed roof, for a week before storing. Make sure they are stored in a dry place with good ventilation.

In case of starvation, try stir-fried pumpkin tendrils.

MELONS OR PUMPKINS IN A WEED BED

See 'Cucumbers'. This method is excellent for all trailers. By the end of the season the weed pile is usually flat enough to plant cabbages or cauliflowers instead.

PUMPKINS IN GRASS

Place a spadeful of compost on the grass, and plant the pumpkin seedling. Water and feed with liquid manure until it starts to spread. It should be vigorous enough to outgrow the grass.

BUSH PUMPKINS

These don't spread. You can grow them neatly in the garden or in a pot, including indoors in winter. Also good in hanging baskets, especially on hot patios. The pumpkins are usually small – one meal's worth – and mature very quickly.

PROBLEMS

Powdery and downy mildew: grow pumpkins on weed-mat or grow the vines in well-mown grass instead of in a humid vegetable garden where the air can't move and is full of moisture evaporating from other vegetables. As a last resort, spray with milk spray. Young and vigorously growing vines are more mildew resistant.

Rotten pumpkins: these may not have been ripe when you picked them. Store pumpkins on their sides so moisture does not collect around the stem.

SEED

The riper the melon or pumpkin, the more likely that the seed will germinate. You can plant the seed from a melon or pumpkin bought in a shop. Unfortunately, most ripe melons and pumpkins come mid or late season. The early ones are rarely ripe enough, so that when you do get the seed it is too late to plant it. Dry it for next year. Melon and pumpkin seed should be hard-shelled when they are ripe, unless they are Pepita or Triple Treat pumpkins with hull-less seeds.

Mesclun mix

This is a mix of salad veg. Grow like lettuce.

Millet

Canary seed will give you millet: small, fine seeds that can be added to stews or bread, or fed to the canary. Sow canary or budgie seed in spring and through summer. Pick the seed heads and dry them for later use, or give them fresh to the budgie.

Mizuna and mitsuba

Chinese green veg. Grows so fast you can eat them six weeks after planting – or a month after the drought breaks and previously dormant seeds in the soil spring into life. Tolerate drought. Let them all go to seed naturally, then you'll always have seedlings coming up, except in the most dry times. Then when it rains you'll have a mass again. Eat small or large. Flowers can be stir fried too.

Mustard

Try red-leafed mustard; eat young leaves boiled or stir fried or micro-waved – they'll be spicy but good. Very, very hardy veg in heat, drought or cold. Sow any warm time of year. Pick leaf by leaf.

Okra

Needs temperate to hot climates. Grows like tomatoes. Quick, and use the pods as small as possible – big ones are woody and tasteless.

Onions

We mostly grow clumps of perennial spring onions. No planting weeding feeding or pests. They just grow, and we pick and eat. Good chopped anywhere that other onions are eaten.

Onions for storage are planted in winter. Onions for fresh eating, and spring onions are planted in spring. They are slow growing and easily smothered by weeds. Try growing them in a box like beetroot, or cut a long line in the weed-mat and plant seedlings along it, very close together – they will grow outwards.

Never plant onions where organic matter like mulch or manure has been dug in: the onions may rot. Like carrots, onions don't need to be in dug soil. They'll force their own way down.

ONIONS AND PANSIES

Grow your onions with a companion crop of pansies. The pansies will keep the weeds down, look beautiful and insulate the onions. You'll get more onions than if you'd planted them by themselves.

ONIONS UNDER THE RUBBISH HEAP

Push along last year's heap of old corn stalks and melon vines. Plant the onions in the bare, weedless ground below. As the onions grow, use material from the rubbish heap to mulch them.

ONIONS AND CLEAR PLASTIC

If you like bare ground, make it weed-free for onions by covering it with clear (not black) plastic for three weeks. This will germinate weed seeds and kill them in the hot, wet, airless area under the plastic. Mulch the onions, to stop stray seeds blowing in and germinating.

TREE ONIONS

These produce several bulbs under the plant and more small ones instead of seed on top of the stalks. Plant the bulbs in spring or early summer.

PROBLEMS

Weeds: grow them in weed-mat or in a weed-free area like last year's weed-mat garden.

Onion neck rot: avoid decomposed organic matter in the soil. Keep it on top and let the worms pull it down.

SEED

Take a healthy looking onion, not squishy in the centre, and plant it so the pointed side is upwards and just poking out of the soil. Wait.

If it hasn't been artificially treated to stop sprouting, two times out of three it will start to sprout again. These sprouts will eventually go to seed, and the seed can be harvested.

Parsley

I let our parsley go to seed, so we always have new plants coming up, both curly and Italian varieties. I also edge the flowerbed in the front garden with parsley – a lovely green froth, and ready by the front door when I need a quick handful. Also good grown in hanging baskets or thickly around trees in tubs. Especially good with fuchsias and citrus.

Parsley seed can be sown any time but is slow to germinate, taking from three to six weeks. Soak it overnight in hot water first to speed it up. Keep the soil moist. We let our parsley go to seed, then replant the wild seedlings, or just let them grow where they come up. This usually means a thicket of parsley – good for tabouli and mashed potato – on the edges of the lawn or in the driveway. Once parsley gets going it's hardy. It also grows well in weed-mat, in pots or as a border along the garden. Plant it where its seed can fall naturally the next year.

Try eating parsley root grated in salads or steamed. It's good.

In dry or cold climates try Hamburg rooted parsley – the big root mean it's hardier. The root is also superb. Beware though: much so-called Hamburg seed sold is ordinary Italian parsley.

PROBLEMS

Yellowing parsley: this is from a root rot. Make sure the soil is well drained. Drizzle with chamomile tea or garlic spray.

Parsnips

Parsnips grow like weeds – if you can get them to germinate. Don't bother with ideas like covering the seed with hessian. If the seed is fresh it will germinate, if it isn't it won't. Parsnip seed only lasts a year and most seed you buy is older than that.

We have parsnips coming up in the lawn, and in the drive: once a plant has gone to seed you'll always have them. Any roughly cleared ground, where you've pulled up lettuce or cabbage for example, will do to scatter some parsnip seed. Plant them in spring or summer and eat them until next spring. They taste better in winter, after a frost.

If parsnips come up in the lawn or under trees give them a few drinks of liquid manure, as they'll need extra tucker with the grass competition or you'll end up with skinny tough parsnips.

PROBLEMS

All top and no bum: planted too early in cold soil, or in need of more tucker.

Gone-to-seed before producing a good root: planted too early.

Peas

Grow climbing peas: the short varieties still tend to collapse, and who wants to crouch down to harvest them?

Plant peas in spring, then from Christmas to winter. Peas won't set in hot weather, though you can try growing a hot-weather crop under a pergola. Any pea can be picked as a snow pea before the pods form, but genuine snow peas are tenderest. Try 'snap' peas too: eat them pod and all. Add pea pods to the soup for extra flavour, and scoop out the pods at the end of cooking.

Peas need rich soil. I grow them along a trellis and mulch them well. Once established, they don't need weeding – they grow above the weeds. You can also grow them in a wire tube: see 'Broad beans'.

PEAS ON A STAKE

Hammer a stake into the grass. Top it with an old bicycle wheel, or radiate more stakes out from the top. Plant pea seed in compost around the stake – three rows deep. Train the peas up the stake, then along the spokes, trailing them over and around until they twine thickly over the lot.

PEAS IN BUILDERS' MESH, CHOOK WIRE OR LATTICE

Place bricks in the garden. Top with mesh, wire or lattice. Plant seeds. As the plants grow through the mesh it'll help support them.

TRAILING PEAS

Plant peas in a window box or hanging basket– and let them trail down the wall.

PROBLEMS

Powdery mildew: plant peas in an airy part of the garden, not in the middle of other vegetables where it will be humid. Mulch well to stop spores splashing up. Clean up pea debris at the end of the season if they are infected.

Birds: cover the pea plants with an old mosquito net or fruit fly netting. Spray the plants red with watercolour. Pick peas ever day so birds don't get in the habit of feasting on them.

Potatoes

Potatoes can grow from seed, but you won't get good tubers for two years. Plant a potato instead – this is really what 'seed potatoes' are – or a hunk of potato with a shoot on it. This will give you more potatoes.

Harvest potatoes when the tops have died down. Put them in bags straight away: they turn green very fast when first dug and exposed to sunlight. Green potatoes are poisonous.

POTATOES IN TYRES

NB Above-ground methods of growing spuds need more water than in-ground methods.

Throw down some straw or sawdust in an old tyre. Throw in a potato, then more straw. As the potato grows, keep it mulched so only the top leaves are showing, adding one or more tyres as required. To harvest, just kick over the tyres – no digging is needed.

Alternatively, dig a hole in the soil with a trowel and bury the potato. Place an old tyre over it. Now throw in any old weeds, hay, or dry lawn clippings. Keep doing this as the potato grows, until only the top leaves show. Even though the potato is in the soil, the tubers will mostly form above the ground, in the loose mulch on either side of the stem.

POTATOES IN A BUCKET OR BOX

Place a thin layer of soil or compost in a bucket or box. Make sure the box has enough holes, so water can drain out. Lay on a potato and cover with mulch. Keep covering until you can only see the top leaves and the bucket or box is full.

When the potato dies down, empty out the bucket – it should be full of potatoes.

Potatoes grown in a bucket can be brought inside during frosty nights and taken out again on sunny days: just like taking the dog for a walk.

130   THE WILDERNESS GARDEN

POTATO TRENCH WITH BROAD BEANS

This is good for dry years. Plant broad beans in autumn. Dig a long thin trench, just wide enough for a potato, in the middle of the beans. In August plant spuds in the trench, about 5cm apart. Fill in the trench with soil or compost. As the beans stop producing use them as mulch for the spud plants.

POTATO BANDICOOTING

We have a wild patch of potatoes. It keeps growing, as we never entirely harvest the crop. I just wriggle my hand down and pull out what we need without disturbing the tops (the definition of 'to bandicoot'). Any weeds in that part of the garden, old corn stalks, prunings, etc. are tossed onto the potatoes – it's the only mulch and feeding they get.

They've been feeding us for 10 years. Note: This doesn't work where lots of people are growing potatoes and aphids may spread disease from one crop to another. In that case you need to buy in fresh seed potatoes every year, and plant in a different part of the garden.

POTATOES IN THE GRASS

Dig a hole just big enough for the potato. Cover it. Throw 30 cm mulch on top. Keep the plant mulched to the top leaves as it grows.

POTATOES IN A PILE OF WEEDS

Tuck potatoes into a pile of weeds. Kick the pile to bits in autumn and harvest the potatoes.

PROBLEMS

Potato moth: hill the potatoes or make sure they are mulched to the top of the plant so the moth can't get into the tubers or their stalk.

Green potatoes: these have been too near the surface, so mulch.

Hard potatoes: these have been infected with a virus; use certified seed potatoes. Make sure you get rid of all infected potatoes. Grow a companion crop of garlic then broad beans after the spuds and cover the soil with clear plastic to help sprout any small tubers left in the ground.

Aphids: mulch heavily, and aphids will avoid the plants.

Ladybirds: mulching up to the top leaves will keep them mostly away. Spray with glue spray. In very bad cases an aluminium foil mulch will repel them, or a diatomaceous earth spray will kill them.

Rotten potatoes: make sure the soil is well drained with no undecomposed organic matter in it. Don't plant potatoes where there have been rotten potatoes for at least five years.

SEED

Technically it is illegal in most states to grow potatoes from any but certified seed. Don't grow non-certified seed in a potato-growing area: you may spread disease. Aphids can carry potato virus for many kilometres. Choose healthy looking potatoes. Avoid ones with long shoots: they may be infected with a virus.

Choosing your seed potato from the supermarket, however, gives you access to gourmet varieties, most of which aren't sold in garden centres as seed potatoes and have to be ordered in bulk if you want them. And even then they are hard to get hold of. Look for waxy yellow potatoes, or white-fleshed perfect baking Colibans. Tasmanian pink eyes are best for potato salad.

The real 'potato seed', produced on the bush after flowering, can also be planted – but you'll need to wait two years for a decent crop. Planting cross-pollinated potato seed is a good way of developing new varieties of potato.

Pumpkins

See under 'Melons'.

Radish

There are long red and short red radish, long white daikon radish (mild and good), green radish, black radish, winter radish and tiny spring radish that mature in three weeks. Once you let radishes go to seed you'll always have them. Grow different radishes at different times of the year.

If you don't like radishes try them steamed or stir fried – much milder and very good. Or pickle them. Or grate them and serve with salad dressing.

Try stir-fried radish seed pods – spicy but crunchy. Good with peanut sauce. Throw monster gone-to-seed radishes to the chooks.

PLOUGHING WITH RADISHES

We grow a lot of radish. In the jungle part of our garden they fill up bare spaces that might become infested with weeds. When I water the ground I pull them out – and find the soil ready dug for me.

Radish seed germinates in a few days. One plant produces a lot of seed.

PROBLEMS

None. A child can grow radish just by throwing down the seed.

Rhubarb

If rhubarb is well fed it will outgrow weeds and grass, but it must be well fed, especially if you pick it often. Plant rhubarb near the kitchen, where you can get at it, both to pick it and feed it. It will tolerate semi-shade under a tree – the stems just grow longer – but will need even more feeding because of competition from the tree roots. I have planted rhubarb into lawn, weed-mat, no-dig straw-and-paper gardens, and on top of a spadeful of compost on a (very) old disintegrating carpet. All grew well.

Keep rhubarb well mulched. If the leaves look small, give it any of the additives listed in Chapter 5 – especially old hen manure or even diluted urine. Rhubarb leaves are thick and can stand occasional doses of high nitrogen. If the stems are short and the leaves are big, you have given it too much nitrogen. The best mulch I ever gave my rhubarb was comfrey leaves – but you need a lot of leaves.

Sow rhubarb seed at any time of the year, though plants won't come true-to-type and you may have to select the best. The problem with using rhubarb seed is that the resulting plants have a tendency to go to seed too. Root divisions are best: just take a slice from the outside with a leaf-bearing knob on it, and plant it in winter or early spring.

Some rhubarb varieties crop all year in temperate areas, others only in summer. Some stems are fat and green, some red and narrow.

Don't wait for green stems to turn red – they won't.

If you have blackened saucepans, try cleaning them by boiling rhubarb in them, or use rhubarb leaves (these are poisonous). Boil up rhubarb root to get a blonde rinse for your hair.

RHUBARB IN HANGING BASKETS

Very drought hardy, this crops even during winter if grown over warm, sunny paving. Looks quite ornamental, especially if you choose red-stemmed varieties.

PROBLEMS

Beetles: Interplant with chrysanthemums or use glue spray.

Rosella

Use the petals to make jams, or stew with apples. Needs a long growing season. Sow in spring. Grow like tomatoes.

Scorzonera (oyster plant)

The long, thin roots taste like oysters. Use them in soups or creamed like mashed potatoes. Sow the seed in spring and harvest the roots through winter and spring. Peel them under water, or the sap will stain your hands. See 'Carrots' for cultivation. Ours go to seed each year, and seedlings come off spasmodically throughout the year, usually after rain.

Silver beet

I grow mostly ornamental beet, with bright red, orange or yellow stems, mostly because I like the look of them, but the leaves are also more tender than the giant green varieties. I leave the best to go to seed each year, and let some self-sow. But self-sown ones often don't start cropping until late summer, so I keep seed to plant each spring too.

Sow silver beet seeds in spring and harvest the plants until the next spring. If you pick off the seed heads you may keep your silver beet producing for several years.

The more you pick silver beet the more you need to feed it. If you only pick it once a week, a regular mulch should give enough nutrients. Otherwise try the additives in Chapter 5, or use liquid manure weekly. Don't worry if the leaves aren't as big and dark as shop-bought ones. As long as your leaves are fat, not narrow with scarcely more leaf than centre, they are adequately fed.

Silver beet grows excellently in weed-mat or no-dig gardens. It also grows well in a pot or hanging basket in a sheltered space so it produces more through winter. I have found that compost-fed silver beet crops better in winter than silver beet fed on artificial fertilisers, blood and bone or dilute urine.

Don't forget to steam or stir fry silver beet stems, too, or serve with olive oil and lemon juice or chilli sauce.

MINIATURE SILVER BEET

Fill a box with compost or potting mix. Scatter seed thickly. Water every two days. Pick the tiny leaves at no more than finger high about three weeks after planting in warm weather.

PROBLEMS

Spots, or brown and soggy stalks: pick off affected leaves, and eat them if you want to. Plant silver beet in an airy spot, say, on a small patch of weed-mat in a well-mown lawn, not among the humidity of tomatoes and lettuce. A fortnightly seaweed spray (see Chapter 5) gives greater resistance to disease.

Spinach

Perennial spinach isn't spinach and it isn't perennial.

Spinach is not silver beet. It is tenderer and much more subtly flavoured. It is well worth growing, even though it doesn't bear as much or for as long as the coarser silver beet.

Spinach goes to seed in hot weather. Sow it at Christmas in temperate climates, in spring in cold ones, and in winter in hot areas. Keep it well mulched wherever it is, and pick it often. Otherwise, see 'Silverbeet'.

MINIATURE SPINACH

As bought in expensive bags in the supermarket ('baby spinach') for salads. See 'Miniature silver beet'.

SPINACH, WARRIGAL OR NEW ZEALAND

A perennial, this grows like a weed, and is drought and frost hardy. One patch can grow to 3 square metres. High on oxalic acid, so blanch in boiling water for one minute; throw out that water and cook again in fresh water. Makes an excellent spinach quiche or fetta and spinach pastries, and a reasonable soup.

Sunflowers

Choose a fresh-looking packet of cockie seed. Plant from spring through summer. If you are short of mulch, plant extra thickly, then pull up the sunflower plants just before they flower when they are still soft and tender. Sunflowers make cheap, quick-growing mulch.

Sunflowers are tall, thin growers and can be planted above carrots, lettuce, parsley and any other plant that does well with a little shade above it. You can also use the stems as poles for climbing beans or peas. Sunflowers grow fast, so you can sow the seeds of both together. Eat the seed raw or fried in oil – you will need to shell them first. Boil the unopened flowers and eat them like artichokes, hot with butter or cold with salad dressing. You can eat the roots, too, though they can be fibrous.

Swede turnips

Sow seeds from spring to late summer. Swedes are hardy and prolific, which is why they are used as cattle food. The cattle are welcome to them, though a very small, fresh swede is good with a baked dinner, occasionally. The big, fat, old ones get thrown to the chooks.

See 'Carrots' for cultivation, if you can be bothered.

Sweet corn (See 'Corn')

Sweet potato

Choose a sweet potato tuber (yellow or white fleshed, or purple skinned) that has started to sprout. Many sweet potatoes have been chemically treated to stop sprouting. Buy organic ones if you can. Plant them in spring or, at any time, in a pot indoors for later planting outside. Sweet potatoes make a good indoor rambling plant. Also good grown in very large hanging baskets in cold areas, over hot paving, or with a rock mulch.

In hot areas sweet potato is a perennial, but in cooler areas it should be treated as an annual. Any of the potato gardens can be used for sweet potato.

SWEET POTATO IN WEEDS

Place a little soil or potting mix in a pile of weeds or a compost heap that hasn't finished. Poke in a sweet potato. The warmth of the decomposing heap does wonders: you'll get a crop this way even in cold areas.

SWEET POTATO UNDER TREES

Sweet potato tolerates broken light, though not deep shade. I find that sweet potatoes under trees are sheltered from frost. Even though it may be as cold under the trees, the tubers don't rot and will crop for much longer. (We are just too cold here to keep them going through winter, no matter how well I mulch them.)

PROBLEMS

No major ones.

Taro

Moist soil, and neither sun nor shade. Excellent in tropical or subtropical groves. Not for cold climates without shelter in a glasshouse. Use in almost any potato recipe.

Tomatoes

Forget about the hard, round cardboardy things in supermarkets: home-grown tomatoes are wonderful. There are hundreds of tomato varieties – eat your way through them. This year we are growing climbing yellow tomatoes (prolific and frost hardy), egg-shaped Roma (sweet), Tiny Tim that come up anyway from the ones I planted 10 years ago, and a couple of large varieties. I usually plant an early-bearing variety in spring and a late-bearing variety in December.

Tomatoes form roots up their stems and stalk if they are mulched. The more roots, the better they grow. So mulch right up to the stem if you can. I don't bother to stake my tomatoes initially, but let the branches that sprawl on the ground take root. Then I stake them up and have another tomato plant.

TOMATO CUTTINGS

Let a branch sprawl on the ground. When it roots, cut it out and plant it somewhere else for a follow-on tomato crop.

'PERENNIAL' TOMATOES

Self-seeding tomatoes: I find that Tiny Tim plants bear for most of the winter if they're sheltered by lots of high vegetables around them. They only die back in the strong frosts of late spring.

Tiny Tims are hardy and almost disease-free. Haul out the dead plants in winter. Grow a quick crop like radish, then leave the ground bare in spring for the tiny tomato seedlings to germinate.

Grafted tomatoes: sadly, most grow from under the graft, and you end up with big bushes and no useful tomatoes! These produce massive plants, but few tomatoes until late in the season. However, they can often be kept until the following year, and will give earlier tomatoes the second year. This saves work, but not space. You'd still be better off with an early annual tomato planted in spring.

Tomatoes can be grafted onto potatoes. This is fun, though you get fewer tomatoes and potatoes than you would from separate plants. Tomatoes can also be grafted onto native solanums like kangaroo berry. This gives very frost-resistant plants, but the grafts often fail and it can be difficult to get kangaroo berry seed.

Potted tomatoes: tomatoes do well in pots. It's a good way to get early tomatoes in spring or to keep tomatoes fruiting through winter.

Sheltered tomatoes: last year I kept my tomatoes growing over winter in terraced beds in a warm courtyard. It wasn't worth it. The tomatoes were soft and tasted of nothing in particular. Tomatoes need heat for sweetness and flavour.

FEEDING

Tomatoes need regular feeding, and lots of phosphorous and potash. Too much nitrogen means lots of leaf and little fruit. Good mulch and compost are perfect. Mulch up to the bottom branches if you can. If in doubt, just buy lucerne hay and keep piling it up every week.

PRUNING

Don't bother to prune tomatoes: they ripen in response to heat, not sunlight. Pruning is just one more task that gardeners have burdened themselves with.

HARVESTING

Pick green tomatoes before they are damaged by frost. Store them on newspaper inside. They'll keep ripening for months, and the flavour will still be much better than shop-bought tomatoes.

SEED

Choose ripe, red tomatoes, then leave them on the window sill to ripen further. When they are too squashy to even tempt you, let them just start to ferment in a jar of water, then separate the seeds and dry them.

PROBLEMS

Splitting tomatoes: these have been irregularly watered. Mulch them and cut down on the watering.

Wilts: make sure your seed is disease-free. Spray plants with garlic spray every week, and include the soil around them. Mulch to stop spores splashing up. If only one plant is affected pull it up and burn it – and burn the other plants at the end of the season. If tomatoes are diseased, don't plant any others there for five years. Covering the ground with clear plastic for three weeks before you plant may kill disease spores.

Fruit fly: grow cherry tomatoes that have thicker skins. Or use fruit fly netting.

Turnips

Fresh, small turnips are infinitely better than the stale ones in shops. Grow them even if you hated turnips as a child. The small white Japanese ones are so sweet you can eat them like apples.

Turnips grow easily (see 'Radish'). I scatter the seed as an in-between crop after lettuce, tomatoes, etc, to eat through winter. They can be sown in spring too, not just autumn – but the autumn ones seem to taste better.

FOLIAGE TURNIPS

These are grown just for the tops, though any turnip top can be eaten. Foliage turnips can be eaten like silver beet, or shredded like lettuce, They are good chopped into mashed potato. They are frost-, snow- and drought-hardy, ignored by pests, and they germinate quickly. They also outgrow almost any weed except for blackberry, lantana, and dock. We grow lots. Any excess just gets turned into mulch.

Water chestnuts

The Chinese water chestnut (*Eleocharis dulcis*) is a great crop – I gather in China they crop up to 50 tonnes per hectare. They'll grow in brackish water by ponds, etc., but they're best grown by sowing them in sandy soils in spring, keeping them moist, then flooding them with about 10 cm of water when they are about 15 cm high. If you really want to maximise your crop, let the water drain away in early autumn, so that the tubers get larger in damp but not wet soil. Feed with orangic manures, compost, etc. during summer. Harvest them in late autumn.

Water chestnuts look like thin rushes, with thin, round leaves to about two metres. I grew mine in a wide deep dish; friends grow theirs in an old bathtub. But true water chestnuts need about seven hot months to get a good crop, and we're too far south for that, so I've never had a really good crop.

A better crop for cooler areas is kuwai (*Sagittaria sagittifolia*), which is also sometimes called water chestnut. The tubers are much the same as Chinese water chestnuts, but they should only be eaten cooked. (Chinese water chestnuts can be eaten raw, with the thin brown skin peeled off, or cooked.) Kuwai won't give you as big a crop as true Chinese water chestnuts, but kuwai are a lot more tolerant of cold weather and drying out if you go on holiday. Ours are totally dry for months most summers, but come back when we get rain. The leaves are a bit like green fat arrows – quite pretty in a glazed waterproof pot outside. Unless you are incredibly keen on water chestnuts, a bath tub full of kuwai will give you masses. Again, plant in spring in damp soil and flood when they have pushed their noses up above the soil, or plant in soggy soil around dams, ponds, etc. Harvest in late autumn.

Store water chestnuts or kuwai on racks in a cool, dark, airy place, like you would onions or potatoes or ginger root. I've also stored them in water in the fridge, and I've seen them stored in unglazed pots of water in South-East Asia – I suppose the water seeps through the unglazed pottery and keeps the pot cool as it evaporates. They can also be grated, dried and pounded into flour, or pickled. (Both kuwai and Chinese water chestnuts are very good indeed pickled.)

Kuwai can be left in the ground over

winter and harvested when needed. Water chestnuts can only be left in frost-free climates or they may rot.

PS Chinese water chestnuts are good for you: high in vitamin B6 especially.

Yacon

This perennial has large tubers like crunchy sweet potato, with sunflower-like flowers. Tolerates tropics, frost, light shade or full sun. Dig the roots as you need them. Good chook food. Drought hardy.

Zucchini

Plant the seed in spring, then again at Christmas in case early bushes are cut by mildew. Young bushes are more mildew resistant. Mulch, and feed with liquid manure every week for four weeks, then leave them alone. Eat the flowers steamed with lemon and oil, stuffed with rice and simmered in stock, or dipped in batter and deep-fried. Good grown in hanging baskets or pots. Try round zucchini – so firm textured even kids adore them, especially if they can pick their own.

PROBLEMS

What to do with too many zucchini? Heap them on your friends! Slice and dry them for winter.

Mildews: plant new bushes at Christmas. Spray with milk spray if really necessary. Mulch to stop spores splashing up. Plants on weed-mat or mulch are less prone to mildew. Choose an airy part of the garden to grow zucchini, and don't plant several together in case one infects the others.

MAKING VEGETABLES PERENNIAL

- Pick lettuce leaf by leaf. Choose cos or frilly-leafed, not iceberg lettuce. Pick out the seed stalk as it appears. The leaves will get smaller as you pick them – and unless you feed it as often as you pick it, the leaves will gradually get bitter.
- Pick broccoli every day, and feed it. Don't let it flower. I once kept one for three years, then went on holiday. When I got back it was inedible.
- Pick silver beet every day and pick out the seed head stalks as they appear – they'll be tall and thick. It will keep branching with smaller and more numerous leaves.
- Pick out the tops of celery. It will branch and become thinner, but if you continue to feed and water it, it will stay tender.
- Graft tomatoes onto a long-lived, frost-hardy native solanum like kangaroo berry.
- Don't pull up all your potatoes. Burrow underneath (a potato bandicoot) and just take what you need – the others will regrow. You can do the same with kumaras (in cool areas), sweet potato (in warm areas), and arrowroot (in hot to temperate areas).
- Don't pull up garlic, eat the tops instead.
- Once you pick a cauliflower, don't pull out the stalk. It will produce more small heads. Pick these while firm or they'll get tough, especially in hot weather. They may turn yellow or purple in summer. Don't worry about it.
- Don't pull out spring onion bulbs. Mine have been in for six years. We just eat the tops and they keep multiplying.

Some perennial vegetables

You can eat quite well all year round without planting any vegetables at all, once your garden is established. Try asparagus, arrowroot, bell peppers, perennial chilli, globe and Jerusalem artichokes, dandelions, warrigal or New Zealand spinach, clumps of spring onions, garlic chives, clumps of Russian garlic, chilacayote melons eaten young like zucchini, sorrel, perennial beans, perennial leeks, taro, yacon, and chokoes. Also try a self-seeding garden.

THE SELF-SEEDING GARDEN

Most of the crops in my garden were planted more than seven years ago. They have simply propagated themselves since.

Apart from the labour-saving side, there are other advantages. Plants that seed themselves naturally self-select the most hardy, the most suited to your area. You always have a number of plants going to seed, and these are one of the best predator attractors you can have. In addition, your ground is never totally bare, and bare ground is an invitation to weeds and results in soil and nutrient loss. The weeds in my garden are parsnips and radishes: I have to pull out handfuls to make space for other self-sown seeds to germinate. Once a bunch of radish is removed, up come lettuce, silver beet and leeks.

Always let the best of your plants self-seed. Stake them well so they don't topple over and rot. If you don't want them to grow in the same spot, transplant them – the shock of transplanting may well send them to seed earlier.

Remember that hybrid plants will not seed true-to-type, and that many plants will cross-pollinate. In spite of that I have found that in actual fact I do get relatively stable, and usually excellent self-sown crops.

AMARANTH
Can't stop it.

BURDOCK
Self-seeds forever and, once started, you'll always have plants available.

CARROTS
Grow several sorts or, depending on the time of year, you may have carrots that go to seed without forming roots. It took several years for my self-sown carrots to produce roots, instead of germinating in autumn and springing to seed in spring. You may have to keep some seed to sow too.

CELERY
Self-seeds surprisingly well, though you may need to wait after the first gone-to-seed plant in summer to get seedlings come up next spring. If they're small or tough from neglect, use the leaves instead of the stems.

CHICORY
You'll soon get a most hardy selection, available whenever you want them.

CHINESE CABBAGE
Chinese cabbage cross-pollinates. You will get some strange results, but all mine have not only been edible but good.

LEEKS
When leeks self-sow you get a clump of very small but very tender leeks. Eat them, top and all.

LETTUCE
Grow varieties that will thrive all year round – like oak leaf, Freckles, red and green mignonette, and cos. Other lettuce will germinate but may go to seed without being useful, or the young plant may be frosted off. Once you have let two or three crops of red mignonette go to seed, you should have them all year round.

MITSUBA AND MIZUNA
These are a delight, as they self-sow, survive years in dry soil, and come up after rain.

PARSLEY
This has formed a thicket that even couch grass can't penetrate.

POTATOES
Don't dig them. Burrow under the mulch, take what you need and leave the rest to regrow. The result: year-round spuds.

PUMPKIN

When you eat a pumpkin throw the seeds into the garden – or hope your compost was too cool and the seeds will survive. A pumpkin left in the garden will slowly rot, and the seeds will germinate in spring. They seem much stronger grown in their own debris.

RADISH

I grow long red and long white radish. They crowded out the short red ones and I no longer get them. The older the radish, the hotter it tastes. I eat them cooked like asparagus – delicious. Radish self-sow so easily they become a weed.

SALSIFY

Self-seeds easily and well.

SILVER BEET

This self-sows readily. Either thin out the plants or let them grow together and pluck them out as you need to use them. The main disadvantage of self-sown silver beet is that you won't get a continuous supply the first year, as the seeds won't germinate until well after the parent plants' prime. But irregular germination will solve that problem in successive years.

SORREL

Once you have French sorrel you always have it. Unlike the weed sorrel it is rarely a nuisance.

SPRING ONIONS

I never pull these. I just pick the tops. The clumps go on expanding: year-round greens that don't have to be stored like bulb onions.

TOMATOES

Cherry tomatoes seem to reseed better than other varieties. But it is a rare tomato patch that doesn't have seedlings the following year. Cherry tomatoes grown in a thicket of other crops will bear throughout winter – or plant them in a pot and bring it indoors.

ITALIAN RED STEMMED CHICORY

Wonderful stuff – drought tolerant and cold hardy. Use instead of lettuce.

MAKING THE MOST OF VEGETABLES

Using waste bits

Parts of vegetables can be 'harvested' even if they aren't really mature. Try parsnip tops. Use them like celery in stews and soup, or finely grated in salads. Beetroot tops can substitute for silver beet, as can turnip tops. If these are young and tender they are also excellent raw. Try young turnip tops grated up in mashed potatoes. Try eating garlic tops instead of the bulbs – again, raw or cooked – and try the leafy tips of broad beans, broccoli or brussels sprout leaves, young sweet corn teased out from next to the stalk, or zucchini or pumpkin flowers.

The latter are wonderful. Stuff them with leftover fried rice and stew them in stock, or dip them stuffed or empty in egg, then breadcrumbs, and deep-fry them. Serve with lemon juice or hollandaise sauce.

You can tell the male flowers, most of which are expendable, by looking for the swelling at the base of the flower.

Using immature vegetables

- Try very young cucumbers. Pick them when they're no longer than your little finger or even smaller. Slice them thinly so they are almost transparent and quickly stir-fry them. A Chinese friend introduced me to them and they have become my favourite vegetable.
- Immature corn cobs can be kept on the stalk by bending it over them, to shelter them from frost and rain so they won't rot before they mature. They will continue to

mature slowly this way until the stalks are almost brittle. Young corn, Chinese style, is delicious. Whenever you pull out a corn stalk, run your fingers down the leaves to make sure an immature cob isn't forming. If it is, pluck, stir-fry and enjoy.
- Pumpkins can be eaten as soon as they form behind the flower – just like small squash, which is, in fact, what they are. They won't taste as sweet as mature pumpkins. They are more mellow and nutty, like zucchini.
- Try pickling small watermelons before they turn pink inside. Use a sweet, well-spiced marinade. Not that the melon will taste of much – all you'll taste will be the pickling solution – but the texture will be excellent.
- Carrots, beetroot, parsnips, turnips and the like can be picked and eaten as soon as you can be bothered. The smaller the sweeter. But all should continue to mature through winter as long as the ground doesn't freeze – especially under a thick bed of mulch.
- Cook lettuce that hasn't hearted, in stock to eat by itself and for lettuce soup, or wrap it round rice for stuffed 'cabbage'.
- Pickle green tomatoes, or make green-tomato chutney or jam.

GETTING DINNER FROM THE GARDEN

It's late, and nearly dark – we've spent too long up in town. Bryan locates the tomatoes mostly by their fragrance: that sun-and-sweetness smell of almost fermenting fruit. I rummage for a lettuce in the garden by the kitchen door, as well as for some chives, cucumbers, tarragon and parsley.

Edward is in the potatoes, bandicooting enough to make potato cakes. Then he takes the torch to hunt for ripe strawberries, raspberries and a few cape gooseberries – though his face is mulberry-stained when he comes in, so he's harvested there as well.

Add an egg or two from the chooks and we've harvested a meal.

If there'd been more light I would've looked for late asparagus or beans, pulled up some carrots, or picked some passionfruit to make fruit salad. It doesn't matter. What we don't eat tonight we'll have tomorrow. And what we don't have tomorrow will just decay back into the soil, to feed us all some other time.

THE 10-MINUTE VEGETABLE GARDEN

A vegetable garden is the proud product of lots of work and perspiration. Right?

Well, not exactly.

With a bit of planning, one hour planting, another hour maintenance each year and a few minutes watering each week, you can have an abundant veg garden with something to pick every day. Impossible? No way.

What you need are low-maintenance vegies, ones that keep growing year after year, or reseed themselves easily. Some of them grow happily in pots; others need a garden of their own, and most can just be tucked into an odd corner of an existing garden.

Amaranth

There are several amaranths around, including the purely ornamental flowers. Buy leaf amaranth seeds, *Amaranthus giganticus*, for your 10-minute vegetable garden and plant them spring to late summer. Amaranth is tall (up to 2 metres), sturdy, drought-, heat- and cold-hardy, with bright red flowers. Pick the young leaves for salads or boil them as a green veg. Amaranth is an annual, but it seeds itself all too readily! Plant them anywhere there is some bare ground – they'll grow in sun or shade, though the plants will be smaller in shade.

Artichokes

We grow these lovely silver-leafed plants in hot dry corners of the garden. They grow from seed sown from spring to mid-summer, or from suckers of last year's plants. Pick the young flower heads – the artichokes – in spring.

Jerusalem artichokes

These are definitely for a corner of the garden – full sun or semi-shade – that you'll never want to use for anything else, as once you have Jerusalem artichokes they are difficult to get rid of! Plant tubers in spring (buy them in autumn or winter at a good fruit shop and keep in the crisper until spring) and they'll grow into 2-metre-tall flowers, like small sunflowers, which is in fact what they are. The tiny ones left in the soil will grow into next year's crop. In winter when the plants die, grub up the knobbly roots; scrub well, don't peel, and bake on an oiled tray until tender. NB Too many make you flatulent. Look for the fat, round variety rather than the longer knobbly ones.

Asparagus

I've planted these in our flowerbeds; we eat the new shoots in spring and enjoy the ferny leaves in summer. I prefer home-grown seedlings (planted spring to mid-summer), to 'crowns' (one- or two-year-old roots dug up in winter), as they are both much cheaper and hardier.

Scarlet runner beans

These are a climbing perennial bean, with bright red flowers all summer and autumn. They don't bear well in very hot weather UNLESS you grow other plants along their roots to keep them shaded, and water well. Plant seeds from spring to mid-summer. Make sure the roots are well covered with soil each winter when the tops die down, or they'll rot. Pick the beans when they are no more than finger size, or they'll be tough. You can also get white, pink and orange flavoured varieties, all with slightly different beans. The old beans are tough – dry the seeds and eat in stews and soups in winter.

Lovage

This looks like a small, wild perennial celery. It gives a meaty celery flavour to soups and stews, and young leaves and stems can be stir fried or tossed into salads. Grows well in pots.

Watercress

Keep this in a pot under your tap so it stays moist. Good in salads, sandwiches and soups, but a bit too peppery if you use too much. Watch out for tiny snails that can transmit liver fluke – in rural areas only use cooked in soup.

Garlic chives

These are TOUGH, and unlike common chives don't die down in winter or shrivel in heat and drought. They are flatter and coarser than common chives, but great in stir fries, sandwiches and salads where you want an onion/garlic flavour. Grow well in pots.

Spring or bunching onions (Allium fistulosum)

I rarely bother growing ordinary onions. If we want an onion flavour I pick a bunch of these and chop them fresh into salads or sauté until soft for other dishes. The clumps grow larger year by year, and tolerate sun or semi-shade. Plant any warm time of year. Grow well in pots. You can also get red-stemmed ones.

Salad burnet

This is a lovely little ferny perenial herb that tastes sweet and nutty in salads or stir fries. It's supposed to give a cucumber flavour to drinks, but doesn't unless you have a strongly cucumbery imagination. Grow in full sun. Grows well in pots.

Bronze fennel

A lovely froth of red leaves. Chop the young ones into salads or sandwiches, but only if you like aniseed. I add finely chopped leaves to potato soup or potato cakes, and just a little in stir-fries. Sow any warm time of year. Grows well in pots.

Warrigal, New Zealand or native spinach (Tetragonia tetragonioides)

This rambling veg grows like a weed, tolerates heat and drought, and is used just like spinach. However, because of it's high oxalic acid content it should be boiled for three minutes each time in two changes of water before eating. Makes a great cheese and spinach pie. sow any warm time of year. Grows well in pots.

Mitsuba, Japanese hornwort, Japanese parsley (Cryptotaenia japonica)

This is mostly grown as an annual, but it's really perennial, and will reseed itself happily too, coming up in bare spots all over the garden. It's like a very coarse parsley – chop the leaves and stems, and use in salads or stir fries or anywhere you would use chopped parsley. The more you pick the more tender new leaves you get. Sow any warm time of year. Grows well in pots

Dandelion

Look for the large-leafed salad varieties; they have larger, more tender leaves than the common weeds! Dandelion leaves are sweetest in spring, but you can blanch them by putting an old flower pot or box over the leaves for a week – this makes them lose most of their bitterness, and the leaves will be larger and more tender too. Sow any warm time of year. Grows well in pots

French sorrel

Loves acid soils and spots where nothing much else grows! It will grow in full sun or semi-shade. The leaves are sour, rather than bitter, but a very little gives a tang to salads and I was served a stunning sorrel soup a few years ago that I've made a few times since: just half a dozen leaves pureed in 2 cups of chicken stock, with a dash of cream, served hot or cold. Sow any warm time of year. Grows well in pots.

Chinese Artichokes

See Jerusalem artichokes – Chinese artichokes are smaller (and not related) but as easy to grow and delicious.

Yacon

A perennial tuber, crunchy even when cooked and cold, heat and drought resistant. Full sun or semi shade.

HOW TO LOOK AFTER YOUR 10-MINUTE VEGIES

Every spring (or winter for the asparagus) mulch them WELL with good quality lucerne hay or compost or other high quality mulch. Sprinkle on a complete plant food like Dynamic Lifter. Cover any weeds with more mulch. Then, in summer, toss on slow release fertiliser.

Water once a week in dry times, though all these plants should survive without watering – they just won't be as productive until it rains. Then pick, cook and munch ... and give yourself a nice pat for your forethought and organisation as you gaze out at what may well be the most productive veg garden in your neighbourhood!

HERBS

Herbs were once wild plants, harvested for their taste or their medicinal properties. Only now have they have been tamed and herded into pots. Herbs are usually tough and fast-growing, with a few exceptions like basil. (Treat basil like silver beet, and feed it well.)

Herbs can be grown in pots, but this doesn't let them spread. Most herbs like to wander. I grow most of ours up the hill in a weed-mat garden, or on a bank by the house.

This was once grass and weeds. I planted the herbs into the grass (mints and marjoram, pineapple and other sages, winter tarragon, coltsfoot, yarrow, thyme, chamomile, garlic, other chives, and many others) and kept the grass mown. And now the herbs have outgrown the grass. Some herbs, like marjoram, oregano, mint, yarrow, tansy, fennel and horehound, can become weeds.

The high-rise herb bed

This saves space. Make a mound out of rocks or old car tyres – anything bulky. Cover it with compost, soil or potting mix: just enough to cover it. Plant your herbs, and let them cascade.

A herb wall

Choose a steep weedy bank. Take as many old cans as you can get, cut out the tops and bottom; pound them into the bank and plant herbs in them. The cans will keep the bank stable until the herbs take over.

For a wall of herbs, take lots of old cans, cut off the tops and pierce holes in the bottom. Fill them with potting mix and plant them with herbs. Nail them to a wall or post, as close together as you want. If the cans are quite close together, the wall should be covered within a year and the cans will be covered too. If you don't like bare tin cans, paint them before planting the herbs.

Herbs in drainage pipes

Ceramic drainage pipes look good up on end, filled with soil and planted with herbs. The herbs trail down and the old pipes turn into pillars.

A herb courtyard

Leave spaces in the paving in your courtyard. Either lever some pavers out randomly, or create a pattern: a large, round space or like the spokes of a wheel. Plant these out with herbs.

A heavily used area can still have one-in-four pavers left out. Feet use the remaining pavers, and wheels may run over the herbs but as they are slightly lower they'll survive.

An edible herb bed

Keep this near the kitchen where you can pick at will: parsley, either curled or Italian, and lots of different sorts of mints. I like Vietnamese mint, to add to red-wine vinegar for dipping fried things, apple mint for a summer drink, and Egyptian mint to chop up for tabouli (very mild, almost like lettuce) and, of course, garden mint for mint sauce. Plant chives for omelettes, garlic chives for when you run out of garlic or to use instead in salads. Plant a few culinary herbs like thyme, tarragon, marjoram and oregano. Plant chamomile for a bed-time tea (dried chamomile flowers taste like compost, but fresh chamomile tea is lovely). Plant lemon grass for adding to Asian cooking or use it instead of lemons for home-made lemonade. Plant perennial Greek basil in frost-free spots and some rocket for a few leaves of salad when you can't be bothered with a lettuce. Plant a few calendulas to rub on stings, and comfrey for juice to rub on grazes or mild burns. Plant caraway seeds for cakes and bread, and a bay tree in a pot: fresh bay leaves are much more fragrant than the stale ones you buy in the shop.

COMMON HERBS

Aloe vera

This forms a cactus-like clump of fleshy leaf blades with prickly edges. It can be grown as a houseplant on a sunny window sill, or in any warm sunny spot outside. Use the fresh juice on burns or sunburn. It can be grown from seed or cuttings.

Angelica

This is a tall biennial, though it can become a short-lived perennial. Candy the stems or use them as a vegetable. Angelica seed is only viable for a month. It must be sown as soon as it matures on the old plant.

Caper bush

This sun-loving shrub has attractive pink or white flowers throughout summer, though the petals drop after a day. The unopened flower buds are pickled, but they don't develop much flavour until they have been processed. Plant the seed in spring, or take softwood cuttings in summer and keep moist.

Chamomile

The perennial is low growing with bright white and yellow flowers. It prefers fertile, well-drained soil and full sun, but tolerates semi-shade. We grow ours between the paving stones. Chamomile flowers are used to make the relaxing chamomile tea, to relieve indigestion, nausea or period pain, or for a brightening hair rinse for blonde hair. Sow seed in spring or divide a clump.

German chamomile is an annual, probably the best for chamomile tea. It does best in sandy or clay soils and needs full sun. Sow seeds in spring.

Chervil

This annual, culinary herb has pale-green delicate leaves and grows to about 70 cm high. It prefers a light, moist soil. Sow seed in spring – it germinates quickly – or sow more in autumn to grow indoors for winter.

Chives

Chives are small, neat onion-flavoured clumps of leaves that die down in winter. They tolerate sun or semi-shade, but not deep shade. Although they'll struggle on in drought and hard soil, they prefer moist, fertile soil for best growth.

Garlic chives are flatter and will grow throughout winter.

Grow chives by planting seed at any warm time of the year, or by dividing a clump.

Coriander

This small parsley-like annual prefers dryish soil and full sun. The leaves are used mostly, much like parsley. The seeds are also good and help digestion, while the roots can be baked like parsnip. Sow the seed in spring or early summer. It may take several weeks to germinate. If your coriander keeps going to seed you may be using a variety grown for seed, not leaves; or try growing it in dappled shade.

Dill

This can become a weed, though a pretty one. It is tall and fern-like with umbrella-shaped umbels of yellow flowers. Use dill seed or leaves as a flavouring for rich food or dill cucumbers. Feed babies dill water for indigestion. Sow the seed at any warm time of the year.

Fennel

This is a perennial – often a weed – with fragrant, ferny, green leaves. There is also a bronze-leafed fennel variety, and one grown for its swollen edible root and stem. Sow seeds in spring or autumn in full sun. Cut off the seed heads to stop the plants spreading and becoming a nuisance. A deep mulch will give a tender, milder root and stem. It's good either raw with salad dressing, or cooked. Can become a major weed.

Feverfew

This pretty, small perennial plant with its pale-green leaves and white and yellow flowers can be used as an insecticide like pyrethrum, though it is much less potent. Use the leaves and flowers to make a very bitter tea, both to prevent and reduce the severity of migraine and tension headaches. It is also a mild sedative. It seeds itself readily, and seeds can be sown at any warm time of the year. Can become a major weed.

Garlic

Garlic can be left to multiply or pulled up when the leaves turn yellow. Plant the individual cloves in autumn, point upwards in fertile well-drained soil, and harvest the bulb the following summer or snip off the garlic-tasting leaves or mild garlic flavoured 'leek' stems as you need them. In warm areas, to avoid harvesting very small bulbs, chill the cloves before planting by leaving them in the fridge for three weeks. Garlic plants are pretty, with tall balls of blue flowers. Plant lots around the edges of the garden to attract predators and help repel pests. Russian garlic has larger cloves and fatter more succulent young stems.

Ginseng, American

This is the source of ginseng tonic. Ginseng needs moist, fertile soil and semi-shade. It is perennial, with small pink flowers in the summer. After several years' growth, you can use the root to make ginseng tea. Sow fresh seeds in spring after winter chilling. Snails love ginseng seedlings. Beware: they will also die in full sunlight. Mulch well.

Indian ginseng, or gotu kola, is a roundish leafed, low-growing perennial for a damp spot in semi-shade. It tolerates mild frosts. Eat no more than a leaf a day, and avoid it if you have high blood pressure. Otherwise it is an excellent tonic and rejuvenator. It grows from seed or division.

Hops

The hop flowers grow on a hardy deciduous vine. We grow ours over the backyard dunny. The flowers are used in beer or for hop 'sleep pillows'. The new shoots are eaten like asparagus. Propagate from root cuttings taken in early summer or late winter. Seeds can be sown in spring, but seedlings are delicate and slow-growing.

Horseradish

This is a perennial, moisture-loving plant. It trails all through the garden, but is cut back by heavy frost, though it should shoot again in spring. The roots are usually grated and added to cream or vinegar for horseradish sauce, though the leaves are also edible, if fiery. I grow horseradish in full sun, in semi-shade under it trees, and around our potatoes to help fungal problems. Horseradish helps reduce excessive mucus from colds, hay fever or sinus problems.

Plant a bit of root in winter.

Lavender

All the lavenders prefer full sunlight and well-drained soils. The bushes help repel pests in the garden, as well as inside the house. The flowers can be used in cooking, or to make an antiseptic or mildly sedative tea. Lavender can either be grown from seed (but seedlings may not come true-to-type) or from autumn, winter or spring cuttings.

Lemon and lime balm

These bright-green perennials will cover any moist fertile spot – and survive happily in dry ones. They seed themselves readily. Seed can be sown in spring or summer, or propagate by dividing a clump.

Lemon verbena

This is a small, aromatic shrub, deciduous in cold areas and tolerating only light frosts. Use the leaves as a mild sedative or to make a refreshing, lemon-flavoured tea to help indigestion or nausea. Lemon verbena grows from spring cuttings or seed. Lime verbena is more fragrant but otherwise similar.

Marjoram

This forms sweet smelling carpets in both shade and full sun. It is perennial, but can be killed by severe frost. Oregano is a more pungent, wild form of marjoram, equally hardy. Sow seed in spring or divide a clump. Tip cuttings may take in autumn or spring. Smell before you buy – some cultivars are more fragrant than others.

Mint

All the mint family like moisture and fertile soil. I grow ours under trees and roses: ginger mint, peppermint, winter mint, eau de Cologne mint, camphor mint and many others. Mint can he grown from seed, but may not come true-to-type. Root or stem cuttings are easier. Mints tolerate sun or semi-shade.

PS Chocolate mint does not taste of chocolate.

Mustard

Black or white mustard seeds are the source of the condiment mustard. The plant is a quick-growing annual, up to knee height, and the seeds are shed quickly when the plant is mature. Mustard is also a good, quick green-manure crop, and useful for choking out weeds. It prefers a moist, fertile soil in full sun, but will tolerate much harsher conditions and semi-shade. Mustard leaves can be chopped up for salads. Sow the seeds at any warm time of the year.

Pyrethrum, Dalmatian

This is the source of pyrethrum insecticide: a low, fringed-leafed grey plant with tall spikes of single white flowers. It is perennial, and tolerates both full sun and semi-shade, and almost any soil. I grow it as a garden border to help repel pests. Sow seed in spring. See Chapter 7 for pyrethrum spray.

Sage

Sage tolerates sun or semi-shade, moist soil or dry banks. It grows from spring-sown seed or winter cuttings. Look for ordinary culinary sage, garlic sage for cooking. Pineapple sage and fruit salad sage are good in fruit salads, but not cooked. The other salvias have stunning flowers but aren't edible.

Tarragon

Russian tarragon is the most prolific. French tarragon has by far the best flavour but is much harder to germinate and to keep alive. Both are perennial, prefer moist, but not wet, soil and full sunlight. Tarragon is said to stimulate the appetite. I love it with chicken, potatoes and in salads and veal dishes. French tarragon must be grown from root division. Russian tarragon will also grow from seed.

Thyme

Edge a garden with thyme to help keep out couch grass. Culinary thyme forms thick clumps, lawn the low mats. All thymes are free-flowering, and bees love them. Sow seed in spring, or divide a clump at any cool time of the year. If your thyme becomes woody or 'leggy', top dress it with compost or good soil. New roots will form along the stem, rejuvenating the bush.

Vanilla

Vanilla comes from the vanilla orchid – and yes, you CAN grow your own vanilla orchids, though for hundreds of years vanilla was only grown in Mexico. Wild vanilla is pollinated by a complex association of bees, ants, humming birds and butterflies only found in Mexico. But once growers discovered hand pollination, vanilla could be grown all over the world. Or the warm parts of the world, anyway. Or, if you have a green house or nice, warm window sill, it can be grown there. Vanilla tends to die fairly quickly if the temperature falls below 16°C. It prefers to be between 26°C and 30°C, and demands high humidity too.

First of all you have to find your vanilla orchid. Specialist herb nurseries are the best place to look, or ask your local nursery nicely if they can order one in for you.

Now find a place for it to grow. Vanilla orchids are climbers, so you'll either need a trellis in semi-shade – under trees is great – or let your vanilla orchid clamber up a tree. Vanilla has a fairly thick stem and long aerial roots that cling to trees or posts so the vanilla can clamber up it.

If you're in an area that gets colder than 16°C in winter, grow your vanilla in a large pot filled with rich compost, with a 2-metre stake for it to clamber up. (Vanilla will grow to about 10 metres or even more – but not in a pot!) Keep the pot outdoors in semi-dappled shade in summer, and take indoors to a heated room by a not too sunny window when it's cold.

Keep your vanilla orchid moist (vanilla shrivels in dry weather) and mulch well – and wait three years.

In the third autumn prune the tip of the vine to encourage flowering – then watch carefully in spring, as each vanilla flower will last only a day, and you have to be quick to pollinate them.

Each flower has two little lips inside, covering the pollen and the female part of the flower – the stigma. Use a toothpick or a kid's tiny paint brush to move the sticky pollen to the sticky stigma. I know this sounds extremely rude, but I promise the plant won't mind! And it really isn't as difficult as it sounds – once you peer into the flower it's easy to work out which bit is which. One vine should give you well over 100 pods, and probably a lot more!

The vanilla pods take about 10 months to ripen. Once the pods change from green to yellow to brown they are ripe. Usually they smell delicious by now, but don't panic if they have no scent at all – they just need to be dried. (Most commercial beans are picked when they are still green, and mechanically dried and sweated until they are fragrant.) Bundle the pods together so they stay moist and sweaty, and keep in a hot place for about two weeks, then separate them and dry them in a hot place out of direct sunlight. However, if you find your vanilla already smells stunning, don't bother with the drying stage – the pods will have dried sufficiently on the tree.

Store your beans in sugar, to flavour the sugar, or add the chopped bean to vodka, for homemade vanilla essence. I love to add the lovely sticky pulp from inside the vanilla bean to home-made ice-cream or choc chip biscuits or custards. The flavour is incredible and the tiny black flecks just add to the charm. But beware – you'll find home-grown vanilla is so much stronger than commercial vanilla, or even old vanilla beans, that you will only need to use a very small amount for a stunning fragrance.

Wormwood

These tall, grey bushes help repel pests. They are incredibly hardy and grow almost anywhere, from dry banks to under trees. Grow them from a piece of hardwood stuck in the ground at any time of the year, though winter cuttings grow best. Seed may be hard to germinate.

Yarrow

This can become a noxious weed – or an indestructible carpet for a little-used area. Yarrow has ferny leaves and white to pink to purple flowers. It tolerates almost any conditions. I grow it under trees and over hard-to-handle banks. Miniature woolly yarrow is small and grey and furry, and makes a lovely lawn.

Grow yarrow from a root cutting and watch it spread. It will also grow from seed, in semi-shade to full sun.

Chapter 10
THE FRUIT GARDEN

THE IDEAL

A tangled prolific jungle that feeds you all year – as well as feeding the birds and other animals that live in your garden. Flowers bloom below the trees year round: nitrogen-fixers to help feed the trees, natural mulch providers, and blossom to attract the predators which control the pests.

- *Instead of well-spaced trees* … plant groves!!! Tangle trees together to help pest control, cut down fruit losses to birds, help weed and moisture control, and provide natural mulch from leaves.
- *Instead of conventionally mulched trees, or trees fertilised with manures or compost* … grow trees in clover, lucerne and herbs, grow your own mulch, throw down everything from fallen trees to road kill under the trees. (Do bury the road kill.)
- *Instead of regular pruning* … use minimum pruning methods and let the trees grow naturally.
- *Instead of pesticides, organic or otherwise* … grow flowering natives and ground covers to attract predators to control your pests; interplant different varieties to lessen pest damage; and let vines tangle through the branches to disguise the shape of your trees.
- *Instead of buying winter cherries from California* … grow 50 kinds of fruit, even in an ordinary backyard, that will give you apples for 10 months of the year, oranges the year round, and at least four other kinds of home-grown fruit to munch every day.
- *Instead of spraying and pruning* … grow maintenance-free fruits like white mulberries, maple syrup and pomegranates.
- *Instead of fences* … have hedges of dwarf apples, or cover fences with passionfruit or grapes.

Fruit trees don't need humans to grow fruit – they've been doing it for millennia. The reason your stunted, yellowing orange or fruit-fly-infested peach isn't doing well is because they've been transferred into a harsh, unsuitable environment – your yard – where the soil was probably turned over when it was cleared; compacted from years of digging and mowing and throwing out the clippings; with no deep roots and falling leaves to replenish and recycle fertility.

Feed your trees, take care of your soil, and most of your fruit-growing problems will vanish. Even a small backyard should be able to grow about 40 trees, thousands of strawberry plants, several dozen berry bushes and climbing berries, and a good number of fruiting shrubs.

Forget the old ideas of well-spaced trees with park-like lawn around them. If you want a range of fruit trees, grow them either as a low hedge or simply plant them close together. We plant ours about two metres apart, and let them grow tall. The branches mingle and you need a ladder to get the fruit – but they give each other wind and frost protection, the mingling branches hide the fruit from birds, and there is a lot more fruit per hectare.

Plant berries under the trees – most were originally forest species and like broken light. (Berries grow better under trees than most grasses.) Ramble brambleberries up fences and pergolas; twine passionfruit around posts.

Stressed plants can be good for you!

The level of flavonoids – antioxidants found in fruits, nuts and vegetables that help prevent diseases and slow down aging – depends on how much stress the plant has endured, according to the US Department of Agriculture. Natural farming methods, with greater insect and disease attack, appear to force plants to release greater amounts of flavonoids and other beneficial compounds. One flavonoid varied from 31 to 114 milligrams in 100-gram samples of the same variety of sweet red cherry.

GROWING YOUR OWN

Fruit-trees from seed

All fruit except bananas (including grapes, some kiwi fruit, strawberry and raspberry varieties, and some passionfruit) grow from seed and, in most cases, the fruit will be reasonably true-to-type, that is, like its parent, although there is an outside chance that it will be very different and that difference can be an improvement or a huge disappointment. I've grown hundreds of fruits from seed; sadly, all have been almost identical to their parents!

Grafting may not be good

Fruit is grafted to ensure it is absolutely identical to its parent – essential for an orchardist, but unnecessary for the home grower. Our fruit comes from a restricted gene pool anyway; seed-grown fruit will almost certainly be close to its parent. Grafting onto dwarfing or semi-dwarfing stock can also keep the tree small and neat, e.g. citrus, apples, pears. But these trees will be far less drought hardy, as they will have smaller (that is, less vigorous) roots, and they'll blow over more easily too. Some root stocks, like passionfruit, kiwi fruit and some grapes, are usually more vigorous than the variety that's grafted onto them, so they grow faster and are therefore hardier. Other 'rootstocks' are less prone to root rots or will tolerate drier, harsher conditions.

If you're a commercial grower, stick to grafted varieties. If you want lots of smaller fruit trees, go for dwarfed trees. Otherwise, take note of suggestions under each sort of fruit – in most cases you may find that seedlings are hardier than grafted trees. The spot where trees are grafted is always a weak spot, especially as the root stock and 'scion' will grow at different rates. Grafted trees may give you one or two fruits earlier; but you'll usually get LOTS of fruit earlier from seedling trees. And seedling trees are often far more cold- and heat-hardy. See my book *New Plants from Old* (Aird Books) for more details on why and how to grow your own fruit trees from seed and cuttings.

AN EASY FRUIT REGIME

Forget about spraying calendars and feeding programs. Just remember that a healthy soil means healthy trees. Never feed trees harsh manures or artificial fertilisers. They result in soft, fast-growing, sappy growth, which is an invitation to pests and disease. Instead, mulch each tree, berry bush or vine to a depth of 10–30 cm each year. Renew the mulch as necessary through the year. Mulch can be seaweed, hay, old leaves, grass clippings – if it has once lived it will provide food for plants living now.

Making mulch scenic

Grow groves, where the skirts of the trees hide the mulch! If you think mulch is ugly, or if you think the neighbours might think so, don't pile it on. A small sprinkle every two weeks will be quickly absorbed. Once fruit trees and bushes are a few years old you can simply mow the grass under them and let that be a substitute for mulch, with a sprinkle of 'additives' on the mown grass in spring.

Remember that once a plant is fully grown it only needs to be fed to compensate for the fruit you harvest each year, and for the leaves that are lost. As well as mulch, give young trees a yearly sprinkle of blood and bone, dolomite and ground rock phosphate, and wood ashes if you have them – again, autumn is best, but any time will do. Mulch can tie up nitrogen in the soil, and these early doses will mean that the soil is fertile enough to break down the mulch quickly. After the first few years the ground will be humus-rich and the 'extras' can be discontinued.

Watering

Plants take up their nutrients through water: a water-stressed plant will starve as well as droop. Too much water is as bad as too little, depriving the plant of air and rotting its roots. Soil should never be wet – just damp.

Water only when the ground under the mulch is dry. Don't train your trees to become dependent on watering: deeper roots will forage moisture as well as nutrients. Deep-rooted plants are also less prone to wind damage.

Pruning

Most trees don't need regular pruning unless you want to win the biggest apple award at the show. The exceptions are peaches, almonds and nectarines, as they develop fruit buds on new laterals and on short spurs from the previous season's growth. If you don't prune you'll get some fruit while the trees are young and growing vigorously, but as they get older they will grow less and less fruit which will be borne mostly towards the end of the branches. BUT – as branches are weighed down by fruit, more new wood will grow upwards … and it will bear fruit.

I haven't pruned ANY tree for over 25 years. And all still fruit.

Unpruned, some old-fashioned varieties produce more fruit than do new varieties.

Advantages of pruning:
- Less fruit is formed. This means the remaining fruit is larger and more attractive.

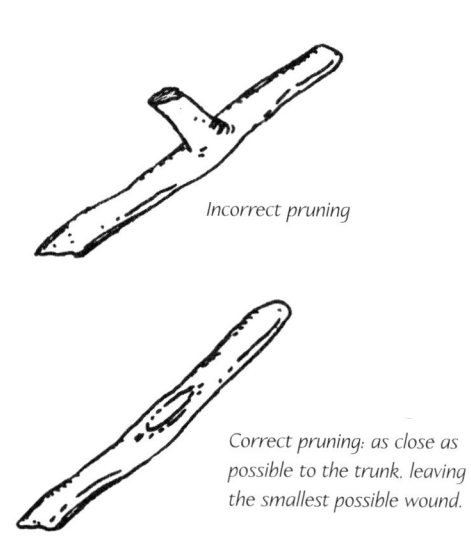

Incorrect pruning

Correct pruning: as close as possible to the trunk, leaving the smallest possible wound.

Promote new fruiting wood by pointing the top leaders downwards, weighed down with stones or tied to stakes. New upright growth will sprout from the old leaders. They, in turn, can be weighed down after five or ten years. This way the tree loses none of its bio-mass to pruning, and isn't exposed to disease by pruning cuts. You end up with a lovely tangle of fruiting wood that birds won't penetrate, and the fruit ripens over a long time. (Often the fruit itself weights down the branches – so you don't need to do anything!)

- The fruit ripens evenly and can be picked over a short period.
- The tree can be shaped to make it stronger or more regular, or smaller with a vase-shape to make picking and spraying easier.
- Hard pruning often means vigorous growth the next year.
- If a tree has been neglected, pruning will remove long and straggly growth.
- More sun can penetrate, which means less mildew and other rots.

Disadvantages of pruning

- Vase-shaped trees weaken near the centre over the years, so that the life of the tree may be reduced.
- Even ripening is not an advantage for the home grower, who may want to extend the fruiting period as long as possible.
- Too much pruning means too few leaves to help nourish the fruit.
- Too open a structure can lead to sunburn in susceptible fruit.
- Some trees, especially apricots, are susceptible to bacterial and fungal infections in the wounds left after pruning. Pruning implements can transfer pests and diseases from tree to tree.
- An open structure means that fruit is more visible to birds.
- Pruning is a lot of work.

A simple pruning regime ... if you really must

Prune peaches, almonds and nectarines every year, thinning out badly placed laterals. Leave about one lateral in three.

Prune the laterals of Granny Smith and delicious apples every year to about half their length. Prune Jonathans every second year to about four or five new fruit buds. Cut back Japanese plum laterals occasionally to about a quarter of their length. Prune European plums every four years or so.

Don't prune grapes, pears, apricots, nut trees, avocados, citrus or cherry trees after their initial shaping as young trees, unless you need to hack them back to stop them taking over. Do, however, cut away dead or damaged wood.

A pruning alternative

Pull down tall branches and tie them to the ground. They will send out new fruiting shoots.

PLANTING

Dig your hole just before planting, about twice as big as the roots. Firm down the soil well after planting: if the tree rocks in the wind, small roots can be destroyed. Don't dig in mulch or compost – put it on top for the worms and bacteria to pull down naturally. Water the tree in well.

Dry-area tree planting

In dry areas, plant trees and bushes in a slight depression. Mulch around the tree when planted. Cover this with black plastic. Keep the plastic in place with rocks, and put down another layer of black plastic, sloping down towards the tree. At night, condensation between the two layers of plastic will run down and water the tree. In wet areas, try planting above-ground: place the tree roots spread out on the ground, stake the tree well, then cover the roots with a sloping pile of mulch and compost. Or better still, dig ditches to drain off excess water.

WHAT TO GROW WITH FRUIT TREES

Never dig under fruit trees – it disturbs fine feeder roots. Either have mown grass (rake it

Water young trees with a bottle of water stuck upside down in the soil near the outer root.

Put a bucket of water next to a mulched tree; hang one end of an old stocking in the water and bury the other end under the mulch; the water will slowly siphon out of the bucket and seep into the soil

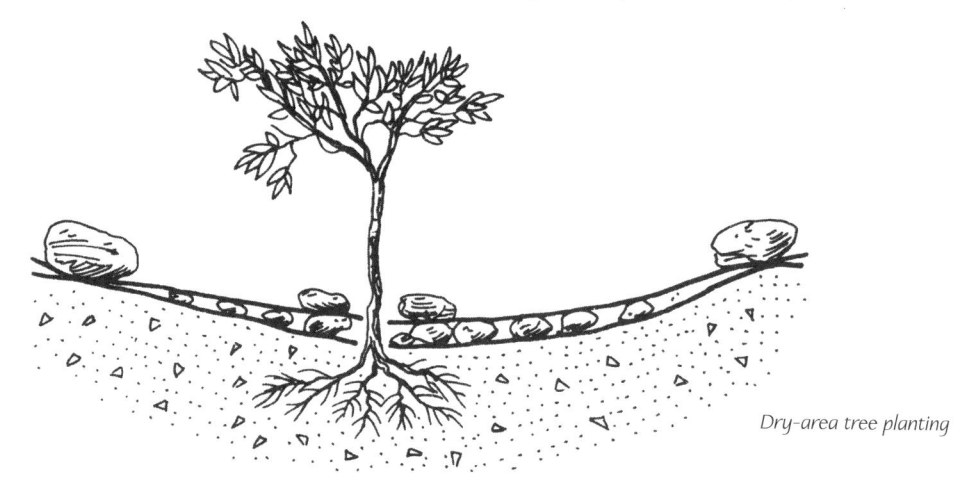

Dry-area tree planting

152 THE WILDERNESS GARDEN

up for mulch) or try other plants instead: mats of chamomile, yarrow, nettles or parsley to stimulate plant growth, and nitrogen-fixers like lucerne, clover, peanuts, lupins, or sweet peas climbing up the trunks, or edibles like Jerusalem artichokes, native ginger, horse-radish, ginseng, tamarilloes, rhubarb or wild strawberries under open branched trees.

In large areas interplant with nitrogen-fixers like wattles, kennedias, false lucerne tree, judas tree, honey locusts, woad, broom (use sterile varieties that won't become a pest), black locust, mesquite or casuarinas (cut back the young branches to use as mulch beneath the trees).

Attract predators with natives flowering throughout the year, and flowering *umbellifera* like parsnip and dill. These will greatly reduce codling moth numbers in apple orchards. Let parsnips go to seed and self-sow. Once started they are incredibly hardy and prolific and will even grow in pasture in the orchard. Repeated mowing simply makes them flower more, and they will rush to seed in late winter/early spring just as you need flowering plants.

Nasturtiums inhibit aphids and woolly aphids. I find yellow daisies twining up the lower branches even better.

Ants, which may carry sap-sucking pests like aphids (the ants feed on their sugary secretions) and may transmit viruses, are said to be repelled by catnip and tansy. I have never found either effective, and rely on grease-banding instead.

ALTERNATIVES TO GRASS UNDER TREES

Ploughed ground is bad for trees – it disturbs their roots, interferes with natural soil associations, may create a hard pan, and in some cases increases moisture loss. (Though in other cases the careful turning over of wet soil may help retain moisture.)

Bare soil is also an invitation to weeds, and bare soil brings dust – and a coating of dust may kill smaller predators without harming pests such as San Jose scale. Ploughed orchards tend to have more pests than similar orchards under ground cover.

Grass is not necessarily the best ground cover for orchards. Couch grass, for example, releases a growth inhibitor from its roots that stunts the roots of several fruit trees. Kikuyu may choke trees and compete for nutrients and moisture. Even if you do choose to have grass under your trees, try mixing several species to make an orchard 'ley'. Instead of grass try some of the companion herbs: chamomile and marjoram or even mint make good under-tree mats.

Lucerne is an excellent crop below fruit trees, as long as it is mown very short. Mown lucerne responds like grass by forming a sward. It is perennial, nitrogen-fixing, and is reputed to encourage earthworms. The roots will continue to travel down year after year – I have known them to go seven metres down a rocky well site. Once lucerne roots are deep enough they will no longer compete with your fruit trees, and the deep roots will bring up leached nutrients which will become available to your plants as the lucerne is mown and the tops break down.

Any grass should be mixed with nitrogen-fixing clover – the sort of clover will depend on your district. Subterranean clovers will also help add organic matter to your soil, as will any mown orchard sward. Don't grow buttercups or other ranunculi or sunflowers in clover – they inhibit it.

All legumes are said to be stimulated by a small proportion of up to 10 per cent of mustard in the mix. Mustard is a quick-growing annual, readily reseeding.

Think about planting flowers under your trees. Dandelions produce ethylene, which will induce your flowers and fruiting trees to bloom earlier, though the flowers may not last as long. The effect will depend on how windy your garden is: a still, warm garden will mean a greater effect from the ethylene. Like lucerne, dandelions are also deep-rooted and they will bring up nutrients leached deep down, returning them to the soil as their leaves decompose. Dandelions also encourage earthworms and generally improve soil condition.

Nettles increase nitrogen-fixing bacteria and improve the quality of the soil, though they are perhaps not the best orchard companions – fruit picking with bare legs can become a problem with nettles around.

COPING WITH FRUIT PESTS

Stop worrying: trees have fruited for millennia without human intervention. With good soil and good planning your trees should thrive with minimal help from you. More trees have died from over-feeding, over-watering and over-digging than have ever died from neglect. Think of it as your ecological duty to simply sit back and enjoy them and their fruit.

How to have a pest-free orchard

- Grow groves. Groves disguise the scent and shape of trees from pests. Grow vines like rambling roses, chilcayote melons, passionfruit, banana passionfruit, chokoes, grapes, and kiwi fruit up your trees too; shrubs like scented pelargoniums or strongly scented lemon marigold (a 2-metre perennial bush with a scent like paradise) tangling in the lower branches.
- Avoid planting all one species or all one age, if possible. That just gives pests a smorgasbord. Interplant with flowering shrubs and nitrogen-fixers.
- Don't plant trees where a similar tree has been before, especially peaches. New trees can be poisoned by the root residues of old trees, the soil may be depleted or there may be levels of pathogens which the old tree gradually got used to but the new one can't tolerate.
- Good soil means fewer pests and disease.
- Orchard hygiene is the best orchard pest control. Pick up any fallen fruit at once or, better still, let animals scavenge it. Remove all dried fruit mummies every winter. Pick off diseased leaves and fruit as they appear. Inspect your fruit for codling moth or fruit fly damage. Pick off any affected fruit, and let it decompose in a sealed plastic bag.
- Never leave fallen fruit on the ground.
- Get some chooks. They eat pests on the ground, and pest-infested fruit.

YEAR-ROUND FRUIT

In a temperate climate you should be able to grow, with a bit of manipulation, enough fruit varieties to have at least several cropping at the same time. Most of the fruits listed below can be grown in all but the very cold or tropical regions of Australia. You can achieve a wide spread of picking times by:

- minimum pruning (more branches mean fruit ripens over a longer period on the tree);
- choosing a wide range of early and late varieties (say, Irish Peach, Jonathan, Beauty of Bath and Lady Sudely apples that ripen from late November to January, and Lady Williams and Sturmer Pippin that can be picked in late July and stored for three to six months after that);
- using micro-climates in your garden.

Micro-climates

Even a small garden has warm and cold areas. In my garden, for example, two delicious apple trees flower and bear two weeks apart from each other: one is in a warm spot, another in a frosty hollow. These micro-climates can be utilised to extend the growing season of your fruit: plants in warm spots bear fruit early, while plants in cold spots bear later. Micro-climates can also extend the range of fruit you grow: A frost hollow may give enough chilling for apples, while a warm sheltered spot by a north-facing wall may let you grow avocados.

Warm areas include north-facing walls, and white or stone walls, which store the heat. Often spots by dams or even fish ponds are warmer: the water stores heat.

You can make a warm garden by piling old tyres a couple of metres high, filling them with compost and growing crops in them. North-facing slopes are usually less frosty, and so are higher areas of the garden.

Cold spots are often hollows where the frost can't drain away; shady spots that get little direct sunlight, especially warm morning light; or exposed sites with cold winds.

Wander round your orchard throughout the year. Some places will feel warmer, some cooler. Mark them on a chart and use them for planting.

AN ORCHARD TO FIT IN A HANDBAG

Longing for an orchard, but you only have a tiny backyard? Sick of yelling at the birds who guzzle your fruit before you can pick it? Tired of either wormy fruit or lots of spraying? Want a gorgeous looking hedge that will give you tucker too?

You need a few dwarf fruit trees – or even a heck of a lot of dwarf fruit trees, because with dwarf trees you can fit a whole orchard into a tiny space. Dwarf fruit trees are grown on 'dwarf' root stocks, so that the trees never grow very large. All dwarf trees will still produce normal-size fruits.

Growing dwarf fruit trees means that almost any garden can have its own orchard. Kids love dwarf fruit trees too – kid-size trees with the great taste of home-grown fruit. If you're having trouble getting your kids to eat fruit, let them grow their own. (The same goes for veg – kids who turn up their noses

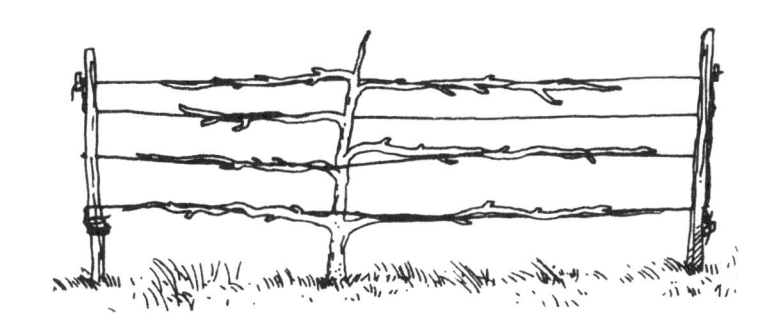

Espalier fruit trees can be pruned and trained to fit along house and garden walls, to benefit from such micro-climates.

North-facing slopes, boulders and stone or brick walls all absorb and store heat, as do ponds, dams and tyres.

THE FRUIT GARDEN 155

at a boiled carrot will eat one they've just picked and washed under the tap.)

Dwarf fruit trees also make great – and edible – hedges. We have a dwarf apple hedge growing up behind our bathroom, and if you want a neat and flowering hedge around your vegetable garden, a dwarf peach hedge may be just what you need. And because dwarf trees are small they are easily netted to keep out birds – or pests like fruit fly, if you use fruit fly exclusion netting. Dwarf trees put out less growth, so they don't need as much pruning either.

HOWEVER: dwarf trees are much more likely to blow over in strong winds, much less drought hardy, and don't work as well in groves.

WHICH SMALL TREES?

Apples

Most dwarf apple trees grow to between two and three metres high and two metres wide, though you can prune them so they stay smaller. If space is really a problem, go for the 'Ballerina' range of 'columnar' apples, that form just one trunk with small shoots and fruits along it.

Specialist growers like Bob Magnus in Tasmania grow literally hundreds of varieties of dwarf apple, but you'll also find a decent range at your local nursery. There are even dwarf apple trees for tropical areas. Dwarf apple trees bear earlier than full-size trees, but I've found that with their smaller root system dwarf apples are not quite as hardy as normal-size apple trees in a drought. In windy areas, young trees should be staked too.

Peaches and nectarines

Most of these in the nursery will be very small trees indeed, like 'Nectarzee' yellow-fleshed nectarine, or 'Pixzee' yellow-fleshed peach, growing no more than a metre high, though some dwarf peaches or nectarines grow to about two metres. These trees have stunning blossom in spring, and don't need the severe yearly pruning that the larger trees do, but their flavour isn't quite as good as some of the larger varieties. But they'll still taste better than any cold-stored commercial fruit!

Pears

Most pears are big trees, but you can buy pears from Bob Magnus that are grafted onto quince stock, which gives smaller trees.

Plums

Dwarf plums exist – again, Bob Magnus supplies them – but you may not find them at your local nursery. 'Gulfgold' is a semi-dwarfing modern plum that is more often available.

Almonds

Most almond trees grow large, and you need two for cross pollination, but the 'All in One' dwarf almond is also self-fertile. Its almonds are pretty good, too.

Mulberries

You may have to hunt through a few nurseries for the 'dwarf black' mulberry, but they do exist! Ours has lived happily in a pot for about seven years, and bears several cups of fruit each year. It will even bear a second time if hard pruned after the first crop. As well as the fruit, you get gorgeous gold autumn leaves in cooler areas, but the trees bear fruit in the subtropics too.

Pomegranates

Most nurseries will stock both dwarf and semi-dwarf pomegranates. Do check the label to make sure your dwarf pomegranate will fruit – some dwarf pomegranates are grown strictly for their flowers and stunning autumn leaves. But the fruit is just as lovely, even if you never cook with it – great yellow and red globulous things that the birds adore.

Cherries

Most cherries are massive trees, but dwarf trees are becoming available. Compact Stella is not only a great tasting cherry but also self-fertile – she doesn't need another variety to pollinate her. She'll also crop in slightly warmer climates than most cherries.

Oranges and other citrus

Seedling orange trees can grow to about 20 metres, but the ones you buy at the nursery have been grafted onto various rootstocks. Trifoliata rootstock produces fairly small trees, and there is a very dwarfing trifoliata variety that produces true dwarf orange trees. As with many dwarf fruit trees though, dwarf orange trees won't be available every year in the nurseries.

Chinotto trees are sometimes sold as a variety of cumquat, as their fruit is cumquat-sized, but unlike cumquats, which are Fortunella, not true citrus, chinottos are really small sour oranges, and the Chinotto tree only grows to about two metres high. Their fruit makes great juice and marmalade, but is pretty sour straight from the tree.

There are no true dwarf lemon trees, but the Meyer lemon (really a cross between a lemon and a sour orange) can be kept to about two metres, and works well in large pots. Tahitian limes, too, though not dwarf trees, can be kept neatly pruned to no more than two metres high.

Cumquats, by the way, can grow to about 6 metres high! But they are very slow growing, and most are grown in pots, or kept half-starved, so their owners may never realise they have a potential monster on their hands. Calamondins, often sold as cumquats, are hardier and faster growing, and will grow to three or four metres high quite quickly, given good soil and tucker. Calamondins are possibly a cumquat and sour mandarin cross.

Some naturally small fruits

Of course there are many other fruits that don't take up much space either!

In cold areas, think gooseberries, raspberries, black, red and white currants, blueberries, or the new jostaberries, the gooseberry-currant cross. In areas with only light frosts or none at all, how about Cape gooseberries, low chill blueberries, and tamarillos? Or strawberries, for just about any climate in Australia if you choose the right varieties, or a passionfruit or grape vine up a pole?

Even if you only have a sunny patio, you still have room for that orchard!

SMALL FRUIT BUSHES, RAMBLERS AND CLIMBERS

Babaco

Bears fruit in one to two years. Though babaco is more frost-resistant than pawpaw, you can grow it like pawpaw: in moist, well-drained soil with regular feeding or mulch. In very hot areas shade the tree for the first summer or two. Ours accepts five degrees of frost but loses its leaves until spring.

Monstera deliciosa

Delicious fruit, but tiny hairs are too irritating to make it worth bothering with. However, it's an attractive plant, great in established groves where it accepts frost to minus 7°C. Otherwise, frost-free tropics to subtropics. Moist soil, but tolerates extreme drought.

Native ginger

Superb ground cover in groves, where it will tolerate tropics to heavy frost. Best in dappled shade and moist soil but survives extreme drought. Use the roots like ginger, or eat the sweet berries. Leaves can be used to wrap food for cooking.

Pineapple

Bears fruit in one and a half to seven years in colder areas. These need acid, well-drained, frost-free soil, and lots of mulch. We grow ours by piling two tyres and planting a pineapple top in the middle with the bottom leaves stripped off. Also good in big pots on warm paving. As it grows, we mulch it. This increases the heat, cuts down frost, and keeps in moisture. Add a sprinkle of blood and bone in spring. Plants will reproduce for years but the fruit will get smaller. Plant new suckers.

BLACKBERRY AND RELATIONS

Domestic 'brambleberries' have just enough of the 'weed' in them so you don't have to break your back growing them, but not so much that they become a menace. There are many blackberry hybrids, but the following are the most common in Australia. In order of ripening:

Silvanberry

These are large, shiny, and VERY prickly, vigorous black berries. They ripen here about late November and fruit from then on until early February – the longest cropping season of all the brambles. They're sweet and luscious, but don't have the rich raspberry hints of some of the other brambleberries. But if you are just growing one brambleberry – and you are sure you'll hack it back every winter – this is a good one to choose.

Loganberry

These are a cross between a blackberry and a dewberry, long rich red fruit, a bit too sour to eat fresh unless you add a sprinkle of sugar or eat with sweet cream or ice-cream – yum. They make wonderful pies.

Like Silvanberries, loganberries are one of the first berries to fruit each year, about early December in our climate, but earlier in warmer climates; but, unlike silvanberries, they only fruit for about three weeks. Old-fashioned ones have thorns. New varieties are thornless and hardier.

Youngberry

These ripen next. They're black and full of flavour and sweeter than loganberries. They're also usually thorny. There is a thornless youngberry, but it is said to be a bit tasteless. Youngberries fruit for about three weeks.

Marionberry

The next to ripen, squishy, dark red berries, with a hint of raspberry in flavour, they aren't as vigorous as the other brambles. You usually get one flush of fruit, then no more until next year, unless the canes are very well fed and tended.

Boysenberry

Boysenberries have a wonderful flavour, and are firm enough to store if treated gently. The plant is also very vigorous – highly recommended for any spare bit of fence.

Blackberry

Thornless blackberries (though they do have some thorns) start to ripen here in mid-February, and keep ripening for about three weeks. They are richly flavoured, though in wet years can be soft and tasteless.

WHERE AND HOW TO GROW

Brambleberries fruit on two-year-old canes. The canes grow for the first year, then fruit and die the second year, while at the same time new one-year-old canes will be trying to tangle themselves up in the older ones.

Brambleberries need full sun and a fence or trellis to climb along, and have to be carefully trained along it unless you want them to turn into a messy clump. Plant them about two metres apart and train the 'canes' up and along the fence. Wear gloves – most brambles do have thorns – just not as many as their weed relatives.

When the canes have finished cropping every year (i.e., in autumn or winter), cut back all canes that have fruited to ground level. It's easiest to cut the canes AS SOON AS THEY HAVE STOPPED FRUITING or they'll become so mixed with the new canes it'll be hard to separate them. Tie new growth to the trellis every few weeks or it will start to spread over the garden instead of upwards.

HARVEST

Leave berries on the vine for at least a week after they look ripe, unless they start to rot or shrivel or fall off. They'll be much sweeter than if you pick them as soon as they begin to colour. Use them the same day you pick them – all brambles lose a lot of their flavour in the fridge. If you really want to taste a good brambleberry, you need to grow your own.

STORE

Berries freeze easily – bung them whole in a freezer bag, a few at a time. But again, they lose delicious pungency and are squishy when thawed. They're best used fresh, or stew them with apple and freeze that.

RASPBERRIES (SEE ALSO ATHERTON RASPBERRY)

Bears fruit in the first year. With thick mulch they don't need staking. We also grow them with comfrey which is slashed to make the mulch. Try growing them through reinforcing mesh to keep them upright.

Theoretically you need to know whether you have summer- or autumn-bearing raspberry varieties; in practice, just cut out the canes after you pick the fruit.

Summer-bearing raspberries

These canes grow in the first year; the second year they fruit. They may fruit after that, but it's best to cut out all canes AS SOON AS THEY HAVE FRUITED, as they next crops wont be much and, anyway, more canes will have grown up from the ground and these are the ones you want to fruit next year.

TRAINING SUMMER-BEARING RASPBERRIES

Tie the canes to a trellis about 1.5 m tall. Bend any tall tops over to one side and tie them to the trellis too. This will encourage more laterals (the short branches that will grow out from the main vine in spring and will have flowers on the end of them.) These flowers will produce your fruit and by that stage the leaves will look dull and tatty.

Autumn-fruiting raspberries

These canes grow and fruit in the same year. Cut back ALL canes to ground level in early winter or as soon as they have finished cropping.

Still confused?

Okay, if you do nothing at all, you'll still get raspberries but the bed will become choked with lots of spindly canes. So cut out plants as soon as they have fruited, to help prevent confusion about what to cut and also to prevent them harbouring harlequin beetles and disease spores.

Then in winter cut out the spindliest looking canes and leave the good fat ones and mulch them VERY well and bung on some tucker too unless your mulch is compost.

More raspberry info

Don't bother about raspberries unless you wear an overcoat in winter as they need

THE FRUIT GARDEN

between 800–1600 hours of chilling and for best flavour you need cool Highland temperatures too. Hot winds will kill them as will intense summer afternoon sun; the only way we can grow ours is in a spot where they get afternoon shade and morning sun.

Raspberries also need moist fertile soil and REPEATED MULCH; they also hate weeds and mulch will control these for you. Basically raspberries are fussy – if the climate is perfect and the soil naturally high in organic matter they'll become a weed but if they aren't totally content you won't get fruit and the plants may die.

Raspberry patches become gradually less vigorous after a few years, although I know of a couple of well-mulched ones (one is fed with deceased rabbits dug between the rows) that are at last 40 years old and thriving. If your canes do decline dig them out and plant new imports in clean ground. Spray canes with Bordeaux in winter to kill disease spores; net against birds (make sure the nets reach the ground and trail a few centimetres across it too); water thoroughly in spring to deter thrips; but a very thick lucerne hay mulch each winter will help keep plants pest- and disease-free (if you don't believe me, try one patch with and one without!)

Berries ripen from November to early winter, depending on variety. Pick EVERY day otherwise the smell of the ripe fruit will attract harlequin beetles (dry berries are beetle sucked berries) and harbour disease; also, birds will get used to picking them before you do. To deter harlequin beetles, use an aluminium foil mulch between the canes, or splash grease around the base.

OTHER BERRIES

Blueberries

Bears fruit in two to three years. Blueberries grow in acid soil throughout most of Australia, but the fruit is soft and bland except in cold areas. Feed your berries well: constant, good quality mulch, or at the very least well-mown grass around them and 'additives' (see Chapter 5) twice a year.

We grow our blueberries under the shade of trees. I throw on sawdust every winter after chainsawing, and hen manure every spring. Not at all drought hardy, they must have moisture.

Currants

Bears fruit in two to three years. Mulch them. Give red and white currants a yearly sprinkle of wood ash or comfrey for potash. Black currants need more nitrogen. Give them a feed such as blood and bone in winter, or mulch them with a kilogram of manure per bush. Currants only fruit with cold winters. Don't prune red or white currants. Thin out black currants every few years as they fruit on new wood. Make a small bird net out of old pantyhose to keep birds away, or better still: we grow our currants under the kiwi fruit pergola; the birds don't find them, and currants fruit at a different time of year from kiwi fruit. All grow VERY easily from cuttings.

Elderberries

Bears fruit in two to three years, but some cultivars never fruit. These small trees grow easily from a cutting in cool weather. When they turn dark, use the berries for pies or stews or in fruit salad. Don't bother with 'so-called' purple- or red-leafed elders.

Cape gooseberry

Bears fruit in the first year. We grow most of ours under other fruit trees – Cape gooseberries do best in light shade. This also protects them from frosts. They are hit each winter, but grow back and fruit each summer. Birds can spread the seeds and in warmer areas they can become a weed.

Grow a thick hedge of thorny gooseberries to keep cats out of your garden.

Slightly frost resistant, especially if grown under a tree, they carry round orange fruit in paper lanterns. They are good space fillers: hardy and fast growing and they fruit within a year. They grow easily from seed. Ours, which are against the house in a sheltered spot, accept five degrees of frost.

Gooseberries

In Victorian times, children were told that babies came from gooseberry beds (the doctor dug them up with a golden spade), because they were so thorny that inquisitive children were unlikely to go down and investigate if any babies were really hidden under the leaves.

Bears fruit in one to three years. Gooseberries only set fruit in temperate to cool climates. They are excellent 'fillers' for bare areas, or can be used as a small thorny hedge to keep out cats from the flower and vegetable bed.

Give good tucker and mulch in autumn. Don't prune them unless you like them neat.

Atherton raspberry

This is a native raspberry, growing like an upright cane-like suckering shrub, and producing about 2–3 kg of fruit per year. Tolerates heat, drought and frost, and is delicious. Just plant, feed, and water if you have it.

Midyim berry

Native. Tiny sweet-fleshed fruit, edible seeds. Accepts heat, sun, dappled shade in groves; cut by frosts but groves protect to about minus 3°C.

STRAWBERRIES

Bear fruit in the first year. Strawberries prefer acid soil with plenty of humus and moisture: a casuarina mulch is excellent and will help prevent leaf spot. Keep strawberries moist: drip irrigation is excellent, mulch almost a necessity. If you get less than 20 mm of rain a week you'll need to water your strawberries.

If you mulch your berries, or grow them under trees where they get each year's leaf litter, you may not have to feed them at all. Otherwise, give them a scatter of blood and bone or old hen manure in winter.

Plant your runners in autumn or winter. Autumn planting is more usual in subtropical areas where a winter crop is wanted. Set the runners out on their own small hills, or just plant them about a handspan apart.

Buy virus-tested runners – next door's spares are probably virus infested, and won't bear well. Commercial growers replace runners every three years: the virus is spread by aphids, and plants are usually infected by then. But the home gardener, who doesn't mind a smaller yield, needn't bother. There are also several superb varieties that grow from seed and don't produce runners.

If you are choosing your own runners, try to take the first runner on a plant, and one that hasn't flowered yet. Thin out beds as they become crowded.

Inter-planting

Grow your berries under trees. After all, strawberries are originally an under-forest species, and do well in broken light, sheltered by trees and fertilised by falling leaves. You can also create your own 'forest' effect. I've grown strawberries under a pergola of kiwi fruit, while a neighbour just rambled hers as ground cover through the flowerbed. This was very successful: the perennial flowers protected the strawberries, the strawberries kept weeds from the flowers, and the berries were also much less obvious to the birds.

You can 'clothe' a clump of berries with bent-over old coathangers covered in clear plastic bags. The plastic will only last one season, but is easily replaced next time you go to the supermarket. This will give you very early or late strawberries.

Cutting back strawberries

Try cutting back your strawberry plants as soon as the first burst of fruit is over. I use a whipper snipper, and just run over them as though I am mowing the grass. This will set the plants back so they will produce fewer runners – but they'll recover in time for an autumn or even a winter crop. Even Red Gauntlet, which produce through most of summer, can be cut back in early autumn and then clothed – this way you should get some berries in early winter.

Strawberries are infected by a variety of leaf problems, all with much the same solutions. Try spraying Bordeaux in winter, use trickle irrigation instead of overhead sprinklers, don't let your beds get overcrowded, and keep mulching. If birds are a problem, grow more strawberries.

Strawberries from seed

Alpine strawberries grow from seed, don't produce runners and aren't attractive to birds. New varieties are sweeter than the old cardboard ones, but are of course more attractive to birds too. Try yellow alpine strawberries – birds may not notice them.

Growing strawberries

Take a nice pile of weeds. Cover with weed-mat. Cut holes in the mat, poke in compost, then the strawberry plants. Water well.

STRAWBERRY BARREL

Fill a barrel with soil. Cut holes in the barrel and plant the berries.

STRAWBERRY TERRACES

Make terraces from old railway sleepers or rocks, and let the berries cascade downwards.

STRAWBERRIES IN TYRES

Pile up irregularly shaped tyres. Fill them with weeds or straw, and top them with compost or potting mix. Plant your strawberries in the holes and crevices.

STRAWBERRY WALL

Build a retaining wall of stone, wood or brick, leaving lots of gaps. Stuff with soil and berry plants.

BERRIES IN A CAN

Take a large can, like a kerosene drum. Slice holes in it, turn down the edges so they aren't sharp, fill with soil, and plant berries in the holes.

THE HANGING GARDENS IN CHAPTER 6 ARE EXCELLENT FOR STRAWBERRIES.

We plant carpets of berries under our trees and under the pergola. If you are short of

Strawberries in a weed-mat covered pile of weeds.

space, plant strawberries down the centre of your drive – a few may squash, but it's better than none at all.

Grapes

Bear fruit in one to three years. We grows ours up fruit trees, never bother with pruning, spraying or feeding and let the leaves fall prematurely if they get downy mildew – and still get masses of grapes. The birds eat most on the pergola (can be covered in fruit bags if necessary), but ignore the ones growing up the prickly bunya or amongst the fruit trees.

There are hundreds of grape varieties in Australia, for cold, hot and humid areas. Don't prune them – they'll just need more feeding, and the birds will have a feast. Grapes are a good deciduous vine to keep out summer sun and let in winter sun. Let them ramble up the pergola, over the fence, or up a tree. Plant the roots away from the tree trunk so they get watered by rain and don't compete for nutrients. Train the grape stem round a bit of string up to the lower branches of the tree.

Our grapes get powdery mildew. Try milk spray, and mulch to stop spores splashing up. Or just let them die down if it's late in the season and they've fruited – a good strong grape vine won't die from an attack of mildew, though a young one or a heavily pruned one might.

If birds attack the fruit, grow more vines, until every tree or post has a vine up it, and let them tangle so the fruit is hidden.

Kiwi fruit

I grow kiwi fruit up other trees – saves space, mulch and water and cuts down pest and bird damage. (Try the 'wild' ones that don't need male and female. They have small fruit but I think better flavoured, if not as sweet.) Bears fruit in three to four years. They are rampant growers which will sneak through the window and choke you as you sleep if you let them go. Hack them back every winter, leaving some of last year's wood to ensure good fruit.

Kiwi fruit tolerate frost, and flower quite late in early November, after most frosts have finished, so they are good for bad frost areas. Once you get them up a pergola they are

Let grapevines wander through your fruit trees: you'll cut down on bird damage and on pests and disease of both vine and tree. Plant the vine out past the branches so the rain will be able to get to it, and so it won't have to compete with the tree for nutrients.

THE FRUIT GARDEN 163

relatively frost-proof. They do, however, need good mulch and moisture the first year, as they are shallow rooted, and can die in the heat. They also can't stand waterlogged soil. Cool winters are needed for fruit set. Once your kiwi fruit are established they won't need much feeding unless you prune them a lot – in which case they will need nutrients to replace lost leaves. I find that a scatter of hen manure once a year is plenty. Don't encourage them too much or they'll take over.

You can also buy red-fleshed kiwi fruit and 'wild berries that don't need a male and female for pollination. They make great decoys to keep birds from other fruit.

Passionfruit

We may use at least six passionfruit a day – no kidding. Passionfruit is an essential in fruit salad, most jellies, and the frozen fruit salad I gluttonise on in summer. And Bryan likes to eat one with a spoon each breakfast. Passionfruit cordial is our favourite drink and the juice is also great over ice-cream, stirred into orange and other juices, on pavlovas, and on iced cakes or in cream sponges. Add pulp instead of liquid in plain cake or biscuit recipes to make them passionfruit-flavoured instead.

Grow the vines:
- on builders' mesh against a sunny wall in cold climates;
- on builders' mesh along fences – the extra height also keeps out wallabies;
- up the chook yard fence (passionfruit love chook poo);
- on builders mesh around a tank in a sunny spot – the retained heat of the water keeps them warm in cold winters;
- as groundcover down a sunny bank – they produce lots of fruit, look green and flowery and black snakes adore sheltering there too;
- up a pole, which takes up much less space than a trellis – they sort of blob out quite attractively, the fruit matures even within the clump; collect them as the ripe ones fall each morning.

Passionfruit also grow very well in large pots on a balcony. They would be worth growing even if they didn't fruit – complex white and purple flowers and glossy leaves. The banana passionfruit, which is even more cold tolerant and vigorous than ordinary passionfruit, has great, vivid pink flowers too (see below).

PS Feed passionfruit WELL – a poorly growing passionfruit usually gets sick. Feed each month with a scatter of hen manure. Give at least one dose of seaweed fertiliser a year, and MULCH!

PPS The plant is very susceptible to viruses, root rots, insect attack – which makes it sound like the least likely to succeed in your garden. EXCEPT – a strongly growing passionfruit vine outgrows almost all problems. Most passionfruit are grafted and the graft suckers. Pull them up at once or they can wander all over the place.

In warm areas the vines fruit most of the year but in colder areas only in late summer. Pick them when they change colour and shrivel just slightly. They will keep for several months in the fridge or a cool cupboard, but will gradually lose their sweetness. The pulp can be frozen in ice blocks for later use.

Banana passionfruit

More cold hardy than black passionfruit. Glorious, pink flowers. Rambles and covers weeds wonderfully.

Granadilla

A passionfruit for hot areas. Delicious.

Pepino

Small fruit like a delicious egg-shaped passionfruit on a small, spreading shrub. Tolerates only mild frost, but is hardier in groves. Accepts dappled grove shade or full sun.

FRUIT TREES

Almonds

Almonds are extremely drought resistant; they also need winter chilling and are one of the earliest fruits to flower – not suitable where there are late frosts or warm winters. Avoid growing them unless you are in an almond growing area with cool winters and dry summers.

For a good crop almonds also need pruning, cross pollinators (or grow a self-fertile variety) and regular feeding. Birds also love them. Plant the tree down the back, with other trees around to hide the fruit from the white cockatoos and where you won't be bothered if it gets curly leaf.

Apples

Try a hedge of 20 varieties of apple, a metre apart, for home-grown apples all year round.

Apples bear fruit in three to four years. Dwarf apples bear in two to three years.

Many varieties, such as Anna, Tropic Sweet, Granny Smith, Gravenstein, golden delicious and five crown pippin, can be grown in subtropical areas, but by and large the cooler climates produce crisper and sweeter fruit.

There are many hundreds of apple varieties available in Australia, so don't be limited to the few in the shops. Hunt around in specialist nurseries. Some are early, some flower late – so choose varieties for your area. Late-flowering varieties won't be hit by late frosts. We have apples fruiting from late November (Irish Peach), December (Jonathan, soft and small) to June (Lady Williams, a red Granny Smith type), and August: Sturmer pippin, which is best after it's been picked and stored for two months.

Apples need cross-pollination. If you don't have much room, buy a double graft, or plant two trees in one hole or nearby – they'll help dwarf each other.

Apples need good feeding when young – mulch in spring and hen manure in autumn are excellent – but, unless they are very heavy bearers, regular mowing and a sprinkle of hen manure should be enough once they are mature. We grow strawberries around apple trees, and let parsnips and fennel go to seed to control codling moth (see pests in Chapter 7).

Pick apples slightly young for storage. A foliar calcium-rich spray or seaweed spray may help their shelf life. Use fruit fly netting if trees are attacked by fruit fly or codling moth. Or grow winter apples – fruit fly free!

Great late apples: French Crab (no relation … and not really a crab either), which is probably one of Granny Smith's parents. Our tree is about 12 years old now and it's fruited well even in the hottest, driest weather. The green-skinned apples are a bit smaller than Granny Smith and they mature much later – in fact, if the birds don't get them you can still be picking them in late August.

BESS POOL

Bess is one of the latest 'dessert apples', maturing about May here and good to eat fresh. Very crisp, dry flesh, absolutely delicious. She flowers late too so she's great in frosty areas.

STURMER PIPPIN

Large, yellow-green apple – best eaten after it's been stored for at least a month or two. It turns even more yellow and a bit wrinkled and looks most unattractive … until you bite into it! Ripens here in June–July but hangs on the tree until August.

LADY WILLIAMS

An Aussie bred, very late, hard apple, with rich red skin, also at its best after a month or two's storage. It's my favourite salad apple, thinly sliced in dressing, and great cooked. Ripens here in late June–July, but we're still eating them in December.

PINK LADY

Daughter of Lady William and golden delicious, a crisp, large, pink-skinned, sweet eating apple.

DEMOCRAT

Very hard, rich red-skinned fruit, a seedling (like Granny Smith) found on a Tasmanian farm. Great in tarts, but a bit hard to eat fresh if you value your teeth. Stores even at home for a year or more.

Apricots

Apricots bear fruit in two to four years.

Sun-ripened apricots are perhaps the most fragrant fruit in the world. Apricots don't need pruning. Unless they are taking over the garden, leave them alone – pruning may spread bacterial gummosis.

Apricots need hot summers and cold winters for fruit set. They are susceptible to late frosts. Groves protect the tree, but not apricot fruit. They like lots of organic matter: mulch well to start with, then keep the lawn mown or eaten down and give compost, mulch or hen manure in autumn. A thick autumn or winter mulch will also delay flowering, which may save your blossom from frost. Too much nitrogen gives fast-rotting, floury, tasteless fruit.

The main problem with apricots is brown rot on the fruit. Avoid this by removing dried-out fruit mummies in winter, spraying with Bordeaux spray in winter, or with seaweed spray every two weeks in summer. I recommend a mixture of seaweed spray and chamomile tea every week once fruit starts to ripen. Apricots also get fruit fly (see Chapter 7).

Avocados

Every home needs at least 10 avocado trees. Try a 'double' hedge of 10 varieties, planted in two rows with 2 metres between each tree, so you can have avocados all year round.

They are one of the easiest fruits to grow as long as you grow them in sheltered groves, drought tolerant and almost pest free, but they will NOT tolerate any wind at all, hot or cold. Shelter them, and any garden can grow them. Use them as chook food, dog food (dogs usually adore them) or even as hair conditioner. Avocados bear fruit in three to 10 years.

They are MUCH more adaptable than most people realise – and make an excellent hedge for privacy. Trees can grow BIG – Wurtz is probably the smallest variety available, but even varieties that like to reach for the sky can be kept severely trimmed; in bad fruit fly areas don't plant thin-skinned varieties. (Hass are pretty tough, and are one of the smaller trees too.)

Avocados are VERY easy to grow from seed – but you (usually) need two varieties to cross-pollinate each other, or you won't get much fruit. Plant masses of seeds of as many different varieties as you can.

Avocados grow happily in clusters – and as they are so close they'll dwarf each other, so your garden won't turn into an avocado plantation.

If you want to grow long-lived avocados, remember they are jungle trees. They need deep, moist soil and plenty of organic matter, and shading from sun and frost for the first three years. I find avocado seedlings grow best in the shade of other trees. We often find wild avocado seedlings – the birds drop the stones as they sit on the branches eating the fruit, and the seeds germinate in the mulch under the trees. We transplant them after three or four years.

Avocados are often found sprouting on the compost heap. Transplant them gently: the tap root is long and easily damaged, and most young transplants die. Feed them with mulch and compost and shade them with hessian or another tree or preferably in groves. I've raised about 70 seedlings: all have borne fruit and come reasonably true-to-type, though avocados are not meant to.

Prune and shape avocados as little as possible. They are subject to a range of root rots but a mulch of lucerne and wattle bark, high in tannin, will suppress it. Make sure the soil is well drained. Use drip irrigation if you can, not weekly flooding with a hose. Give a sprinkle of dolomite to acid soil every year or two. Feed with phosphorous – and magnesium-rich food like lucerne hay, hen manure, and blood and bone at least once a year.

HARVEST

Avocados any size are edible – but the longer you leave them the better; different varieties and different climates crop at different times. If it comes off easily in your hand, it's ripe. Avocados don't soften for at least 10 days after they're picked. I leave some of ours on the tree for 18 months, long after the new crop is ready – and these elderly ones are SUPERB. (With luck – and if the birds don't get them – you may well have avocados all year round.)

Avocado trees fruit after between three and 10 years, depending on the climate. They can grow up to 10 metres high and wide, but this takes about 30 years. Lop them when you need to, and plant them close together. I find they grow better this way anyway: there is less moisture loss, less heat stress, and more protection from wind – which is the main reason for poor fruit set after frost. Avocados will tolerate up to eight degrees of frost, but not cold winds. Make sure they are very sheltered. Avocados need pollinators, though fruit does set sometimes without them.

Bananas (*Musa paradisica*)

This was the 'tree of neglect' in many warm backyards when I was a child in Brisbane. They need subtropical to tropical, mostly frost-free, conditions. The smaller, sweeter sugar banana is more cold tolerant than the larger varieties.

Bananas bear fruit in two to five years. They are very hungry fruits, and must be well fed and watered, though backyard trees in fertile soil in reliable rainfall areas survive total neglect for decades. In cooler areas, cover bananas with blue polythene bags or other protection against low temperatures in autumn, winter, and spring. Bananas can be propagated by removing suckers or part of the underground rhizome; they prefer a rich soil and shelter from winds – perfect for that patch behind the garden shed where you've piled the rubbish for the past 10 years. Mulch young plants to protect against drying out and summer heat. (I know this doesn't sound like a low maintenance plant, but once it's established it can be left alone for decades – and you'll end up with a banana grove down the back.)

Grow them from suckers about 20 cm high and keep them weed-free. They are heavy feeders: sprinkle the soil with dolomite, add wood ash for potash, and give blood and bone or decayed hen manure every two or three months.

Wrap a banana leaf around ripening fruit to help protect it from flying foxes, birds, and the wind and the sun. Covered, or even indoors, the fruit ripens as well as in the sunlight.

I use banana leaves as 'green' disposable plates. And even in our cold climate they grow – if protected by the rest of the garden.

Sprout an avocado seed (the pip) by balancing it on a pair of toothpicks (use bluetack) over a glass, with the pointed end poking into the water.

Black sapote

Black sapotes bear fruit in three to five years. They are tall, frost-prone trees with long, sweet fruit, slightly like a chocolate pawpaw. They need deep soil and plenty of room, though they can be kept pruned. In cold areas they must be grown deep in a grove to survive – and will take many, many years to grow and fruit.

Brazilian cherry

Extraordinarily hardy, accepts drought, frost, heat and grasshopper plagues. Purple berry fruit. Makes a great hedge. Accepts semi-dappled shade or full dry sun.

Bunya nuts

Bears fruit in 10 to 20 years. The bunya pine is not for small gardens. It can be grown wherever you can grow a lemon tree. The nut cones are enormous. If you want a bunya, plant it in the corner of your block and keep the lower branches pruned. This way you'll be able to use the ground around it. Beware of falling nut cones: they weigh up to 12 kg. I grow chilacayote melons up ours. (Beware of falling nuts AND melons). You could also try grapes.

Bunya trees are either male or female. Ostensibly you need both to produce nuts, though I have known females to bear when there is no male in the vicinity.

Grow the trees from seed – patiently. They take about a year to germinate. The seed should be planted point down in moist soil and kept warm. The trees quickly develop a long tap root. Allow for this when you are planting them out, and transplant carefully. Make sure the young trees are kept moist and free of weeds and grass – in the wild they grow in the bare ground under a parent tree, and you should try to duplicate this.

Burdekin plum

A native rainforest tree, it is great in frost-free groves. Pick purple plums and allow to ripen off the trees for a few days until soft, before eating. Good in jellies too.

Bush lemon

Superb hedge to keep stock in or out, prickly and drought resistant, but not ornamental in droughts, as they can lose their leaves. Will fruit when few other trees survive. Bush lemon bears fruit in two to four years.

In the past, most citrus trees were grafted onto bush lemons. If the main tree died, the rootstock often grew instead. Bush lemons are round, knobbly, thick-skinned and seedy, but very cold- and heat-tolerant, and fast-growing. Try them in difficult areas. They grow quickly and true-to-type from seed.

Candle nuts

A native rainforest tree, its nuts MUST be roasted, not eaten raw, or they are toxic. Nuts are also high in oil and will burn like a candle. Great in frost-free groves.

Calamondins

A very tough prolific citrus, which many people confuse with cumquats. Much sourer and tougher. Grow lots as 'decoy plants' for the birds, then they'll leave your other citrus alone. Birds adore them. They also look gorgeous indoors in vases during winter. Good for jam or jelly or sliced with gin and sugar.

Capulin cherry

Small, purple cherries with a large stone, but the hardiest of trees – drought, frost, and heat hardy, with fruit borne from spring to February. Full sun or dappled shade, in groves.

Carob

Carob bears fruit in three to five years. You need a male and female tree. Full sun or dappled shade in groves. Carob grows quickly from seed. They need very little feeding once established and are drought tolerant. Grind the pods, not the seeds, for carob flour or cocoa.

Cedar bay cherry

Large lilypilly type fruit, bright orange red, tolerates light frost in groves, otherwise warm climates only.

Cherries

Cherries bear fruit in three to four years. You need two varieties for pollination (or a self-pollinating variety such as Stella), cold winters to set fruit, and otherwise a regime of benign neglect. Once they are large enough to fruit, don't feed or water cherries too much or the fruit will split. Don't mulch the trees. A well-mown lawn or, at most, a sprinkle of blood and bone in autumn is plenty once the trees are large. Cherries like sure, slow growth and no pruning.

Try growing four or more cherries about a metre apart. They'll stunt each other's growth, the pollination will be excellent, and birds will be confused by the tangle of branches. Cherries will usually be attacked by pear and cherry slug (see Chapter 7).

Chinotto

Chinotto bears fruit in two to four years. This is a small, ornamental mandarin, used to make 'chinotto' or 'Italian coca cola'. The juice is sweet and musty. It tolerates mild frosts and is much smaller than a mandarin: a good tub tree with pretty, spiked leaves. Like all citrus, it needs plenty of feeding.

Chestnuts

Chestnuts bear fruit in 10 years from seed. Grafted trees may bear earlier.

They need deep moist soil, cold winters to set fruit, though will fruit in the subtropics if there are enough cold winter days, and protection from winds. They are massive trees but we keep ours pruned quite small. Excellent as starter shelter trees for groves.

Cherry of the Rio Grande

Small, purple fruit in spring, hardy trees in frost heat or drought. Good hedge or understorey trees, or they can take full sun. Must be grown in sheltered groves in frosty areas.

Chilean nut

This evergreen tree requires a temperate to subtropical climate. The nut is similar to a hazel nut, but sweeter and usually larger. It is usually eaten roasted. The Chilean nut grows to seven metres and is a good windbreak.

Citron

Citron bears fruit in two to three years. This is the oldest recorded fruit in the world, a frost-hardy citrus like an overgrown lemon, but with a thicker and much more fragrant skin. The tree is smaller than most citrus. Use it for lemon peel or use the juice. Tolerates semi-shade in groves; takes tropical heat or can be grown in frosty areas in groves or pots.

Coffee

Needs frost-free spot, or grow it as an indoor plant in a large pot. Will flower and fruit indoors but needs hand pollination with a small paintbrush. See *New Plants from Old* (Aird Books). Fruits in three years. Accepts dappled shade or full sun. Makes a superb and ornamental hedge in subtropical areas.

Cornelian cherry

This is a small, attractive tree with reddish bark and slightly sour but tasty red fruit.

Children will eat Cornelian cherries straight from the tree. Adults usually find them too tart. But they are good stewed with sugar, used in pies or added to fruit salad – and make a wonderful, glowing red jelly.

The Cornelian cherry will tolerate subtropical to cool climates but prefers a limy soil. It can be propagated by seed or cuttings.

Crab apple

Crab apple bears fruit in two to four years.

Some crab apples are simply ornamentals. Others give fruit large enough to eat – it can be sweet and good. Crab apple jelly or pickled crab apples are divine. Crab apples tolerate almost total neglect. They'll grow from fresh seed: just plant a crab apple fruit and you'll get a new tree, or chill the seeds from older fruit in the fridge for three weeks before planting. Accepts dappled shade or exposed sun.

Cumquat

Cumquat bears in two to four years.

If you think cumquats are bitter you probably have mistaken them for calamondins. Modern cumquat varieties are as big as a small mandarin and as sweet. Cumquats are a small, cold-tolerant tree that can be grown in a pot or a corner of a courtyard. Feed them well with a yearly mulch. If the old leaves turn yellow, the tree needs more nitrogen. But otherwise be careful of high-nitrogen 'additives' as they will make the fruit thick-skinned and sour. Accepts dappled shade in groves but fruits best in full sun.

Curry leaf tree

Supposed to be tropical but survives up to minus 8°C here, in a pot on sunny paving. In warmer areas it is a good grove tree. Use the leaves in curries.

Custard apple

Survives heavy frosts in groves, but only grows to 2 metres with a few smallish fruit. Prefers the subtropics. Treat as an avocado.

Davidson's plum

Tall native, grows best in groves where it will tolerate frost to minus 7°C; otherwise tropical to subtropics. The plum-like fruit is eaten fresh or cooked.

Date palm

These are plants suitable for almost every area – including cold ones. They tolerate high wind (cyclones and tornadoes), drought, salt and limited flooding.

Date seed will germinate but seedlings are variable; suckers are more reliable, or buy commercially cloned trees. Protect all young palms from frost. Must have male and female. Survive cold climates but grow very slowly. Protect all young palms from frost.

Elderberries

These can be stewed, or used for wine, jelly or jam. Some cultivars are sweeter than others. All grow happily in neglected gardens.

Feijoa

Feijoa bears fruit in three to 10 years. An almost maintenance-free tree, it is very hardy in heat, drought and frost, but not high winds. Accepts dappled shade, but most fruit in full sun. We grow ours in a mass of citrus and ginger lilies. A good mulch once a year is plenty. Too much nitrogen means less fruit. No pruning is necessary, but you can prune them to keep their shape. You may need two feijoas for fruit to set.

Figs

Figs bear fruit in one and a half to five years. Will grow in dappled shade but you get less fruit – though still quite a lot. Good hedge tree, though deciduous. I grow grapes through ours.

Fig trees grow from Tasmania to Queensland, but protect them from heavy frost: grow them against a wall in cold climates. Mulch them or keep them in mown grass as they are shallow-rooted. They tolerate drought, grow fastest with plenty of moisture, but cannot stand being waterlogged. They grow easily from winter cuttings.

Figs, native

Native figs bear fruit in two to 10 years. Excellent decoy tree to keep birds from other fruit. All native figs are edible, and a few are good, including the common Morton Bay fig, sandpaper fig and Port Jackson fig. The figs should be eaten when they're very ripe and purple. Some trees seem to produce better figs than others. Try to find out what native figs once grew in your area. They need moist, fertile soil and, to begin with, plenty of mulch – later they make their own.

Ginko

Slow growing, needs moisture, accepts heat or frost, needs male and female for fruit to set. Fallen fruit stinks. Eat the nuts – the seeds – baked. Raw nuts can cause dermatitis, so wear gloves. Leaves have medicinal uses. Extremely lovely trees with stunning autumn leaves.

Governor's plum

Subtropical or tropical, or in the middle of a sheltered grove, this tree won't take frost. Small, drought hardy native fruit, with large berries.

Grapefruit

See oranges.

Grumichama

This small tree is frost and heat hardy. The black clusters of fruit are sourish but reasonably good either raw or stewed.

Guava

STRAWBERRY GUAVA

Tolerates extreme frosts and drought. Great base tree to establish groves in difficult climates. Its insipid, strawberry-flavoured fruit is best marinated with a little lemon and sugar to bring out the flavour.

YELLOW CHERRY GUAVA

Sweet and delicious. Tolerates frost in groves, otherwise frost free to tropical. Drought hardy.

HAWAIIAN

Pink flesh, juicy. Tolerates frost in groves, otherwise frost free to tropical.

INDIAN

White fleshed, lots of seed, juicy. Tolerates frost in groves, otherwise frost free to tropical.

MEXICAN CREAM

White fleshed, delicious. Tolerates frost in groves, otherwise frost free to tropical.

Hazelnuts

Hazelnuts bear fruit in two to six years. Many people grow hazelnuts, but few trees fruit. This is often because they need two varieties to pollinate and most nurseries only sell one. You also need cold winters for flowers. Dig up suckers for more trees, or plant the nuts – they won't grow true-to-type but this won't matter in the home garden. Hazelnuts fruit best as hedges. Will fruit in dappled shade at the edges on groves, but not good in the centre.

Ice-cream bean tree

Fast growing, great as central tree for groves, tolerates drought, light frost and tropical conditions. You eat the pulp surrounding the inedible seeds. Also nitrogen-fixing.

Jaboticoba

Tolerates shade in groves where it's protected from frost. Plum-size fruit grows on the tree's trunk.

Jackfruit

Jackfruit bear in five to seven years. This will grow as far south as Ballina, though ostensibly a tropical tree. It produces enormous, strong-flavoured fruit, too strong if the fruit is overripe. It has a tough rind. The seeds can be peeled and used like breadfruit. The sawdust of the jackfruit tree can be boiled to produce a strong yellow dye – used by Buddhist monks in Asia to colour their robes.

Protect the tree from frost until it is five years old and give it a moist, deep well-drained soil. May not fruit in cold areas even if protected. Tolerates deep shade in groves but grows very slowly.

Japanese raisin tree

The Japanese raisin tree produces quite delicious dried sap in raisin-like clusters when it is about 10 years old.

This fast-growing tree tolerates almost any climate and can be raised from a seed. Don't eat the fruit – the 'raisins' are the accumulation of gum in the corners of the branches. They are superb. The trees are fast-growing and problem free. Great in any spot in groves.

Jelly palm

Soft, sweet fruit on a frost hardy palm. Also drought hardy.

Juniper

Juniper berries are a traditional condiment. Pick the berries when they are black, dry them in the sun until they are shrivelled, then store in a dry spot or sealed jar. Add them whole to a marinade or a bouquet garni, or crushed to stews and gravies. Juniper takes the gamey taste away from wild meat. Juniper jam can be served with cold meat, especially mutton or pork.

The juniper bush is exceptionally drought hardy and frost tolerant, and will grow in poor to rich soil. To get berries you must have a male and a female tree. The berries take three years to ripen, first green, then blue, then black. Juniper can be grown from seed – which is slow to germinate – or from cuttings taken in autumn or late winter.

Kaffir plum

This is a broad, densely shading tree with an invasive root system and fruit like a sour plum suitable for jam, drying or stewing with sweet fruit. It accepts moderate frosts, and any soil as long as it is well drained. Incredibly hardy trees, they make a good hedge, and yield sourish fruit all summer. Good in groves.

Kakadu plum

A tall, skinny tree, this native yields small fruit in autumn – yellow, red or purple. Tolerates frost in the centre of established groves, otherwise it's for frost-free climates. Needs moist soil for good growth, but tolerates drought.

Kei apple

Prickly, incredibly hardy, good hedge to keep stock in or out, sweet plum-sized fruit. Not suitable for young children, because of thorns. Good 'base' tree for groves in difficult, dry conditions.

Kurrajong

The kurrajong bears fruit in three to 10 years. These trees tolerate slight frost. They need deep, fertile soil and good drainage. As with most 'wild' trees, the quality of the fruit varies.

Lilypilly

Lilypillies bear fruit in three to 10 years. There are many kinds of lilypilly – we grow about 13. To my surprise even the ones that come from Cape York (I collected the seed on a visit there) survive our winters. And even though they do MUCH better with lots of water, they survive drought too, as long as they are grown in groves for extra shelter from hot, dry winds. Lilypillies hate hot, dry winds.

The young foliage is frost tender but the trees survive light frost, especially if they're grown in the shelter of larger trees. Lilypillies need moist soil. The fruit ranges from edible to tasty: like most trees that are not selected for their fruit, the quality varies. The berries range from green to blue to red, depending on the cultivar. Riberries is the most popular fruit to eat raw, but all are good cooked.

NB! Pick fruit for eating and cooking before it is fully coloured – over-ripe and fully coloured fruit may have a turpentine taste. You may need a few years of tasting to learn when your lilypillies tastes best.

Lilypilly isn't a sweet fruit, but once you add sugar and a touch of lemon juice, you have a stunner. Lilypilly cordial is real 'grown-ups' cordial. But DO pick the fruit before it is quite fully coloured – when it's bright red to purple it becomes a bit astringent.

LILYPILLY CORDIAL

Simmer 6 cups of fruit in 6 cups of water until soft. Strain. Add 6 cups of white sugar and the juice of 3 lemons. Bring to the boil. Take off the heat. Keep in the fridge for a month. Bottle. Throw out if it starts bubbling or looks odd.

Lemon

We grow Eureka, the most cold-, heat- and drought-tolerant lemon, with large knobbly fruit all year round if picked regularly. Meyer lemon is the LEAST frost hardy lemon! Avoid it! It is, however, small and will grow in pots – hence the myth about being hardy. Eurekas will lose their leaves in winter but regrow them in summer, and then fruit. They also tolerate dappled shade in groves. Grows fast from seed but needs well-drained soil. It's shallow rooted, so mulch heavily, but away from the trunk in case of collar rot.

Lemonade tree

(See lemon.) Very lemony fruit; grows well in semi-shade as well as full sun.

Lime

KAFFIR AND TAHITIAN

The lime bears fruit in two to four years.

These citrus trees are small. Mulch them every year or give additives in spring and mow the grass regularly. Don't give too much nitrogen or the fruit will suffer. For the best flavour, pick the limes while they are still pale-green. They tolerate dappled shade in groves or full sun. Not drought hardy so don't stint on the mulch. Kaffir limes are mostly used for their fragrant leaves but the fruit will give some juice. Tahitians are juicy winter croppers.

ROUND LIMES

Possibly the most easily bought native citrus is the round lime (*Microcitrus australis*). It's a tall, slender tree (up to 9 metres) with narrow leaves and round fruit that turn yellow when they are ripe, like lemons. As a fringe rainforest tree it will grow happily in full sun or dappled shade, in just about any climate – it tolerates light frosts as well as baking hot summers. Our round lime tree has survived three minus 7°C frosts, but it's protected by a plastic guard and grown by a large, sunny rock – I wouldn't try a round lime in an exposed, frosty position.

Give your round lime plenty of water, mulch and feeding in early spring and mid-summer, but once established they are quite drought tolerant.

To use: round limes are small, round (naturally) and juicy, but like all native citrus, very, very sour! But they make great cordial and marinades.

FINGER LIMES

Finger limes (*Microcitrus australasica*) come from the subtropical or warm rainforests of Queensland and Northern New South Wales, but despite this our finger lime grows quite well in our frosty climate in the shelter of other trees – like most rainforest shrubs finger limes prefer dappled shade.

Their branches are very thorny, with longish leaves, a bit like a lemon's, that will fall in cold or very dry conditions, then regrow; the flowers are fragrant white. The fruit is oval, and slightly curved, about 6 cm long, and green when they are young, then ripening to yellowish green, or purple, or blackish green.

Finger limes are slow growers to about 6 metres, and bear after about four to five years. Like most plants they grow faster with plenty of moisture and feeding, though ours has survived two years of heat and drought!

To use: finger limes taste like very slightly bitter, slightly oily lemons. (I prefer the cleaner taste of round limes) You can squeeze out the juice, or use the fruit to make the cordial or vinaigrette dressing given below. They make a very good, if slightly unusual, marmalade.

Cordial: make a sweet syrup of 1 cup sugar to 1 cup water, boil for 5 minutes, then add thinly sliced finger limes, and simmer for 10 minutes, then cool in the syrup. Store in the fridge for up to a fortnight. These sweet treats are stunning on ice-cream, as cake decoration, or on lemon tarts.

DESERT LIMES

Like many desert plants, desert limes tolerate baking heat, endless drought and searing cold. They grow up to 6 metres, with thorny branches and narrow little leaves. Some trees are incredibly thorny, and sucker to form big, impenetrable thickets, but if you cut off suckers and keep the lower branches trimmed you'll get a well-shaped tree. The leaves will fall in very dry times, but will grow back again, so don't panic.

Desert limes do best in full sun, but will also tolerate dappled shade. They fruit incredibly quickly after flowering (the trees naturally flower after rain). It only takes eight weeks from flower to ripe fruit!

To use: you can eat desert limes whole, like knobbly cumquats, if you're brave enough – their yellow-green skin is thin, and they are very juicy. But they are also very, very sour – they really do need sugar to make them taste good.

Linden

Linden fruit can be made into jams or jellies, or stewed with sugar or honey. It makes a good sorbet – mix a sweetened purée with equal quantity whipped egg white and freeze, stirring twice as it sets. Linden trees tolerate heavy frost.

Loquat

Loquats bear fruit in two to 15 years. Excellent as a base tree in the middle of groves. This is one of the earliest fruits to ripen. Young trees are slightly frost tender when small but, once established, they tolerate extreme cold – as well as heat, drought and temporary flooding. Seedlings take up to 15 years to fruit – one of the few fruits where grafted trees do bear earlier. Loquats grow without any extra feeding at all but, while they are young, a yearly mulch is good. Good base to grow vines up.

Longan

Delicious. Similar to lychees, but slightly more frost tolerant, and generally hardier. See lychees.

Lychees

Delicious tropical fruit but will grow slowly in established groves in frosty areas. Grafted or marcotted trees fruit faster in hot climates; home-grown seedlings establish best in cold areas, as they suffer less transplant shock than when they've been brought from a hot climate. Need moist soil to fruit well, and good feeding. Mulch heavily.

Macadamias

Macadamias bear fruit in three to seven years. I grow *tetraphylla* macadamias – frost tolerant and such hard nuts the cockatoos ignore them. (Buy a GOOD nutcracker.)

They need frost protection when young, and regular watering during spring and early summer for fruit set. They are susceptible to a range of soil deficiencies, so regular mulching is excellent. Will survive drought well but won't fruit much until it rains. Ours gives a few nuts every day.

Mandarin

Bears fruit in two to four years. Tolerate semi-shade but don't fruit as much as in full sun.

For good fruit, mandarins need a slightly warmer climate than oranges, but they are also more frost resistant. Pick them young, or they become dry and tasteless. Feed them well. Thorny mandarins are probably the most cold-, heat- and drought-tolerant. See Oranges for more details on growing.

Mango

You can grow mangos in frosty climates in a grove but they may not fruit for decades, and won't be sweet. Try Nam Doc Mai variety in cooler areas. Use fruit fly nets – they also keep off fruit bats. Mulch heavily – with a good mulch, it doesn't need feeding.

Medlar

A medlar bears fruit in two to five years. They are hardy trees and take any amount of neglect and lack of feeding. Pick the fruit after the first frost when they turn soft. They grow well surrounded by hungry bushes like blueberries.

PS Medlars used to be known as the 'open arse' fruit – have a look at them from underneath and you can see why. And the ripe fruit looks like dog turds, all brown and squishy. But they are one of the most fragrant of all fruits, and they make the most wonderful jelly I know. Stunning gold autumn leaves.

Miracle fruit

After tasting the fruit, everything you eat seems sweet, although miracle fruit itself isn't sweet at all. Tolerates frost in groves, otherwise frost-free to tropical. Needs moist soil and masses of mulch.

Mulberry

Bears in two to five years. Mulberries can grow from Queensland to Tasmania. The trees can grow to an enormous size, but can be pruned or root-pruned with a sharp spade. Mulberries can be either red, black or white. Fruit quality varies a lot – choose good cultivars. Black fruit is the sweetest. White mulberries grow the fastest and tolerate more humidity. Very sweet but a bit tasteless, they're better dried. A well-mown lawn is sufficient feeding.

Narranjilla

This orange, green-fleshed South African fruit is eaten fresh or juiced. The tree grows to 1.5 metres and suits tropical or subtropical conditions as far south as Sydney. It is very drought hardy.

Nashi

The nashi bears fruit in three to four years. They are frost-, drought- and heat-tolerant, fast growing and early fruiting. Mulch is the only feeding needed. Tolerates dappled shade in groves.

Natal plum

Thorny, good hedge, very hardy, large pinkish plum fruit, fairly sour and tasteless.

Native tamarind

Delicious. Related to lychees. Hairy brown fruit with orange flesh. Makes a stunning ice-cream or cordial. Can be eaten fresh.

Nectarines

See Peaches.

Olives

Olives bear fruit in three to seven years. They are the classic drought-resistant tree. They require some chilling for fruit set, and are best with cold winters and hot summers. The more you feed your tree, the faster it will crop. However, I planted ours on a stony, dry hillside and ignored them – they are bearing, but only half the size of other, better tended ones lower down. Once olives stop bearing after 20 years, they should be lightly pruned to stimulate new wood. Harvest olives when they turn light green or black. Excellent base to grow grapes or passionfruit on.

Orange

An orange tree bears in three to four years. Tolerate dappled shade in groves, and shaded fruit will ripen over a three-month period, the ones that get the most sun ripening first.

Seville oranges are the most cold tolerant: they are bitter and used for marmalade. Valencias tolerate moderate frost, once established, and navels take mild frosts. Blood oranges with deep-red juice are a type of valencia, and quite cold-hardy. Feed oranges with mulch in winter. If it's good mulch, that should be all that's needed – otherwise add blood and bone, hen manure, etc. on top. Too much nitrogen gives thick-skinned, less flavoursome fruit, which keeps badly. (Some of our oranges have kept for years in a neglected fruit bowl.) So be sparing with 'additives'.

Pale-yellow old leaves indicate a nitrogen deficiency. Pale-yellow new leaves indicate a phosphorous deficiency. Hen manure will solve both problems. Pale-yellow new leaves with green veins indicate iron deficiency. Scatter on iron chelate or use a regular seaweed or comfrey spray, and add mulch to make the soil more acidic.

Always pick up fallen oranges – they attract fruit fly and citrus bugs. To ward off citrus bugs, try flowering yellow daisies twining in the lower branches, or an aluminium-foil mulch or glue spray.

Panama berry

Small pink sweet berries all year round. Tolerates light frost in groves, otherwise frost free to tropical. Mulch deeply. Fast growing.

Pawpaw

Pawpaw bears fruit in one to three years. Tolerates dappled light to deep shade in groves – will grow up towards the sunlight.

Their flavour is best in the subtropics, but they can be grown in any area with only light frost. Acid, well-drained soil is essential to prevent root rots. Pawpaw are either male or female or hermaphrodites. Hermaphrodites produce poorer fruit and may revert to males in cooler areas. If your tree grows too tall you can cut it down to a side shoot and cover the wound with a tin can. Mountain pawpaw tolerates colder climates than ordinary pawpaw, but their fruit isn't as large or sweet. Ours loses its leaves in winter, but they regrow in spring.

Peaches

A peach bears fruit in three to four years. They are adaptable, with varieties for most areas except very cold or tropical ones. They are drought tolerant. Unlike most fruit trees, they need annual pruning as they fruit on last year's wood. Without pruning you get less fruit each year, and only on the tips of the branches. However, we never prune out trees, and 30 years later still get lots of small fruit. Try cutting out two out of three shoots in winter if you want larger fruit. Stimulate wood production with good feeding: an annual mulch, and one or two dressings of additives.

To reach fruit on high branches, make your own fruit picker from a stick, some wire, an old knife, and some netting.

Spray peach trees with Bordeaux in winter against curly leaf, brown rot, and peach rust. I have found our compost-fed trees much more resistant than new ones I brought in.

Peachcott

Cross between a peach and an apricot. Have never pruned ours. Frost-, heat- and drought-hardy, it is resistant but not immune to fruit fly. Easier to grow than either a peach or an apricot, it bears masses of superb fruit after three years.

Peanut tree

Native, rainforest nut tree. Superb grove tree and good 'base' tree in hot climates. It tolerates frost in groves, but otherwise needs a frost-free to tropical climate. Mulch very deeply. Needs moist soil, but tolerates short droughts. Nuts can be eaten raw or roasted.

Pear

Pears fruit in three to four years. They need deep soil but tolerate wetter and dryer soil than most trees. Very drought hardy. Grow climbers up them. Good 'base' tree for the centre of groves. You are supposed to have pollinators, but pears are sometimes self-fruiting. Don't rely on it though: plant a multi-graft or, if you are short of room, plant two trees in the same hole. Pear trees grow large. Don't overfeed pears, they are susceptible to disease. A yearly mulch is fine, or a well-mown lawn sprinkled once a year with blood and bone. Himalayan pears are grown as frost-hardy ornamentals. The pears are hard but make stunning, gold jelly. Low chill varieties can be grown in the subtropics. Others are good in the most frosty areas.

Pecan

Pecans bear in three to four years. Good base tree for the centre of groves. Long lived. They need hot summers, and cold winters for fruit set. They need deep soil and will tolerate occasional flooding – they're good on the edge of rivers to hold banks together. Pecans can grow to 15 metres high. In small areas, I'd let them grow tall and prune off the lower branches. You may need a long ladder to get the fruit, but they'll take up much less room this way. Grow climbers up them.

Persimmon

These bear fruit in four to seven years. Fruit hangs from the bare tree all winter – or until you and the birds eat them. Drought tolerant, but won't bear without moisture. Survive dappled shade but fruit less. Best planted by themselves, so you can appreciate their glorious shape.

Modern varieties are less astringent and can be eaten crisp, like an apple. Older ones must be left until they are mushy. Persimmons are slow to start growing. They are very ornamental, well-shaped trees with wonderful autumn colours and golden globes of fruit in dark leaves. In hot areas they can become evergreen. Plant them where you can see them. Persimmons need little feeding: a well-mown lawn and a dressing of blood and bone, etc are fine.

Pines

COULTER'S PINE (PINUS COULTERI)
Very large seeds on a tall, hardy tree.

MEXICAN STONE PINE (P. CEMBROIDES)
This is a small pine, to 8 metres, very frost-, cold- and drought-hardy and grown almost anywhere, though wind protection is needed when young. Ours fruited five years after planting.

STONE PINE, SWISS OR ITALIAN
Majestic ornamental tree, very slow-growing, with large edible seeds which take three years to ripen. Slow-growing and incredibly long-lived, it may take several decades to fruit.

ITALIAN STONE PINE OR UMBRELLA PINE (P. PINEA)
This tall pine is the best known 'nut pine', with decorative cones containing up to 100 nuts. The 'nuts' are sweet, oily and tasty. Eat them raw, steamed, roasted or ground to flour. *P. pinea* grows from seed in cold to subtropical climates. It is easily grown.

SWISS STONE PINE (P. CEMBRA)
This is very slow growing (it may take 20 to 40 years to fruit), very hardy and produces abundant but small nuts. Tolerates altitude, frost (but not more than a few days below minus 12°C), heat and drought and, once established, locusts, rabbits and wallabies. Doesn't do well on alkaline soils.

SUGAR PINE (P. LAMBERTIANA)
This is grown for its sweet sap that exudes from the bark. It needs cold, dry summers and is only suitable for southern or mountainous areas.

ARAUCARIA PINES
These also produce edible nuts, including the Chilean pine or monkey puzzle tree (*A. araucana*), the salt-tolerant Norfolk Island pine (*A. heterophylla*) and the Morton Bay Pine (*A. cunninghamii*). The bunya pine (see above) is also an araucaria.

COLLECTING PINE NUTS
Pick the cones while large and full grown but still slightly green. Place them in a brown paper bag and hang them in a warm dry place. As the cones open they can be shaken so the nuts fall out.

Pines grow from seed or tip cuttings in autumn. Cuttings produce cones earlier than seedlings – often within five years instead of up to 15. Take an 8 cm cutting with a strong bud, do not remove needles, plant 6 cm deep and keep moist.

Pistachio

Pistachios bear fruit in four to six years. This tree tolerates drought, frost, and poor soil, though it grows better without them. You need at least one male to every six female pistachio trees. Only tolerates very light, dappled shade.

Pitaya (Dragon fruit)

A climbing cactus with delicious fruit. Will grow in light shade but must have heat and a frost-free spot. I grow ours under the eaves against a sunny stone wall. Drought hardy. There are yellow and red varieties. It needs cross pollination of two varieties.

Plum

A plum bears in two to four years. Excellent 'base' trees for groves, frost and heat and drought hardy. Try a tangle of six plum varieties for five months of fruit. Also grow rambling roses up them – lovely combination.

Plums, especially European ones, like feeding, though they are a hardy tree, which tolerates neglect. I give about 2 kg of hen manure per adult tree after the fruit has set.

European plums have higher potash needs than most trees: sprinkle wood ash once a year, or mulch with comfrey or compost instead of giving them hen manure. European plums bear on two-year-old spurs and should be pruned a little every four to five years, though I have never bothered in the past 30 years and ours fruit well (too well some years). Japanese plums need no pruning, but a little regular pruning will improve cropping. European plums need more cold for fruit set than Japanese plums. Some plums need cross pollination; others don't. All plums tolerate drought and occasional waterlogging. Plums are far more fruit fly resistant than other stone fruit.

Plum pine

Native rainforest fruit, sweet and grape like with a hint of turpentine. Excellent hedge tree, great in groves and a good 'base' tree for frost-free groves. Tolerates frost in groves, otherwise frost free to tropical. Mulch deeply. Needs moist soil for good growth but tolerates short extreme droughts.

Plumcotts

These are a cross between a plum and an apricot, apricot-sized with a flavour somewhere between the two. Plumcotts are slightly more frost resistant, cold hardy and drought hardy than apricots and recover better after damage by stock or native animals. Fruit fly don't seem to like them.

Pomegranate

Pomegranates are cold tolerant, heat tolerant, drought tolerant and indestructible. They have stunning orange, spring blooms, glorious gold autumn leaves, and the fruit hangs in winter until you or the birds eat it. Tolerates semi-shade and is great in groves. Good 'base' tree for groves too. They need little feeding and little watering, and they look lovely. Eat the pulpy seeds on ice-cream, eat the soft immature seeds in salads and other dishes, or make cordial.

Pomelo

A thick-skinned, giant grapefruit-like fruit that suits tropical to cool climates; very hardy. Grow it in groves for shelter from frost in cooler climates.

Quandong

Quandongs bear fruit in three to five years. This native tree grows anywhere in Australia. The fruit can be eaten fresh or stewed, and it makes good jam. Pick it when it starts to fall from the tree. The tree is a partial parasite and needs a good host tree – plant it in the middle of other bushes or near other trees. Drought hardy, excellent grove tree, but wallabies adore them. Survives frost in groves, otherwise needs a frost-free spot.

Quince

Bears fruit in three to four years.

Give it acid soil, lots of mulch and, at planting, a little ground-up rock phosphate. Quinces are very cold tolerant. Pick them after the first frost.

Where to grow: full sun; almost any soil; tolerates cold heavy soils and light dry ones; will fruit even in cool wintered subtropical areas.

Which variety: Champion and Smyrna are the only commercially grown quinces in Australia. Both crop mid season and have good fruit. Specialist fruit nurseries will sell many other varieties – we have about 12 growing here. Feed in early to late spring. While neglected quinces will bear, well-fed and watered ones do a heck of a lot better.

Quinces can get codling moth and fruit fly, but usually don't. The fruit bruises in high wind. Quinces bear fruit even in drought but it may become woody. The main problem is that some trees sucker – prune off suckers or just let your tree turn into a clump, though the suckers possibly won't bear good fruit. Another problem is fungal leaf and fruit spots – spray with Bordeaux at leaf fall and again just as leaf buds are swelling. Spray pear and cherry slug with pyrethrum.

HARVEST

Fruit ripens from March until June, depending on variety. Ripe fruit is yellow, not green, and smells wonderfully fruity when you sniff it close up. Fruit fall is a sign that either fruit is ripe or the tree is moisture stressed. While it's best to know what variety of quince yours are, you can still tell when to pick them:
- Look at them once a week to see when they change from green to yellow.
- Sniff once a week too – when they smell fragrant and ripe they're ready to pick.
- When a few drop naturally from the tree, i.e. not from wind, possums, drought, etc. they are probably ready.

But don't wait for them to soften on the tree – quinces are still hard when ripe. Quinces picked too early taste like mud. I've tried ripening them indoors, but they rot before they turn fragrant – I suspect they are really best ripened on the tree.

Quinces store well in the usual cool dry place, i.e. a shelf. They do put out a lovely scent when stored – a great way to scent the house, but if you store spuds or apples near them they'll also smell a bit disconcertingly of quince.

Quince trees often fruit very young – just count your blessings, and your quinces, before birds, rats, fruit bats or possums eat them. You can buy fruit fly exclusion bags that will keep off quince marauders – too much work to bother with when you have a giant crop, because when you have giant crop there's enough for everyone. But they'll protect your first few crops of a dozen or so. Repellent sprays (either commercial or homemade) will also keep off possums and fruit bats by disguising the scent – but they'll also disguise the scent for you too if you're relying on the quince's perfume to tell you when they're ripe.

STORE

Fruit stores for several months, and even longer if individually wrapped in newspaper.

EATING

Quinces are both sour and astringent. Very ripe ones, however, can be eaten raw, but only if you've got a strong set of chompers. If you really want to eat them raw I find they are best cut into very thin slices, dipped in lemon juice so they don't discolour, and served as a contrast to slices of sweeter fruit like plums and kiwi fruit. They can also be added thinly sliced or chopped to fruit salad, as long as they are marinated for at least four hours in the sweet syrup of other fruits. But quinces really come into their own when they are cooked.

Rose apple

Yellow fruit for six months of the year at least. Heat and drought hardy, it needs grove protection in frosty areas.

Sapote

Survives here down to minus 7°C with shelter from other trees. Moist soil to grow well but survives extreme drought. White or yellow flesh, susceptible to scale – use an oil spray. Mulch deeply – it may need no other feeding if the mulch is lavish. Superb grove tree for any climate.

Soursop

Tropical tart fruit; immature ones are cooked as vegetable. Look for grafted varieties as many seedlings around are too astringent, but if you find a good fruit, plant the seeds. Makes the most superb ice-cream.

Star apple

Tropical to subtropical, this is a delicious, ornamental tree. Good in groves, but even in groves it tolerates no more than light frosts.

Tamarillo

A tamarillo bears fruit in one to two years. Invaluable in groves as it prefers growing in dappled shade and will even tolerate heavy shade. May lose its leaves in frost or drought but they're likely to regrow. Not drought tolerant – we mulch ours with about 1 metre of loose material which usually allows them to survive.

Grow them from a cutting or a seed. Mulch them well, and protect them from frost when young. Give them blood and bone or hen manure once a year, unless the mulch is good.

Tamarind

Subtropical to tropical tree; good in groves. Good acid fruit for tamarind sauce and in curries. Tolerates light shade as well as sun. Tall tree with small trunk and large canopy. Very drought resistant. Tolerates rocky and shallow soils and slopes. The leaves, pods, immature pod and flowers are all edible, and it is the source of tamarind sauce. Not suitable for wet sites, it needs protection from frost when young. Once established, it is almost indestructible – survives fire, drought, locust plagues, etc. and still flowers and fruits.

Tangelo

This mandarin-grapefruit cross is quite delicious – better than either of its parents. Tolerates light shade in groves or full sun. Needs grove shelter from heavy frosts; more frost hardy as it gets older. Fruits in winter. Grows from seed. See Oranges.

Tangor

Mandarin-orange cross. Delicious. See Tangelo.

Tea camellia

Great in groves; enjoys semi-shade. Pick young leaves and twigs for green tea or ferment for 'ocker' tea. Excellent hedge.

Ugni

Great hedge shrub or on the periphery of groves. Very pretty, fluffy white flowers and glossy leaves with red new growth. Also excellent in large pots, especially in cold areas where it will survive by sunny walls on warm paving. Otherwise, light frosts only to tropical areas; survives short but severe droughts.

Walnut

Walnuts bear in five to 10 years.

If you don't have deep, well-drained soil don't grow walnuts. Mulch every winter. Walnuts inhibit other species: nothing much grows under them, except grass. Unless you have a lot of space, it's better to avoid them – or grow them on the nature strip.

FRUITS THAT BEAR IN THEIR FIRST YEAR

Raspberries, strawberries, most brambleberries, blueberries from a large bush, limes from a well-grown tree, pawpaw (in warm areas), mountain pawpaw, passionfruit (in warm areas), banana passionfruit (two years in cooler areas), tamarillo, babaco, pepino, melons, cape gooseberries, gooseberries (if the bush planted was well-grown), and rhubarb.

Dwarf trees usually bear in the first year of planting. Many citrus, especially cumquats, are often sold at close-to-bearing size.

Grafted fruit usually, but not always, bear before seedlings do.

The better a tree is treated, the sooner it bears fruit.

A PLANT IT, PICK IT, AND IGNORE IT ORCHARD

A bloke asked me last year what he could plant on his hundred acres. 'The trouble is,' he said, 'we only get down there every six weeks, and the neighbours' cattle (I could sympathise with that) break through the fences and there are wallabies and feral goats …' And, of course, this was all in the middle of the drought. (Please, please let it be the middle of the drought – I hate to think we may still be near the beginning … droughts would be so much more bearable if you knew exactly when they'd come and, better still, when they'd finish!) Anyway, back to his acres. My first thought was to tell him to stick to thistles, blackberry, broom and a few briars (at least they'd keep the cattle out). But the trouble with requests like that is that they keep whispering inside your brain. Anyway, I came up with a few possibles. No guarantees, but these should at least have a good chance of survival … just.

1. Plant well – i.e., don't just scratch out a hole, but plant a tree, pile up dirt around it, find the hole isn't deep enough, so pile dirt up higher anyway. Make sure the hole is half as deep and wide again as necessary to fit the plant in and hoik out any massive rocks too that might block its root spread. Pack the soil down firmly, water it with at least 10 L per tree. Leave a slight depression around the tree for water to pool in rather than run away.

2. Put a tree guard around each tree. Feral goats will eat anything, the neighbours' cattle will have a taste of anything, wallabies will too, and will break branches to get to it. Tree guards are a nuisance to make and fit (and take off when the tree is out of wallaby height), but they can be used again and again – and without them there is no use planting the tree! (Guards are much better than fences; most fences are bad fences, i.e. everything can get through, under or over them if they really want to. And even good fences will be broken by starving or thirst-crazed cattle – and it is amazing how high a wallaby can jump or how small a hole they'll wriggle through.)

Put the netting guards about 30 cm up from the ground. This will mean wombats can get their noses in and eat the grass and weeds around the tree – which will save you the bother of weeding, and also means that the wombats won't decide to knock the tree and guard over to get to the grass.

As well as netting guards, consider plastic water-filled tree guards. Again, it's more cost, but that cost is worth it if it means the tree grows well or survives. And the guards can also be re-used when the tree is established. Last year (when we got two and half inches in 11 months), the trees here with plastic guards lived. All the young ones that didn't, died.

3. Water every six weeks for the first three years. This can be by the 'hold the hose and trickle' method, except the water will probably trickle OFF the soil, not into it. Or you can put in a drip system, except ants may clog up the drippers or wombats rip them out to get the water or the cattle's feet shred them; drippers are not really for the total absentee. And, of course, unless you are there to turn the water on and off at the tap each time you want to water your trees, a dripper that loses its top or is damaged by animals will then drain your water system. The idea of automatic watering systems controlled by mechanical or computer timers sounds wonderful (and absolutely what the absentee landowner dreams of) but can lead to BIG system failures. Another example of going to biggery, come to think of it.

But 'eco bags' are good – the plastic bags holding about two weeks of trickled water that also help mulch and keep grass away from the trunk. They don't work well on slopes though, and in very dry times animals may learn to rip them open to get the water. (Depends how experienced your local wildlife is at working out how to get the best from human activity. Ours are pretty expert by now at human exploitation.)

Alternatively buy two-inch polypipe (sorry for the lack of metric here) and when you plant the tree, plant a two-metre length of polypipe half a metre deep with each tree. Fill pipe with water as often as possible – the water will seep down to where you want the roots to grow, instead of sitting on the surface where the roots ought not to be. Also very good on steep hillsides where the water just wants to flow downhill regardless of your small dykes, banks and saucer-shaped depressions.

4. Mulch. Except the cattle may eat the mulch, unless you use rocks. I'm serious here. Rocks are one of the best drought mulches. Nothing eats them, they cool the soil and keep it warmer at night – and definitely keep the moisture in. The shrubs that really did well through last year here are the ones planted in clumps of rocks – they even get a tiny (I do mean TINY) dribble of water each night as the air condenses around the hot rocks (even drought air does have a little moisture in it). Rocks around your plants may mean the difference between dying and surviving.

A STORY OF ABUNDANCE

There were four of us at afternoon tea. I was the youngest by about 40 years. They were talking about the orchards of their childhood, when food was mostly home-grown, and supermarkets not even thought of.

Cherries by the bucketful, so many peaches you had to feed them to the pig, watermelons so fat they cracked when you opened them, and fresh peas or beans and beetroot at every meal.

They had an impoverished childhood by modern standards: no cars, videos, TV or telephone, and one pair of shoes for Sunday while the rest of the week they had to go barefoot. But they had an abundance few children today will ever know.

There's no need for those days to be lost forever. Any suburban garden will feed you through the year – as well as your friends, and the birds and animals that share your garden. All you need to do is plant and wait.

Chapter 11
THE FLOWER GARDEN

THE IDEAL

A source of joy and colour and insects – a place to gather bunches of blooms for friends and for the house. A place filled with perennials and other flowers that mostly reseed themselves, and where birds and other predators feed and flourish.

And the lawn? This can be lucerne or clover, a source of 'living mulch'. Or it can be a no-mow lawn of scented chamomile, flowering lawn thyme, or woolly yarrow. It can be filled with bulbs and daisies, a place where geese or guinea pigs or even wombats graze.

- *Instead of mowing your lawn* … plant a 'no-mow' lawn, let small animals graze it, or harvest it as home-grown fertiliser.
- *Instead of separate flower and vegetable gardens* … plant flowers among the vegies, and vegies among the flowers.
- *Instead of feeding your flowers with compost, mulch and bought manures* … provide natural fertility with flowering nitrogen-fixers like sweet peas, and 'living mulch' from other flowers.
- *Instead of neat beds of flowers planted at well-spaced intervals* … grow closely-planted 'free-range' flowers to maximise leaf cover. Dying annuals leave weed-free room for more annuals, and then become the mulch that feeds them.
- *Instead of planting flowers every year*…. choose masses of drought-hardy shrubs and perennials that will give you armfuls of flowers every day of the year.
- *Instead of watering* … get rid of the lawn and put in paving or shrubs and mulch.

TEN REASONS FOR GROWING FLOWERS

1. They make the world more beautiful.

2. They attract predators that will help kill the pests in your garden.

3. You never feel poor if you have bunches of flowers to give away and masses through your house.

4. Flowers like sweet peas can fix nitrogen and help fertilise your garden.

5. Flowers lead to seeds – to replant your garden.

6. Flowers help hide the shapes and scents of your vegetables, making it hard for pests to find them.

7. Flowers like chamomile, borage and foxgloves appear to make the plants they grow with more vigorous.

8. Most flowers have 'cottage kitchen' uses: you can eat them, make wines with them, make calendula ointment if you cut yourself in the garden.

9. Flowers can help weed control: marigolds repel couch grass, dahlias will stop grass intruding in your garden, a thick crop of poppies will help clean up weeds, cornflowers stop some weed seeds germinating, thickly sown sunflowers will stunt weeds and choke them out.

10. Any sourpuss smiles if you give them flowers.

FREE-RANGE FLOWERS

All flowers once grew wild – or their ancestors did. Many still haven't had the original hardiness bred out of them. But be careful with plants that reseed too easily in country areas: they can become a weed and compete with native bushland. Calendulas are lovely, but a whole world infested with them would be almost as bad as a world littered with McDonald's. The world is infinitely variable and it's a pity to muck that up.

FEEDING ON FLOWERS

The division between flowers and vegetables is fairly arbitrary. Many vegetables are beautiful, especially when they 'go to seed'. At the moment we have great clusters of yellow flowers in our garden (they are last year's turnips), there are tall spikes of pale blue flowers (winter radish), and there are lovely white umbrellas (from flowering carrots), all this at a time of year when last year's annual flowers are finishing and the summer blooms haven't yet come on.

It is ironic that we pull out vegetables as no longer of any use just as they start to look their best, while going to a lot of trouble to cultivate less spectacular flowers in another bed.

But not only are vegetables beautiful – their flowers can be eaten. There are too many recipes to list here; it could go on for pages.

Still, just as a start:
- Grow masses of amaranth. Eat the leaves and seed, enjoy the flowers.
- Enjoy the blooms of Jerusalem artichokes, tea camellias, coffee, pomegranates, apples, cherries, pears or the bright orange winter citrus fruits.
- Try stewing poppy leaves like silver beet or, for a bright and natural colour, try pounding poppy petals in your icing.
- Stew rosehips with sugar to make rosehip syrup, which is nicer than most cordials.
- Stuff hibiscus flowers with leftover rice and stew them in stock, or sautée them in butter.
- Use violets for flavour and sweetening in a baked custard instead of sugar and vanilla (bruise the violets first).
- Use nasturtium flowers in the same way, chop a few nasturtium leaves into a salad, or pickle nasturtium or broom buds for use instead of capers.
- Scatter primulas into your salad.
- Use orange or lemon blossom instead of vanilla.
- Make jam from elderberries or rosehips.
- Gather poppy seed for cakes and bread.
- Use dianthus (clove pinks) or carnations for flavouring instead of cloves and cinnamon.

Edible beauty

Red-flowering perennial beans, hops with its drooping prolific flowers, pink-flowering banana passionfruit (the long yellow fruit are pretty too), ornamental grapes (stuff the leaves or use them as disposable plates – toss them in the compost when they're dirty).

Some useful ornamental shrubs

- Tea camellia with its small, white single flowers. Use the tips for Chinese green tea.
- Coffee bush with bright red berries. Roast the seeds for coffee.
- Jasmine sambac: the jasmine found in jasmine tea.
- Bay tree: use the leaves in cooking or to repel pests.
- Arrowroot: this canna lily also produces edible roots. Bake them like potatoes or grate them and wash out the 'arrowroot flour'.
- Native ginger: eat roots and edible berries.
- Tree lucerne and wattles: slash the leaves for nitrogen-rich mulch. Feed tree lucerne to animals; grow edible wattle seeds.
- Elder tree: edible flowers and berries.
- Calamondin, cumquat, chinnotto and other citrus: fruit give colour all winter.
- Persimmon, medlar, sugar maples, apples, pomegranates: glorious autumn leaves.
- Apples, pears and cherries: wonderful spring blossom.
- Pomegranates, persimmon and others: their fruits can be more stunning than any flower.

SOME 'DIFFERENT' FLOWER GARDENS

Try:

A herbal seat: a stone or brick flowerbed at seat height, planted out with chamomile or matting caraway thyme, with pennyroyal or orange peel thyme – a wonderful scent to sit on.

A flowering wall: tin cans, nailed to walls or posts, filled with cascades of nasturtiums or trailing geraniums.

Window boxes: fill with climbing sweet peas trained up strings: a living curtain.

'Hills' of flowers: a heap of rocks, or even old tyres, covered with soil and planted out with flowers.

Flowering paths: plant yarrow or *Prunella grandiflora* with its pink, white or blue flowers through most of summer, or periwinkle in shady areas, or white or purple flowered bugle, or yellow archangel.

In between paving: plant white alyssum 'dividers'.

A paving garden: leave out every sixth paving stone and plant with flowers. Less care and watering than grass, and far fewer weeds.

And try any or all of these:
- Grow thickly planted dahlias or gladioli to choke out weeds.
- Grow tall tree dahlias and let perennial beans clamber up them.
- Let nasturtiums range up fruit trees to help repel pests.
- Grow pansies and alyssum between veg to choke out weeds.
- Edge garden beds with frothy parsley.
- Don't just grow sweet peas up a trellis – let them climb up corn stalks in the vegetable garden, twine them round a pole, and inter-plant them with climbing beans for beauty and for the crop.

SHRUBS AND OTHER ORNAMENTALS

Some roses will get black spot and balled flowers even if you hold an umbrella over them every time it rains. If you love roses, but don't want to prune, spray, or worry, try rugosa roses. These are hardy and thick-leafed, with enormous single or double flowers. Their foliage is pretty too – unlike hybrid teas, which are poor, spindly things when they are not flowering. Rugosas flower early and late, many are recurrent, pests and even possums mostly ignore them, and they tolerate heat, cold and drought.

China roses are also hardy. Ours flower for 10 months of the year without a break – small, neat bushes of single flowers. Or try some of the old-fashioned roses: great arching bushes that need no pruning and are vigorous enough to survive any pest, weed or leaf spot. Our most vigorous ones are 'Climbing Albertine', 'Madame Alfred Carriere', a host of hybrid musks and 'Sparrieshoop' – but there are thousands more. Floribundas usually need less tending than hybrid teas.

Other ornamental shrubs should be chosen to suit your area. Wander round your suburb and see what grows wonderfully in neglected gardens. Then plant them. They'll flourish and flower without you having to worry, and you can spend your time on more delicate plants with a reliable, no-care framework around you.

Our no-care shrubs include camellias (with roses and camellias you have cut flowers most of the year), elderberries, grevilleas, thryptomenes (a range of grevilleas and thryptomenes give you year-round flowers too), buddleia, rhododendrons and cistus or rock roses. In fact, most shrubs are hardy if they suit your climate and soil – and are much less work for the number of flowers than the same area would be as a dug garden bed.

MIRACLES FOR DRY SHADE

The more groves, trees and climbers you have, the more shady your garden will get. And the hotter our world becomes, the dryer your garden will be too… Luckily, a few – a very few – plants have evolved that LIKE it dry and shady! These odd creatures can even be stunning.

Agapanthus: there are many varieties to choose from, all hardy. Some will NOT accept shade. Check.

Miracle of Peru: bright pink or yellow blooms all mid-summer to late autumn. Perennial, drought hardy, stunning.

Perennial pineapple marigold: two metres high and wide, divine scent, massed yellow blooms all winter, repels pests and sometimes mozzies, loves dappled shade and is drought tolerant. Grow lots!!!

Japanese anemones: some are surprisingly drought hardy, especially white ones.

Red flowered sage: fragrant leaves, bright winter flowers.

Hellebores: once upon a time hellebores were pretty boring, but now they come in a glorious range of colours, from green to a glowing pewter grey, or plum coloured, bright white, cream, pink or dappled with pink spots. Some of the new hybrids have blooms that flower well above the leaves too, making them even more spectacular. Look for *H. foetidus* too, with its knee-high green flowers in winter and the elegant finely dissected leaves. Hellebores flower in winter. They make great cut flowers – very elegant indeed. Cut out ALL the leaves in early summer, after they've finished flowering – the old leaves soon turn brown and mottled (otherwise they can hand on a nasty fungus disease year after year) but once you get rid of them the new, brighter green leaves can take their place.

Best look: en masse, under trees, along walls and paths.

Lamium: this groundcover's dappled green and white leaves look good all year. The yellow or pink spring flowers are pretty enough, not really dramatic, but if you have a stretch of dusty grey under a tree, this is the plant for you. It can become a weed, so be careful.

Best look: lamium is THE groundcover for dry shade under trees, as long as you can mow its edges to keep it from straying – and unlike many would-be weeds, it doesn't seem to spread by seed, just runners.

Flaxes (*Phormium spp.*): flax isn't supposed to like shade, but it does wonderfully under our eaves. It survives if we forget to water it for a month too, though the poor thing does get limp and dry looking; however, it recovers after a good drink. There are dozens of glorious flaxes around now: reds, greens, pinks, yellows, striped and dappled, miniatures and those that will grow taller than you. Choose to suit your site, and mulch them well … and do water the poor things when you remember, even though they'll forgive you when you don't.

Best look: like all plants, flaxes look best with more flaxes! One looks lonely; a group looks elegant and sculptural.

Hen and chickens (*Echeveria spp.*): this succulent gets its name from the 'chickens' that the mother plant puts out each spring. One 'hen' will give you several chickens every year – and your echeveria will just keep spreading. Again, echeveria aren't supposed to tolerate shade, but I find them quite shade tolerant, as long as they are surrounded by a good, dry pebble mulch – the pebbles help reflect more light onto the leaves.

Best look: spilling over a bank, or edging a path.

Euphorbia spp.: these come in a variety of sizes and personalities: some are aggressive muggers (but still immensely attractive) and others are large, well-mannered and slow-growing. Grey-green sounds boring but these aren't – lovely sculptural darlings with great columns of yellow-green, penny-like flowers in giant flower heads in winter or spring. They last and last … watch out for the white sap though. It's caustic.

Best look: At the back of a border or along a wall.

Miscanthus spp.: this ornamental grass copes with just about anything. Miscanthus flowers in autumn, but the blooms are pretty insignificant. Cut down the whole plant in spring, to encourage rich, new, cream and white growth.

Best look: miscanthus are great to edge a garden; also marvellous en masse. I grow ours in shallow concrete pots – they'd kill just about anything else, but the miscanthus thrives.

Mondo grass (*Ophipogon planiscapus 'Nigrescens'*): black grass in shade sounds boring, and, to be honest, many plantings of mondo grass are dull. But if you give it some contrast – like pale rocks – it can be stunning. There is also a bright green mondo grass, *O. japonicus*. It can get brown edges if it doesn't get enough moisture, as can the far darker form, so they're not plants for the driest shade you have. Trim back if they do start looking streaky and give a bit more moisture.

Best look: as an edging for bigger plants, or along a path.

New Zealand rock lily (*Arthropodium cirrhatum*): this is a dramatic looking foliage plant: big, broad, strappy leaves with a blue-grey bloom, up to a metre high and with even taller sprays of small white starry flowers through spring and summer. Once established it will cope with very dry positions (and look surprisingly lush), although it will grow bigger faster when given adequate moisture. The variety 'Matapouri Bay' is a particularly fine plant. Guard against voracious snails and slugs which can make the big fleshy leaves look sad and tattered.

Best look: where its shape can be admired!

Blue flax lily (*Dianella spp*): this is another good survivor in dry shade (although it flowers better with a bit of sun) and the leaves keep their bright, fresh green colour even when they are struggling.

Best look: dianella is good for colonising the ground beneath trees, where it looks attractive and natural.

Pouched coral fern (*Gleichenia dicarpa*): this thicketing native fern will colonise poor ground beneath large trees. Look after your new fern with a bit of extra moisture until it is established, but once it's contented it will make a ferny thicket a metre and a half high which seems to be particularly attractive to blue fairy wrens.

Best look: en masse under big trees, or along the shady side of the house.

Best roses in the shade

Yes, you can grow roses in the shade – SOME roses. Others just slowly wither away. Look for the magic words 'shade tolerant' on the label. There are shade tolerant ground covers, hybrid teas, and floribundas. My solution to an increasingly shady garden is to grow ramblers up my fruit trees and let THEM find the sunlight. Also look for the new 'patio rose' especially bred for shady patios.

Good points: roses AND lots of shrubs, trees and shade.

Bad points: roses in shade don't produce as many flowers as roses grown in sunlight.

How to cosset: shade may mean competition with other roots for food and moisture. Be liberal with both.

Best roses: 'Seven Sisters', 'Climbing Albertine', 'Climbing Souvenir de la Malmaison', 'New Dawn', 'Mme Alfred Carriere', 'Alberic Barbier', 'Lamarque', 'Shady Lady'.

SECRETS OF YEAR-ROUND EASY-CARE 'PICKABLE' REWARDS

STEP 1

Plant at least two climbing roses up the walls of the house, or pillar roses up a pergola (if you don't know which are which, the kindly – or at least profit-aware – staff at the nearest nursery will tell you).

Plant at least three rambling roses over the fence.

Forget about hybrid tea roses unless you are really, truly sure you'll get round to pruning, feeding and spraying them for black spot. (If your last indoor plant died alone and neglected, do not answer 'yes' to this.) Instead, bung in a few 'shrub' roses – good, strong growers that will give flush after flush of blooms for damn all work, though a touch of food once a year will be welcomed. (Hybrid teas are the most common rose, bred for long straight stems and pickable flowers. They can be a heck of a lot of work.)

My favourite 'can't kill 'em bloomers' are:

- *Rosa mutabilis*, which most people don't realise is a rose when they see it in our garden – it almost always has masses of single butterfly-like flowers that change from pink to red to cream to orange. It sounds horrible but isn't.
- 'Berlina' (sprays of small pink flowers all summer).

Tips for dry shade

- Mulch! Mulch stops dry soil turning into concrete, as well as keeping in moisture.
- Feed! Often dry shade is caused by large trees, which can rob smaller plants of tucker.
- Water! Even plants that like dry soil do best with a bit of water. Use drippers if you can, but do give your plants an overhead water at least once a month as well, to kill pests like red spider mite and wash dust off the leaves.

- 'Sparrieshoop'
- Also consider the world's most planted rose, 'Iceberg', and its climbing form, and there's now a pink form too. It's planted so often for a reason – flush after flush of flowers for about nine months of the year, fast growing, hardy, disease resistant. They're not flowers to stick in great, tall vases, but a nosegay of them does look pretty in an old teapot on the kitchen table.

The 'Great Reliables' (roses that bloom and bloom forever with minimal care) include 'Freesia', 'Climbing Gold Bunny', 'Iceberg', 'Pink Iceberg', 'Archiduc Joseph' (used to be known as 'Monsieur Tillier'), 'Frau Dagmar Hastrup', 'Buff Beauty'.

Care needed: trim as necessary. Feed any warm time of year.

Groundcover roses are great, no-work roses ... 'Heidesommer', 'White Meidiland', pink 'Flower Carpet'. Feed in spring and ignore. Good grown in paving.

By now you may have started down the long lurid path of the rose addict. (Roses are very, very easy to fall in love with once you realise they don't all have long thorny arms and prickle bare legs.) You will also have masses of spring, summer and autumn flowers.

STEP 2

Plant at least ten camellias – early, medium and late varieties, in shady spots, like under trees and along the gloomy spots by the side of the house. Just make sure they aren't shaded by the eaves: if the leaves don't get wet they may get infested with sap sucking mites. These camellias will give you flowers all through winter and into early spring too. (Stick to japonicas, not sasanquas – check the labels. Sasanquas bloom too early to be decent winter blooms – unless you have REALLY cold winters.)

STEP 3

Plant a hedge of cumquats along yet another fence (you'll get gaudy fruit all through winter and spring, and flowers in summer), or a hedge of dwarf pomegranates – brilliant orange-red flowers in spring and early summer, then fruit for most of the rest of the year until the birds eat it – or you do.

STEP 4

Plant six relatives of *Grevillea banksii* – or any grevillea that suits your area and that will bloom all year (have a look at the label).

STEP 5

Plant at least six sorts of salvias for masses of drought-hardy blooms for you, the birds, bats and insects.

STEP 6

Plant another dozen flowering shrubs – ask at your local nursery for the best they can recommend for your area. (The most constant bloomers in our garden are marguerite daisies, pineapple sage and fruit salad sage – the last two tolerate only mild frosts.) A few other hardy bloomers include winter roses (*Helleborus spp*.), great for shady spots; Earlicheer jonquils (but don't plant them by hot walls – most other daffs won't do well unless you need to wear a jumper AND a coat each winter, but Earlicheer will do okay anywhere as cold or cooler than Sydney); a hedge of canna lilies if you get light frost or less. If you love a million flowers in a dozen different shades all summer, stick in a packet of Yates dahlia seed; each one will have about four or five fat tubers after two or three years; hoik some out and start a new bed with them.

STEP 7

Resist any temptation to plant a flowerbed, unless you feel a similar urge to feed, feed and trim it every two weeks. Instead, get a couple of giant pots or half barrels, or an elderly wheelbarrow or half dozen LARGE hanging baskets. Place them where you'll see them most often – this will probably be by the front door or out the kitchen window.

Plant them with masses of primulas in late summer, to bloom all through winter and spring, then plant either pansies or Californian poppies in spring. Both come in a wonderful range of colours now and both will bloom for at least another 12 months or more if trimmed and regularly fed. You can also bung in alyssum, which will bloom for at least a year.

STEP 8

Now add some Federation daisies, gazanias and at least six assorted native shrubs.

STEP 9

Plan to fall in love at least once a year with something new – russet-coloured sunflowers or naked ladies (a brilliant, opulent, light-pink-flowered bulb that loves hot dry spots and neglect). And no matter what else you do or don't do with your garden, you will at least have a thousand flowers.

RE-THINKING THE LAWN

I love lawns – whatever they are made of. They are places to sit, places where kids can play and dogs can roll and scratch their backs. But if you actually look at the grassy areas of most gardens, very little is really used. The bit at the front is too public, the bits at the sides too narrow or too shady and the patches round the shrubs too hard to get to.

Look at your garden, decide what bits of lawn are actually used, then plant the rest. What with? If you need a flat area, look at the lawn alternatives below. Or think of ground covers, roses left to ramble on the ground, prostrate grevilleas or rosemary in dry areas – all plants that don't need tending. Plant smaller bushes near large ones, dig in bulbs – once you cut down your lawn you have an enormous area to plant, even in a suburban garden, and the possibilities are endless.

In our garden we have several staples for filling up unwanted grassy patches:

- Daisies – in all but heavily frosted areas these flower most of the year, attract insect and bird predators and – best of all – grow easily from cuttings: just bits of hardwood thrust into the ground and kept moist. Daisy cuttings take at almost any time of the year except when it's stinking hot or the ground is frozen.
- Rosemary and lavender – these take almost as easily as daisies, are wonderful hedges, and have a multitude of uses.
- Wormwood – this is a good pest repellent, grows from a stick pushed into the soil, and has a lovely, soft, grey colour that harmonises with almost anything: a touch of colour in the garden when there's nothing much flowering.
- Geraniums (pelargoniums) – nothing can kill a geranium, except a heavy frost. They grow from a cutting, flower for most of the year, and are happy in cold areas in a pot inside or on the verandah or under the eaves, or in warmer areas as a hedge by the fence.

  If you don't have any of these, wander round until you find a garden that does – then knock on the door and ask for cuttings. (By and large, gardeners are generous people – or they wouldn't enjoy growing things so much.) Within a few years, one plant will give you dozens more.
- Bulbs – buy them in bulk (they are much cheaper that way) and thrust them into the soil by scooping up a bit of turf with a tablespoon, placing the bulb in the hole, and then replacing the grass. You can plant hundreds in an hour that way. We grow daffodils for spring, dahlias (tubers rather than bulbs), watsonias and gladdies for summer, and early jonquils for winter: they, and many others, all multiply like mad and form carpets beneath the trees.

  You never feel broke when you've got an armful of flowers to give to friends or to scatter through the house.

- Grevilleas – these grow from seed, but may not come true-to-type if they are hybrid (not that that matters, usually) and from cuttings (which are often hard to strike), but they are cheap in small pots from the Forestry Commission in your state. Grevilleas give you masses of flowers in mid-winter and mid-summer when other flowers are rare. They attract hosts of birds and insects, are incredibly hardy, make a wonderful hedge, and are as tough as an old boot. We grow dozens here. Every bush we put in seems to bring more birds.
- 'Small fruits' – from blueberries to pepino, pineapple to cumquats (see Chapter 10 for ideas). Half the average lawn could give enough fruit for a whole family.

Different gardeners will probably prefer different 'fillers'. Fillers may need to be cheap, so it often depends on what cuttings you can scrounge.

Just keep planting! Remember that the average gardener uses perhaps one-hundredth of the available space in their garden properly. A backyard should be able to feed you, entertain you and give you joy – a good garden should be as thick as a fulfilled life.

'No-mow' lawns

Lawns can frame a house, cool it down, shield it from bushfires, and become a play space – or sitting room. Mowing the lawn probably takes more time than any other garden activity. You can avoid mowing by having a lawn of something other than grass.

Lawn alternatives

PAVING

This is wonderful for garden chairs, pets, skateboards and roller blades – and if you plant the spaces in between with herbs or other creepers, paving doesn't have to look like an expanse of concrete.

SHRUBS

Many 'native' or 'jungle' gardens get rid of the lawn altogether, and plant shrubs and groundcovers thickly. The result is less work and less noise and pollution – shrubs and trees will help block both.

THYME LAWN

Thyme lawns are good to sit on (they smell wonderful), to play cricket on, or to let the dog roll on (it may help repel fleas). Matting thymes are small-leafed and not prickly. They are good in hot, dry areas and are drought tolerant once established, but respond best to regular watering.

Lawn thymes need close-carpeting, small-leafed prostrate thymes, which don't clump or turn woody like culinary thyme. They make excellent mats between paving and will tolerate some traffic – and they smell wonderful when trodden on. They also attract bees, with carpets of varied-coloured flowers in late spring and summer.

Shakespeare's thyme is the original carpeting thyme, pink flowered and fragrant. *Thymus albus* has small, round leaves and white flowers, *Thymus coccineus* deep-red flowers, and *Thymus minimus* has small white flowers and extremely tiny leaves.

Grey woolly thyme is almost fuzzy, the softest of them all. This is the only thyme that can comfortably be sat on, golden thyme has pale-purple flowers and long, yellow leaves, which unfortunately look as though the plant is starved of nitrogen.

Caraway thyme does not produce a thick mat, but the scent is incredible on a hot day.

Grow thyme from seed, or from cuttings.

CHAMOMILE LAWN

The Queen's garden parties are said to be held on chamomile – I wouldn't know, I've never been to one. But chamomile does stand considerable traffic, smells lovely in summer, and doesn't need mowing. It does need fertile soil.

The classic chamomile lawn is 'Treneague',

a non-flowering form of Roman chamomile, *Anthemis nobilis*. It can only be grown by planting runners, then waiting until it spreads. The flowering variety of Roman chamomile will grow from seed; it is perennial, and the flowers can be used for chamomile tea. Annual German chamomile, *Matricaria recutita*, is not suitable for lawns, but is more commonly used medicinally.

Chamomile lawns will grow in both broken light and full sun. They're not drought tolerant but will take quite heavy traffic. Make sure your ground is very well weeded, however, before you plant them: chamomile is shallow-rooted and easily disturbed by weeding, and its matting habit means that weed roots seem irrevocably trapped beneath it. Sow seed in spring or transplant runners at any time.

AJUGA LAWN

This is a rampant grower and can become a problem. It has glossy, green leaves and white flowers, grows best in semi-shade, but will expand anywhere and tolerates frost and light traffic. Bronze-leafed and variegated forms are also available. It is an excellent lawn substitute if you want to avoid mowing, and is lovely under fruit trees. It is also an excellent groundcover in places where grass won't grow as a result of tree competition.

PERIWINKLE LAWN

Periwinkle (*Vinca*) can be grown in shady areas and in broken light under trees. It doesn't need mowing and can form a carpet of white, pink or mauve flowers throughout summer. They are too bushy, though, to walk over or sit on comfortably.

MOSS LAWN

These can be beautiful, but are only suitable for temperate areas with lots of water.

DICHONDRA LAWN

This is a low, prostrate creeping plant that is a good lawn substitute in damp, shady areas like under trees where it is difficult to get grass to grow, or where mowing is difficult. It grows well in exposed areas too, and while it doesn't need mowing, regular cutting will thicken the sward. Seed should be sown at 100 g for every 10 square metres.

CORSICAN MINT LAWN

This is a tiny-leafed mint that makes a thick, very low carpet in shady areas. It smells wonderful when you tread or lie on it, but won't take much traffic. It is best grown from runners.

GROUND IVY LAWN

Miniature ground ivy forms a flat, interwoven mat on most soils. It grows quickly, but don't try to skateboard on it.

VIOLET LAWN

Violets make lovely ground covers under trees or in quite deep shade, where grass is unsuitable.

Lawns to harvest

LUCERNE

Lucerne is perennial, deep-rooted, and will form a fine sward if regularly cut. The more it is cut, the more it thickens. The residue will be excellent mulch or animal food, higher in protein and calcium than grass. Lucerne fixes nitrogen and will bring up leached nutrients. It also needs less fertilising than grass and is more drought hardy than many grass varieties.

MINT

Mint can be grown thickly in moist areas, and can even be mown – as long as you keep the mower fairly high. Apart from Corsican mint, most mints will need mowing as they can become tall and bushy. Mint grows best from cuttings as seeds may not be true-to-type. Most pieces of mint stem will root when planted.

Grass is not very good in heavily used areas: instead, plant herbs like prostrate thyme, rosemary or pennyroyal between stepping stones.

STRAWBERRIES

Strawberries can be an excellent ground cover. Spread stepping stones through the garden and plant strawberries between them. This is not suitable for cold areas where strawberries die off each year, leaving unsightly brown patches – though Alpine strawberries are more frost resistant.

Strawberries do need a lot of water, but they will take a surprising amount of traffic if you don't mind squashing the odd berry.

CRESS AND MUSTARD

These can be grown in damp stretches instead of lawns. They are annuals, and more seed should be scattered as soon as they start to flower, though flowering will be delayed with regular cutting. The more you cut them, the thicker and lower they will grow. But cress and mustard can't stand heavy feet.

PENNYROYAL

This is a small-leafed, flat carpeter with tiny, mauve flowers in spring: wonderfully scented to walk on, and the leaves can be used in pot pourri or to make flea repellent. It's best in a moist or shady area, and grows from seed or runners.

PROSTRATE YARROW

This is smaller leaved than conventional yarrow, with delicate feathery leaves. Surprisingly tough, it withstands quite heavy traffic, once established, and is very drought hardy. The dense, narrow, greyish green leaves make a tough and unusual lawn. It grows best from cuttings, though seeds can be sown at any warm time of year. Yarrow tea is an excellent plant tonic.

Heavily used areas

- Grow plants between stepping stones.
- Use paving (it needs no mowing), but leave spaces for small clumps of plants.
- Pave with bricks designed for wiring, with holes at each end, and plant herbs in the holes. These are suitable for wheeltracks in a driveway.

GRASS LAWNS

If you do choose to have a grass lawn:
- Don't feel you have to shave it every weekend. Birds like grass seeds – I'd rather have flocks of silver-eyes and red-browed finches than a lawn that looks like green carpet.
- Never mow too short. Low-set blades on the mower won't mean a longer time between cuttings: the lawn will just grow faster but unevenly and, without enough leaf to feed them, you'll weaken the roots and weeds will encroach. Leave your grass longer and just trim off the tops to make it look even if you want to minimise mowing. Many lawns look untidy because weeds grow faster than grass. 'Spot-weed' them with undiluted urine on a dry morning, and you'll be able to go longer between lawn mowings without the grass looking a mess.

Leave lawn clippings where they are – unless you want to use them elsewhere – or your soil will become harder and your grass less healthy for want of organic matter.

Feeding

Clover-rich lawns, which get to keep their clippings, rarely need feeding. Feed your grass with a scatter of blood and bone, dry compost (in summer, it disappears into the lawn within a few days), liquid manure (see Chapter 5) or pelletised hen manure. A sprinkle of rock phosphate and dolomite every five to 10 years will keep up phosphorus levels, and help keep the lawn green without a lot of watering.

Learn how to mow

Too many people (mostly men) use their lawnmower like a rotary hoe. Shaving your grass down to its roots doesn't mean you have to mow less often – it'll just make the grass (what little of it survives) grow faster. You'll also leave bare patches that weeds will rapidly colonise.

Only ever shave off a few millimetres of grass. You don't need short grass for a neat lawn – just grass that's all one length (and if you get rid of weeds your grass will look neater for longer periods of time). Longer grass grows more slowly and tolerates more cold and heat and dryness without going brown. If a friendly male offers to mow your lawn – CHECK THE HEIGHT OF THE MOWER BEFORE THEY START.

Men often get carried away by the potential of machinery and overdo the whole thing ... with the best of intentions, poor things. They think that mowing it short means it'll stay short long – but the opposite happens! If you (or your resident male) got carried away with mowing last year and there are bare patches in your lawn, Yates have put out an excellent 'patch repairer' – a combination of lawn seed and paper mulch. Just scatter it on and you'll have new grass in a couple of weeks.

Don't bully your lawn!!!!

Grass doesn't like to grow in the shade or where size 14 boots keep clomping over it. If your grass refuses to grow somewhere or just fades away, plant violets instead – say under the trees – or other groundcovers and put paths or paving in heavily used areas.

Don't put your lawn on a diet

I hate diets – for me and my lawn. If you feed your grass properly it'll stay green longer, without so much water.

Give your grass a gentle sprinkle of pelletised hen manure or sieved compost or any lawn food with trace elements (not just nitrogen, phosphorous and potassium – look at the contents label on the packet) once or twice a year.

But just as I'm getting ... well ... tubby ... lawns can also be overfed.

Most lawn food just washes down the gutter and eventually pollutes some overburdened waterway. A very light sprinkle once or twice a year (just pretend you're scattering icing sugar on a cake), and ONLY when it's growing strongly, is all any lawn should need.

In fact, if you don't rake up your lawn clippings you may never need to feed your lawn once it's established. If you take away your lawn clippings you're taking away nutrients that would otherwise decay and feed the grass again. We use a 'mulching' lawnmower. It chops everything up finely – including the weeds I toss over my shoulder when I'm weeding the flower gardens. Bryan just snarls at them (and me) and mows over them. A mulching lawnmower also doesn't leave trails or clumps of clippings.

Tired of straggly grass under trees? Replace it with:
- a bed of hellebores for winter flowers;
- a mulch of bright pebbles or crushed rock;
- a groundcover like yellow or pink flowered variegated lamium;

THE FLOWER GARDEN

- a wrap-around garden seat;
- half a dozen hydrangeas for a stunning summer display.

Lawn weeds – the vampire technique

The best way of getting rid of annual weeds is to mow regularly. Grass likes being mown – or being chomped by grazing animals. Tall growing weeds dislike being regularly chopped in half. See also the chapter 'Living with weeds'.

Lawn pests and diseases

Forget about them. If they appear, just feed and water and mow – properly. See above. Concentrate on growing things, not killing things, is my motto – and your lawn (and your bank balance) will be all the better for it.

The very best of all

Every now and then I'm asked 'Okay, if you had a small garden, what would you plant?' Which isn't easy to answer, as one of the reasons we have a 4-hectare garden (and getting bigger all the time) is that I like to have EVERYTHING …

But the very, very best? Well, here goes!

The most glorious flowers

Rambling roses, like 'Climbing Albertine'. They ramble up trees and don't need pruning, weeding, or spraying – and possums won't eat their glorious tangles!

'Climbing Iceberg' rose: it flowers all year round and, again, you can twine it up trees or posts or over the front door.

Japonica camellias: they bloom in shade in dull winters, and are much more drought tolerant than sasanquas!

Grevilleas: birds adore them (so do I), and you can find varieties that bloom all year round.

Ginger lilies: a scent like paradise and they bloom in shade.

Salvias: like pineapple sage, blue sage, bog sage, fruit salad sage, tequila sage. I collect sages – hardy, no matter how bad the drought, and we have more birds per square metre sipping at their nectar or picking off nectar-feeding insects than anywhere else this side of the black stump.

And, of course, I could keep going … and have, for the last 30 years of gardening! Come to think of it, the REAL essentials are the plants you love. Forget about what the neighbours are growing, or the garden you grew up with (unless you have a rush of nostalgia when you get a whiff of a special fragrance). What plants do you adore? Cinnamon and oranges? Pepper vines and lillipillies? Don't settle for second rate in your garden. Plant what you adore.

Chapter 12

GARDENS BY MAIL

One of the nicest things a gardener can hear (apart from 'Let me carry that for you, darling!') is another gardener exclaim in a mix of envy and rapture: 'Where did you get THAT?!'

And the answer is usually 'Mail order'.

Don't get me wrong: garden centres are lovely places. But if you want something DIFFERENT from the run of the mill shrubs; if you're bored with orange carrots and want to munch on purple ones, or striped beans or climbing yellow tomatoes; if you have a passion for roses or violets or scented pelargoniums and want to browse through descriptions of hundreds of them in drooling detail, then you need to go mail order.

I am a mail order devotee. Another catalogue in the mail means I can curl up on the sofa while Bryan watches a submarine movie and dream of 20-metre clematis, and apples that ripen in December before the fruit fly can get their fangs into them, and make lists of the 20 roses most essential to my happiness next season. (With luck I'll forget to post the order form because we really have enough roses …)

Most mail order firms are specialists, which means you can get exactly what you want.

Many sell in bulk, so even though you are also paying postage costs, you can often get plants cheaper than you would in the garden centre. But, mostly, mail order catalogues are just great to drool over and dream of the garden you might have if only you had 50 hectares under cultivation and a million dollars, but never mind, at least this rose will be a stunner that none of your friends has seen before.

If it wasn't for mail order catalogues I wouldn't have my 125 apple trees that fruit from late November (Irish Peach) to early August (Sturmer Pippin).

I wouldn't have my forest of shaggy tree dahlias or rare quince trees, or grow my own saffron and tea, or have dozens of varieties of mint or thyme or lavender dotted about the garden. I wouldn't have found the old-fashioned yellow trumpet daffodils and straw jonquils that survive the 40°C summers here, or the fragrant camellias or the metre-high true geranium that is one of the stunners of spring.

I wouldn't have … well, okay, enough boasting. Our garden is a product of 30 odd years' browsing through mail order catalogues and saying, 'I'll have this, and this, and this, ... well, okay, maybe I can only afford THAT, but next year ...'

A WORD OF WARNING

Okay, quite a lot of words.

1. Most mail order plants come through the mail or by courier, and this means they are usually smaller than similar plants in the garden centre and have either been stripped of their soil and packed in damp paper or similar, or are in very small pots.

Some mail order places pack their plants better than others – in fact some are really awful and plants arrive as wilted bits of mildew. I haven't had that happen with any of the places below, but you have been warned!

2. You'll need to send a cheque or credit card details. I've dealt with all the places below and found them reputable but that doesn't mean that all mail order companies are, and when you have to pay in advance you are risking losing your dough for stuff that may not arrive or may not be what you expected.

If it doesn't arrive, contact the company. If it isn't want you want, let them know, and ask either for your money back or for the correct plants to be sent to you, at their expense. (The few times I've had mail order problems the places concerned have offered to do this without my asking, as soon as I mentioned there'd been a problem.)

Be tactful (says she who tends to jump in gum boots and all yelling 'Consumer fraud!'). The people who run most, if not all, garden mail order companies are real garden enthusiasts. They can get very, very hurt if you insult their product. Only start yelling if you begin to suspect a con job.

3. New products from overseas often haven't been grown for long in Australia, and have usually been trialled only in one place.

In the past year I've bought a dozen 'bright blue' salvias that turned out to be dull blue grey and reasonably hideous; two 'purple leafed' elderberries that look suspiciously green; two 'red' kiwi fruit, but the fruit so far have had a distinct lack of redness; a gorgeous pair of 'dwarf' dahlias that grew to waist high (but were still gorgeous anyway) and several climbing roses that just sit there as though they're saying, 'Climb? Us? No thanks, we're scared of heights.'

Most of these are offered in good faith; but when you buy new varieties you have to expect that they sometimes don't live up to their promise.

In other words: buyer beware, because it's a lot harder to take something back if you've bought it from 1000 kilometres away!

Some of the best

This isn't a list of the best mail order places in Australia, because I haven't ordered from everywhere yet. (Just give me a few more years and $$$.) But these are all places I buy from regularly, and I can promise they have catalogues to drool over.

If any place is NOT in this list it probably just means either I haven't come across it yet or the editor refused to let me list my favourite 501 mail-order firms and limited me to these.

Bulbs

LAKE NURSERIES

Will send you a free catalogue.
PO Box 336, Monbulk, Vic. 3793
T 03 97566157
www.lakenurseries.com.au

TESSELAARS BULBS AND FLOWERS

357 Monbulk Road, Silvan, Vic. 3795
T 03 9737 9811
E enquiries@tesselaar.net.au
www.tesselaar.net.au

Contact them for one of their three seasonal catalogues. I've bought luscious liliums, a black iris, winter-flowering red hot pokers, and fragrant clematis from Tesselaars.

BROERSEN BULBS

Contact them for a free catalogue.
365-367 Monbulk Road, Silvan, Vic. 3795
T 03 9737 9202
E sales@broersen.com.au

Herbs

HONEYSUCKLE COTTAGE

Lot 35, Bowen Mountain Road, Bowen Mountain, NSW 2753
T 02 4572 1345
E kamcleod@zeta.org.au
www.honeysucklecottagenursery.com

MARSHALL'S NURSERY

Contact them to enquire about their catalogue. You can also order everything from valerian to licorice from their web site.
1321 Candelo – Wolumla Road, Candelo, NSW 2550
T 02 64 932 932
E marshall@asitis.net.au
www.herbsalive.com.au

Antique Tools

THE OLD MOLE

Contact them for their free catalogue of stunning antique and old and reproduction tools that LAST. Also sell great steel garden tripods for plants to climb up, and turned hardwood garden stakes – really lovely things.

PO Box 984, Armidale, NSW, 2350
T 02 6775 0208
E oldmoletools@bigpond.com

Roses

ROSS ROSES

PO Box 23, Willunga, SA 5172
T 08 8556 2555
E orders@rossroses.com.au
www.rossroses.com.au

See also MISTYDOWNS NURSERY (Perennials) and HONEYSUCKLE COTTAGE.

Gourds

THE GOURDFATHER

Fresh and dried gourds in a stunning collection of shapes, sizes and colours, books on growing gourds and what to do with them (a gourd banjo? kids' toys? grow your own storage containers?) and an extraordinary range of gourd seeds. Send four x 50 cent stamps for a catalogue.
PO Box 298, East Maitland, NSW 2323
T 02 4933 6624
E gourdfather@kooee.com.au
www.thegourdfather.com

Seeds

THE DIGGER'S CLUB

A wide range of hard-to-get and heritage seeds (like multi-coloured carrots, striped beetroot and black- or yellow-striped tomatoes) and ornamentals like tree dahlias. The first catalogue is free; after that you need to become a member, and once you pay your $29.50 membership fee there are five catalogues a year. Non-members can buy plants at a higher price.
105 La Trobe Parade, Dromana, Vic. 3936
T 03 5987 1877
www.diggers.com.au

NEW GIPPSLAND SEEDS AND BULBS

Good quality veg, herb and flower seeds and a great range of reliable and hard-to-get varieties. Apply for their free catalogue by post, telephone or email.
PO Box 1, Silvan, Vic. 3795
T 03 9737 9560
E newgipps@bigpond.com
www.possumpages.com.au/newgipps/index.htm

EDEN SEEDS

Great tropical and subtropical range, but I buy a lot of my cold climate seeds from there too. Apply for their free catalogue.
MS 905, Lower Beechmont, Queensland 4211
T 07 5533 1107; free call, orders only 1800 188 199
www.edenseeds.com.au

GREEN PATCH NON-HYBRID ORGANIC SEEDS

To order a catalogue send them $2.50 or stamps to the same value, or contact them to find out when their next open day is.
PO Box 1285, Taree, NSW 2430
T 02 6551 4240

Organic remedies and tropical seeds and plants

GREEN HARVEST

Contact them to order their really superb free catalogue, *The Australian Organic Gardening Resource Guide*. This is the most comprehensive catalogue of its kind I know. I order from them regularly – everything from water chestnuts to nets to keep out fruit fly to really good quality garden tools or a boracic acid puffer to get rid of silverfish.
52 Crystal Waters, MS 16, via Maleny, Queensland 4552
T 1800 681 041 (orders only) or 07 54944676 (general enquiries)
www.greenharvest.com.au

Perennials

Lambley Nursery
Fabulous quality stock with many really tough plants including the best range of Kniphofias, agapanthus, wonderful grasses and phormiums. Good descriptive (non-pictorial) catalogue issued twice a year.
'Burnside', Lesters Road, Ascot, Vic. 3364
T 03 5343 4303
E lambley@netconnect.com.au
www.lambley.com.au

Fruit trees

DALEY'S FRUIT TREE NURSERY

A superb range of really good quality subtropical and tropical fruit, but I've grown a lot of their trees down here in the frosty chill. A great range of avocados, plus many unusual fruit like chocolate sapote, tropical cherries, coffee bushes and ice-cream bean tree. Ask for their free catalogue.
Daley's Nursery Lane, Geneva, via Kyogle
PO Box 154, Kyogle, NSW 2474
T 02 66321 441
E donna@daleysfruit.com.au
www.daleysfruit.com.au

BOB MAGNUS

A great source of rare and heritage apples, pears, plums and quinces, mostly grafted onto dwarf stock so you can fit more in a small garden. How about a fruit-tree hedge of a dozen different apples (Irish Peach, Macintosh, Sturmer Pippin, or giant Twenty Ounce cooking apples) along your front fence? Most of these are varieties you'll never see in the garden centre. Send them 3 x 50 cent stamps to get their catalogue.
C/- PO, Woodbridge, Tasmania 7162
T 03 62 674 430

CALENDAR

Note: The times given in this calendar suit our garden in southern New South Wales. Other gardens may be a few weeks earlier or later.

JANUARY

This is the main time to plant the vegetables you'll be eating in autumn and winter. I know it seems crazy, planting for the cold weather now – but if you don't you'll be buying stale, sprayed stuff from the supermarket. Remember that you don't have to prepare a garden: just spread your weed-mat on the lawn, snip holes, and slip in your cabbage, cauliflower and broccoli seedlings. Keep mulch up to trees; watch out for fruit fly.

WHAT TO PLANT

VEGETABLES

Winter crops like cauliflowers, cabbage, broccoli, brussels sprouts, peas, and collards. In warm areas you can still plant small cucumbers, melons, and bush pumpkins. Plant Tom Thumb tomatoes in a pot, to bear through winter. Plant more beans, corn, lettuce, carrots, silver beet, cabbage, and potatoes, strawberries, sweet potatoes, choko, herbs, artichokes, asparagus, basil, beans, beetroot, burdock, cabbage, capsicum, carrots, celery, celtuce, chicory, corn salad, cress, cucumbers, eggplant, endive, fennel, kale, kohlrabi, leeks, lettuce (may not germinate over 26°C), melons, okra, parsley, pumpkin, radish, salsify, scorzonera, sweet corn, tomatoes, turnips, salad greens like mizuna and mitsuba, and zucchini.

FLOWERS

All the ones you want to flower in autumn: ageratum, dianthus, gladioli bulbs, forget-me-nots, iceland poppies, lupins, pansies, stocks, and sweet peas. Autumn flowering bulbs like autumn crocus, nerines, tuberoses, vallota lily, or zephyranthes, plus seeds or seedlings of achillea, ageratum, alyssum, amaranthus, calendula, calceolaria, cleome, Iceland poppies, lunaria, lupins, nasturtiums, pansies, sunflowers, zinnias.

WHAT TO HARVEST

VEGETABLES

Just about everything you planted in spring should be bearing now.

FRUIT

Late cherries in cold areas, peaches, nectarines, plums, late apricots, early apples like gravenstein, passionfruit in warmer areas, mulberries, gooseberries, early grapes, early almonds, cape gooseberry, Valencia oranges, lemons, avocados, babaco, pawpaw or mountain pawpaw in warm areas, strawberries, mid-season raspberries, loganberries, fruit from flowering prunus (good for jam), red, white and black currants, blueberries, banana passionfruit, and mangoes in hot areas.

FLOWERS

Alyssum, dahlias, gladioli, lavender, liliums, pansies, petunias, roses, and zinnias.

WHAT TO PRUNE

Nearly all plants will keep flowering and fruiting without any pruning, as long as they are growing strongly. To maximise productivity, though, January is a good time to prune:
- native shrubs, fuchsias and roses (lightly – just the tips); and
- strawberries – take off the runners to encourage late summer fruit.

WHAT TO FEED

Give dahlias a sprinkle of pelletised hen manure, or any of the 'extras' listed in Chapter 5, to keep them flowering through autumn.

Cut the grass or other plants around fruit trees to keep tree roots cool and moist and to provide food for the autumn growing 'flush'.

Cut comfrey, lucerne and other 'natural mulch' plants around the garden.

LAWNS

Mow as little as you can, and set the mower as high as possible: heavily cut lawns will suffer in the heat, resulting in weeds through your grass by winter.

PESTS

Check apples every week for signs of codling moth.

Remember that fruit fly and stink bugs are attracted to ripe fruit and breed mostly on the ground. Pick all fruit just before it gets ripe, and never leave windfalls for more than a day. Watch out for fruit fly breeding in 'compost heaps': piles of rubbish and food scraps that aren't heating up at all. Add blood and bone or sprinkle them with urine to get them going. Check for 28-spot ladybirds. These like potatoes, tomatoes, and pepinos – they speckled our eggplant leaves brown last year before I noticed what was happening. A reflective mulch (like aluminium foil or reflective insulation) will repel them. As a last resort, use glue or commercial diatomaceus earth spray. For a long-term solution, attract birds and keep cats away.

FRUIT ROT

Try a weekly seaweed, nettle or even weed spray. The best spray I know is a mixture of chamomile flowers, chives, nettles, seaweed, casuarina leaves, horsetail and comfrey – or as many of these as you can get. Cover them with water, and spray on the foliage when the liquid is light brown. Spray just before picking, to minimise post-arrest rot. Thin out the fruit if necessary. After picking, try and keep the fruit as cool as you can: hot and humid storage conditions, even for a short time, can start them rotting. Pick out any bad fruit at once. You can also try dipping fruit for a second or two in boiling water – or in hot, very salty water or hot chamomile tea. But make sure the fruit is dry before it's stored. (I leave it to dry on newspaper.)

WHITEFLY

If your plant leaves are wilting, mottled or speckled, look underneath for clouds of small, white flies. Hose thoroughly underneath the leaves, every second day, or use a glue spray, and increase the potash in your soil with wood ash, comfrey, or compost.

FEBRUARY

This is the harvest month – the month when you start to wonder why on earth you put in a dozen zucchini and two dozen tomatoes, and where to store all the apples fattening on the tree. Alternatively, you're beating off the birds and grasshoppers or next door's goats who think they're going to get a good feed too.

Put out traps for the grasshoppers, fresh water for the birds (see Chapter 7), and tell the goats that roast kid is delicious. Then start picking quickly before fruit fly, stink bugs and other pests come zooming in, lured by the scent of rotting fruit and vegetables.

WHAT TO PLANT

Subtropical and tropical areas

FOOD PLANTS

Sweet potatoes, passionfruit vines, parsley and other herbs, hand pollinate pumpkins and melons if heat or rain is preventing fruit set, plant beetroot, capsicum, carrot, caulies, celery, cucumber, eggplant, lettuce seedlings (lettuce seeds may not germinate in the heat), pak choi, pumpkin, radish, silverbeet, sweet corn, tomatoes, watermelon.

FLOWERING PLANTS

Hibiscus, bougainvilleas, tropical evergreen fruit trees, ageratum, celosia, cosmos, coleus, Iceland poppy, salvia, sunflowers.

Temperate to cold areas

FOOD PLANTS

Passionfruit and banana passionfruit, rhubarb, blueberries, artichoke, beans, beetroot, broccoli, cabbage, carrots (try the tiny, fat, fast-maturing ones in cold climates), sweet corn (fast-maturing varieties only), leek, lettuce, white onions, salad greens like corn salad, mizuna, cress, red Italian chicory, silverbeet, spring onions, spinach.

FLOWERING PLANTS

Spring flowering bulbs like iris, daffs and jonquils (look for heat tolerant ones in warmer areas, like Earlicheer jonquils) alyssum, stocks, and LOTS of flowers to give you colour and cheer through winter – pansies, violas, primulas, Iceland poppies, wallflowers, polyanthus.

BULBS

Early planting of bluebells, daffodils, Dutch iris, grape hyacinths, lachenalia, jonquils, and nerines.

FRUIT

Strawberry runners.

WHAT TO HARVEST

VEGETABLES

Much the same as for January. Late maturers like capsicum and eggplant will be ripening now. Stick large pumpkins on a hot roof to harden. Onions for storage, planted last winter, should be lifted now when the tops die off.

FRUIT

Brambleberries, raspberries, peaches, nectarines, plums, apricots, apples, passionfruit, mulberries, gooseberries, cape gooseberries, hazelnuts, almonds, grapes, figs, babaco, pepino, pawpaw or mountain pawpaw in warm areas, orange, lemon, avocado, strawberry guavas, strawberries, pears, early melons, tamarillos, and banana passionfruit.

FLOWERS

Agapanthus, ageratum, asters, bergamot, dahlias, gladioli, lilliums, lobelias, pansies, penstemons, petunias, thyme, roses, zinnias.

WHAT TO PRUNE

This is a good time for summer pruning, especially vines like kiwi fruit now the fruit has set. (Summer pruning's other name is 'hacking back the jungle'.) Bending back unwanted growth now will check plants far less than a rigorous pruning in winter, and cuts will heal quicker. If you must prune apricots or cherries because the trees are getting too big, do so now.

Prune hydrangeas back to about half their size, to encourage flowering.

Native shrubs, fuchsias, and shrubs that have just finished flowering can be lightly pruned.

WHAT TO PROPAGATE

February is probably the best month for budding stone fruit.

Take softwood and semi-hardwood cuttings, and keep them moist.

LAWNS

Restrain yourself and try not to mow too often or too hard. February is too hot for severely disciplined lawns.

Scatter pelletised hen manure to encourage clover for a green winter lawn.

If lawn mowing, lawn watering and the heat are driving you mad, dig up part of the lawn for a lily pond or a cooling fountain – and pave the rest with stones and herbs.

PESTS

At the first sign of mildewed vines, pull off the infected leaves and compost or burn them. Make sure the soil is well-mulched to stop contact between the vines and damp soil – and any leaf residues in the soil. Spray with chamomile tea or milk if the infestation is light. Spray under the leaves as well, and on top of the mulch where spores may linger.

Brown rot should have been partially controlled by removing infected twigs and 'mummies' in winter and spraying with Bordeaux. Pick any infected fruit before it harms the rest. Stone fruit for storage can be treated by dipping them in hot water for about 30 seconds. If their skins shrivel hold them under for a shorter time. You'll need to experiment according to the heat of the water and the moisture content of the fruit.

MARCH

March is a gentle month. The sun isn't so fierce and there's a touch of lushness in the growth: the autumn flush before the winter. The cooler air and warm soil start to tempt you into the garden again after the harsh days of summer.

- Move shrubs and small trees while the weather is cool, but still warm enough for them to put out new roots
- Take rose cuttings – snappable wood, about as long as your hand. Fill a box with clean sand and plant so just the top third is poking out. Keep moist and in semi-shade; plant out your new roses next winter.
- Leave pumpkins in a sunny spot (e.g., the shed roof or on paving) for a few days to 'cure' so their skins will harden before storing them (on their sides – moisture collects in the tops and bottoms and the pumpkin may rot).

Hot climates

Plants to eat: Garlic, macadamias, avocados, bananas, custard apples, lychees, sapodilla, star fruit, pawpaws, mangoes, passionfruit, citrus, strawberry plants, capsicum, carrots, chilli, cauliflowers, eggplant, okra, potatoes, silver beet, sweet corn, zucchini.

Plants for beauty: Hibiscus bushes, calendula, poppy, primula, snapdragon, sunflower, salvias; fill bare spots with ferns.

Temperate

Plants to eat: Garlic, macadamias, avocado trees, citrus, strawberries, beetroot, broccoli, broad beans, cabbage, carrots (mini or 'French round' carrots mature fastest), cauliflower, garlic, leeks, parsnips, spinach, celery, fast maturing Asian veg like tatsoi, pak choi and mitsuba.

Plants for beauty: Bulbs, including liliums, agapanthus, iris; multi-stemmed jonquils, heat-hardy tulip varieties, flowers like alyssum, dianthus, pansies, primulas, salvias, poppies, sweet peas, stock. Grevilleas for nectar for the birds (superb and 'Robyn Gordon' and her relatives bloom throughout the year).

Cold climates

Plants to eat: Garlic, strawberry runners, broad beans, spinach, onions, seedlings of broccoli, cauliflower, Brussels sprouts, fast-maturing Asian veg like tasto, pak choi and mitsuba.

Plants for beauty: Bulbs like daffodils, jonquils, tulips, anemones, hyacinths, freesias, ranunculi, seedlings of Iceland poppy, primulas, pansies, polyanthus, sweet peas.

WHAT TO HARVEST

VEGETABLES

Melons and okra will be ripening. As well as most summer vegetables, early cabbages and other winter vegetables may be starting to mature. This is a good time for peas, and for digging sweet potato roots.

FRUIT

Olives, oranges, lemons, cumquats, calamondins, chilacoyotes, macadamias, citrons, native limes, native raspberries, figs, late peaches, late nectarines, apples, passionfruit, pepino, babaco, pawpaw or mountain pawpaw in warm areas, sapote, mulberries, hazelnuts, almonds, orange, lemon, tamarillo, strawberries, raspberries, brambleberries, early quinces, early persimmons, pears, melons, pecans, bunya nuts, late grapes, and banana passionfruit.

FLOWERS

As for February.

WHAT TO FEED

Scatter blood and bone or any of the 'extras' (Chapter 5) on citrus and other evergreen fruit trees.

Keep picking off dahlia heads and keep watering with home-made liquid fertiliser for a good autumn display of flowers.

PESTS

Most pests will be vanishing as the weather cools down. Keep up fruit fly lures until none have been caught for three weeks.

OTHER JOBS

- Plant more peas or broad beans for 'green manure': slash them in late winter or early spring, just as they start to flower, to provide mulch and fertiliser for spring planting in a 'no-dig' garden.
- Start to prepare for frost now: work out which trees are vulnerable – like avocados, citrus and tamarillos – and start building shelters for them. See Chapter 10.
- Cover part of the garden with weed-mat or clear plastic to make a weed-free area for winter-planted onions.
- Get rid of most of your tomato glut by drying them: just halve the tomatoes, place them on aluminium foil in the sun, and take them inside or cover them at night. They should take about three to four days to dry. Place them in a jar, and cover them

with olive oil – and garlic and herbs if you want to.

APRIL

This is autumn: soft skies and lush growth. Everyone expects spring growth, but autumn usually takes us by surprise – the last flush and profusion before winter. Roses start weighing down the bushes again, strawberries begin to swell, and the last of the raspberries are hidden in the tangle of summer canes.

- Gather seeds from flowers and trees to germinate and grow your own spring seedlings.
- Rake up fallen leaves to use for mulch.
- Cut back dead stems and summer flowers.

WHAT TO PLANT

VEGETABLES

Anything you plant now will go to seed in spring. So plant broccoli, cauliflower, broad beans and peas – you want them to go to seed, because it's the seed heads you eat. Plant to eat them in spring. Start putting in brown-skinned, long-keeping onions now. If, in temperate areas, the soil is still warm enough to sit on, put in winter lettuce, winter radish, Chinese mustard, kale, corn salad and Swedes.

FOOD GARDEN

Fruit trees, pots of herbs, artichoke suckers. Coriander rushes to seed in hot weather – try it now! Plant seedlings of broccoli, Brussels sprouts, cabbage, cauliflower, Chinese cabbage, lettuce, leeks, mustard, silverbeet, spinach, seeds of broad beans, onions. In frost-free areas you can also plant beans, capsicum, parsnips, carrots, beetroot, scorzonera, burdock and potatoes.

FLOWER GARDEN

Ornamental shrubs and climbers, spring bulbs; in cold areas plant seedlings and in frost free areas plant seeds or seedlings of alyssum, amaranthus, balsam, bellis perennis, calendula, California poppy, honesty, Iceland poppy, larkspur, pansy, primula, snapdragon, statice, sweet pea, viola, Virginia stock and wallflower. Frost-free areas only: nasturtium, petunia, ornamental chilli, salvia and sunflowers.

FRUIT

In warm areas, plant evergreen fruit trees. Start checking catalogues for the deciduous fruit trees you want to plant in winter – or you may have to stick with the nursery selections.

WHAT TO HARVEST

VEGETABLES

All the 'year-rounders' (like celery, silver beet, carrots and beetroot) plus Chinese cabbage and the last of the summer vegetables. Chokoes will be fruiting now, even in cool areas. Dig up kumaras or Jerusalem artichokes. Potatoes should be ready too.

FRUIT

Pomegranates, medlars, Valencia oranges, lemons, early limes, olives, late figs, quinces, Granny Smith apples, passionfruit, tamarillos, late grapes, chestnuts, walnuts, persimmons, grapefruit, guava, feijoa, strawberry guava, late strawberries, raspberries, bananas, avocados, Irish strawberry tree fruit, melons, chilacoyote melons, macadamias, hazelnuts, kiwi fruit, and pecan.

FLOWERS

Alyssum, dahlias, proteas, roses, sweet peas and summer-planted annuals.

PESTS

This isn't a bad time of year for pests: the great population explosions have come and gone, and predators should have built up to cope with the remnants.

If you have winter-maturing fruit, keep up your fruit fly traps and orchard hygiene. Otherwise, just make sure that you don't have any old fruit in nice, warm, slowly decomposing compost heaps or pits – places where fruit fly can cosily over-winter.

Check any late-maturing apples, like Democrats or Grannies or Lady Williams, every few days for the sawdust-like deposits from codling moth larvae. If you find any, pick the apples and either feed them to the animals or stick them in a plastic bag to anaerobically compost over winter.

Remove any old ladders or boxes from around the trees where codling moth can hibernate, pick up any windfalls or let the chooks do it for you.

If your garden is troubled by harlequin beetles – sometimes called push-me-pull-yous because of their active sex lives – stick some broad pieces of cardboard on the ground around the garden. Check each afternoon for sheltering beetles. This should considerably reduce the numbers in your garden the next season.

If you can, stick hens or other animals under fruit trees and in the old tomato patches now – they'll help clean up any fruit residues which might help fruit fly over winter.

OTHER JOBS

Now is the time to bed your garden down for the winter.
- Don't mulch. Mulching insulates roots and stops them from freezing. It will also increase frost damage to the leaves above. So choose: frozen roots or frozen leaves.
- Dust plants with potash-rich wood ash – potash helps make plants more frost resistant. So does a weekly foliar spray of seaweed spray or home-made nettle or waterweed spray. (Just cover the plants with water until it turns brown, and spray the leaves in the early morning or late afternoon.)
- Gather up whatever will be spoiled by winter cold: green tomatoes to ripen on newspaper indoors or to make into green tomato pickle; immature cucumbers and pumpkin to slice and stir fry or to hang by their vines in the garage to keep ripening for a few weeks. Dig up tomatoes and capsicum bushes with as much soil as you can, and try to pot them for a continuing crop.

Hang capsicum bushes and pumpkin vines in the garage, away from the frost, to allow the fruit to keep ripening.

In autumn, dig up capsicum bushes, soil and all, and put them in pots to shelter indoors over winter.

- Scatter radish seed for a quick crop to help protect other plants. The radish will go to seed in spring and can be hauled out easily, leaving your garden relatively weed-free and deeply dug – and with a weed-free mulch.
- Don't clean up the garden. Leave those corn stalks, radish going-to-seed and patches of weeds alone. The weeds probably won't seed or run about until spring anyway – and they'll protect the soil and help insulate your plants.

Gardeners who recommend you spend your peaceful winter months 'tidying up the garden' just have a fetish for straight rows and nice chocolatey, bare earth. This may help their spirits but won't help the garden. Gardens are wasted on people with a passion for sweat and blisters. Gentle pottering and a bit of contemplation are more effective than maniacs with mattocks.

MAY

This is a time of blue sky and warm soil. It's a joy to be outside. This is a month for all the major garden jobs it's usually too cold or too hot for: lugging tyres for tyre gardens (in most areas, you can still get potatoes through winter in tyre gardens), putting down paving instead of lawn, and building terraces or compost bins. May is perhaps the one month of the year when it's a pleasure to do some hard work.

Watch out for: slugs and snails as snail-eating lizards grow sleepier.

Spread: the contents of your compost bin, so you can fill it with prunings and perennials that die back in winter.

Plan: a rose garden to plant this winter; a hedge of fruit trees; a scented plant beneath your bedroom window; a tall native tree for the birds.

Harvest: rose hips for winter teas and syrup ... every rose bush will produce some hips, and as long as they haven't been sprayed with pesticides or fungicides you can use them in cooking, or save the seeds to plant in spring. Roses too can be grown from seed! The seedlings probably won't be like their parents, though – each one will be an adventure!

WHAT TO PLANT

Frost-free climates

Plants to eat: Just about anything can be grown now! Put in lots of mixed salad leaves, apple cucumbers, basil, butter beans, huge New guinea beans, coloured capsicum, Chinese cabbage, chillies, chokoes, sweet potatoes, long oval eggplant, melons, okra, rosellas, pumpkin, shallots, sweet corn, tomatoes. Try above ground beds for parsley – the roots may rot in hot damp soil.

Plants for beauty: Alyssum, calendula, cleome, coleus, gerbera, petunias, phlox, salvia, torenia, zinnia.

Cold to temperate climates

Plants to eat: Don't be tempted by blue sky and warm breezes. If you live in a very frosty area stick to onion seedlings and broad beans and lots of seedlings of broccoli, cabbage and cauliflower. In temperate areas: seeds of radish, onions, winter lettuce, silver beet, spinach, broad beans, peas, snow peas, winter lettuce, spring onions, parsnips, fast-maturing Asian veg like tatsoi, pak choi and mitsuba. Seedlings of beetroot, broccoli, cabbage, cauliflower, chicory, leeks, lettuce, leeks, onions, spinach.

Plants for beauty: Seeds of alyssum, calendula, lunaria. Seedlings of Californian poppy, evening primrose, gazanias, primulas, pansies, polyanthus, Iceland poppies, viola. In cold areas the annual flower planting time is nearly over. Put in native shrubs now, before the

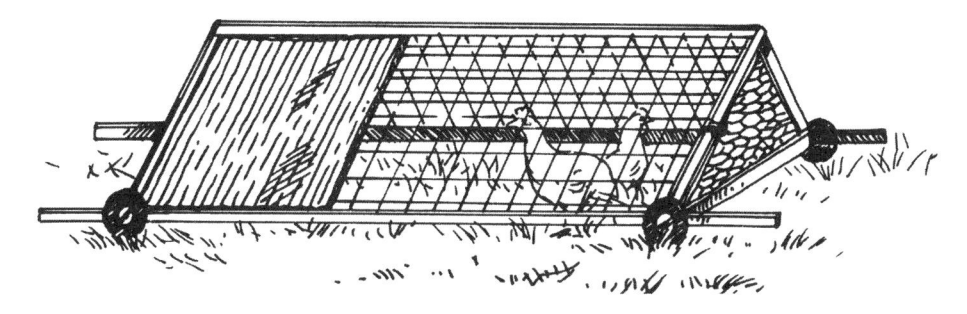

Build a mobile hen run, to keep down the grass and fertilise it at the same time.

ground gets cold. Plant camellias before they start to flower. Keep putting in daffodil bulbs for spring – though these late-planted ones will bloom later. Plant tulip bulbs now. (In warm areas, first keep them in the refrigerator for a month to encourage them to flower.)

FRUIT

In warm areas, evergreen fruit trees can be planted now – they won't be burnt by harsh summer sun. In cool and temperate areas, deciduous fruit trees can be planted from now until the beginning of spring.

WHAT TO HARVEST

VEGETABLES

Potatoes, year-rounders like celery, beetroot and silver beet. Strip corn stalks for 'baby corn'. Root vegetables are good now – much sweeter after the first frost. You should have a glut of chokoes. Dig up sweet potatoes now in cool areas; in frost-free areas, dig them when you want them.

FRUIT

Early mandarins, limes, pomegranates, late apples, late Valencias or early navel oranges, tangellos, citrons, cumquats, tamarillos, early kiwi fruit, late passionfruit (high up on the vine), late raspberries, late strawberries (if grown on a high garden away from early frost), olives, persimmons (if the birds haven't finished them), feijoa, bananas, avocados, banana passionfruit, elderberries, medlars, olives, melons, guavas, chilacoyote melons and sapotes.

FLOWERS

Late roses, dahlias in warm areas, late summer annuals, chrysanthemum and proteas.

LAWNS

Keep your grass trimmed fairly high – it will survive frost better. Keep mowing it right into the cold weather to stop lawn weeds from setting seed.

PESTS

This is a month of prevention. Prune off dead twigs and 'mummies', band apple trees with grease, corrugated cardboard or old wool to help control codling moth and oriental peach moth, and clean up old ladders and fruit boxes where moths may shelter. Let hens scavenge round the orchard to pick up old fruit or insects on the ground.

Check that there are no stink bugs on your citrus – spray with glue spray so the birds can find them, or just slow them down with soapy water.

OTHER JOBS

- Clean out greenhouses now, and leave them open to the sun for a time. Take shelves out to air, and wash them in disinfectant or vinegar if there's a chance

they're harbouring fungus or disease spores.
- Make use of a slow garden and the warm weather to revamp the chook house for next spring's chickens; build a mobile hen run to keep down the grass; build more compost heaps; and make potpourri with the last of the rose petals and scented leaves before they are frosted.
- Don't rake up the autumn leaves. They attract frost and keep the soil cold so that trees and shrubs will shoot later in spring – and so avoid being nipped off by late spring frosts.

JUNE

This is hibernating season. Things move slowly in winter. It's also a 'bare' time – a good time to look around the garden and plant.

Winter is the time to move shrubs in the wrong place – but most native plants don't transplant well. It's best just to plant new ones!

Water! Cold days – and especially cold windy days – dry plants and soil more than you think. a lot of 'cold damage' is often just lack of water!

Prune most vines now, thinning out messy wood, but not spring flowering ones – leave those until after they've bloomed.

WHAT TO PLANT

Frost free climates

Plants to eat: Passionfruit vines and seeds mixed salad leaves, apple cucumbers, butter beans, huge New guinea beans, coloured capsicum, Chinese cabbage, chillies, chokoes, sweet potatoes, long oval eggplant, melons, okra, rosellas, pumpkin, shallots, sweet corn, tomatoes. Try deep pots of parsley – the roots may rot in hot damp soil.

Plants for beauty: Alyssum, calendula, cleome, coleus, gerbera, petunias, phlox, salvia, torenia, zinnia,

Cold to temperate climates

Plants to eat: Seeds of radish, onions, winter lettuce, silverbeet, spinach, broad beans, peas, snow peas, winter lettuce, spring onions, parsnips, fast maturing Asian veg like tatsoi, pak choi and mitsuba. Seedlings of beetroot, broccoli, cabbage, cauliflower, chicory, leeks, lettuce, leeks, spinach.

Plants for beauty: Seeds of alyssum, calendula, lunaria. Seedlings of Californian poppy, evening primrose, gazanias, primulas, pansies, polyanthus, Iceland poppies, viola.

FRUIT

Keep planting deciduous fruit trees and berries; put in rhubarb crowns.

WHAT TO HARVEST

VEGETABLES

Year-rounders like celery, beetroot, silver beet and carrots. Winter vegies planted in January: cabbage, broccoli, brussels sprouts, cauliflowers, winter lettuce, parsnips, swedes, turnips, foliage turnips, broad bean tips, tampala, spring onions, collards, parsley, winter radish, spinach, leek, oyster plant, celeriac and parsley root.

FRUIT

Apples (Lady Williams, Democrat), feijoa, navel oranges, kiwi fruit, limes, mandarins, citrons, grapefruit, bananas, avocados, late passionfruit (high on the vine), banana passionfruit, guava, strawberry guava, quinces, medlars, olives, late tamarillos (above the frost), a very few late raspberries, and winter rhubarb.

FLOWERS

Primulas, daisies, winter rose or helleborus, jonquils and most natives – especially grevilleas.

WHAT TO PRUNE

Lock up your secateurs until summer. The more you prune, the more you'll have to feed your trees and shrubs to make up for the lost foliage – and they'll be set back in spring when they should be producing flowers. Summer pruning is far better: wounds heal quickly. Heavy pruning attracts sap suckers like woolly aphids, so practise light pruning after flowering instead.

If your apples are growing too tall and flower mostly at their tips, try weighting down the end of the branches, or tying them onto a stake in the ground. This will encourage new growth along the branch. In five or 10 years, repeat the process.

PESTS

In most areas there are few pest outbreaks at this time of year. But you may have over-wintering populations, especially of fruit fly and codling moth, and any remaining fruit or windfalls should be rigorously checked to prevent an early pest build-up when the weather warms. This is also a good time to think about planting to reduce pest problems next year.

If you have apple trees, let parsnips or other umbellifera go to seed now, to spring up wild around the orchard to reduce codling moth infestations. This is extraordinarily effective, though I don't know the mechanism – whether the flowers attract predators or inhibit the moths. Tansy planted under apples is also supposed to reduce codling moth, but I haven't found it works here – in fact, pungent tansy just seems to make fallen fruit less attractive to wombats, sheep, etc, and uneaten fallen fruit is the best way to breed codling moth.

Mid-winter is the classic time for preventive spraying with Bordeaux against curly leaf (pinkish, raised blisters on peaches and almonds), rust, shot hole (small holes in leaves, most common on apricots), brown rot (exactly that: a brown, soft rot on fruit, sometimes with a furry outside), black leaf spot, bacterial blight in walnuts, and other fungal and bacterial conditions.

I try to avoid preventive spraying. Even curly leaf, which is disfiguring, usually doesn't harm the tree unless the tree is very young or the disease is so bad that new shoots wither and fruit sets badly. But if you have had problems with these conditions in the past, or your neighbours have, or you have young trees you wish to cherish, it is probably best to give them a Bordeaux spray when they are dormant. In very bad cases, spray at leaf fall and again at bud swell, just before buds start to colour. Otherwise, one spray should be enough.

Make snail fences now (see Chapter 7) and put them round the beds in which you want to plant young seedlings. If you leave this until later, you may be fencing in the slugs and snails – instead of fencing them out of your garden.

JULY

This is the slow time of year: the time to watch the garden through the window; to see where the frost falls and what bits get the sunlight first; to dream of what and where you'll plant when the shadows grow small again.

- Spray 'Stressguard' on frost-sensitive plants to help protect them. I put plastic tree guards on some youngsters – many plants become more frost resistant as they grow older.
- Clean up dead palm fronds; use for mulch.
- Divide clumps of perennials, for lots of free new plants.
- Pour almost boiling water on bright green frothy patches of young bindii eyes and watch the bindiis shrivel.

WHAT TO PLANT

Cold to temperate climates

Don't plant veg and flowers unless you're absolutely longing to get your fingers in the dirt! Seed may rot in cold ground, veg and flowers won't grow much before they bloom and die. Stick to onion seedlings, rhubarb, strawberry, asparagus and artichoke crowns, bare-rooted trees, shrubs and roses.

Frost free climates

Plant just about anything and keep watering! Pop in some of the new spreading petunias too, for a touch of colour.

FRUIT

Deciduous fruit trees, berries and rhubarb crowns.

FLOWERS

Any spring bulbs that haven't sprouted. A few flowers can be sown: primulas, violas and sweet peas – coat them in salad dressing to help prevent rotting in cold, wet conditions – but they are best left until next month.

WHAT TO HARVEST

Root vegetables are sweetest now, after frost and cold nights. Try them grated into salads with lots of parsley. Winter fruit will be at its best now, too – frost makes citrus softer and sweeter, and seems to give late Lady Williams apples a unique zing.

VEGETABLES

As for June.

FRUIT

Apples (Lady Williams, Sturmer Pippin), navel oranges, kiwi fruit, limes, calamondins, Kaffir limes, native citrus, native gooseberry, mandarins, citrons, grapefruit, bananas, avocados, tangelos, medlars, alpine strawberries, late quinces, Himalayan pears, winter rhubarb, and cape gooseberries grown in a pot or sheltered spot.

FLOWERS

Jonquils and other winter bulbs, winter rose, and natives (especially grevilleas), daisies, euryops, camellias, some lavenders, pansies and violets.

WHAT TO PROPAGATE

Take rose cuttings and thrust them deep into semi-shaded soil under a tree.

Divide perennial clumps like shasta daisies and hollyhocks.

Take chrysanthemum cuttings and thrust them into moist sand.

Transplant the new dahlia bulbs (which grew last season) to other parts of the garden, to increase next year's display.

OTHER JOBS

- Scatter potash-rich wood ash on bulbs and around broad beans to lessen the chances of leaf spot and rotting.
- Mulch asparagus beds – or plant comfrey and other 'living mulches' to do it for you.
- Surround next year's beds with comfrey, lemon grass or dahlias to keep grass out and provide 'living mulch'.
- Daydream through seed and fruit tree catalogues, planning for next season. Clean up garden rubbish and make a final winter compost heap.
- Make a bird table and start putting out old bread and other scraps to attract birds so they'll be around to help clean up spring pests.
- Don't clean up the garden. Don't tear down last year's dead vines or chokoes – they'll provide tangles for birds to nest in. Don't pull up weeds – just trample them down for next year's garden beds. Don't pull out old corn stalks, etc. – they are helping protect your garden from frost. Don't even worry about that pile of weeds that is supposed to be a compost heap but isn't doing anything – you can plant it with potatoes or pumpkins in spring.
- And take a break.

AUGUST

The air is getting warm, but the soil isn't – restrain yourself, except in hot areas. There's something in spring that gets to gardeners: they go out planting things long before the world is ready. I still do it, year after year.

Water! Up to 80 per cent of the year's growth may happen in spring. It's worth being lavish with water in spring, then using just enough to keep plants alive for the rest of the year.

If you get hay fever ask someone else to mow your lawn and spread your mulch. Use a drier for your sheets too – pollens can cling to wet sheets, and you don't want to sleep all wrapped up in pollen.

WHAT TO PLANT

Frost free climates

Good tucker plants: fruit trees like limes, tropical apples, avocados, grape, choko, sweet potato and passionfruit vines, seeds of amaranth, artichoke, asparagus, basil, burdock, carrots, celery, chilli, corn, celeriac, choko, collards, eggplant, gourds, kale, leeks, lettuce, mustard greens, okra, onion, parsnip, parsley, peas, pumpkin, radish, rockmelon, salsify, shallots, silver beet, tomato, watermelon, zucchini.

Plants to eat: Spring crops can be planted when the soil is warm enough to sit on, bare-bummed.

Plants for beauty: Any ornamental shrub in the nursery! Seeds or seedlings of alyssum, Californian poppy, calendula, cleome, coleus, gerbera, helichrysum, honesty, impatiens, kangaroo paw, marigold, pansy, petunias, phlox, salvia, sunflower, Swan River daisy, torenia, zinnia.

Temperate climates

Good tucker plants: any fruit tree, vine or shrub, bare-rooted or evergreen, seeds or seedlings of baby carrots, beetroot, lettuce, parsnip, peas, radish, swede, turnips, celery, celeriac, leek, lettuce, onions, mizuna, mitsuba, seed potatoes, rocket, silver beet, spinach. Pots of tomatoes or chilli plants can be grown on a warm sunny patio.

Plants for beauty: seeds or seedlings of alyssum, calendula, heartsease, lunaria, bellis perennis, Californian poppy, English daisy, evening primrose, Iceland poppy, love lies bleeding, primulas, pansies, polyanthus, Iceland poppies, viola. For a touch of early colour pots of petunias or impatiens should stay warm on a sunny patio.

Cold climates

Good tucker plants: last chance this year for bare-rooted fruit trees, gooseberries, currants, grape vines. Plant seedlings of onions, cauliflower, collards, kale, mustard greens, peas, salad greens like mizuna, mitsuba, spinach, also rhubarb crowns, artichoke suckers, asparagus plants and seed potatoes. Plant early tomatoes, zucchini, melons and pumpkins in pots on a sunny windowsill to give them a head start.

Plants for beauty: seedlings of alyssum, bellis perennis, calendula, Californian poppy, Iceland poppies, lunaria, primula, pansy, stock, sweet peas

Avoid pale straggly seedlings in nurseries that may be left over from autumn. Otherwise, buy seed and sow it in pots indoors – take them out during the day. Restrain yourself from planting camellias or azaleas in flower – they will be badly set back, even if you plant carefully. It's best to leave them in their pot until flowering has finished.

FRUIT

Deciduous trees can still be planted now – with care, as they may be shooting. Evergreen trees do well if planted when the fruit trees are blossoming.

WHAT TO HARVEST

VEGETABLES

Carrots, beetroot, parsnips, turnips, foliage turnips, early broad beans or peas in warm areas, winter lettuce, celery, spring onions, garlic tops, cabbage, Brussels sprouts, broccoli, cauliflowers, celeriac, corn salad, silver beet, potatoes if you've kept them growing over winter, leeks, parsley, winter radish, and oyster plant.

FRUIT

Navel and late Valencia oranges, lemon, tangelo, mandarin, calamondins, cumquats, lemonade fruit, chinotto, chilacoyote melons, macadamias, citrons, chestnuts, hazelnuts, edible wattle seed, kiwi fruit, grapefruit, avocados and limes, early banana passionfruit, late tamarillos, and early rhubarb.

FLOWERS

Jonquils and daffodils should be carpeting the area under your deciduous trees now. Violets should be blooming in shady corners, and some lavenders will be flowering. Camellias will be wonderful, as will primulas, calendulas, Californian poppies, pansies, violas, daisies, ranunculi, anemones, Spanish bluebells, buttercups, daisies, euryops and banana passionfruit. Many early flowering trees and prunus will be spectacular by now.

PRUNE

Winter flowering shrubs: cut out straggly growth, trim off flowers just behind the dead flowers. Most native plants do well with a light 'tip prune' every spring

Summer flowering shrubs: buddleia, fuschias, santolina, lavatera all flower best on new growth made in spring. Trim back straggly branches to the base or main stem. Prune back hibiscus, tibouchina, oleander, heliotrope and other shrubs now too.

Hedges: trim them back until they're neat but don't cut back into bare wood past the leafing area, or the branch will probably die back.

Climbers: give winter flowering jasmines good hair cut – cut out straggly growth and trim it all back by about a third. Prune summer-flowering jasmines by taking out some of the major stems – if you just give them a haircut you'll end up with a shaggy mess.

ROSES

Modern hybrid tea roses need to be pruned to get more flowers – though they'll give some flowers with no pruning at all. Prune them lightly now. Early pruning just encourages early shoots which can be snapped off by frost – leading to dieback problems later. I cut off any spindly growth and cut back other branches by about a third. There are more expert ways to prune, but this is a simple and effective method for the amateur.

Mulch roses heavily now. You'll not only provide food for late-spring flowering, but you'll also keep the soil cool – so that the roses will shoot later and are less likely to be damaged by frost. Scatter blood and bone or hen manure on top of the mulch if you have pruned heavily – the rose will need more feeding to make up for the bits you've amputated.

If you don't like pruning roses consider rugosa roses. They're old-fashioned Japanese roses that are incredibly disease, drought and salt resistant – and don't need pruning. Some varieties are very thorny – wonderful for a rose hedge planted very close together to keep out dogs, cats and wallabies.

WHAT TO PROPAGATE

Take chrysanthemum cuttings and strike them in sandy loam.

Snap off bits of lavender and wormwood and stick them in any bare patch round the garden, both for their beauty and to help repel pests and attract predators.

Dig up bits of comfrey root (you only need small bits), and plant them around garden beds to stop the grass encroaching, and under fruit trees as deep-rooted 'living mulch'.

LAWNS

Scatter on pelletised hen manure or blood and bone. This will give the grass a boost and stop weed seeds germinating.

Mow the lawn as soon as it starts to grow. This will kill annual weeds which are just starting to flower, and stop them spreading their seeds through your lawn next year.

Look for bright green bindii patches. Throw day-old urine over them, or scatter on sulphate of ammonia, to kill them. Bindii eyes are easy to see at this time of year – they're a much brighter green than the rest of your grass.

PESTS

Clean up piles of rubbish. (Dowse with hen manure or blood and bone and hope they turn into compost.)

Pick off all dried fruit 'mummies' that may infect next season's crops.

Put out snail traps and snail fences.

Keep feeding your birds – they're the best pest prevention method I know.

OTHER JOBS

- Lay down weed-mat for next month's gardens.
- Build no-dig beds.
- Put down clear plastic to kill grass and weeds for a spring carrot crop. Don't be in a hurry though to pull out last year's debris to make room for new crops – the debris will protect the remaining plants from late frost.
- Throw potash-rich wood ash on perennial flowers like hollyhocks and delphiniums, to harden the stems and improve the flower colours.

SEPTEMBER

Spring usually comes with a bump – one day you're shivering and the next the lawn needs watering and you're racing to get your spring vegies in. Don't panic – a few days or even weeks won't make much difference to the time they crop.

September is the main planting time. I put in enough carrots, silver beet, celery, beetroot and parsnips to see us through the year. Anything you want to put in, put it in now: melons, tomatoes, masses of corn. While conventional gardens need to be kept small so you can weed them, if you use the weed-mat and other low-work gardening methods you can plant everything you want. Go wild.

WHAT TO PLANT

VEGETABLES

As for August.

FLOWERS

As for August, plus gladioli bulbs (early gladioli flower before thrips build up), sweet peas and lupins (for garden fertility) and delphiniums. Move dahlia tubers and divide chrysanthemum clumps. Make sure you plant sunflowers for quick-growing mulch. (The young flowers can be boiled and eaten like artichokes.) Lawns are best planted now – growth is very rapid in early spring.

FRUIT

Evergreen fruit trees can be planted now before it gets too hot. So can deciduous trees, as long as they are in pots or transplanted with plenty of soil, then kept moist and well-staked so their new roots aren't broken as they rock in the wind.

WHAT TO HARVEST

VEGETABLES

All-rounders like celery, silver beet, carrots, etc, as well as peas and broad beans in warm areas, lots of asparagus, and early artichokes in warm areas. Small potatoes can be harvested from plants that over-wintered. Winter vegetables may start to go to seed. Pick out seed heads regularly to delay them. Mulch heavily to keep the soil cool – this will also delay plants going to seed.

FRUIT

Navel orange, lemon, limes, tangelo, mandarin, cumquats, calamondins, macadamias, early loquats, chinotto, Kaffir limes, native limes, lemonade fruit, satsumas, citron, grapefruit, pommelo, shaddock, blood oranges, avocado, small alpine strawberries (not the large new varieties that fruit later), cape gooseberries (if they haven't been frosted off, autumn's will mature now), tamarillos (same as for cape gooseberries), and rhubarb.

FLOWERS

Spring bulbs should be spectacular, as should azaleas, late camellias, rhododendrons, daisies, primulas, pansies, violas, late violets, calendulas, euryops, banana passionfruit, flowering fruit trees like crab apples, pelargoniums, a mass of natives, jasmine and many others.

PESTS

Pests like spring: growth is soft and sappy and there are few predators around.

Pests attack early plantings. Most start breeding at about 3°C – most predators at about 12°C. Wait until the world is ready to receive your bean seeds and capsicum plants – don't try to hurry spring along.

How do you know when to plant? One bit of folklore wisdom says to plant tomatoes when the soil is warm enough to sit on with bare buttocks. In suburban areas, use the back of your wrist. Another old saying has you planting corn when the peach blossom falls. I do this every year, and it works – unless of course your peach blossom happens to be frosted off.

On the other hand, there is also the 'spring flush'. This really exists – spring-grown crops grow faster than ones planted later. Up to 80 per cent of the year's growth happens in spring! You just have to use your judgment. Get plants in early enough to catch the spring tides, but not so early that they're stunted or frosted off.

As another anti-pest precaution, try not to water spring crops and don't fertilise them until the spring flush is over – and never give high-nitrogen fertiliser.

Let some vegetables go to seed and flower around your garden. This is perhaps the most important bit of spring advice there is. Flowering vegetables are one of the best ways I know to attract pest-eating predators. Most adult predators eat nectar from flowers (it's only their offspring that are carnivorous), and most prefer the nectar from the plants which their offspring will forage over for pests – in other words, your vegies.

Letting vegetables go to seed will also give you a stock of home-grown seed for next year – fungicide-free and suited to your area.

Spring is the classic time of year for sap suckers like aphids. Make up the glue spray (Chapter 7) or just hose them off. If thrips are a problem in blossom, hose them too (water kills thrips better than any pesticide), and next year plant low-growing flowering groundcovers to keep the thrips down there. (Thrips prefer to feed low down – they only start advancing in the world when the low-growing winter weeds and flowers have finished.)

OTHER JOBS

- Graft fruit trees just before bud burst but before the sap is flowing. The timing will vary from district to district.
- Just keep planting – the rest can wait.

OCTOBER

October is exciting: vegetables are growing, trees have set fruit, and the world is a carpet of flowers. October has all of spring's growth without summer's heat to knock it back. It is a wonderful time to be in the garden – which is good, because it is also an excellent time to plant things.

MULCH! Now the weather has warmed up mulch EVERYTHING (with the possible exception of the cat).

WHAT TO PLANT

VEGETABLES

Cool areas will start spring planting now.

Food plants: choko, lemon grass, sweet potato and passionfruit vines, Jerusalem artichokes, pawpaw and Cape gooseberry seeds. Also the seeds of artichokes, basil, beans, beetroot, capsicum, carrots, celery, celtuce, chicory, cucumbers, eggplant, endive, fennel, tropical lettuce, melons, okra, parsley, peas, peanuts, pumpkin (not in humid areas), radish, rosellas, sweet corn, tomatoes and salad greens like mizuna and mitsuba.

Plants for beauty: seeds or seedlings of ageratum, alyssum, amaranthus, carnations, celosia, coleus, cosmos, dichondra, echinops, erigeron, gaillardia, gazania, gloxinia, gourds, hymenosporum, impatiens, nasturtiums, phlox and salvia.

Cold and temperate climates

Food garden: seed potatoes, sweet potatoes, choko, strawberries; seeds of artichokes, asparagus, basil, beans, beetroot, broccoli, burdock, cabbage, capsicum, carrots, cauliflower, celery, celtuce, chicory, collards, coriander, corn salad, cress, cucumbers, eggplant, endive, fennel, kale, kohlrabi, leeks, lettuce, melons, okra, parsley, peanuts, pumpkin, radish, rosellas, salsify, scorzonera, sweet corn, tomatoes, turnips, salad greens like mizuna and mitsuba, and zucchini.

Flower garden: achillea, ageratum, alstromeria, alyssum, amaranthus, aster, balsam, bellis perennis, bells of Ireland, brachycome, calendula, candytuft, Canterbury bells, carnation, celosia, clarkia, cleome, coleus, coreopsis, columbines, cosmos, delphinium, dichondra, echinacea, echinops, erigeron, euphorbia, foxglove, gaillardia, gazania, globe amaranth, gloxinia, godetia, gypsophila, helichrysum, heliotrope, hellebores, honesty, lavender, marigolds, nasturtium, petunia, phlox, Flanders poppy, portulaca, rudbeckia, salpiglossis, salvia, scabious, sweet william, viola, zinnia and snapdragons.

FRUIT

Evergreen fruit trees can still be planted now, except where it's getting too hot – though, if necessary, trees can be sheltered in hessian shelters for a few weeks. Don't be tempted by leftover bare-rooted trees in nurseries, even if they are cheap – they may not shoot, or their new roots will break off when you plant them. Trees which are badly set back when young don't recover for years.

WHAT TO HARVEST

As for September. Asparagus and early artichokes will be yielding now. In warm areas, lettuce, Chinese spinach, corn salad and peas may be starting to yield if planted in August.

FRUIT

Loquat, navel orange, lemon, lime, tangelo, mandarin, avocado, early strawberries, very early raspberries (in warm areas), rhubarb, banana passionfruit and tamarillos (ripening from last season).

FLOWERS

Early roses, late camellias, azaleas, rhododendrons, magnolias, primulas, rock roses, lavender, daisies, ranunculi, late daffodils, grevilleas, early sweet peas, irises, lawn daisies and freesias – I could keep going for paragraphs. Sometimes it seems as though the whole world is flowering now.

PESTS

No matter what pests are bugging you, try not to do anything about it for at least another two weeks – see if natural predators will start doing the job for you.

Put out codling moth lures now to see if you need to start spraying. Put out fruit fly traps if you have any fruit, or fruit-like vegetables, near ripening.

Look for snails. Snails love spring – the lizards that keep them in check are still sleepy. (Frogs do a good job at snail killing too.) Try a cup of bran or old muesli and a quarter cup of derris, moistened with molasses. Place bits in an old margarine container with a gate cut out of it, so that rain won't wash the bait away. Derris makes snails and slugs froth up and die. Dogs and cats can eat this amount of derris without having to be rushed to the vet.

OTHER JOBS

- Stake tall, flowering perennials – or use reinforcing mesh.
- Chop up vegies gone-to-seed, and stew them into a rich vegetable stock – either have it for lunch or freeze it. A friend grates them up, adds wheat germ and bakes them into crisp dog biscuits. (Many vegetables like carrots and celery that have gone to seed can be eaten simply by peeling away the tough outer membrane – the centres will be soft and sweet.)
- Plant green-manure crops that can be slashed and ready for January plantings of winter vegetables – broad beans (cut them at flowering, don't wait for pods to set) or sunflowers, buckwheat or even radish if you pull them out before the bulbs form.
- Plant passionfruit vines and chokoes now, before it gets too hot – though they can be planted at any time as long as they are well established by winter, and kept mulched and watered.
- Mulch strawberries and rhubarb now, and cut off any rhubarb heads going to seed. Mulching now prevents leaf disease later.
- Buy young chooks now – they'll lay through until next spring. If you don't raise your own chickens, try buying alternately black, white or red ones, to 'colour code' each year – or leave different colour roosters with the females each season.
- Don't dig (use the no-dig gardens in Chapter 6).
- Don't weed (see Chapter 8).
- Don't rush out and buy pesticides for every bug you see. Most pest outbreaks will be controlled naturally as the season warms up (see Chapter 7).

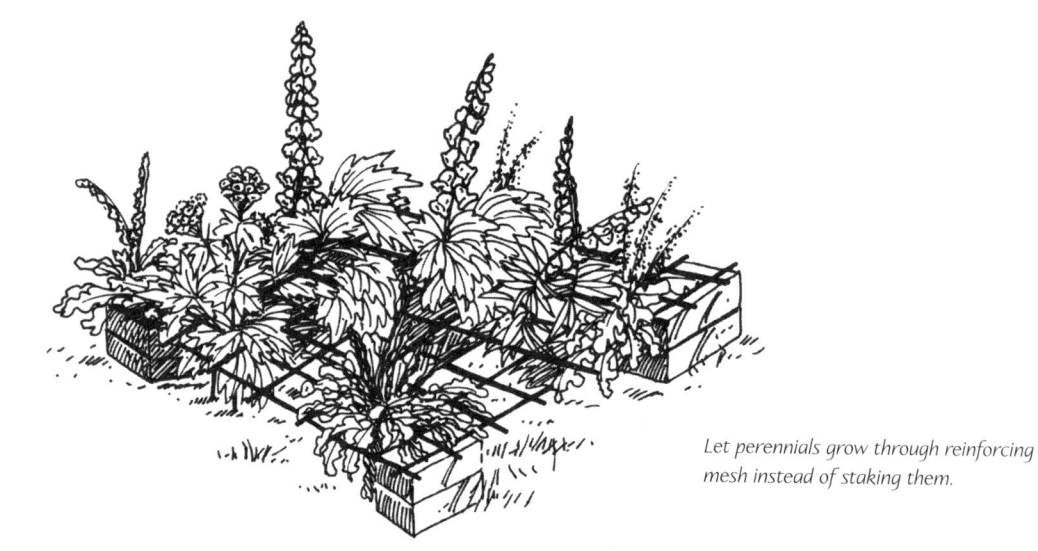

Let perennials grow through reinforcing mesh instead of staking them.

NOVEMBER

This is the time at which gardeners who have dug their beds will be hauling out the weeds (or watching their seedlings disappear under unwanted greenery), while those who have started minimum-work gardens (see Chapter 6) will be feeling smug.

Prune spring flowering shrubs and climbers once the petals fall.

Splash out on slow-release fertiliser pellets for the whole garden – great for busy people who don't have time to cosset their plants.

This is the best month to buy hanging baskets of annuals, to enjoy them for the whole summer.

Remove all fallen and ripe fruit so you don't attract fruit fly.

Trim hedges before they get too leggy.

Try to water often – hard baked ground repels water.

This is THE gorgeous time for gardens. Treat yourself to a weekend looking at the Open Gardens in your area, to get great ideas for yours.

SUMMER LUXURIES

- the scent of freshly mown grass;
- the smells of a summer garden at dusk as you water the garden beds;
- birds splashing in a bird bath; and
- kids painting the garden chairs a dozen different colours.

WHAT TO PLANT

VVEGETABLES

As for August. Keep planting successions of vegetables – more corn and beans and lettuce.

FLOWERS

As for September. Plant more for a late-autumn display.

FRUIT

In cool areas you can still plant evergreen fruit trees.

WHAT TO HARVEST

VEGETABLES

Most winter crops will have gone to seed; broad beans and peas will be fruiting; early silver beet can be snipped small and young; mignonette lettuce sown in August will be ready; parsley will still be plentiful; dandelions will be leafy and sweet; and you can gorge on asparagus and artichokes.

FRUIT

Cherries, early peaches, early nectarines, early apricots, small early plums, Irish Peach and Jonathan apples (late November to December), loquat, orange, lemon, lime, grapefruit, strawberries and raspberries, cumquat, kei apples, chinnotto, lillypillies, macadamias, mandarin, grapefruit, avocadoes, early loganberries, and red, black and white currants.

FLOWERS

Roses should be glorious and summer annuals are beginning in warm areas. Gladioli will be starting to flower, and so will miniature gladioli – delicate and lovely. Watsonias will be spectacular and summer natives are just beginning – there are too many flowers to list for November.

PESTS

Start spraying fruit with chamomile tea or seaweed spray every week if you are worried about brown rot. Thin the fruit, too, and keep bad ones picked off. Put out fruit fly and codling moth traps.

Spray pear and cherry slug with debris or pyrethrum spray – or leave them alone if they're not killing the tree.

OTHER JOBS

- Lightly prune roses and spring-flowering shrubs by cutting back spent flowers.
- This is the best time to plant 'no-mow' lawn thyme.
- Compost and rubbish heaps will be rotting well now, fed with winter debris – poke in some potatoes or pumpkin seeds for a quick crop.
- Feed lettuce seedlings, celery, silver beet and corn with liquid manure.
- Weeds are the worst problem now. Don't pull them out. Cover them with newspaper or strips of weed-mat weighed down with rocks. Feed your plants more while they die and turn to fertiliser beneath their mulch. Whippersnip or mow annual weeds, and use the residue to mulch your plants.
- Mulch beans, tomatoes and potatoes heavily now to get more roots on their stems – and to become healthier, more productive plants.
- Take tomato cuttings now (see Chapter 9). Cuttings are an easy way of getting successive crops, and they fruit much earlier than seedlings. In frost-free areas, if you take a cutting from your tomatoes every time the bush is large enough, you should keep yourself in year-round tomatoes.

DECEMBER

December is busy enough without worrying about the garden. This is a month for doing as little as possible – except for harvesting your produce. In December you really begin to reap what you sowed in spring. Remember that the more you do, the more you have to do:

- the more you dig, the more you'll have to weed;
- the more you water your lawn, the more you'll have to mow it; and
- the more you prune, the more you'll have to feed your shrubs and trees to make up

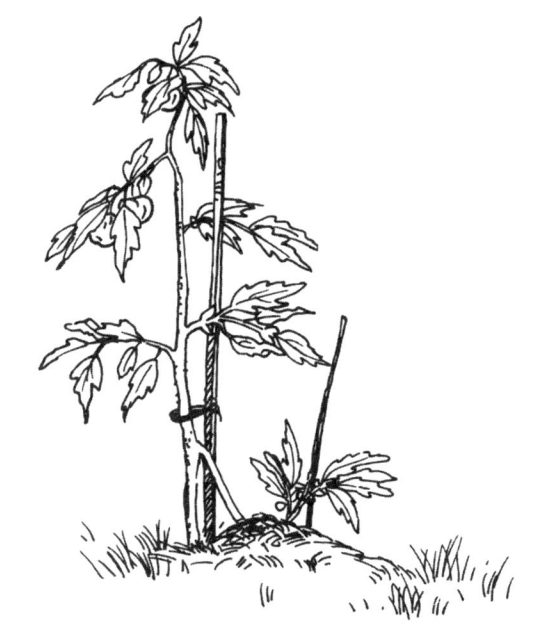

To take a tomato cutting, bury a branch under some mulch and stake the end to force it to grow upwards. When new roots form after a couple of weeks, cut the rooted branch off near the stem of the parent plant, and replant the offshoot somewhere for a new, vigorous tomato plant.

for the lost material. So don't – just sit back and wait until Christmas is over.
- Scoop out weed from ponds before it chokes them.
- Watch out for suckers or watershoots on trees and roses. Pull them off – if you snip them neatly they'll regrow.
- Snip off dead blooms.
- Water pots OFTEN – dry pots become water repellent.
- Drape shade cloth over salad veg in the vegie garden – it'll stop them wilting and turning bitter.
- Feeling humid? Tall trees will shade you from the sun, but too much greenery around the house can also block breezes and add to the humidity. Sometimes a little thinning of the jungle can greatly add to summer comfort.
- Dry soil can repel moisture. If your soil is

still dry just under the surface after you've watered, use a wetting agent like Wettasoil so that the next lot of water can really penetrate.
- Pick a few baskets of summer veg and flowers if you've been following previous garden tips!

WHAT TO PLANT

VEGETABLES

As for November. Keep up successive plantings.

FLOWERS

In cool areas, summer annuals sown now may be frosted off before they flower. Stick to dianthus, snapdragons, hollyhocks, wallflowers, marigolds and calendulas. In warm areas, you can continue November's plantings.

FRUIT

Don't.

WHAT TO HARVEST

VEGETABLES

New potatoes (planted in August), Tom Thumb tomatoes (in warm areas or where they are pot grown), peas, silver beet, baby carrots, lettuce; tiny beetroot, celery tops, zucchini (in warm areas), dandelions, bush pumpkins (in warm areas or where they have been started in pots), asparagus and artichokes (in cool areas).

FRUIT

Late cherries, peaches, nectarines, plums, late apricots, early apples like Gravenstein, Irish Peach, Jonathan and Lady Sudely, passionfruit in warmer areas, mulberries, gooseberries, early grapes, early almonds, cape gooseberry, Valencia oranges, lemons, avocados, babaco, pawpaw or mountain pawpaw in warm areas, strawberries, mid-season raspberries, loganberries, fruit from flowering prunus – good for jam, red, white and black currants, blueberries, banana passionfruit, grapefruit, lillypillies, sapote, Davidson's plum, Capulin cherry, kei apple, dates, jelly palm fruit, native ginger berries, macadamias, and mangoes in hot areas.

FLOWERS

Summer annuals planted in spring (petunias run riot in December); roses if you remembered to cut them back lightly when they flowered in spring; gladioli; summer-flowering natives; sweet william; and lilies will be flowering now – spectacular for Christmas.

PESTS

Keep up fruit fly and codling moth traps. Put out fruit fly netting. Make a ginger beer trap (see the author's *Natural Control of Garden Pests*), and use the rest for Christmas dinner.

Inspect apples every fortnight for codling moth holes or fruit fly – feed the infected ones to the chooks or seal them in garbage bags.

Watch for black spot on the roses.

OTHER JOBS

- The spring weeds you pulled up and flung in a bucket of water should be decomposing now – just tip the brown water onto celery and silver beet and onto anything else that needs a nudge.
- If you're going away on holidays place containers of water, topped with oil, under ripe fruit trees to catch fallen fruit and stop the spread of fruit fly. Fill bottles with water and upend them in the soil to keep your young plants damp, and mulch heavily to keep moisture in.

INDEX

abundance, a story of 184
acidity deficiency in soil 69–70
aerobic compost 65
air conditioning, natural 29–31
ajuga lawn 193
algae 62
almonds 165
    dwarf 156
aloe vera 143
amaranth 115, 138, 140
angelica 144
aphids 90
    predators of 95
apples 165
apricots 165
arrowroot 115
asparagus 115, 141
Atherton raspberries 161
avocados 166

babaco 157
bacterial problems, control 84
baits and traps, pest 94–5
balconies 32–4
bamboo, control 110
bananas 167
banana passionfruit 164
bats, fruit 95
beanfly, predators of 96
beans 116
    in bottles 117
bees 67
beetles
    Christmas 91
    staghorn frond 93
beetroot 118
bindii eyes, control 110
birds
    attracting, methods of 97
    control of 7
    fertility sources 67
    as pests 94–5
black sapote 168
black spot 89
    spray 87
blackberries 158
    control 110
blueberries 160
Bordeaux mixture 87–8
Bordeaux paste 88
borers 91
    control 84

bottles, plastic
beans, grown in 117
    celery, grown in 122
boysenberries 158
box gardens 78, 130
bracken, control 110
brambleberries 158
Brazilian cherry 168
briars, control 110
broad beans 118
broccoli 119
broom, control 110
brown rot of fruit 89
Brussels sprouts 119
buckets
    kumaras, grown in 125
    potatoes, grown in 130
'budgy method' of fertility 67
bugs 93
bunya nuts 168
Burdekin plum 168
burdock 119, 138
burglar proofing 32
bush lemon 168
bush pumpkins 127
bushfire protection 45–9
    fire resistant plants 45–9
    mulch 49

cabbage 119
    Chinese 138
calamondins 168
candle nuts 168
cans
cucumbers in 123
    hanging garden 77
    in herb wall 143
    strawberries in 162
Cape gooseberries 160
caper bush 144
capsicum 119
Capulin cherry 168
carob 168
carrots 120, 138
caterpillars
    predators of 96
    heliothis 96
cats 4, 95
cauliflower 120
Cedar Bay cherry 169
celery 121, 138
celeriac 122

chamomile 144
    lawn 192
cherries 169
    dwarf 156
cherry of the Rio Grande 169
cherry slug 92
chervil 144
chestnut 169
chicory 122
Chilean nut 169
chilli 119
Chinese artichoke 142
Chinese cabbage 138
chinotto 169
chives 144
    garlic 141, 144
chokoes 121
chooks (see also hens) 57, 67
    weeding with 107
Christmas beetles 91
chrysanthemum, edible 122
citron 169
citrus, dwarf 157
clay spray 88
climbers 30
clover 60
    garden bed 62, 76
codling moth 91
    predators of 96
coffee 169
collar rot 90
collards 122
colour for happiness 38
comfrey 58, 59–60
companion planting 97–102
    instead of pesticides 98
    herbicides 99
    fertilisers 99
    fruit, for 101
    roses, for 102
    vegetables, for 100
compost 63–7
    alternatives to 66–67
    aerobic 65
    heap 66
    how to make 64–6
    kitchen 66
    plastic bag 65
    trench 65
    two-week 66
compost spray 88
convolvulus, control 110

cooling house, garden 29–32
coriander 144
corn 122
corn salad 123
Cornelian cherry 169
Corsican mint lawn 193
couch grass, control 110
crab apple 170
cress lawn 194
cucumbers 123
cumquat 170
curly leaf 90
currants 160
curry leaf tree 170
custard apple 170
cutworms
    bait 94
    predators of 96

dahlias as herbicide 109
damping off 90
dandelion 124, 142
Davidson's plum 170
date palm 170
dichondra lawn 193
dieback 85
dill 144
disease control 89–90
dock, control 110
dogs 4, 95
downy mildew 90, 163
drip irrigation 43
drought protection 7, 40–5
drought-tolerant plants 41–2
dry shade
    plants for 187
    roses for 189
    tips for 189
dry-area tree planting 152
ducks 67
dwarf trees 9
    fruit 156

earthworms 4, 68, 70
earwigs 92
eggplant 124
elderberries 160, 170

failure to grow 85
feijoa 170
fences 18
    plants for 80
fennel 144
    bronze 141
fertilisers
    artificial 56, 57
    liquid manure 57
    organic 56
    urine as 56
fertility 55–71
    'budgy' method 67
    companion plants 99
    for flowers 190
    for vegetables 100
    from flowers 184–5
    quick fixes 57–8

small animals as sources of 67–9
weeds, from 104
feverfew 144
figs 170
    native 171
firebreaks 45–9
    plants for 45–7
fire resistant plants 45–9
fish 68
flower gardens, different 186
flowers
    as food 185
    for picking 189
    free-range 185
    ten reasons for growing 184
    the most glorious 196
flying foxes 95
foliage turnips 136
food
from flowers 185
from fruit 39
from herbs 143
from vegetables 39, 140
from weeds 104
fragrance 31–2, 38
free-range flowers 185
frost
    predicting 24
    preventing damage 25–26
    repairing damage 26
    zones 23–6
fruit bats 95
fruit falling 5
fruit fly 92
    baits 94
    predators of 96
fruit picker, home-made 177
fruit trees
    companions 101, 152
    dry area planting 152
    dwarf 155
    from seed 149
    grafting 149
    pests 154
    planting 152
    pruning 150
    watering 150
fruit, in first year 181
fruit, year-round 154
fruiting times 7
fungal problems, control 84
fungicides 82, 87

garden beds, conventional 81
garden design 17–19
garden health 4
garlic 145
    spray 88
garlic chives 141
geese 68
ginko 171
ginseng 145
gladioli as herbicide 109
globe artichokes 124, 141
glue spray 86

goats 68
gooseberries 161
Governor's plum 171
granadilla 164
grapefruit see oranges
grapes 163
grass, see also lawn alternatives
    barrier 106
    lawns 194
    mowing 194
    under fruit trees, alternatives 153
grasshoppers 92
    bait 94
    predators of 96
grease bands 90
'green' spray 89
green manure
    as fertiliser 59
    weeding with 108
greenery 31, 38, 92
grey water 43–4
ground ivy lawn 193
groves 6–9, 17, 27, 40
grumichama 171
guava 171
guinea fowl 69
guinea pigs 68
    weeding with 107

hanging baskets
    cucumbers in 123
    rhubarb in 132
hanging gardens 76–8, 162
happiness garden 38–9
hazelnuts 171
heated frost frame 26
heating the house, naturally 32
heliothis caterpillars, predators of 96
hens (see also chooks) 68
herb wall 143
herbicides
    natural 99, 108
herbs 142–7
    food from 143
hops 145
horseradish 145
    ice-cream bean tree 171

inter-planting 98
    strawberries 162

jaboticoba 171
jackfruit 171
Japanese raisin tree 172
jelly palm 172
Jerusalem artichokes 125, 141
jungle, modified 79–80
juniper 171

Kaffir plum 172
Kakadu plum 172
kale 125
kei apple 172
kids and gardens 50–4

food games 53–4
picking food 51, 53
safety 54
kikuyu, control 110
kiwi fruit 163
kumaras 125
kurrajong 172

lantana, control 110
lavender 145
lawns 9, 18, 42
   alternatives to 192
   clippings 60
   feeding 195
   mowing 195
   no-mow 192
   pests and diseases 196
   re-thinking 191
   to harvest 193
   weeds 196
lawn daisy, control 110
leaf eaters, control 84
leaf fall 85
leeks 125, 138
lemon 4, 173
lemon balm 145
lemon grass, as mulch 60
lemonade tree 173
lemon verbena 145
lentils 116
lerp psyllids, predators of 96
lerps, predators of 96
lettuce 126, 138
lilypilly 172
lime 173
   desert 174
   finger 173
   Kaffir and Tahitian 173
   round 173
   lime balm 145
linden 174
liquid manure 57
loganberries 158
longan 174
loquat 174
lovage 141
lucerne 61
   garden bed 76
   lawn 193
luxuries, in the garden 19–20
lychee 174

macadamia 175
maize 126
mandarin 175
mango 175
manure
   green 59, 108
   hen 58
   liquid 57
manure-heated pit garden 25–6
marionberries 158
marjoram 146
marrows 126
medlar 175
melons 126

mesclun mix 127
messy gardens 36–7
mice 69
micro-climates 154
midyim berries 161
mildew 6, 90, 163
millet 128
mint 146
   lawn 193
miracle fruit 175
mites 92
mizuna and mitsuba 128, 138, 142
monstera deliciosa 157
moss lawn 193
mulberries 175
   dwarf 156
mulch 40, 49, 58–61
   as weed control 108
   high fertility 58–9
   what to use 58
mustard 128, 146
   lawn 194
mycorrhizae 71

narranjilla 175
nashi 175
Natal plum 175
native ginger 157
native plants, feeding 71
native tamarind 175
natural herbicides 108
nectarines *see* peaches
   dwarf 156
newspaper 72, 81
nitrogen sources 58
nitrogen-fixers 56, 60, 61
no fruit 85
no-dig gardens 72–80
no-mow lawns 192
nutgrass, control 110

oil spray 88
okra 128
olives 176
onions 128
orange 176
   dwarf 157
orchards
   easy care 182
   in a pot 35
   pest-free 154
   dwarf trees 155
organic gardener 2–3
ornamentals 186
oxalis, control 110
oyster plant 133

Panama berry 176
parsley 129, 138
parsnips 129
paspalum, control 110
passionfruit 164
paths 36
patios, plants for 34–6
paving
   heat of 31
   lawn alternative 192

pawpaw 176
peaches 176
   dwarf 156
peachcott 177
peacocks 69
peanut tree 177
pear 177
   dwarf 156
pear and cherry slug 92
   predators of 96
peas 129
pecan 177
pennyroyal lawn 194
pepino 164
pergolas 18–19
periwinkle lawn 193
perennial vegetables 137
persimmon 177
pests 45
pest control 7, 82–9, 90–102
   regime 84
   for fruit 154
pest repellents 98
pest-like symptoms 85–6
pesticides 2, 3, 37, 82
pheasants 69
phosphorous
   deficiency in soil 69–70
   sources of 70
pigs, weeding with 107
'pile of weeds' garden 75
   cucumbers in 123
   potatoes, in 131
   pumpkins, in 127
   strawberries, in 163
   sweet potato in 134
pines 178
   nuts 178
pineapple 158
pistachio 178
pitaya (Dragon fruit) 178
plastic
   bottles, *see* bottles
   sheeting, clear, *see* solarisation
plum 178
   dwarf 156
plum pine 179
plumcott 179
polluted areas 22–23
pomegranate 179
   dwarf 156
pomelo 179
possum control 7, 95
potatoes 130, 138
   in grass 131
   in 'pile of weeds' 131
   in trenches 131
   in tyres 130
powdery mildew 90, 163
predators 82–3
   methods of attracting 97
   of pests 95
preventive spray 86
privacy 26–7
problem spots 20–3

frost-prone areas 23-6
nasty neighbours 21
patch of shale 28-9
polluted areas 22-3
seaside areas 23
waste areas 19
wet areas 21-22
prostrate yarrow lawn 194
pruning 9, 36-7
alternatives to 151
disadvantages of 151
fruit trees 150
pumpkins 126, 131, 138
bush 127
in grass 75, 127
pyrethrum, Dalmatian 146
spray 89

quandong 179
quince 179

rabbits 69
radish 132, 138
raisin tree, Japanese 172
raspberries 159
Atherton 161
rats 69
red spider mites 92
repellent spray 89
rhubarb 132
rocks as mulch 39, 41
rock gardens 39
root rots 90
control 84
rose apple 180
rosella 132

sage 146
salad burnet 141
salsify 139
sap suckers, control 84
sapote see also black sapote 180
sawflies 92
predators of 96
scale 92
predators of 96
scarlet runner beans 142
scorzonera 133
seaside areas 23
seaweed spray 89
seedling problems, vegetables 115
self-seeding garden 138
self-sufficiency 27-8
shade 32
shade tolerant plants 10-16
annuals 15
climbers 15
fruit trees 10-11
hardy coloured plants 15
roses 15-16
herbs 11-14

sweet-scented plants 16
vegetables 14
shale 28-9
sheep 69
shrubs 186, 192
silvanberries 158
silver beet 133, 139
slugs 93
bait 94
snails 93
bait 94
predators of 96
soil deficiencies 69-70
soil health 83
solarisation 108
sorrel, control 110
sorrel, French 139, 142
soursop 180
spinach 133
warrigal or new Zealand 133, 142
spitfires 92
sprays 86
black spot 87
glue 86
preventive 86
spring onions 139, 141
staghorn frond beetle 93
staking 9
star apple 181
stink bugs 93
stock, backyard
strawberries 162
as lawn 194
sunflowers 134
Swede turnips 134
sweet corn see corn
sweet potato 134

tamarillo 181
tamarind 181
tangelo 181
tangor 181
tanks 43
taro 134
tarragon 146
tea camellia 181
terracing 29, 162
thrips 93
predators of 97
thyme 146
lawn 192
tomatoes 134, 139
cuttings 135
'perennial' 135
trailing plants
cucumbers 123
peas 130
strawberries 162
trap crops 98
trellises 80
trench compost 65

trench gardens 44-5, 131
turkeys 69
turnip-rooted celery
turnips 136
Swede 134
tyre gardens 78-9
corn in 122
kumaras in 125
potatoes in 130
strawberries in 162

ugni 181
urine 56
quick-fix fertility 58
weedicide 108

'vampire method', weed control 110
vanilla 146-7
vegetables 112-42
crops, fast 114
harvesting 139
healthy, rules for 113
making perennial 137
10-minute garden 140
vertical gardens 80
violet lawn 193

walnut 181
waste areas 19
water 31, 38
grey 43-4
tanks 43
water chestnuts 136
water cress 141
water stress 45
watering 9, 114
efficient 41, 44
drip irrigation 43
weather control 6-7
weeds 103-11
as fertiliser 104
as food 104
as ground cover 104
control 7, 105-11, 114
mowing 110
weed gardens 75, 127
weed-mat 72-4
alternatives to 73
corn grown in 122
windbreaks 45-9
plants for, 47-9
wind protection 7, 9
wombats 2-3, 69
woolly aphids 94
wormwood 147

yacon 137, 142
yarrow 147
yellowing leaves 85
youngberries 158

zucchini 137

THE WILDERNESS GARDEN 225

OTHER BOOKS BY JACKIE FRENCH

Backyard Self-sufficiency $19.95
Paperback, 164 pages, illustrated
ISBN 978 0947214241

Organic Control of Common Weeds $17.95
Second Edition
Paperback, 124 pages, illustrated
ISBN 978 0947214517

Organic Control of Household Pests $17.95
Second Edition
Paperback, 138 pages, illustrated
ISBN 978 0947214470

Growing Flowers, Naturally $19.95
Paperback, 192 pp, illustrated
ISBN 978 0947214234

Jackie French's Guide to Companion Planting $13.95
Small paperback, 128 pages, illustrated
ISBN 978 0947214197

The Pumpkin Book $16.95
Paperback, 116 pages, illustrated
ISBN 978 0947214494

Soil Food $18.95
1372 ways to add fertility to your soil
Paperback, 184 pages, illustrated
ISBN 978 0947214449

Jackie French's Chook Book $16.95
Paperback, 120 pages, illustrated
ISBN 978 0947214401

Jackie French's Top 10 Vegetables $16.95
Paperback, 162 pages
ISBN 978 0947214388

Natural Control of Garden Pests $21.95
Completely Revised 2nd Edition
Paperback, 192 pages, illustrated
ISBN 978 0947214555

Switch! $21.95
Home-based Power, Water and Sewerage Systems for the 21st Century
Paperback, 180 pages, illustrated
ISBN 978 0947214302

New Plants From Old (2nd edn) $19.95
Simple, natural, no-cost plant propagation
Paperback, 128 pages, illustrated
ISBN 978 0947214562